Confessions of a
Catholic Schoolboy

Confessions of a Catholic Schoolboy

Jesus Runs Away and Other Stories

♦ ♦ ♦ ♦ ♦

Joe Farrell

To order additional copies of this book, contact:
Xlibris Corporation
1-888-795-4274
www.Xlibris.com
Orders@Xlibris.com
69444

CONTENTS

This book is dedicated in loving memory to Grace S (Casey) Farrell

Her Laugh, Her Smile
Her Kindness, Her Love
Left Footprints on The Hearts Of Many
She Made The World a Better, Brighter Place
And Left an Example For All Of Us To Follow

In Defense of Grudges

Recently I was talking with a friend about an incident in my past and he said, "You're not still holding a grudge, are you? A good Catholic school-educated man like you?" "Yes," I replied, "of course I am." It was true and I was surprised at the question. Later I got to thinking about holding a grudge and why it is regarded as a bad thing. To me, it is natural. In fact, I'm proud of my grudges. Webster defines a grudge as "a feeling of deep-seated resentment." These I have! Holding a grudge is also seen as an Irish trait or stereotype. You've heard of Irish Alzheimer's? You forget everything but your grudges. I'm Irish, so maybe it's in my genes. I choose, however, to think of holding a grudge, or having a feeling of deep-seated resentment, as a function of having standards or embracing a certain code of conduct violating which is beyond being forgiven easily. If you have no standards, you can forgive anything and you'll never hold a grudge.

Even God holds a grudge. Isn't Hell the *ultimate* grudge? Hell, Purgatory, and even Limbo are all examples of holding a grudge, after certain standards of behavior were violated. While Hell and Purgatory are still in full operation, I believe Limbo has been cancelled and I hope that the souls there got promoted to Heaven.

I was taught that God has His standards and He makes them well-known and when you die, you are judged on how well you lived up to His standards or met His expectations. (In my experience, God has always been referred to as a male.) I was taught that you could go to Hell for eternity for eating meat on Friday or missing mass on a Holy Day.

So holding a grudge is a sign of being civilized and of having good taste. Who wants a friend who has no standards, who can forgive anything, who doesn't have *some* expectations of fellow human beings? Not me. I have standards and when they are violated, I hold a grudge!

I am not saying that I hold a grudge against anyone who ever did anything I didn't like, or who had hurt or disappointed me, or who attained something I wanted. Not at all. Perhaps the following stories will help explain my stand more clearly.

CHAPTER ONE

♦ ♦ ♦ ♦ ♦

"JESUS RUNS AWAY"

"Our Father, who art in heaven, Harold be thy name . . . ."

In the spring of 1959, I was in the seventh grade at St. Andrew Avellino School. At this particular time in education history there was a program called "Released Time." This program allowed for early dismissal of Catholic School children so that public school children could receive religious instruction at the local Catholic school. I thought this was great. We got out at 2:00 p.m. every Wednesday instead of the normal 3:00 p.m. For this reason, Wednesday was the best school day of the week. Except during Lent.

During Lent, instead of early release, we got punished for our sins by having to go attend the "Stations of the Cross" at two o'clock. This ritual ceremony took far longer than an hour, as Monsignor Oechsler pompously visited fourteen different stops commemorating the passion and death of Jesus Christ. At each stop he would read from a little "Stations of the Cross" book, which we were all issued, that recounted the somber events at that particular point, and then say a series of prayers.

After doing this *fourteen* times, he would go to the altar and begin Benediction. Benediction was another strange and somber ritual that took fifteen to twenty minutes, easily. It involved incense, candles, bells, a strange gold vessel, and lots of Latin. The entire ceremony, somber, repetitive, and filled with "agony," "scourging," "crowns of thorns," "cross carrying," "crucifixion," not to mention "death," took an average of *one hour and forty-five minutes*! We were twelve years old and were supposed to get out *early*! We had to do this each Wednesday throughout Lent. I, for one, thought this was outrageous. After two or three weeks of this, a regular 3:00 p.m. release time would have been welcomed.

On this particular Wednesday in seventh grade, our teacher, Sister Charles Marie, was to teach the public school kids. She told us just as two o'clock approached that she would take us to the church, but that she had to return to the school to teach today's lesson, but that we were to be on our "best behavior." In other words, the usual garrison of nuns would be short in number. The other nuns would be there, but guarding an extra twenty-five boys and thirty-two girls would be difficult.

Things started out different right away. Michael Scansaroli had forgotten his Stations booklet. This was a punishable offense. Anyone who didn't have his or her booklet and got caught would receive some sort of punishment. This would most likely a slap in the face or sometimes a written punishment, such as copying the booklet's contents in longhand for homework or both, depending upon the whim of the nun and how she felt about you. Michael Scansaroli had no doubts where he stood. He could do nothing right since his name changed from Michael Weiss to Michael Scansaroli in the fifth grade. You see, Michael Weiss's mother got a D I V O R C E from Mr. Weiss. Exactly when this occurred no one seems sure and it might have gone unnoticed except that this "bold and brazen article" of a mother got remarried to Mr. Scansaroli and he apparently adopted Michael as his son.

I remember when Michael announced the name change in school to Sister Sereta. He raised his hand and announced his name henceforth would be Scansaroli, not Weiss, and that his mother had remarried and he had a new father. Sister Sereta was dumbstruck. She stood catatonic and glared at Michael for what seemed like five minutes. I think she thought he was making it up. That it was some sort of prank. Michael was so uncomfortable with Sister Sereta's reaction that he began to shake and look like he was going to cry. He had announced it with happiness, almost pride, but now he realized his mistake. Sister Sereta, finally realizing that this was no joke, asked him to spell it for her, made the change in the grade book and asked him to tell his mother that she would like to see her. None of us ever heard the results of that meeting, or if it ever even occurred, but Michael never again got an even break at St. Andrew Avellino School.

So, at Stations of the Cross, when he looked at me and said with dread in his voice and that I'm-as-good-as-dead look on his face, that he didn't have his booklet, I promptly and cheerfully said, "Here, have some of mine." I carefully pulled two pages from the middle of my booklet, so that he could look as though he had one too. It worked! As Sister Mary Thomas walked by, slowly checking pew by pew if everyone had their booklet, she failed to detect that Michael Scansaroli had only a few pages and that I was short a few. Once she passed and I realized that it had worked, I smiled proudly at Michael and we laughed.

Ralph Azanza, and Francis Baxter, both altar boys, were sitting directly in front of us. Ralph Azanza had something like a Jekyll-and-Hyde personality. He was always the teacher's pet. He was the top student in the class, his parents were rich, and they gave a lot of money to the church. But, outside of school, Ralph was cool. He liked girls and sports, had a great laugh, and was full of hell. In school he was an angel. He had terrific self-control and never got sucked into anything that would get him in trouble. He thought I was a riot.

When he heard Michael and I laugh, he turned to see what was happening and seeing Scansaroli with his two pages, he cracked up. He immediately turned around and bowed his head, but his shoulders shook with laughter. This got Baxter's attention and he too, upon seeing Michael kneeling with his two pages, and an angelic look on his face, cracked up.

To have two altar boys broken up in laughter at a somber, serious, pompous, holy church service was quite an accomplishment—a feat that did not go unnoticed by Eddie Haggerty. Eddie and I were the best of friends and normally Sister Charles Marie split us up to ensure we weren't anywhere near each other at any school function. But on this fine day, Eddie was sitting next to me on my right. Scansaroli sat on my left. Eddie was so challenged by my getting laughs, that in a bold and risky move he reached across me and snatched the pages from Michael Scansaroli, tore them in half, and quickly returned them to him! The sight of Michael kneeling with four tattered half pages of the booklet completely broke us up. It was so bad, in fact, that our laughter caught the attention of others, but remarkably not of a nun.

Robert Hutchinson, Michael Boyle, Cathy Garrity, and Rosemary Moore were all looking in our direction and either laughing or stifling laughter. Yet no nun seemed to have detected our having fun. Suddenly, *every* thing seemed funny. Pontius Pilate's name was funny, Scansaroli pretending to be reading his booklet by turning over one of his half pages was funny, and Monsignor announcing the station, "Jesus is Stripped of His Garments" was funny.

Don't forget, we were only twelve. Still no reaction from the nuns who seemed really taken up with the dour drama, that was unfolding before them for perhaps the hundredth time, while we should have been out having fun, playing ball, and releasing our energy, before we started our three hours of homework, for the average student, that they assigned us *every* day, even on weekends!

Toward the end, I contributed two new Stations of the Cross. With flawless timing, I announced, "The Apostles Get Out of Town" and finally, "Jesus Runs Away." Each brought audible laughter, shaking shoulders, red faces buried in hands, and the approval and admiration of all who heard it. After we were released, everyone was cracking up at what we had done and reporting pain at having to stifle their laughter and amazement that no one got in trouble.

The next morning, Sister Charles Marie (who we affectionately called Charlie Horse) was conducting class normally when Sister Cirylla suddenly knocked on the door and said she had some very bad news for Charlie Horse. It seems she was in the choir loft during Stations of the Cross and "some of your boys were having quite a time." Sister Charles Marie looked stunned and embarrassed. Sister Cirylla taught eighth grade and said she hadn't punished the culprits because she thought Sister Charles Marie would prefer to do it herself.

"Well, who was it?" Charlie Horse asked. "Mr. Baxter, Mr. Scansaroli, Mr. Haggerty, and Mr. Farrell," said Sister Cirylla. They often called you "Mr." when they were angry. Charlie Horse thanked Cirylla for telling her and assured her she would take care of it. Charlie Horse seemed very angry and stunned. She was slow to react. You could tell she was thinking of what to do.

"Stand up, you four," she said, "and everyone else who was involved." Baxter shot a look at Ralph Azanza, who was looking straight ahead with an innocent look on his face. "Who is going to tell me what this is all about?" demanded Charlie Horse. When she got no reply, she remarked that we had embarrassed her and this whole class, and demanded to know what had happened. Again no reply.

"Mr. Baxter, you are an altar boy," she screamed. "Tell me what you were doing." "Nothing, Sister," he said. A loud smack rang out as Charlie Horse slapped Baxter hard across the face. "I was laughing at Farrell," he immediately responded. "You sit down and pray you don't get thrown off the altar," she yelled as she turned her attention to Scansaroli.

"What's your story, Mr. Scansaroli?" She sneered at him with contempt. "I don't have any story," he began. He had hardly gotten the words out of his mouth when Charlie Horse's right hand smacked him in the face. She was a big woman, and Scansaroli was rocked. We didn't call her Charlie Horse because she was petite. Pow! The left cracked across his face from the other side.

"I was laughing at Farrell," he said softly, reluctantly. "Sit down! I'm not surprised at you! You're worthless!" she yelled as she moved toward Haggerty. The rest of the class sat quietly in shock. Sister Charles Marie was in a frenzy.

"Mr. Haggerty, what do you have to say?" Eddie knew what was coming and almost in defiance, had put his hands in his pockets.

"Nothing, Sister." Crack! "Don't tell me 'nothing'." Eddie put his hands deeper in his pockets. "What were you doing?" "Nothing, Sister." Crack! Eddie was tough and stubborn and he could take punishment. He was also a good friend.

"Where do your hands belong when you are being corrected?" Charlie Horse screamed. Eddie shrugged. "Take your hands out of your pockets and keep them at your sides." Crack! A third slap rang out. "Were you laughing at Farrell, too, Mr. Haggerty?"

"No, Sister," Eddie said firmly and stubbornly. I knew how tough Eddie was and knew he wasn't going to blame me no matter what. I was proud of Eddie. I loved Eddie. "Sit down, you disgust me," said Charlie Horse as she walked away from Eddie and started across the room toward me. I should have been able to think of something to say during all this, but my mind went blank as she stood in front of me in a rage.

"Well, Mr. Farrell, let's hear what was s-o-o-o-o-o funny!" she screamed. She was feeling the adrenaline in her blood and was literally screaming. I, of course, gave the standard answer in this type of situation. "Nothing, Sister." Crack! Crack! She hit me twice on the left side of my face. The second one caught me by surprise and really stunned me. "I want to know what was so funny about the Stations."

"There is nothing funny about the Stations, Sister."

"Then tell me what everyone was laughing at!"

"Nothing, Sister."

Crack! Crack! This time once on each side of my face.

"Tell me," she screamed, "or do I make them tell me?" I figured there was no point in resisting any longer. Her rage was not subsiding. She was not content with hitting me and insulting me, as was so often the case. This time she wanted to get to the bottom of it for some reason.

"I was making fun of the Stations," I blurted out, hoping to lighten things up a bit.

"You were making fun of the Passion and Death of Our Lord and Savior?" she shrieked.

"Yes, Sister." Crack! Crack! Again, both on the left side of my face, which was now numb.

"You find the death of Jesus funny, Mr. Farrell?"

"No, Sister."

"Then what *was* funny?"

"The stuff I made up." Crack!

"Tell me something funny about the Stations. We all want to laugh."

"I said things like, 'Jesus runs away'."

A few snickers and titters of laughter broke out from the class, but another smack on my face brought them to an immediate halt. Now I could taste blood in my mouth. The inside of my cheek had apparently been cut on my teeth and was bleeding inside.

While Charlie Horse glared around the room to silence anyone who thought this was funny, I slid my tongue around in my cheek, checking out the damage. The blood was coming from right near my lips on the left side. In the quick exploration with my tongue, I apparently pushed a small trickle of blood outside my mouth. Charlie Horse's next slap somehow made it run out more. Mary Lohan saw it and started to cry.

"Sister, he's bleeding," Mary cried out. Anne Dooley and Joan Conte had their hands up to their faces in horror. "Oh, it's nothing," said Charlie Horse. "Think of what Jesus went through." Charlie Horse began to back off. "*You* would run away, Farrell. Jesus would never run away. Wipe your face off and go rinse out your mouth. You sicken me!"

Apparently, the good sisters weren't of the school of educational thought where the child's self-image was important. In a span of fifteen minutes, Sister Charles Marie has called Michael Scansaroli worthless, told Eddie Haggerty that he disgusted her and told me that I sickened her, all while smacking us in the face in front of the rest of the class. Hardly the classroom management technique of the future.

I went to the bathroom, rinsed out my mouth, and returned to class. My thoughts were on what further punishment there would be. No matter how many times she hit me, it would not be as bad as involving my mother.

My mother took this nuns, brothers and priests thing entirely too seriously. Whenever a nun, priest, or brother told her about me being a problem (which was often), she would heap punishment on me, and rant and rave for days. Some kids could tell their parents that Sister beat them bloody and the parents would be upset at the school, not the kid. I was not one of those and had learned that lesson well in fifth grade.

It seems every May at St. Andrew's the "Month of Mary" was celebrated by circulating around the class a statue of the Mother of God, which contains a set of Rosary beads. The statue was about eighteen inches high, hollow, and with a base that screws off. Inside the statue was a fifteen-decade set of Rosary beads. The Rosary, you see, has fifteen sets of ten beads, separated by one bead. Each "decade" consists of one Our Father on the single bead, ten "Hail Marys" on the ten beads, and one "Glory Be" on the single bead. There are fifteen decades in a complete Rosary—five Glorious Mysteries, five Sorrowful Mysteries and five Joyful Mysteries. There is also a preliminary set of prayers—consisting of the Apostles Creed, the Our Father, three Hail Marys, and a Glory Be—that I never really understood.

The idea here was to celebrate the "Month of Mary" by passing the statue around the class so that each family would say the Family Rosary together—all fifteen decades. An ordinary set of Rosary beads has only five decades, but a Family Rosary has fifteen.

Because there were fifty-six kids in our class, this "celebration" started in April and went into June. During each day of May, one boy and one girl were designated as having "Honor Day." On this day, they didn't have to wear their school uniforms. They were supposed to honor Mary, the Mother of God, by wearing nice clothes to school that day and leading the prayers we said, usually a decade of the Rosary, each afternoon.

Many kids brought flowers on their Honor Day, to put in front of the statue of Mary that was prominently displayed in a corner of the classroom. At the end of the month, there was a "May Crowning." A boy was selected to carry a crucifix on a pole, and a girl was selected to carry the Crown on a satin pillow, and place the crown on the Statue's head—after a small procession around the classroom and a lot of prayers. If all went well, we usually got ice cream or a bottle of Coke as a reward.

Sister selected the boy and girl for this honor and the exact criteria were never explained, but it was never me. I thought the whole thing was stupid, except for the laughs, and missed class time. And usually the day of the May Crowning we didn't get any homework.

There usually were some laughs. One year, Billy Hamberger was sent to bring up the cases of Coke from the cafeteria in the basement. Hamberger was a great kid. He was poor and lived in a small apartment with his mother and brother John. He was very smart, but didn't care about school and loved to laugh. He was always happy. His poverty and irreverence eliminated him as one of the nuns' favorites, but Billy could take being slapped around and it never deterred him from laughing and being happy.

This day he had been given a rare opportunity and was not going to let it pass. He was given his instructions to go to the cafeteria and tell the custodian he was there for the three cases of Coke for Sister Rene. Since three would be too much for one boy to carry, David Brinkmoeller went with him. Brinkmoeller took the first case and Hamberger followed with the other two, only Hamberger shook his as much as he could the whole way back. He returned about two minutes later than Brinkmoeller, because he was shaking the cases of Cokes every step of the way.

When he got to the room, the Cokes were distributed and then Sister Rene gave an opener to each side of the room to pass around to open the Cokes. Jeffrey McGrath was already chugging his Coke since he used his Cub Scout knife-combination-bottle opener to open his. Jeffrey McGrath thought it was extremely cool to be a Cub Scout and wore his uniform to school once a week on meeting day, as was allowed by Monsignor Oechsler.

The knife, which opened up and had an opener on one of the blades, was an official Cub Scout Knife, and hung from his official Cub Scout Belt. He and Billy Rusie were, as far as we knew, the only Cub Scouts in our class. Unless, of course, there were closet Cub Scouts who didn't wear their uniforms to school. Jeffrey had gotten a Coke that David Brinkmoeller had brought up from the basement. He was attracting attention to the fact that he had opened his with his official Cub Scout Opener by chugging it.

"Hey, that's cool," said Billy Hamberger, "open mine." Jeff McGrath began opening Hamberger's Coke with his Official Cub Scout knife/opener and Coke sprayed all over his Official Cub Scout Uniform Shirt and Neckerchief! Hamberger went nuts laughing and so, too, did Eddie Haggerty and I.

Sister Rene's immediate reaction was that McGrath had done something wrong since the opener hadn't gotten to him yet. She started yelling at him, which we loved, but was soon distracted by a commotion on one side of the room and then on the other. Anne Dooley had opened her Coke and been sprayed and Jimmy McVann had opened his Coke and it was foaming up out of the bottle and all over his desk. Vincent Digilio began shaking his Coke vigorously and trying to get his hands on an opener.

"Everybody *stop*!" yelled Sister Rene. "Don't anyone else open their Coke!" "Aw, shit," said Digilio, loud enough for everyone to hear him. "Collect all the Cokes and put them back in the case," Sister Rene said, looking at Brinkmoeller.

Many in the class groaned their disappointment as Sister Rene was saying something like, don't be babies, and carry on because you can't have a Coke. Brinkmoeller was collecting the Cokes and seemed to be enjoying the whole thing a little *too* much. Digilio's "Aw shit" had really cracked him up. Suddenly, Sister Rene had a brainstorm and started walking fast toward Brinkmoeller.

"Mr. Brinkmoeller, do you think this is funny?" she screamed.

"No, Sister," he answered, but he still had traces of a smile on his face.

"Did you shake the Cokes up?"

"No!" he yelled back.

"What did you say?"

"No, Sister," he yelled.

Sister Rene swung an open hand at his face, but Brinkmoeller, not accustomed to being hit in the face by nuns, instinctively raised his hand in defense. These were two very bad offenses committed by David Brinkmoeller in a matter of seconds. He omitted "Sister" on his first reply, and raised his hand and flinched when swung at. For a kid who, seldom, if ever, did anything wrong in school, he was suddenly in deep water. You might even say, water over his head.

"Stand up straight with your hands at your sides," yelled Sister Rene. "I asked you a question and I want a truthful answer."

David Brinkmoeller was a sorry sight. He was standing rigid with his hands at his sides like a soldier at attention. His eyes were closed tightly and his lips were quivering as if he was about to cry. His face, neck, and ears were as red as a bad sunburn.

"Did you shake up the Cokes?"

"No, Sister," he said without opening his eyes, but almost crying.

It was a painful sight to see someone so uncomfortable. While Haggerty and I and Hamberger, Scansaroli, Heaney, Hutchinson, and a few others were used to the nuns' threats and physical abuse, to some, including David Brinkmoeller, it was absolutely terrifying. The class was shocked and completely quiet. Mouths were literally hanging open as David Brinkmoeller began to shake as he stood at rigid attention with his eyes closed.

"Open your eyes and look at me," Sister Rene said right in Brinkmoeller's face.

"Yes, Sister," said Brinkmoeller as he began to cry and painfully and slowly opened his eyes. "I did it, Sister," suddenly rang out from a few rows over. Billy Hamberger was on his feet and confessing. He couldn't bear seeing Brinkmoeller in so much pain over something *he* did.

Sister Rene admired honesty. She told Brinkmoeller to sit down and behave himself and told Hamberger to remain after school.

I waited outside after school. I just couldn't leave until I knew that Billy knew that someone appreciated what he did. After about a half-hour, he came outside with a box of blackboard erasers. As a punishment, he had to wash the blackboards and take all the erasers outside and clap them together to get the chalk dust out. He seemed happy. Sister Rene appreciated his honesty and didn't hit him or send for his mother.

"I'd do this every day just to see McGrath get Coke all over his uniform," he laughed. We both laughed at McGrath and at Brinkmoeller being so shook up.

He finished clapping the erasers and as he picked up the box to go back inside, he said, "You can go home now, I'm all right." I hadn't told him why I was there and he hadn't asked. He just knew. I walked home feeling pretty good about knowing Billy Hamberger and to tell the truth, feeling pretty good about Sister Rene. She chose a good punishment for Billy Hamberger, one he actually seemed to enjoy. He seemed to feel good about helping out, about being useful. I was never sure if she appreciated Billy's honesty, was embarrassed at her intimidation of a weaker David Brinkmoeller, or thought that Hamberger was just taking the rap for Brinkmoeller and wasn't really guilty.

So on this particular day in May in fifth grade, I was scheduled for the Family Rosary Statue. On the walk home, I began to think about the prospects of spending a good bit of my free time saying the Rosary with my parents and sisters. If I took the statue in the house for sure my mother would see it and insist on doing what was expected for fear if we did not, the nuns would somehow find out and she would be embarrassed. As I approached the house, I had to make a decision.

The prospect of 153 Hail Marys, 16 Our Fathers, 16 Glory Be's and an Apostles Creed instead of watching TV or listening to the radio in my room was overwhelming. I stuck the statue in the hedges that surrounded the front of our house. Without my mother seeing the statue, she would not know it was our night and when I returned the statue to school the next day, no one would be the wiser. Great Plan, except in the morning I forgot the statue and returned to school without it!

Sister Sereta was understanding. "You forgot the statue, Joseph?"

"Yes, Sister. I'll bring it in tomorrow. I promise."

"Well, tonight it was supposed to go home with Barbara Gannon. Barbara, is it alright with you to wait until tomorrow?"

All Barbara Gannon had to do was say yes. Instead, she says, "Well, my whole family is looking forward to it tonight, Sister. They'll be very disappointed."

"Okay, Joseph, what is your phone number? I'll call your mother and ask her to drop it off."

"Sister, I'll go home and get it," I offered.

"No, I can't let you do that during school hours."

"I'll run home after school and bring it right back."

"I can't wait around after school, Sister. My mother expects me home by 3:15" whined Barbara.

"Flushing-8-5756," I said, desperately hoping that she wouldn't be home.

But, of course, she was. Sister Sereta had gone to the office and asked the Principal, Sister Kieran to call and ask my mother to return the Family Rosary Statue and quickly returned to our classroom. A few minutes later, Sister Kieran's voice came over the PA system.

"Sister Sereta, would you please send Mr. Farrell down to my office?"

I knew this was trouble. They always call you Mr. when they're pissed off. When I got to the office, Sister Kieran was talking to my mother on the phone. She handed me the phone and said, "Mr. Farrell, would you be kind enough to tell your mother where the Family Rosary Statue is, since she apparently never saw it?" My mother was surprisingly civil on the phone and nicely asked me what Sister Kieran was talking about. I tried to talk very low when I got to the part about the Statue being in the hedges, hoping Sister Kieran wouldn't hear it. But, of course, she did. My mother said she would find it and bring it right down to the school. Sister Kieran told her to drop it off at her office. After she hung up, she folded her arms in front of her chest and said, "Let me see if I understand this, Mr. Farrell. You stuck the statue of The Blessed Virgin in the bushes outside your house? Pause. "Is that right?"

"Yes, Sister."

"You stuck the statue of The Blessed Virgin that is the property of the parish and left it overnight in some bush outside? Pause.

"Yes, Sister."

"You never said the Family Rosary?"

"No, Sister," I said, trying to look contrite.

"You never told your mother anything about the statue or the Rosary or even took the Statue in your house?"

"No, Sister."

"Were you just going to leave it in the bushes to rot?"

"No, Sister, I was just going to bring it back today, but I forgot."

"Well, Mr. Farrell, you go back to class now and I'll have a talk with your mother. Maybe you should go to Public School. Are you a big disappointment to your parents? Are you as big a disappointment to your parents as you are to me and to St. Andrew's? I bet you, none of the public school kids who come here on Wednesday afternoons to learn about their faith would show such disrespect. I'm going to suggest that your mother send you to Public School with the pagans and riff-raff. You don't deserve to be here."

I went back to class completely despondent. I told Sister Sereta that my mom was bringing in the statue and sunk into my seat. For the next half-hour or so I was unaware of anything that was going on in class. I just kept thinking about this being my last day at St. Andrew's and having to go to a new school with Pagans and Riff-Raff and not seeing my friends. I was struggling not to cry.

The next thing I remember was Sister Kieran coming into the classroom with the statue. She gave it to Sister Sereta and said that it had some scratches on it that were probably from spending the night in the bushes.

"Mrs. Farrell is very nice. I feel sorry for her. She deserves a better son," Sister Kieran said loudly. "I told her he belongs in Public School, but she wants us to try to shape him up. Let me know if he causes any trouble whatsoever. If he does, he's going to P.S. 22 (the local public elementary school).

22

I felt greatly relieved despite the embarrassment and humiliation being heaped on me in front on the whole class. At least I wouldn't have to go to a new school and never see my friends and have to make new friends with Pagans and Riff-Raff.

Sister Sereta didn't pile on. She said, "Okay Sister" to Sister Kieran and actually seemed sorry for me. She gave the statue to Barbara Gannon so the Gannon family wouldn't be disappointed and have to wait one day to say the Family Rosary in the presence of the Statue.

When I arrived home I didn't know quite what to expect. My mother was nice on the phone but that might have been because she thought Sister Kieran was listening. I actually felt grateful that she had saved me from being kicked out of school.

I was hardly inside the door before I was greeted with a flurry of punches, kicks, curses and hair pulling. "You son of a bitch" was yelled quite a few times. "I have never been so humiliated in my life. What kind of mother must they think I am? I can never show my face in St. Andrew's again." These were recurrent themes amidst punching and kicking and hair pulling. I went to my room and closed the door.

"You just wait 'til you father gets home."

It wasn't long before my father came home and I could hear her ranting and raving to him about her "humiliation" and "embarrassment." "Why do we bother? We should send him to Public School. We should send the rotten son of a bitch to Public School and the hell with him."

This threat secretly bothered me. I did not want to go to Public School with the Pagans and Riff-Raff and this was a new threat that I had never thought about.

My father yelled for me to come downstairs. I don't know how upset he really was, because he had to act upset to appease my mother.

"What the hell is wrong with you?" he asked.

"There is nothing wrong with *me*."

"Mom says we have to go to St. Mel's from now on."

"That's bull. She's making a big deal about nothing."

"You embarrassed your mother and don't say it's not a big deal or I'll knock you on your ass!" he yelled. "You're not leaving this house for a month," my mother chimed in. "Not after school and not on weekends. "And no television either," Dad added emphatically. "So you think it's not a big deal? Maybe you'll think differently in a month."

"Okay, like *you* wanted to say the Family Rosary," I said with a sneer, which pushed him over the brink. Now he was truly mad and started hitting me in the head. "Don't hit him in the head!" my mother yelled. Not "don't hit him," but "don't hit him in the head."

"I'll break both his legs if he doesn't wise up!"

So I suffered through a month of being grounded and missed some television. It was hard to deny me television completely, since my sister would watch some of our favorite shows upstairs in my parents' bedroom, which was next to my room, and I could hear it and watch it with her. If I heard someone coming up the stairs, I would rush quickly to my room a few steps away.

Some weeks later, Paul Pirro brought in a box for the Family Rosary Statue that his father had specially made. It was a wooden box with a felt lining, a handle, and two latches. This made the statue easier to carry and also protected it from the elements or from being scratched, as Paul so kindly pointed out. It seems Paul must have discussed the episode with his parents and his father decided to make a box to donate to the parish to protect the Statue of the Blessed Virgin Mary from the likes of me. Paul got to bring it in and present it to Sister Sereta, who fussed over it, sent him to Sister Kieran's office to show her, and wrote a note of thanks for Paul to take home to his father.

I was embarrassed that Sister Sereta was again reminded of this incident. It was more than Eddie Haggerty could stomach. He looked at me with a disgusted look on his face and made the gesture for "brown-noser" (making a fist around your nose and turning it). When we got outside he yelled to Paul, "Next time you take my turn, since you like it so much!"

So you see, I couldn't tell my parents that Sister Charles Marie had lost it and beat me bloody in front of the whole class for the Stations of the Cross incident.

So, given the aforementioned events, who did I hold a grudge against? Who violated my standards of behavior? Francis Baxter, perhaps? After all, he ratted on me after one smack in the face. No, I didn't hold a grudge against Baxter. He wasn't used to being in trouble and not used to being slapped across the face. Plus, he had the threat of being thrown off the altar, which would have been a *huge* deal in the Baxter family. He later said he would have run away, rather than face his father, if he had been thrown out of Altar Boys. When I asked if his mom would have been mad, he said she would've helped him pack before his father found out! Plus he didn't really do anything except laugh.

I also didn't hold a grudge against Scansaroli. He hadn't asked for my help, I offered it. Although he had been in the middle of it, why get in deeper if a short answer would do? Under pressure, giving the same answer as Baxter and getting past it was reasonable, although not the most noble thing to do and since his mother was d-i-v-o-r-c-e-d and remarried, I figured he had enough trouble.

Eddie Haggerty was my best buddy. He took a beating and didn't give me up. This was typical of Eddie. It was partially loyalty and partially stubbornness. I never would have betrayed him nor would he betray me. This was the basis of a friendship that endures more than fifty years.

How about Ralph Azanza? Once again, Ralph escaped trouble. Baxter was no more guilty of anything but Ralph did not get named and certainly he could not be expected to jump up and say, "I laughed, too, Sister, hit me in the face!" So no grudge against Azanza although I would have liked to see him get hit one time.

How about Sister Charles Marie? She beat me bloody and tried to inflict serious damage on my self-esteem in front of the whole class. Strange as it may seem, no, I did not hold a grudge against Charlie Horse. First of all, she was caught by surprise and embarrassed by Sister Cirylla. I do not know their relationship, but she was shaken by how this had unfolded. Perhaps Sister Cirylla was mentoring her in classroom management? But this wasn't in the classroom and Sister Charles Marie wasn't there. Secondly, Sister Charles Marie kept me after class and we had a nice talk about me. I think she was embarrassed at having lost it and wanted to put the beating in a different context. She said she liked me, but was worried about me because I lacked self-control. She smiled and almost laughed when I told her she couldn't possibly conclude that I had no self-control, unless she knew how bad I really wanted to be.

The conversation then took a strange turn. If I had some semblance of self-control, she asked, why was I looking up girls' skirts when they went by my desk? I wasn't, I protested! Are you telling the truth, she asked, because impure thoughts and actions were a mortal sin and if I am doing it willfully, then I'm guilty of mortal sin and if you die with a mortal sin on your soul, you go to Hell. (Apparently even twelve-year-olds.)

"I am absolutely sure," I said, but felt embarrassed and my face getting warm.

"Then why do girls hold their skirts when they walk past your desk?"

"I have no idea, Sister!"

She reiterated that she liked me and was concerned about my future (particularly if it involved Hell) and urged me to examine my conscience and go to confession if I was in a state of sin. I was mortified!

A few days later, I noticed Jean Reed coming down the aisle on my right, holding her skirt down. As she walked past Claire Burns, who sat directly across from me, Claire tried to grab the bottom of her skirt. It seems Claire would playfully grab the bottom of her girlfriends' skirts as they walked by with her hand down near the floor nonchalantly. When I saw this, I jumped up and said, "Sister, it's Claire Burns!"

25

"Miss Burns, are you grabbing other girls' skirts when they walk by?"

"Yes, Sister, I'm sorry."

"Well, cut it out now!!" she yelled. "Mr. Farrell, it seems I owe you an apology. I never expected such childishness from Claire Burns."

An apology goes a long way toward mitigating a grudge.

Thirdly, she didn't involve my parents. So, no, I didn't hold a grudge against Sister Charles Marie. How about Sister Cirylla? What kind of person would see something going on that they feel is wrong, and let it go on when they could easily stop it? Why not come over during the Stations and hit me herself? Why not give Sister Charles Marie the names of those who she saw misbehaving either that evening or in school the next day and let her handle it? Why did she need to surprise everyone, embarrass Sister Charles Marie, and make such a big deal out of it?

These are questions I never got answers to. But I did hold a grudge against Sister Cirylla. To me she had violated some standard of normal human behavior and decency. As far as I was concerned, she didn't exist for the rest of seventh grade and all of eighth grade. I never spoke to her or made eye contact again. Not that she ever noticed or cared. I got Sister Mary Mark in eighth grade and so had minimal contact with her, but when our paths did cross, I would not acknowledge her in any way.

I certainly bore no grudge against Billy Hamberger. To this day, I wonder what ever happened to him. He was funny, loyal, willing to take chances and own up to the consequences. He was not a follower nor did he seek to lead others. He was wild, mischievous and not a good student, yet he was smart, honest, and not liked by the nuns. He was unusual in St. Andrew Avellino's Class of 1960.

David Brinkmoeller was more typical. He was a very serious, studious, sensible kid who in many ways seemed a lot older than he was. I certainly couldn't resent a kid for not being accustomed to being hit in the face.

I bore no grudge toward Sister Rene or Sister Sereta. In fact, I liked them both. They were good teachers and actually seemed to like the kids. Also, they weren't prone to episodes of psychotic rage, like many of the nuns. In meetings with my mother, Sister Sereta actually told her I was "funny" and she enjoyed my sense of humor and seeing me laugh. She also had a strategy for working with me. She told my mom she purposely kept me involved in the class work because when I was bored is when I got in trouble.

Sister Rene told my mother I was a "leader" and that she had to work hard to keep control of me and the classroom. She told my mother that the other children liked and respected me and I could take the class either up or down. I was secretly very proud of those comments. Of course, they also told her many of the bad things I had done and that Eddie Haggerty and I together were more than any teacher should have to bear.

Sister Kieran had shaken me like no one before with the threat of expelling me from St. Andrew's. She may have been completely bluffing, and looking back, I'm sure she was, but it seemed like a real possibility to me at the time. Despite the beating and punishment I got at home and the berating she gave me in her office and in front of the class, I didn't hold a grudge against her. I had screwed up and she had a job to do! She did it well.

I did, however, hold a grudge against Barbara Gannon. All she had to do was say "no problem" to the one-day delay in the Joy of the Family Rosary and none of this would have happened. Why couldn't they say the Rosary together without the official set of Rosary Beads and Statue if they were so set on that night? All she had to do was show a little flexibility. Postpone it for one night, say it without the Statue or wait for me to go home and get it after school. Barbara Gannon was a pain in the ass then and I bet remained a pain in the ass. That kind of phony, pompous, rigid behavior in a sixth grader was surprising, unusual and in my opinion, unforgivable. Most of the class felt the same way. She hadn't even acted like she wanted to help me out, even though Sister Sereta put the pressure on her. She seemed to enjoy having some power and seeing me uncomfortable.

How about that brown-noser Paul Pirro? Surprisingly, no I didn't. Paul Pirro was an altar boy and always looking for opportunities to kiss up. There were certain kids who always seemed to get special treatment. Paul Pirro was one of these, although I never knew why. Rosemary Moore always got special treatment because her uncle was Father Moore, one of the parish's priests. She didn't seek special treatment, but many of the nuns seemed to want to please Father Moore or felt that just having a priest in the family made you a better person.

Leroy McNally transferred into St. Andrew's and somehow when he did, it became known that he wanted to be a priest. There was a special high school in the Brooklyn Diocese for boys who wanted to be priests. It was called Cathedral High. Somehow, the fact that Leroy wanted to go to Cathedral became well known and made him a favorite with the nuns. Leroy was also an altar boy. Paul Pirro was one of those who got special treatment, probably because of his parents' involvement in parish activities. So Paul Pirro's brown-nosing didn't bring resentment. I had come to expect it. The fact that Eddie Haggerty had recognized it and commented on it was satisfaction enough.

Lastly, my parents. I did then and still do resent that my mom was always so freaked out by the nuns. It wasn't that my behavior was so troublesome or a sign of some serious character disorder. I never hurt anybody and I got good grades. I liked to laugh and make others laugh and was rebellious when I thought something was unfair or just plain bullshit. It was always about her embarrassment, not my well-being.

My father I forgave, even though he was the muscle behind her ranting and ravings. He just wanted peace. She would carry on so that he would be mad at me for getting her upset, not for whatever prank had caused the bad report.

My father was an oil burner service man and worked hard all day in the hot noisy boiler rooms all over the City. When he got home from Brooklyn after fighting traffic, he was tired and filthy dirty. He always went right down to the basement to take off his work shoes and wash the grease and fuel oil off with a special abrasive soap he bought. It would take him quite a while to get the dirt off his hands and face and arms and he would scrub his fingers with a brush to get the dirt from under his fingernails. Even though he took great pains to get clean, he would still have the faint smell of fuel oil when he came to dinner. All he ever expected from his day was to read the evening paper, watch a little television and go to bed. I know he wouldn't have wanted to, nor seen the need to, get on his knees and say the entire fifteen decades of the Family Rosary.

CHAPTER TWO

◆ ◆ ◆ ◆ ◆

"BABY BOOMER BLUES"

You might have heard I run with a dangerous crowd
We ain't too pretty, we ain't too proud
We might be laughing a bit too loud
But that never hurt no one.
                    Billy Joel ~ "Only the Good Die Young"

In the fall of 1959, we felt the first concrete evidence of being Baby Boomers. We were born in 1946, the first year of the Baby Boom generation. As we went through St. Andrew's, there were always three classes of our grade, and we were always whatever grade dash three. We had been 7-3 and now we would be 8-3. This was unusual as most grades, in fact, all that I can remember, had only two classes. The eighth grade at St. Andrew's School traditionally occupied two cool basement classrooms. These classrooms were unique to St. Andrew's in that they had moveable desks, where the desktop opened up on hinges, green blackboards and were in the basement; but there were only two of them.

When we reported to school in September, we found our classroom was in the basement of the Rectory, i.e. the home of the parish's priests. It was certainly less than an ideal situation from an educator's perspective. It was totally isolated from the rest of the school not even being in the same building. It had no windows, and four support poles that obstructed the view. It had a hard, highly polished tile floor, poor acoustics, and a powerful noisy exhaust fan that Sister Mary Mark always called The Blower. Every time she asked someone to turn "the blower on" or "turn the blower off," there would be chuckling from most of the boys.

Sister Mary Mark never understood the snickering every time she mentioned The Blower, but she did understand that the education system like St. Andrew's had not prepared for the increase in numbers that the Boomer generation was bringing. She understood and told us almost *every day* that admissions to Catholic High Schools were going to be very competitive, unusually competitive. There was a great shortage of spaces available in the City's Catholic High Schools and because of this; a new exam would be administered, which would determine who got in and which poor souls would have the great misfortune to have to attend the NYC Public School System.

Up until now, each high school would give its own admission test and let you know if you were accepted. Now only one test would be given, in February, and the results would be sent to four schools of your choosing. The program was called the Cooperative Entrance Examination Program and we were about to learn the downside of being the first class of baby boomers. Sister Mary Mark announced that because of the Co-op exam, we would not be dismissed at our normal three o'clock, but instead we would be kept until four o'clock to drill for the test.

Sister Mary Mark was new to St. Andrew's but was a veteran teacher. I would guess her to be in her late fifties, but it's hard to be sure when judging from about three-quarters of a face. Dominican nuns wore habits that covered their full body from head to toe. We never saw nuns' hair or even their ears (which made hearing even more difficult I'm sure) or neck. The headpiece came down on their forehead to just above the eyebrows. The body of the habit went to the floor and a long string of rosary beads were hung from the waist. (Sister Charles Marie used to flip her rosary beads around her hand and then back in an intimidating manner, sort of like a cop with a nightstick.)

Sister Mary Mark wore glasses, was short, and probably wore dentures, as her teeth seemed a little too perfect. She obviously was called on to handle a large group of eighth graders in a tough competitive situation. St. Andrew's reputation was at stake and Sister Mary Mark was running class like a drill sergeant in boot camp. She seemed very determined that we do well on the exam. Now that all the eighth graders from all the Catholic schools in the Metropolitan Area were taking a common exam, there was no way St. Andrew's would be made to look bad. Every day from two-thirty. until 4:00 p.m., we would drill, drill, drill, for the Co-op exam. We were issued special workbooks that had the various types of multiple-choice questions and each day we would go over a section of the workbook.

Math, vocabulary, grammar, history—were all reduced to multiple choice, fill in the blanks, or matching column questions. Since the test was to be timed, we were told we had to work quickly and thus Sister Mary Mark tried to drill us quickly.

So at about two-thirty when everyone was tired and at wit's end, Sister Mary Mark would tell us to get our workbooks out and she would get her pointer out and start reading questions to us and then randomly point to someone for the answer. By setting a quick tempo and using her pointer, Sister tried to simulate the pressure of the real timed exam.

Sister Mary Mark and some of the kids in the class took this very seriously. Eddie and I saw it as an opportunity for breaking the boredom with a few laughs. We started feeding wrong answers to kids when they were called upon. The acoustics were horrible in our subterranean classroom and Sister Mary Mark's hearing wasn't the best and she seemed to never hear us whispering an answer to someone she called on.

What made this so funny to us was Sister Mary Mark's reaction to the answers. She would show her frustration when someone got something wrong and rant and rave about how we better wise up and take this more seriously. She would slam the blackboard or her desk when someone missed something she thought simple or something we had recently been over. This created a situation where simply wrong answers weren't funny—they had to be really stupid answers.

Now why would other kids who know us, give an answer we fed to them when they know we might be giving them a wrong answer? Well, for one, we frequently whispered the *correct* answer to someone who was stuck and starting to feel the heat. We helped out way more often than we hurt. The key was when someone was not paying attention and had no idea whatsoever. Then was the time to feed them a ridiculous answer and watch Sister Mary Mark have a minor stroke. The key reason kids were willing to take a chance on our suggested answer was the enormous pressure they were under.

One day Sister Mary Mark read a question from our workbook asking who was the second president and first vice president of the United States. She had been firing off questions and getting correct answers for quite a few in a row and was picking up momentum. She pointed to James Connolly for the answer. Connolly was in the midst of a daydream as he often was and had no idea what the question was. He stood up at his desk and pretended to be trying to recall the answer, but in truth, had not heard the question. Eddie sat in the front of the room and I in the back, as Sister Mary Mark had been told in advance about us. I could see Eddie whispering to Connolly but Connolly was reluctant to give the answer. Again Eddie offered a suggestion. Connolly feigned being in deep thought; Sister Mary Mark pressed for an answer.

"Let's go, Mr. Connolly. This is simple stuff. You shouldn't have to waste time thinking about this. This is not a tricky question. Let's have an answer." Eddie made a big stretching motion and a yawn and offered his answer again.

Connolly was desperate and not knowing the question, had two options. Admit that he wasn't paying attention or take a chance that Eddie was giving him the correct answer. Not paying attention was always inexcusable and made you subject to some punishment. You could get smacked or you could get a written assignment or remain after school for detention, which could mean manual work, written punishment, getting smacked or any combination of these. So Connolly decided to take a chance and after pretending to wrack his brain blurted out, "Howard K. Staph."

Sister Mary Mark looked puzzled. "What did you say? I didn't quite hear you. Speak up!"

"Howard K. Staph," repeated Connolly loudly.

"Who in God's name is Howard K. Staph?"

Eddie's hand shot up.

"Haggerty."

"He's St. Andrew's swimming coach," said Eddie, laughing. I was already doubled over with laughter at the incredulous look on Sister Mary Mark's face.

"Are you trying to be funny, Mr. Connolly?"

"No, Sister."

"Then why would you give such an answer?"

James Connolly was in a tough spot. How does he explain giving such a stupid answer? Eddie is cracking up at getting Connolly to go for it and

Kevin Connolly, who sat next to his brother, is also laughing at his brother's predicament and even James himself is now smiling and trying not to laugh.

Sister Mary Mark was getting angry fast when she saw Connolly fighting back laughter and Kevin and Eddie laughing. She slammed her pointer on the side of her metal desk! "Who knows the answer?" she screamed. A number of hands went up. She points at Cathy Kain who says "John Adams, Sister."

"Did you hear that, Mr. Connolly?"

"Yes, Sister."

"Well, you can start writing 'John Adams was the first Vice President and second President of the United States' a thousand times for homework tonight and maybe you won't think it's so funny."

Connolly slumps into his seat and amidst a lot of kids chuckling and laughing he sees Eddie in stitches and shoots him the finger. Sister Mary Mark sees Connolly do it and swings the pointer at him, hitting him in the shoulder, and snapping the pointer in half! Many in the class are stunned and quiet, some are laughing, Eddie is laughing so hard he is almost falling out of his chair, and I am struggling for breath.

"Okay, knock off the laughter," she screams. "This isn't funny." "You big baby," she yells at Haggerty. "You won't be laughing if you don't get into a Catholic high school," she yells, shaking half a pointer at Eddie.

Joe Heaney raises his hand and asks Sister Mary Mark if she wants the other half of her pointer back, holding it up. She walks down the aisle and takes it from him and sensing he might be making fun of her, tells him to take the next question, then me, then Eddie. We each, in turn, get the answers correct. Then she delivers her first warning about getting her recommendation for Catholic high school.

"They will not accept you without my recommendation no matter what you score. I'm giving you fair warning, people. If I don't think you're trying and taking your schoolwork seriously, then you don't deserve a seat in a Catholic high school and I won't recommend you. So . . . just keep laughing."

The drill resumed until four o'clock when Sister Mary Mark suddenly asked James Connolly to give her what he was writing. Connolly had started on his punishment and once again was caught by surprise. He slowly got up and tried giving Sister Mary Mark one page, but she said, "Give it all to me!"

He handed her five or six pages which she tore into little pieces, threw up in the air, and told him they better be all picked up and put in the trash when she returned from dismissing us. Since we were in the basement of the rectory, Sister Mary Mark always led us in line quietly up the stairs and down the hall to the door and watched us march in line to the corner.

Once we broke ranks, Eddie and I laughed so hard we couldn't stand up. Eddie was so proud. Even Kevin Connolly was in stitches as we waited for James to come out and recounted and reenacted the story over and over.

Soon James came out and at first he acted sullen because of the punishment he had to do for homework, but soon was cracking up at the memory of Sister Mary Mark shaking the remaining half of her pointer at Eddie.

"I can't believe you went for Howard K. Staph," said Eddie. "I can't believe she saw me give you the finger," said James. "I can't believe she broke her pointer," said I. "You better hope Mom doesn't find out," said Kevin. Eddie and I offered to write a few pages each of his punishment, but James was worried that she'd notice handwriting differences and he'd get in even more trouble.

The Connollys left and Eddie and I who lived in opposite directions from school talked for a while. I asked him if he was worried about Sister Mary Mark's threat of possibly not recommending us to Catholic high school. He wasn't. He was the fifth Haggerty child to attend St. Andrew's and his parents had done a lot over the years for the parish. His mother, it turns out, was a big wheel in The Mother's Club. I didn't know there really was a Mother's Club. As we split for our walks home, Eddie said, "We have a long way to go until June, but I don't think I'll laugh that hard again." He was wrong.

My most memorable victim of this diversion was Joe Rubbone. Joe and I had both loved sports and often played whatever sport was in season together after school. Joe's father was a rich doctor and his mother a beautiful redhead who hated me. She didn't want Joe playing with me and so he always lied about who he was with when we were together. The Rubbones lived a half-block from the school and Mrs. Rubbone was frequently involved with parish activities. She had heard something about me and decided I wasn't a good influence on her son. Joe told me he thought it was bullshit, but not to let on that we hung around together. Eddie and I both liked Rubbone, but our families ran in different social circles. He had a lot of pressure on him to be a model child, which is why getting him in trouble was so much fun.

Sister Mary Mark was using a yardstick now to conduct her drills. On this one fall day, she suddenly called on Rubbone and caught him completely asleep. The question was 'what number multiplied by any number is always zero?' Rubbone hadn't heard the question and sprung to his feet completely helpless. He hesitated groping for a clue to what the question was.

"Forty-nine," I whispered.

He smiled, suspecting I might be goofing on him.

"Mr. Rubbone, how about an answer."

"Forty-nine," I whispered again.

Joe Rubbone closed his eyes as if doing a calculation in his head.

"Mr. Rubbone, this is simple and shouldn't require a lot of . . ."

"Forty-nine," he said quickly, as if he had just figured it out.

"*Forty-nine!*" said Sister Mary Mark. Any number times forty-nine is *zero?*"

Rubbone smacked his forehead with his palm as if to say 'how could I be so stupid?'

Sister Mary Mark didn't like his reaction and came down the aisle and slapped him in the face. "Either you weren't paying attention or you are being a smart aleck. Either way, that's what you get and I'll tell your mother when I see her."

Even Rubbone, with one red cheek, laughed when he glanced around and saw Eddie, and then me, red-faced with laughter. Many in the class were laughing and smiling and murmuring, but Sister Mary Mark never quite understood what was going on.

Although this was my best execution of the prank, it was far from the best one. Eddie scored heavily again in late January about three weeks before the Cooperative Exam.

As any Catholic school kid knows, "Ejaculations" are little prayers such as "Mother of God, pray for us" or "Jesus, Mary and Joseph, pray for us." Sister Mary Mark was very big on Ejaculations and frequently used them. It seemed like cursing to most of us, but she frequently defended herself and encouraged us to use these short prayers whenever we could. Whenever you are frustrated or angry or distressed, say an Ejaculation and offer it up to God, Sister Mary Mark would urge us. She never quite understood why there was so much smiling and chuckling every time she mentioned "Ejaculation."

On this one day in late January, we were drilling for the exam and someone messed up a grammar question. Sister Mary Mark was annoyed at three consecutive people she called on not knowing the correct answer. "It's very late in the game to be getting this wrong," she yelled. "Don't let dependent clauses throw you. They just modify independent clauses," she yelled, smacking the blackboard with her yardstick.

"Let's get back to basics." Suddenly she scrawls on the board: John hit the ball. "What is the subject of this sentence Helga?" "John," she answered.

"And what part of speech is 'John' Carol Bishop?" Carol Bishop was one of the weaker students in the class, because she daydreamed a lot and true to form, she had no idea what she had just been asked. She got to her feet and looked at the board, hoping for a clue.

"Preposition," whispered Eddie.

Sister Mary Mark, already frustrated, saw doubt on Carol's face and asked with a scowl, "Were you paying attention?"

"Yes, Sister."

"Then, answer my question."

Eddie whispered, "Preposition."

Carol looked down at her workbook on her desk and mumbled something. "Speak up, we don't have all day!" Sister Mary Mark screamed. "Preposition," Carol said almost yelling. Preposition?" Sister Mary Mark screamed. "Jesus, Mary, and Joseph," she slammed her yardstick on her desk and it broke in two pieces. She throws the piece in her hand on her desk and clasping her hands together and looking up at the ceiling says, "Mary, Mother of God, Help *Me!*"

I didn't think I could laugh any harder, when Billy Hamberger suddenly is on his feet and walking up to Sister Mary Mark who is standing behind her desk in the front of the room. There is a lot of commotion in the room—some laughing, some murmuring. Hamberger had the other half of the yardstick and he handed it to Sister Mary Mark, turned around and as he started back to his seat, he put his finger to his lips in a be-quiet gesture and said, "S-h-h-h-h-h, Sister's ejaculating."

As I lapsed into a near convulsion, Sister Mary Mark called it quits for the day and let us go. As we packed our books up and got our coats, she lectured us about how it's *our* future, not hers. If we want to rot in Public High School, that's our business. She took advantage of the opportunities God gave her. If we want to slap God in the face, that's our choice. We will pay for it in this life and in the next. The path to heaven is a much tougher one through Public School, she warned us. Many lose their faith and fall away from God and ultimately lose their souls. I figured it was worth it to get out early.

So the fall of 1959 was not going especially well for me. My parents were fighting more frequently and more violently, my classroom was in the basement of the Rectory, completely separate and isolated from the rest of the school, there were no windows, as if to cut us off from the world completely, Sister Mary Mark conducted class like a drill sergeant and we had class till four o'clock! To top it all off, the Dodgers had tied for the National League pennant and won a play-off to get into the World Series where they beat the White Sox in six games. This was very depressing to me because I had been a fanatical Brooklyn Dodger fan. I was born in Brooklyn and my father worked in Brooklyn and the whole family, especially me, were *huge* fans.

I loved baseball and my summers were centered around it. If I wasn't playing ball, I was watching it. One year I played on three teams in three separate leagues. The Dodgers were the center of my world up until 1958. I had a complete Dodger uniform and would dress in it to watch each game on TV. I played first base and Gil Hodges was my role model. I had a Gil

Hodges glove and bat. I could imitate every Dodger at bat and did so in front of the TV.

This kind of behavior was not unusual for Dodger fans in New York. The Dodgers had rabid fans that lived and died with them all season long, despite their team never winning a World Series until 1955, after sixty-six years of trying. The rabid fandom became sheer lunacy when the Dodgers played the hated Giants from the Bronx. When the Dodgers played the Giants, I would watch it in our living room with my parents. My mother would make popcorn and we would sit in the dark and watch the game on our black and white TV.

We especially rooted for Jackie Robinson, who remains one of my heroes to this day. It is a well documented story how Jackie Robinson broke the color barrier in major league baseball. He did it with great poise, dignity, and exceptional talent, despite having to endure terrible harassment and indignities from both players and fans. We pulled for Jackie Robinson every at bat, and when he stole home in the World Series against the sanctimonious Yankees, my mother cried.

When Roy Campanella was paralyzed in an automobile accident, my parents broke it to me gently and urged me to light a candle for him in church, which I did. In 1955, while I was in the fourth grade, the Dodgers won their first World Series and removed that terrible weight from the shoulders of their fans. The Giants had won in 1954 and the Yankees were the elite of baseball history, so the burden of *never* having won became unbearable.

One of my fondest childhood memories was going to Ebbets Field with my father to see the Dodgers play. My father's company had season's tickets and once in a while they would offer them to him and we'd go. It was an indescribable pleasure. I remember telling my Dad that I couldn't wait until I grew up and had a job and could afford to go to all the games. One night when we were supposed to go, the game was rained out. It had been raining all day and the game was called a couple hours before game time. I was despondent beyond words. I refused to eat dinner, instead sat in my father's car wearing my Dodger hat and my first baseman's mitt, and cried. I had been praying all afternoon that this wouldn't happen, and I felt bitter and angry. How often did I get to go to a Dodger's game? Why did God do this to me, I wondered. Was it punishment for something? Was he preparing me for something in the future? Was it to protect me from something, perhaps an automobile accident on the way to the game or on the way home? If it is punishment, I should at least know what for or what's the good of it?

If a person is being punished for something but they don't know what, how will they know to stop doing it? Of course, I never found out.

After dinner, my father came out to the car. "Mom saved you some dinner, Joey. You should go in and eat. I'm sorry about tonight, but there's nothing anyone could do about it."

"Bull."

"What do you mean, 'bull'? Nobody can control the weather."

"God can and I prayed all afternoon."

"God has a little bit more to do than worry about the Dodger game."

"Oh, yeah," I said. "Then why did Gil Hodges ask the people of Brooklyn to pray for him when he was in a slump? And why did he go four for four the next day?"

"Go eat, and I'll try to get tickets for some other night."

In the summer of 1957 I heard rumors that the Dodgers were going to move. Eddie Haggerty, a Yankees fan, chided me about it. I asked my Dad if it was true and he said the Dodgers would never move out of Brooklyn. After that, whenever people teased me about it, I told them they were crazy—the Dodgers would never leave Brooklyn.

Then on October 8, 1957, the Dodgers announced that after sixty-eight seasons in Brooklyn, they were moving to Los Angeles. I was calm at first. The season was over and I figured they probably wouldn't go through with it. How could the "Bums of Brooklyn" move to California? Unimaginable. Unthinkable. Every time a bastard Yankees fan would taunt me, I would just say, "We'll see" and move on, but inside I felt sick and angry. When Peter Ross, who lived two doors down from us, and was a Yankees fan, pushed me too far, I beat the shit out of him. He went home a bloody mess and his mother came to our house all upset. I apologized to Mrs. Ross just to make my mother calm down, but I didn't really mean it.

The two families were never friendly again. I really was sorry later for what happened. My heart was broken and no one seemed to understand. For six months or more each year, my life was involved with the Dodgers lives on a daily basis and now it was suddenly over. I quit watching baseball until 1962, when the Mets came to Flushing.

CHAPTER THREE

◆ ◆ ◆ ◆ ◆

"IMPUDENCE"

*I believe in God, the Father Almighty, creator of Heaven and Earth,
and in Jesus Christ his only son, our Lord, who was conceived in liberty
and dedicated to the proposition that all men are created equal.*
Vincent DiGilio, 1958

As if having class until four o'clock wasn't bad enough, I frequently had to stay after school to do my homework or to do my homework over. St. Andrew's gave a lot of homework. In fact, many parents even thought it excessive at times and some complained about it. The answer was that you should expect up to three hours of homework every night. I felt this bordered on child abuse and was determined not to let homework interfere with my busy schedule of sports, girls, music, and television. In the lower grades, I could race through my homework in what seemed like no time. I was a good student, or should say, a successful student, in that I always got excellent grades. By the time I hit eighth grade though, the work was harder, my social life busier, and my home life more chaotic. My parents were fighting more frequently and more violently and at times, I simply could not concentrate on homework. At other times, I was too tired or busy to do it and simply ran out of time.

When this occurred, which was often, there were two options: either don't hand in the homework and take a grade deduction and then stay after school to do it, or copy someone else's. Copying was my preference! The difficulty in doing that was whose, when, and where. On a typical day, I would rush to school, which was about a mile walk, and arrive about ten minutes before the bell. I would feverishly look for someone to let me copy their homework and then hurriedly copy it; often lying on my stomach on the ground or leaning on a car hood, sometimes even up against a tree. The rush and the conditions often made my paper a sloppy mess. If I couldn't find anyone before I got to school, I had to find someone to let me copy their homework in class and return it to them before it had to be handed in. This could be very problematic, since it involved risk for the homework "donor." Even in the schoolyard, it involved risk, but inside the school, there was a much greater chance of getting caught.

The last resort was doing it myself in class before it had to be handed in. In any instance, the work was hurriedly done and very often Sister Mary Mark would glance at it or specifically look for mine and return it to me often crumpled up in a ball. What this meant was that I had to stay after school and do it neatly, so as not to get a zero for the assignment. Many times after doing it over neatly and handing it in, Sister Mary Mark would say, "Now, why didn't you do it like this the first time?" or "When are you going to learn to do your work neatly?" or "How many times do I have to punish you before you learn, you big lazy lug?" She apparently had no appreciation for speed. I would have liked to challenge *her* to neatly diagram complex sentences on the trunk of a car in the rain, or while walking under rigid time constraints, or with fingers that were freezing!

Copying homework was not easy. It was not because of laziness or stupidity. Copying homework successfully, over a long period of time, required a lot of skill and thought. It required sensitivity, determination, stamina, skill, charm, courage, and self-esteem, all of which seemed to go unappreciated by the nuns at St. Andrew's.

It wasn't as if I could ask just anyone in the class for their homework and they would give it to me. Some of my best friends like Eddie Haggerty and Billy Hamberger didn't do theirs either and were in the same boat as I was. Michael Scansaroli and Barbara Murphy were two others who were frequently scrambling around looking for homework donors. Some of my other classmates like Cathy Kain and Paul Pirro would threaten to turn you in and Julianne Fenchak actually *did* turn me in once. Not only couldn't you ask these particular people for homework to copy, you had to be careful they didn't see you doing it or find out about it. Many others would simply say, "No—I don't want to risk a zero" or "I couldn't get it, it's probably all wrong" or "I didn't do it," which I knew was a lie, but I got the message.

Many others would help me out reluctantly. Eileen Quinn, David Dyke, and David Brinkmoeller fit into this group. They wanted to help, but were uncomfortable with the risk. With this group, I had to build a relationship where I would only ask when I was really in a jam, copy it in a safe place not near them, and promise not to copy all of it-or to change things around so as not to get caught.

One of the easiest ways to get caught was copying exactly a unique mistake. I can't tell you how many times people got caught by having the same unusual mistake. Sister Mary Mark's response was to give a zero to both people. The way her system worked was that homework couldn't help you, it could only hurt you. You either got a checkmark or a zero. If you handed it in and it was complete, had a few reasonable mistakes or at least showed that you had attempted the work, you got a check. Every zero in her grade book was a point off your final grade, in that subject, for that marking period. I was sensitive and smart enough to never copy homework and have it identical. I frequently changed something that was correct to something incorrect to avoid detection. So by providing this protection to these donors and by not using them often and only when desperate, I created a safety net for when my usual channels failed.

My usual channels were numerous under the right conditions. Eddie, if he had it, Michael Boyle if he was there in time. Once Eddie and I jokingly chastised Michael Boyle, calling him "selfish," for not getting to school early enough for us to copy his homework! Baxter would let me copy it only if we weren't near school. Ralph Azanza would let only me copy his, but not near school, and he would stand right there while I did it, urging me to hurry. Claire Burns was very generous when she had it, but was often also looking for someone else's to copy. Rosemary Moore would tell you the answers or help you do it, but not give you her paper to copy. I am grateful to these and many other classmates who helped me get by, but especially to Cathy Garity and Kathy Lynch.

These two were special people. Both were bright, good-looking, funny, good students, athletic, loyal and ironically, lived across the street from one another. My earliest memory of Cathy Garity was after she had been in a horrible accident. On the way home from school one day, Cathy was hit by a garbage truck and seriously hurt. The original story as we heard it was that she was pushed in front a garbage truck by Michael Scansaroli. Later Cathy told me that was untrue. She said she had darted in front of the garbage truck to get away from Michael Scansaroli, who was in pursuit, trying to kiss her.

At the time this happened, we were learning our multiplication tables. Day after day of drill and recitation, alone and as a group . . . 1 × 3 = 3, 2 × 3 = 6, 3 × 3 = 9. Each night the next table to commit to memory.

Cathy Garity missed all this while in the hospital recovering from her collision with a New York City Garbage Truck. When she returned, she established herself as the times-tables Queen. It was amazing. While in the hospital, Cathy mastered the times-tables and when she returned, she could not be beaten. She actually beat Ralph Azanza in a times-tables contest. Neither Eddie nor I remember Cathy prior to this, but apparently Michael Scansaroli does. Kathy Lynch did not start at St. Andrew's with us. She transferred in, what I believe was, fourth grade. I don't know where she came from and didn't care either. I just thought she was pretty and I liked her and made no bones about it!

These two were great friends and in the seventh and eighth grades, I spent a lot of time uptown in the more affluent part of Flushing on their block of 168th Street. Kathy Lynch taught me how to swim at the Whitestone Pool, and they both taught me how to dance. We spent many hours listening to rock and roll in the Garity basement or on the back porch. The girls would almost always dance and eventually try to get me or Eddie or whoever else was there to dance too. They taught me dances like the cha-cha, the lindy, and something called the savoy. I hated dancing, but I liked girls. If I had to dance to get girls, then I'd dance. I can still remember cha-cha-ing to "Hushabye" by the Crests and "Little Darlin" by the Diamonds, savoying to Dion & the Belmonts' "Teenager in Love" and doing the Lindy to "At the Hop" by Danny and the Juniors.

The Garity home was huge and beautiful. Mr. Garity was a doctor and apparently doing well. He was always pleasant, but contact with him was infrequent. Mrs. Garity, however, was frequently around and I thought she was wonderful. She always talked to me, joked with me, and called me by my name. "Hello Joe Farrell," she would yell out the window or down the stairs. If I was leaving, she'd say, "Take care of yourself Joe Farrell" or "Nice seeing you Joe Farrell" or "See you soon I hope!" This really struck me as unusual. I didn't know if that was the way rich people behaved or if possibly, for some weird reason, she liked me. I always felt welcome and grown-up there and was always on my best behavior so as not to disappoint Mrs. Garity. I used to hope that she would have a talk about me with Mrs. Rubbone at some Doctors' Wives Club card party, over a highball.

Cathy and Kathy not only helped me out countless times, but they would often actually ask me if I had done my homework, if it was neat enough, or should I be doing it over? Sometimes while I was copying their homework, they would explain certain parts of it to me so that I would understand it. If they were unsure of something they would tell me it was hard and caution me not to copy it exactly. It was from them I first caught on to putting JMJ (Jesus, Mary, and Joseph) at the very top of my homework paper in hopes of Sister being impressed with such holiness. Maybe she would be impressed with this ejaculation and realize that I offered up my effort to God and she would accept it and overlook a little sloppiness. It didn't seem to work. Balled up homework papers were being thrown back at me at an alarming rate.

On some occasions, I was unable to get all my homework copied before class. In these cases, I would do it myself during school. Luckily, every day was started with Religion. Religion was often boring, usually easy, a good opportunity to do homework, and appear to be taking notes. Most of the time, I would be feverishly doing homework but listening to the exchanges between my classmates and Sister. Once in a while one of the priests would come in for Religion and answer our questions. There were three priests in our parish and, of course, Monsignor.

Father Moore was the senior priest and was Rosemary Moore's uncle. Almost everybody liked Rosemary and so nobody gave Father Moore a hard time. By hard time I mean asking questions about sex.

Father Denning was the youngest and he was shy and, we thought, pretty cool. He liked sports and never acted like a priest and was frequently out of "uniform." The lines at his confession box were always long and full of grade school and high school kids. We never had many questions for Father Denning. Father Botino, on the other hand, was middle-aged, pompous, and lived in another world. He always looked like had he just woken up. His confession lines were full of old ladies and very pious men. When he came to the Religion class, we liked to pepper him with questions, particularly on sex. He would be awkward and looked stunned. He frequently didn't understand the question and his answers were pathetic. After he left, we usually got scolded by Sister Mary Mark for our outrageous behavior and for embarrassing Father Botino. She called the girls "bold and brazen articles" and called the boys "impudent."

Robert Hutchinson, Joe Heaney, Vincent DiGilio, and Louis Climent (the oldest kid in the class) were the most active during the Religion class. Kissing, making out, petting, looking at nude pictures, and impure thoughts were all prime topics. Masturbation, although ever present in our minds, was never discussed.

Eighth graders are at a point where most of us were consumed with sex and after seven years of having the "mysteries of faith" drilled into us, we were becoming a little skeptical. This made these discussions often a real pleasure to listen to. Questions like: Is kissing a sin? Is petting a sin? Is looking at nude pictures a sin? were more complicated in our minds than they appear. Father Botino once answered that prolonged kissing was a sin.

"How long is prolonged?"

"More than a few seconds."

"Mortal sin or venial sin?"

"Mortal sin!"

"You mean we could go to hell for a kiss that lasts, like, five seconds?"

"Yes!"

"How about petting, Father?"

"Mortal sin!"

"How about looking at nude photos, Father?"

"Mortal sin!"

"We could go to hell forever just for looking at *Playboy*?"

"If you have impure thoughts!"

"Why else would someone be doing it?"

"I don't know. Impure thoughts alone is a mortal sin."

"Murmur." "Murmur."

"How about impure thoughts that just come into your head from nowhere?"

"Not a sin unless you entertain them."

"What does entertain them mean?"

"Once you realize that you are having impure thoughts, you must get them out of your mind. If you don't try, then you are entertaining them, and it's a mortal sin."

"Is there any time limit on that?"

"No!"

"Suppose you try to get rid of them, but they keep coming back?"

"You must keep trying."

"How do you keep impure thoughts from coming into your head?"

"Prayer and meditation. Think of Jesus, hanging and bleeding on the cross. Say 'The Act of Contrition.'"

"So every time we find ourselves thinking about sex, we should immediately think of Jesus hanging on the cross?"

"That's right! Remember Jesus suffered and died for you and your sins and that sin is in the will. You don't actually have to commit an immoral act."

"Murmur." "Murmur."

Vincent DiGilio was big and tough. He also stuttered. Actually outside of school, he seemed to talk fine, but in school, he stuttered badly and almost never asked a question. When called on, he would nervously rock from side to side, actually lifting one foot slightly off the floor, shift all his weight, and then lift the other. He would answer questions in a very bad stutter and didn't care if the answer was right or wrong, just so he could sit down and be done. No one ever made fun of Vincent, however. At least not to his face. I once whispered an answer to him when Sister Mary Mark was momentarily distracted and he whispered back, "If it's wrong, I'll break your fucking head!" No stutter there!

It was on this particular day when Father Botino had upset Vincent with his talk of sin being in the will, that he raised his hand and stood and asked a question.

"F-f-f-father, if you-you t-t-try to k-k-k-kiss and t-t-t-touch a g-g-girl but she-she stops y-y-you, it's not the s-s-same as if-if you-you actually d-d-d-did it. Is-is-is it?"

"Yes! It's a mortal sin and if you die without forgiveness, you will suffer in Hell for all eternity."

Stunned by Father Botino's unequivocal answer, Vincent slumped slowly back into his seat and said, "H-h-h-holy shit."

A lot of us had difficulty with the idea that in God's eyes, looking at a nudie magazine or wanting to kiss or touch a girl or guy was equal to murdering someone. Both were mortal sins and if unconfessed and unforgiven, carried the same punishment! Father Botino had no trouble with this. "Murder violates the Fifth Commandment, while impure thoughts and actions violate the Sixth and Ninth Commandments."

No matter how we argued that we weren't talking about adultery or our neighbor's wife, Father Botino would not hear of it.

Many of us had difficulty that "Thou shalt not commit adultery" or "Thou shalt not covet thy neighbor's wife" could be interpreted to mean no willful sexual stimulation, even if it's just in your mind. (Many of us didn't even know what 'covet' meant, but took it on faith that it meant something bad.) Often, these discussions of morality would bog down on how a just and merciful God could punish murder and rape the same as French kissing Jean Reed or Vincent DiGilio just *wanting* to French kiss Jean Reed!

However, Father Botino was adept at logic, and would escape these theological conundrums by reminding us that "you can also go to hell for missing Mass on Sunday or eating meat on Friday!" A brilliant logistical move by Father Botino. Certainly a God who would commit your soul to hell for all eternity for eating meat on Friday or missing Mass, wouldn't think twice about doing it for "entertaining" an impure thought about Jean Reed or Laurel Kramer or yes, even about Vincent DiGilio.

These sessions with a priest were rare—perhaps twice a month. Most of the time the Religion period was conducted by a nun and the conversation wasn't usually about sex. Whenever sex came up and Sister Mary Mark felt uncomfortable, she would tell you to take it up with a priest. The discussions were often spirited, however, and humorous, at least to me and Eddie Haggerty.

Robert Hutchinson was fascinated with the concept of Indulgences. We were taught that every prayer carried with it an Indulgence of a certain number of days. Our Religion textbook even had the Indulgence amount in parentheses after the prayer. A "Hail Mary" carried a thirty-day Indulgence, and an "Our Father" carried a sixty-day Indulgence. Various prayers and rituals carried Indulgences of various weights and occasionally there was an opportunity for a Plenary Indulgence, which removed all the punishment due for all the sins you ever committed!

As it was explained to us, each and every sin carried a punishment with it. If you died with a Mortal Sin on your soul, you went straight to Hell *forever*. However, even when a Mortal Sin was confessed and forgiven, a punishment remained due. Venial Sins also carried punishment. This punishment was called temporal punishment and was redeemable only by time spent in Purgatory. Purgatory was a lot like Hell, only not forever. You knew it would end when your time was up and you would go to Heaven. Indulgences were days off your time in Purgatory.

Robert Hutchinson found this fascinating and tried to get Sister Mary Mark to reveal what the punishment was for various sins. If he could find that out, then he could say enough prayers to stay even, he reasoned. He once asked if a person can get ahead of the game and actually have negative time in Purgatory, or could commit some sins, and due to the surplus of Indulgences, have no penalty.

Sister Mary Mark, of course, wouldn't cooperate. "No one knows how much punishment is given for each sin, Mr. Hutchinson. We know how many days or years of Indulgence you get, but not how much punishment is due—that is up to God."

"Who decided on Indulgences, Sister?"

"The Pope."

"Then why can't the Pope decide on punishment?"

"Because the punishment can depend on circumstances."

"Like what?"

"Like, how often you commit the sin, how hard you try not to, and how sorry you are."

"Sister, you pray a lot and I bet you hardly ever commit a sin, so do you have negative time in Purgatory, like a credit?"

"I'm sure I do not, Mr. Hutchinson. Although I try to be like the Blessed Mary, I fail. I do not have enough patience."

"Does anyone bypass Purgatory and go straight to Heaven?"

"Yes."

"Who?"

"The Blessed Virgin did and anyone who dies after receiving a Plenary Indulgence. I'm sure some of the saints and martyrs did."

Robert was relentless.

"So, how much time do you think cursing would get?"

"I don't know, Mr. Hutchinson."

"Well, what do you think, Sister? Do you ever curse? Did you ever disobey your mother?"

"That's between me and the Lord."

"Do you think you will go to Purgatory, Sister?"

"I don't know, but I have faith in God's mercy."

"I'd feel better if we knew the rules and knew what to expect. Maybe if the punishment is severe, like a thousand years, praying won't make much of a difference."

Sister was losing her patience. "Such impudence!"

"I'm sorry, Mr. Hutchinson, if God didn't create the world to your satisfaction, but I think most people would be interested in any reduction of the terrible pain, suffering, and misery of Purgatory."

"Suppose you do a lot of praying and good works all your life, but die with a Mortal Sin on your soul?"

"You would burn for all eternity in Hell."

"And all the prayers and Indulgences are wasted?"

"Yes."

"But, suppose you were sorry for it, but didn't get a chance to go to confession?"

"If you die with a Mortal Sin on your soul, you go to Hell!"

"If God knows you are sorry, but you didn't have a chance to confess it and God is merciful, why would he send you to Hell?"

"God is also just. He has told us his Commandments and you disobey at your peril, Mr. Hutchinson."

"But, Sister, if you make the nine First Fridays and go to confession and communion within seven days, aren't you guaranteed that you wouldn't die without a priest?"

"Yes."

"So, let me get this straight, I could do the nine First Fridays and then be bad and have lots of Mortal Sins on my soul, but confess them just before I die and go to Heaven?"

"Confessing them alone won't save you, Mr. Hutchinson! You must get absolution from your sins, which requires . . . Anyone want to help Mr. Hutchinson here? LeRoy?"

"You have to be truly sorry . . ."

"That's right, *and* . . . ?"

"You have to have a firm purpose of amendment."

"Correct! Now, Mr. Hutchinson, would a person who commits Mortal Sins and waits until he is on his deathbed to confess, be truly sorry . . . and did he make a firm purpose of amendment?"

"Maybe, Sister."

"Very doubtful that a just God would see it that way. Don't forget that sin is in the will and God knows your every thought."

It was amazing how deflating it was to hear those words. And how often we heard them.

The whole concept of the Nine First Fridays was fascinating to us. We were told that in 1699, Our Lord appeared to St. Margaret Mary Alcoque and promised, among other things, that anyone who attended Mass and received communion on nine consecutive First Fridays of the month, would not die without a priest, and the final sacrament.

We were strongly urged to do the Nine First Fridays and, in effect, ensure ourselves of Heaven. No reason or logic was given for why Our Lord chose Friday or the first Friday or even the magic number nine. We were told it was true and we should believe it as a matter of faith. During a discussion of this, I once asked if anyone had considered that Margaret Mary Alcoque might be nuts. The class erupted in laughter and Sister Mary Mark slapped me in the face . . . for "impudence."

Not all the skepticism was about just good and evil, however. The concept of the Blessed Trinity was one that eighth graders wrestled with as well. No matter how many times the nuns told us about St. Patrick and the Shamrock, it was still hard to grasp the concept of three persons in one God. God the Father was easy to understand. Apparently, God is male and a fatherly being who is all-Just, all-Wise, all-Merciful, and all-Knowing—but God the son was a bit more profound.

He was a male who was sent by his Father to save the world. But although he was sent by his Father, he was equal to him and not subservient in any way. He was God, just like God the Father, but a different person who had taken on human form and was tortured and executed by the Romans to atone for our sins, even though we were centuries from even being born.

And then there was the Holy Ghost, who apparently sits on God the Father's left hand side but is equally powerful. The Holy Ghost comes to us during the ritual called Confirmation. He makes us soldiers in Christ's Army and gives us strength. When a person receives Confirmation, he or she takes an additional name for some reason. I took Patrick. I figured if this made sense to *him*, maybe he would help it make sense to me.

You see, St. Patrick, we were told, converted all of Ireland to Catholicism by using the shamrock to illustrate the Blessed Trinity. He must have been quite a sight, proclaiming that the shamrock had three petals, but was one plant, and this is like the three persons in one God. Of course, the Irish were probably drinking Guinness and after a few pints it's no doubt probably easier to grasp this phenomenon. I was thirteen, Catholic, Irish, loved the shamrock, and took Patrick as my confirmation name, but I still had trouble with this concept, as did many of us.

Once when Sister Mary Mark mentioned angels, Laurel Kramer asked if angels were real or were they, as she had heard somewhere, just a symbol of souls in heaven. Sister Mary Mark was quick to respond and quite definitive. Not only are angels real, but there are nine different ranks of angels, called "choirs." There are Angels, Archangels, Principalities, Powers, Virtues, Dominions, Thrones, Cherubim and Seraphim! With *that* kind of specificity, we figured she must know what she was talking about. When Joe Heaney suggested, in a sarcastic tone of voice, that surely the idea of guardian angels, i.e. each one of us has an angel watching over us, was bogus, he got slapped in the face by Sister Mary Mark for . . . "impudence."

The notion of going to hell for eating meat on Friday seemed particularly egregious to some of us and was often questioned. Since it isn't in the Bible and not in the Commandments, we'd reason, how can it be so wrong?

The answer was that the Pope says so. The Pope makes the laws of the Church, he's Christ's Vicar on earth and therefore, infallible. He says it's a mortal sin and therefore it is. Simple enough! We understood the answer, but it just didn't sit well. Murder and rape and eating meat on Friday just didn't seem to balance on the scales of justice. And who in the right mind would purposely, knowing full well that they could go to Hell and suffer horribly for Eternity, choose to eat meat when there they could stay in God's graces and eat a grilled cheese or tuna fish sandwich or macaroni and cheese or fish sticks and French fries?

Sister Mary Mark seemed to notice, that I, with a few exceptions, was never giving her or the priests a hard time during Religion period. I was too busy copying or doing my homework. Other than the St. Margaret Mary Alcoque question, I can only remember two instances of me causing Sister Mary Mark any trouble at all during our opening hour of class.

Once, I was questioning praying to Mary or the Saints. Eddie Haggerty had been asking about why all through grade school nuns had always told us to offer up any suffering or difficulties we may encounter for "the poor souls in purgatory." We often were told to pray for them and mentioned them in our prayers in school every day. Eddie was merely questioning the wisdom of using the indulgences that could be reducing the temporal punishment on *his* soul for whoever was in purgatory. The answer was that if you help souls in purgatory, they will remember and help you when *you* are in purgatory. How would they help you? Sister Mary Mark said they could "intercede" on your behalf and ask God to forgive some of the punishment due your soul. Eddie asked "What if they are still in purgatory when you get there?" Eddie was smart and cynical, even at thirteen.

Sister Mary Mark muttered some answer about if Eddie were more humble and less impudent, he wouldn't worry about having a lot of punishment *due* on his soul. "Practice humility and try to avoid sin and maybe you won't worry so much about your punishment," she said.

Eddie's line of questioning, however, made me wonder about why anyone should pray to saints or angels or to Mary, when they could pray to God himself. So I asked.

"Sister, why should we pray to saints and angels and the Blessed Mother, when we can eliminate the middle man and pray directly to God?" I wasn't being difficult. I thought it was a good and legitimate question.

"You pray to whomever you want, Mr. Farrell, and you better pray hard and often. As a matter of fact, you and Haggerty better pray for each other, because I don't think anyone *else* will," she screamed. I was amazed at such a hostile answer to my sincere question and sat down slowly, shook my head in frustration, and went back to copying my homework.

A few minutes later a note was passed to me from Cathy Garity. It read, "Don't worry. Kathy and I will pray for you!" As we broke for lunch, my path crossed Vincent DiGilio's. "Hey Vinnie, will you pray for me?" I whispered jokingly. "F-f-f-fuckin'-A!" he whispered back without hesitation.

The other time I admit I was going for a laugh. Sister Mary Mark was discussing "The Annunciation," which was one of the fifteen mysteries of the Rosary. "The Annunciation" was when the Angel Gabriel appeared to Mary and told her she was going to conceive by the power of the Holy Spirit and have a son, who will be Jesus, the Son of God. We were told that an angel came to Joseph in a dream and told him that Mary was pregnant of the Holy Ghost. He accepted this and prepared to become the foster father of God.

St. Joseph was my patron saint. He was a carpenter and apparently not a very good one, because he was very poor. My question was simple and I thought obviously funny. Perhaps too funny.

I raised my hand just as Sister Mary Mark was discussing how Joseph, knowing the child was not his, had had a dream in which an angel (apparently the angel who appeared to Joseph preferred to remain anonymous) told him that it was God's child.

"How did Joseph explain this to the guys at work?" I asked.

Most of the class burst out laughing. Sister Mary Mark did not. Eddie was hysterical and was reacting to the same mental picture I had when I asked the question.

"Mary's pregnant and it's not yours, it's God's?" "Yeah, right," Eddie answered. More bursts of laughter.

Sister Mary Mark clapped her hands loudly and shouted for silence. "You can both stay after school today for your impudence."

"Oh, great," I said, "I haven't even finished copying my homework for today and already I have to stay after school." I said it just loudly enough for those around me to hear, but not loud enough for Sister Mary Mark to. Most of those who heard me cracked up again! Claire Burns, Cathy Garity, Francis Scully, Michael Boyle, Eileen Quinn, even Robert Shullman, were all laughing.

Sister Mary Mark started down the aisle toward me. As I prepared to get smacked in the face, she stopped halfway down the aisle and looked at those around me and said, "Please, don't laugh at him. He's not funny. Please." She was practically begging. "Those who laugh at him will wind up just like him and that's not going to be good."

After school, Sister Mary Mark talked to Eddie and me about Catholic high school. How could she recommend us when there are so many worthy young boys and girls and a limited number of spaces?

"What's the problem?" Eddie asked. "We laugh, we joke around a little, what's the big deal?"

"Do you want to go to Catholic high school?" she asked.

"Yes, Sister," we both answered.

"Well, very shortly you'll be making your choices of schools and they'll be asking for my recommendation. You will *not* be accepted without my recommendation and I'm telling you right now I won't be recommending you if I see any more disrespectful behavior."

"Sister, I'm not trying to be disrespectful. Are my grades good?" I asked.

"Very good. Both of you have excellent grades. I have no doubt that you can do the work. The problem is your attitudes."

"But, Sister, some things are funny and we laugh, but we're not being disrespectful. If St. Joseph told that story today, nobody would believe him. They'd think it was somebody else's child. Things have changed since those days. We don't mean any disrespect to St. Joseph, but when you think about it in today's world, it just seems funny."

"Well, wouldn't we all be better off if people didn't question everything and they just believed? That is what our Catholic high schools want. They don't want students that laugh and make others laugh, they want serious students. They want boys and girls who believe what they are taught, who have faith and don't question or challenge everything."

CHAPTER FOUR

♦ ♦ ♦ ♦

"A SNOWBALL'S CHANCE IN HELL"

You'll never know the pain I feel or the suffering I rise above; and I'll never know the same about you; your holiness, your kind of love; and it makes me feel so sorry.

Bob Dylan ~ "Idiot Wind"

Our first quarter report cards came out in November and Sister Mary Mark was correct about our grades. As usual, we both did very well. To the best of my memory, Eddie had a 96% average and I had a 93. There were only a few above Eddie. Ralph Azanza was number one, as usual, with a 98, then came Carol Anderson, Robert Shullman, Kevin Connolly, Paul Pirro, and maybe Kathy Kain. A few more between Eddie and me, but basically, we were crushing Grade 8A. This seemed to me to make an impact on Sister Mary Mark. I thought I detected a small change in her attitude toward me. Two incidents reinforced this idea.

The first involved Francis Scully. Francis Scully was a weird kid. He was tall and gangly and had a deep voice. He wore strange clothes and didn't play or follow sports. He didn't seem to notice girls at all and was smart, but unenthusiastic, almost lethargic in class. He had older brothers and seemed to spend time on mechanical things. He seemed to always be talking or reading about something unusual, like books on aircraft or weapons or vehicles.

For a short while in eighth grade, Francis sat in front of me. I sat in the last desk of the first row, for about six weeks, after being moved a few times. The first time Sister Mary Mark sat us alphabetically, I was too close to Eddie. After a few days, she realized her mistake and put Eddie up front and me in the far right hand corner of the classroom, or storeroom, as it was originally designed. Shortly after that, she moved me to the left corner behind Scully.

Her reasoning for the last shift was that, in the right corner, I was near too many "immature" girls who "foolishly" thought I was funny. By switching a few people around, as if in a chess game, she thought she had me pretty much isolated. She put me in the last seat against the wall, behind the loner Scully and next to the humorless, ambitious Robert Shullman.

Many of my best comments and observations went unappreciated in this seating arrangement, although I occasionally had Shullman biting his pencil or taking off his glasses and rubbing his eyes to cover up laughter. Shullman was a very serious and efficient young man who in the eighth grade seemed about forty-two. He was very organized, hardworking, kept a pencil behind his ear, and seemed to realize that Sister Mary Mark expected him to not laugh at me. He was exactly the kind of person I would want to operate on me, if I needed serious surgery, but a real challenge to get to laugh out loud. The nuns, of course, loved him.

Even Shullman found it difficult to relate to Scully, who was disorganized and pretty much lived in his own little world. Whenever called on, Scully would stand, as was required, and answer, but he would always flop down hard into his seat and make a weird sound effect, like escaping air. He did it almost every time. Even Shullman rolled his eyes when Scully flopped down.

Scully was upset about his report card and gave Sister Mary Mark a hard time about it. He said *his* records indicated that his average was higher, and asked to see his homework records. When Sister Mary Mark explained it to him after school, he left grumbling. I, of course, was there because I was doing my homework over after school. I'm not sure what role Scully's questioning and hostility played in the upcoming event, but it was probably a factor.

One afternoon, just before the bell that would end our lunch break sounded, Scully was hovering over and intensely studying a large document that appeared to be a blueprint. He had it spread on the ground and had stones on two corners to keep it from rolling up on itself. As I walked by, I asked, "Scully, what's that?"

"Hmmm," was all he answered.

"Scully, what is that?"

"What? Oh, you wouldn't understand."

I bent over to get a better look and as I did, Scully quickly started to roll up the document. "It's blueprints," he said, with a strange smile.

"Blueprints for what?"

"You'll find out soon enough," he said as he put rubber bands around the roll of papers, which were about a yard long. "You'll find out soon enough." And he walked away, smiling smugly.

When I got to my seat a few minutes later, Scully had the blueprints on his desk and as soon as class resumed, Scully's hand went up. I could barely believe what I heard.

"Yes, Mr. Scully?"

"Sister, I'm building a helicopter and I want permission to land it on the roof."

As I looked around to see the reaction of others, wondering if I had heard correctly, there were snickers, and hands were covering mouths to stifle bursts of laughter. Eddie had a huge smile on his face and a look that said, "this ought to be good." Shullman looked at me with his mouth hanging open in disbelief.

"What?" Sister Mary Mark said, squinting as if she couldn't believe it either.

"I have blueprints right here, Sister," said Scully, holding up the roll of papers, "and I would like permission to land on the roof when I fly to school."

"Sit down, Mr. Scully, before I *knock* you down," she yelled. "We don't have time for your nonsense."

While Scully was on his feet, I had inched my movable desk and chair forward slowly, quietly pushed his chair in under his desk, and moved back slowly to the wall, as far away from him as possible. This time, when Scully slowly and dramatically tried to plop into his chair, he instead went down on his ass like a ton of bricks, blueprints flying! Eddie later told me that when he looked back, Scully's face suddenly disappeared and Eddie saw Scully's feet come up as he hit the floor. I heard Shullman laugh out loud for the first time ever, as he completely lost it.

Sister Mary Mark hadn't seen Scully fall since she was looking down at her desk trying to find the place where she was before the interruption. When she heard the commotion, a mixture of Scully crashing onto the floor and others gasping and laughing, she raced down the aisle toward us.

As I prepared to get hit, I immediately regretted what I had done. I realized as Scully was struggling to get up that he could be hurt and that I was responsible. That wasn't my intention. I also realized as Sister Mary Mark was flying toward me in a rage, that this could be serious trouble. I mean not doing homework, making a wisecrack, asking a funny question—those were all one thing—but doing physical harm that hurt someone, that was another matter completely.

Shullman was still laughing loudly and uncontrollably, but suddenly I wasn't enjoying it. It occurred to me that if Sister Mary Mark was looking to get rid of me, this might be her opportunity. To my complete astonishment, when she reached the back of the room, she slapped *Scully* in the face! "I don't know what's gotten into you lately, Mr. Scully, but you better get over it!" she screamed. "I'm not putting up with any more of your foolishness. Do you understand me?"

Scully was stunned. He was not used to being slapped in the face, much less falling on his ass on the floor. He couldn't seem to grasp what was happening.

"Do you?" she screamed in his face.

"Yes, Sister," he said quietly, as he looked down for his blueprints, which had rolled away.

My heart was beating fast and I had a terrible sense of dread as I waited for Sister Mary Mark to turn her wrath on me. The only other sound I was aware of was Shullman. He was now in convulsions of laughter. Sister Mary Mark turned to Shullman.

"Would you kindly go out in the hall and get control of yourself?"

Shullman was quickly on his feet and heading for the door with his hands over his mouth to contain himself.

"Mr. Hamberger, get back in your seat."

Billy Hamberger, who sat in the opposite corner of the classroom, hadn't seen what happened and was standing up on his tiptoes and craning his neck trying to figure it out.

Sister Mary Mark started back toward the front of the room and I started breathing again. I could just barely hear Eddie saying something to Scully about crashing and burning from his seat up front, but I dare not look at him. I had had a narrow escape and couldn't afford to draw any attention to what had happened.

About fifteen minutes later, Shullman returned to his seat, but would not look at me, just as I would not look at Eddie. I did not know if Sister Mary Mark had any inkling of what had happened to Scully or not. Maybe she did and had cut me a break. Maybe Shullman's convulsions of laughter had helped me. Maybe she just had it in for Scully.

The second incident was a real shocker. Traditionally at St. Andrew's, a number of eighth grade boys were chosen to be "Patrol Boys." This was a position of trust and honor, one that required monitoring the schoolyard at lunchtime and also walking each class quietly and in a double line to the end of the block for dismissal.

The job came with a white belt that went around your waist and diagonally across your chest and a badge that was pinned to the belt in the front of the chest area. It was cool to be a Patrol Boy. You had authority over all the other students and you got to leave school ten minutes early at lunch and a half hour early, around 2:45 p.m., at dismissal time. I found this part to be particularly attractive, since I found the confinement for long periods in class to be unbearable.

The boys in 8A1 had been the patrol boys up until now and apparently it was us, 8A3, who would serve for the second third of the year. Who was selected was up to Sister Mary Mark. It was usually the best students or the biggest brown-nosers who were picked. I can't remember the exact number, but I think it was six.

Sister Mary Mark was in the front of the room with a cardboard box with all the belts and badges in it. She reviewed the responsibilities of a patrol boy and asked if there were any boys who couldn't be here early enough in the morning (thirty minutes before school) or at lunchtime. A few boys raised their hands and disqualified themselves for one reason or another. I thought for a moment about raising my hand to avoid *not* being picked, but the only reason I could think of to give would be that I needed the time to copy my homework!

"Ralph, would you like to be Captain?" she asked Ralph Azanza.

"Yes, Sister."

She held out the belt and the silver and red badge that said "Captain" on it. Ralph went up to the front of the room and got it.

"Robert Shullman, would you like to be Lieutenant?"

"Yes, Sister," answered Shullman, as he started up to her desk for the belt and badge.

Sister Mary Mark could go a lot of ways now. If she did it by grades, I would be picked, as would Eddie. Or she could pick the altar boys McNally, Pirro, Baxter, Rusie, and McVann. She could throw in some brown nosers, like Jeffrey McGrath and David Dyke or parish favorites like Joe Rubbone and John Daly.

Instead, she asked Ralph and Robert to discuss who they wanted to be on their team. They talked quietly together as my hopes rose. Ralph and I were pretty good friends. I spent a lot of time at his house, playing wiffle ball, watching TV, and copying his homework. In fact, I called him by his nickname, "Bing," which nobody at school knew.

His older brother, Roman, showed me *Playboy* magazine for the first time in their bedroom. Roman went to Xavier High School in Manhattan. This was a Jesuit military academy and Roman wore a strange maroon and gray uniform to school that had stripes on his sleeve, indicating some sort of rank. We would make fun of him whenever he arrived home from school, but once out of uniform, Roman was cool. When he showed us *Playboy* and Ralph mentioned that he would burn in hell, Roman told us that it wasn't a mortal sin to look at naked women.

"That's just the crap they tell you in grade school," he said. "I go to Xavier and, at dances, we all make out with our dates and the priests never say anything about it." This was great news!

The Azanzas hosted the first boy—girl party I ever attended in sixth grade. Roman had all the latest hit records and taught us how to play kissing games. When Ralph first proposed having a party, he asked me who he should invite. I think I was Ralph's link with the cool kids. We made up the list in his bedroom and he called each one personally and very politely invited them.

The party was a big success and started a chain reaction of such parties, mostly at girls' homes. Bing was invited to some, but not all of them. When he wasn't, it really bothered him. He would say, "I hope the party sucks. I hope nobody comes." He would mock the person and draw unflattering pictures of them. Once he put a hand-drawn picture on a tree and threw a sharp knife at it! When he couldn't get the knife to stick in the tree, he asked for Roman's help. Roman threw it and it stuck.

"What's the secret?" asked Bing.

"The secret is you're an asshole," said Roman as he again got the knife to stick in the picture on the tree.

Bing saw the key to Roman's success and threw the knife, handle first, holding the blade—and it stuck.

"Take that, you fuck," he said to the drawing, extracting the knife.

The whole thing made me uncomfortable, but it illustrated Ralph's desire to be popular and be a part of the "in crowd." I think Roman was very popular with his age group and Ralph wanted to be, but wasn't. I often felt caught up in this sibling rivalry.

Now, however, it was time for old Bing to show his colors. Would he pick who he thought Sister Mary Mark would want or pick me and risk Sister Mary Mark's disapproval? Shullman used to avoid me like the plague, but since he sat next to me, had grown to like me. I saw Shullman glance at me once during this discussion, as if to see if I was watching. I realized they were probably discussing me and I felt really strange. I wanted this badly! I felt sure that Sister Mary Mark would never approve, but if they picked me it would be a moral victory. If her two favorite boys picked me, I felt it would definitely send her a message about me. My heart was beating fast and my ears felt hot. I wasn't prepared because no one knew this was going to happen. I saw Ralph and Robert look at Sister Mary Mark and say something quietly. I could not hear what they said nor could I see their faces.

I looked down and feigned interest in a book on my desk as they discussed their choice. I didn't want to show disappointment.

"Mr. Farrell, would you accept assignment as Patrol Boy?" was the next thing I heard. I looked up at Sister Mary Mark and she was holding out a belt and badge for me to come up and accept! I got up and walked to the front of the room, trying not to show any emotion. I didn't want anyone to know how much I wanted this. I was elated that her two hand-picked boys had picked me and felt like letting out a triumphant yell. I was astonished and stunned that Sister Mary Mark was going to accept it. As she handed me the belt and badge, she said, "This is against my better judgment, Mister. Don't embarrass me or yourself."

"Yes, Sister."

I returned to my seat quietly and showed no emotion; at least none I could control. Inside I felt like exploding! I wanted to scream, "Yeeeesssssssss!" I wanted to pump my fist in the air. I wanted to jump up in the air, pumping my fist and yelling "Yes!" For the next few minutes, I don't remember anything. The rest of the patrol was picked, including Eddie and Billy Rusie was picked as the alternate. If any patrol boy was sick, or going to miss school or unable to perform his patrol boy duties, Billy Russie would fill in.

Our first patrol was at 2:45 p.m. that day. I was ecstatic. As soon as we got outside, I thanked Bing and Robert Shullman. It felt so good to get out of class, even if only for a half hour!

I'm not sure why Sister Mary Mark allowed me to be a patrol boy. Was it a conscious decision to see how I responded to responsibility? Was it to win me over? Was she caught by surprise and didn't give it any thought at all? I'll never know!

Twice before teachers had given me special responsibility and both times, it worked out well—sort of. In the fourth grade, Mrs. Headen was my teacher. She and Mrs. McGarry were the only two lay teachers at St. Andrew's. Mrs. Headen was well-off. Her husband made a lot of money and she was a trained teacher and could afford to teach in Catholic school. She was an excellent teacher. All the students liked her and she had complete control of the class. I liked her and liked school at that point in time. I cannot recall Mrs. Headen ever hitting anyone. She maintained classroom discipline by being liked and respected and by involving those who needed special attention.

A few weeks after school began, she amended her initial seating arrangement, which was alphabetical, by sex, that is, boys first, starting on the left alphabetically, then girls alphabetically. The boys took up about two and a half rows and the girls three and a half. This arrangement had me, Haggerty and Hamberger all together in a row. This would not endure! After a few weeks, she decided to make a change. No significant event triggered it. She just announced one morning that she was changing some seats. She moved me to the first seat in the fifth row, right beside her desk. Along with this move, however, she announced that I was to be her assistant and help her with a variety of chores, hence the move and location. She also moved Billy Hamberger to the front of the first row and gave him the responsibility of neatly lining up all the students' book bags and boots when worn.

My duties were to take charge of the blackboards and erasers. I was to erase the boards whenever requested, as Mrs. Headen came to school dressed to kill. As a matter of fact, we could always hear her coming from a distance because of her jewelry clanging as she walked. She didn't want to get chalk dust on her expensive clothes and I guess figured my uniform didn't matter.

I was to completely clean the blackboards at the end of the day and clap the erasers outside to clean the chalk off and return them to their place in the chalk trays. I was also to count and pass out things to the first person in each row when she had something to be passed out, which was frequently. I would count out nine and hand them to the first person in each row to pass back. Likewise, when something was to be collected, everyone would pass the item forward and I would collect them from each person in the first seat in her prescribed manner and place the pile on her desk. In this way, the papers were in the correct order.

Looking back on this decision, Mrs. Headen seems to have been very smart. I secretly loved my assignments, even though they were a masked punishment for goofing around with Haggerty and Hamberger. I took my jobs very seriously and did them well. I didn't want to disappoint Mrs. Headen and I loved the getting up and moving around. Mrs. Headen was always thanking me and I liked it. She called me Joseph and after erasing the blackboard or collecting the papers or opening or closing the windows with a six-foot long window pole, she would almost always say, "Thank you, Joseph."

I got good grades, liked school, never got hit and the whole thing worked out great, except for one unusual incident. In the spring of that year, St. Andrew's was dedicating their new rectory. One morning, Mrs. Headen was late coming to class. The class was supervised by a nun no one knew, while Mrs. Headen attended the dedication ceremony. It seems the Headens were generous contributors or played some role in the fundraising efforts and were therefore honored guests at the ceremony. When she came to class in mid-morning, she was extremely dressed up, including a mink coat!

Mrs. Headen thanked the nun who had filled in for her and, anxious to get going with class, asked me to hang up her coat for her in the cloak room. I had never done this before, since she was always there before we were. I took her mink back to the cloak room and hung it on a hook, like I assumed I was supposed to. At the end of the day, I was just returning with the clean erasers when I heard Mrs. Headen.

"Oh, my God! Joseph, did you hang my coat on a *hook*?"

"Uh, yes, Mrs. Headen."

"Well, look at this—you ruined it!" she screamed, holding up her coat and showing her finger through a hole made by the hook! Apparently the weight of the coat forced the hook through it.

"Didn't you see the hanger back there for my coat?"

I shrugged.

"Well, I want your parents to pay to have it repaired."

"Okay. How much will it cost?"

"I don't know, but I'll let you know when I find out."

That night I felt compelled to prepare my parents. I told them at dinner what had happened. When I said Mrs. Headen wanted them to pay for the repairs, it caused an uproar.

"I will like Hell," my father said.

"Joe, we have to," argued my mother, "or I'll be ashamed to show my face down there."

"So don't show your face, but I'll be God damned if I'm paying to fix her mink coat! I break my ass in boiler rooms six days a week and don't even buy lunch, so we can have a decent home and the things we need. I'm going to pay for her mink coat? Like Hell!"

My father refused to discuss it any further. This had not gone as I expected and I was unhappy about it. I expected them to be pissed off at me and rant and rave and punish me, but to agree to pay Mrs. Headen. Now I was faced with the awful proposition of having to tell Mrs. Headen that we wouldn't pay to have her coat mended.

After dinner when my father had calmed down and he was reading the evening newspaper, I asked him quietly what to say when Mrs. Headen gives me the bill for her coat. I was trying to make him realize the awkward position I was in.

"Tell her to roll it up real tight and shove it up her ass."

I went to my room and laid in the dark and tried to figure out what to do. My mother came in and asked me what was wrong. I told her what dad had said and she laughed. If she gives you the bill, bring it home and we'll see what we can do. I can squeeze a few bucks out of grocery money. We'll see how much it is. You have money in the bank that you got for your First Holy Communion. Maybe we'll use that."

As it turned out, Mrs. Headen never gave me the bill. In fact, she never mentioned it again. Maybe she expected us to offer or ask about the damage, but I never did. It appeared to just blow over, but I always felt sheepish about it.

In the sixth grade, Sister Rene had a similar brainstorm and made me "cloak room" monitor. Ten minutes before dismissal at midday and at the end of the day, I was to go to the "cloak" room, in this case in the back of the classroom, and open the doors and put on the light. Then I was to signal for the first row to come get their coats.

As a row moves through, I signal the next row and so on. When all rows have gotten their coats and hats or whatever, I get mine, check for anything that may have been forgotten or dropped, turn out the light and close the doors. I did this job well. I frequently found gloves, hats, scarves and even sweaters left behind or accidentally dropped on the floor, and always made sure they got back to their owner. Sister Rene seemed pleased with me and acted like she counted on me to help her through her day. Our relationship meant a lot to me. The entire strategy worked out great, but I almost blew it.

In early spring, I was getting bored with this daily routine and one day, while the "cloak room" was filled with kids, I flicked the light out for just a few seconds. Everyone in the room stopped in their tracks and went silent and then laughed when the lights came back on. This little prank caught on and escalated. I would do it almost every dismissal on a different row and it soon became a game.

There were no windows in the cloak room and when the light was out, it was pitch black. To sixth graders, this was fun. Whenever it seemed that kids were reacting too strongly and that they might attract attention, I would not do it for a while. After a while I added a twist—I started to take coats of certain friends off the hooks and drop them on the floor or change where they were hung so that they would have to hunt for their coat. This was fun for a while and then I added searching for coats to searching for coats in the dark. I was careful not to do this while certain people like Barbara Gannon or Julianne Fenchak were in the cloak room, because they were likely to tell Sister Rene.

One day I noticed Jimmy McVann, a frequent victim of this prank, putting his coat up on the hat rack. Later, he would come in and just grab it off the hat rack and go. He thought I wouldn't notice this and therefore wouldn't change where he hung his coat or throw it on the floor.

The cloak room also had a closet in it where Sister Rene stored supplies. On this one particular day, there was a glass vase on the floor of the cloak room, just outside the closet. Apparently Sister Rene had meant to put it away, but had forgotten. Frequently, brown-nosers would bring flowers to the nuns and they put them in vases until they died. The flowers, that is. Anyhow, this one day I decided it would be fun to booby trap Jimmy McVann's coat by putting the vase on it. Somehow, I thought he would discover the booby trap and realize his counter-move had been trumped and I was fully aware of his clever scheme.

Jimmy came into the cloak room, grabbed his coat off the hat rack, never saw the vase and it broke as it crashed to the floor! Sister Rene came running back. Her first concern was that no one had hurt themselves. She got a broom and a dustpan and gave them to me to clean it up. Then she wanted to know how it happened. I was busy sweeping up glass in the cloak room and pretended not to hear her ask. I was grateful not to be in sight of her because I knew I couldn't lie to her. I was praying somehow Jimmy wouldn't rat me out. My prayers were answered. Jimmy said he didn't know how it happened. Jimmy McVann was a nice kid. He came from a well-to-do family that lived very close to St. Andrew's. His father was a lawyer and he had older siblings who had gone through St. Andrew's. Jimmy had a lot of spirit but was a nervous wreck. He always seemed to avoid big trouble but enjoyed laughing and was often on the fringes of trouble. Right now he could have told the truth and exposed me. Instead, he claimed ignorance but offered to pay for the damages.

"It was an accident, Sister. Somehow I kicked it or knocked it over with my coat, but it wasn't on purpose and I'll be glad to pay for it."

"How did the vase get near you?" Sister Rene asked. "It was in front of the supply cabinet."

"I don't know, Sister. I never saw it until I heard the crash."

"It's all swept up, Sister," I interrupted, hoping to move this line of questioning along. "Do you want me to do anything with the pieces of glass?" I was hoping to distract her and get Jimmy off the hook. She told me to go dump the glass in a barrel under the stairwell in the basement.

When I returned, the class was praying as we always did before dismissal. Once I got outside, Jimmy told me that he had to pay seventy-five cents for a new vase. I thanked him profusely for not ratting me out and promised to pay him the seventy-five cents.

That night, I took seventy-five cents from my father's work pants pocket to pay Jimmy McVann. My father usually had a lot of change in his work pants to pay tolls as he drove all over the metropolitan area answering service calls. I rationalized it by telling myself my father would rather I take the money than tell them what happened and cause a big scene.

The next morning, I gave Jimmy the money and again thanked him and praised him for being a stand-up guy. He paid Sister Rene and she told him to be more careful, as somebody could have gotten hurt. I never again pulled any pranks as "cloak room" monitor. I had had a narrow escape and didn't want to risk it ever again. The year ended with my tour of duty as "cloak room" monitor a success.

So now I was given another opportunity to be responsible and this one was really big. This wasn't just in our class of fifty-six, but in front of the entire school! I loved it and I was good at it. St. Andrew's is between 157th Street and 158th in Flushing and both were used as "play streets" and traffic was blocked by signs that Patrol Boys put out at the appropriate times.

I patrolled 157th St. I liked being looked up to by the younger kids, particularly the kids in my sister Ronnie's class and in my cousin Tom Nash's class. Tom was in sixth grade. During the morning before school and at lunch time, the Patrol Boys were to watch for any unsafe behavior or violation of any rules. Whenever we saw anyone fighting or on private property (neighbor's yards) or climbing trees or fences or throwing balls too hard or playing too rough, we were to "pull them in." This meant they had to stand at the entrance of the school behind the open doors until the bell rang, at which time everyone ran to get in line to enter the school. Each class had a designated spot to line up. When the nuns came to lead their class into school, we were to present them with any kid who had been "pulled in" and tell them why. This, of course, would lead to punishment.

A lot of Patrol Boys were hated for getting kids in trouble. I personally had never had trouble with a Patrol Boy because I was always either arriving just in time for the bell or busy copying homework.

I was a popular yet effective Patrol Boy. I never "pulled in" a kid without a warning first. And unless the kid gave me a hard time, I would tell him to go get in line as the bell rang and thus spare him further punishment by the nun. I never got any kind of resistance from any kid. This probably came from me being well-known, especially by those who would cause trouble, well-liked, and bigger than almost every other kid. I never wore my belt as designed but rolled it up into a ball with just a six-inch piece extended. I put the badge on the rolled up belt and, holding the extended part in the palm of my hand, twirled it back and forth around my hand. This was cool. Wearing it around your waist and across your chest with the badge pinned to your chest was not.

Many kids were surprised to see me as a Patrol Boy and sometimes made comments such as, "They must be desperate for Patrol Boys in 8-3" or "Did you steal that badge from someone?" I just smiled and continued doing my job. A few of the nuns were surprised at first, some happily and some not. When Sister Cyrylla first saw me on patrol, she stopped dead in her tracks and looked at me wide-eyed. "Don't tell me you're a Patrol Boy, Mr. Farrell?" She didn't seem to realize that I was still holding a grudge from Stations of the Cross. I just walked away without saying a word.

All the expressions of surprise or dismay just made me like it even more and served to motivate me more to do an exemplary job. I loved it! I loved being responsible. I loved being a leader. I loved getting out of class for patrol duties. I was even doing most of my own homework! In the six weeks I was a Patrol Boy, I did an excellent job and once Sister Mary Mark let it be known that she was pleased with the feedback she had gotten from other nuns and teachers.

One day in mid-January, it began to snow in the early afternoon. By four o'clock there was a couple of inches of fresh, wet, easy-packing snow on the ground. On this day I had to remain after class to redo a report I had done for homework that was, according to Sister Mary Mark, sloppy and illegible. The report was on the Pullman Strike of 1894, the first national strike in United States history. I had been given the assignment by Sister Mary Mark as part of an exercise to learn to use a library. Each student had an assignment similar to this. Unfortunately I had written mine while watching "The Rifleman" on television.

I had gone to the library and gotten material on the Pullman Strike and needed only to put it into a few coherent paragraphs. That episode of "The Rifleman" must have been captivating, because there were a few mistakes in my report. It took me about half an hour to redo the report and head out the door.

St. Andrew's had a very strict policy about snow. This policy was developed after a number of incidents involving snowballs. Kids throwing snowballs seems like a natural enough thing, but after some neighbors complained about a snowball fight in their yard during lunchtime, Sister Kieran cracked down and made it absolutely forbidden to throw snow on the school block during lunchtime. A short time later, a group of boys were reported by the police for pelting a city bus with snowballs. This event was blocks from school, but the boys were identified as St. Andrew's students because they were in uniform.

Throwing snowballs at buses was common and great fun. It was neat to startle passengers with a direct hit on a window. When there was a group of us, we'd all fire at once and try to hit every window on one side of the bus. A dozen snowballs would suddenly hit the side of the bus and splatter all over the windows. It seemed harmless and was fun. Most bus drivers didn't think so.

After this one episode, Sister Kieran made a much harsher ruling. No St. Andrew's student was to *touch* snow in uniform, anywhere, anytime! Sister Kieran made this announcement over the public address system every time it snowed or even when snow was forecast. Not throw snowballs! Not on school property! Not during lunchtime! We were strictly forbidden to *touch* snow *anywhere* at *anytime* while in uniform. Patrol Boys were instructed to report anyone seen touching snow in uniform anywhere or anytime. This policy seemed clear enough and seemed to be working to the nuns' satisfaction. Once out of uniform, you could do whatever you wanted and it wouldn't be blamed on St. Andrew's.

On this particular day in January 1960, I left the Rectory at about 4:30 p.m. and as I headed up the street, I suddenly got hit with a snowball in the shoulder and then almost immediately in the back as I turned away. Another came right at my face and I instinctively blocked it with my hand and as it broke, my face got sprayed with snow. I was under attack from across the street!

Joe Rubbone, Jimmy McVann and John Fracchia (a friend and neighbor of Jimmy's) had stockpiled snowballs and, using a parked car to shield them, had lain in wait for me. I took refuge behind a tree and thought about my options. The three of them were laughing and taunting me with glee over the seeming success of their ambush. They all lived within two blocks of school and had gone home and changed clothes. I could have turned and run away from them and gone home a slightly longer way. I'd soon wish I had.

Returning fire seemed futile, as they were behind a car, but I saw an opportunity I liked and moved quickly. I left my book bag behind the tree, made two snowballs, and put them in my left coat pocket, made a third for my left hand and in a sudden maneuver grabbed the lid to a Rectory garbage can, which was on the curb a few feet away. Using the lid as a shield, I charged my opponents. The shield worked great and I caught them by surprise. I stomped on their supply of snowballs and used mine to get some good shots at them. I got Fracchia good once, in the ear, and McVann two good shots before they began to run away empty-handed.

Rubbone had grabbed a couple of snowballs from the pile and had taken off. As they ran between the Rectory and the Convent, I made two more and took off after them with my shield. I had just yelled, "Stand and fight, you bastards!" when I heard clapping and my name being yelled.

There, making her way slowly through the snow from the Rectory to the Convent, was Sister Mary Mark.

"Joseph Farrell, you stop that right now!" she screamed. My heart sank. Here I had practically run over Sister Mary Mark, cursing, with snowballs in my hand and pocket, and with a Rectory garbage can cover being used as a shield, in my St. Andrew's uniform on school property! She was apoplectic! She groped for words and finally managed, "Give me your Patrol Belt."

"It's in my book bag, Sister."

"Go get it and bring it to me at the back door of the Convent. I'll be waiting.:

"Sister . . ."

"Go!"

I went back to where I left my book bag and returned to the back door of the Convent. Sister Mary Mark was not in sight. I thought about just going home, but figured that might just compound things, so I rang the bell. Just as I did, two snowballs whizzed by, thrown by Joe Rubbone from about fifty yards away. He took off running and laughing. Sister Mary Mark answered the door and held out her hand. I gave her the belt and badge.

"Sister, I couldn't help it—I was ambushed. They were waiting for me to come out," I said apologetically.

"Are any of them Patrol Boys?"

"No, Sister."

"Are any of them in uniform?"

"No, Sister."

"Did you return the garbage can lid?"

"Yes, Sister."

The door slammed.

That night when I went to bed, I prayed that Sister Mary Mark would change her mind and give me back my belt and badge in the morning. I fell asleep saying Our Fathers and Hail Marys. In the morning when I arrived, I found that Billy Rusie had been told by Sister Mary Mark that he was to take my place. Joe Rubbone and Jimmy McVann were looking for me to apologize. They both felt badly and assured me they never intended to get me in trouble. They assumed I would not fight back, since I was in uniform, and they would pelt me with as many shots as they could while I ran by. "It was all in fun," Jimmy McVann repeated somberly.

As the bell rang and we lined up, more and more kids were noticing me in line, instead of on Patrol, and were asking, "What happened? Why aren't you on Patrol?" I didn't answer. I thought I might cry if I talked, so I just put my head down and marched into class.

I felt very angry and it didn't go away. For the next few days, I was angry and depressed when the Patrol Boys left for duty. I felt so frustrated by the situation. I wasn't angry at anyone in particular, but somehow felt Sister Mary Mark should have understood. She acted like she had given me a chance and I had blown it, just as she had expected. I felt like there was no recognition of the great job I was doing, the arriving early each day, doing my own homework and trying to be a role model. My friends and classmates realized it and many of them said so to me in the days following my being kicked off Patrol.

I remember being very depressed. I had had a lousy Christmas break because of my mother fighting with my father. I was sick of doing drills every day until four o'clock and now I had been kicked off Patrol. The worst part of it all was Sister Mary Mark's attitude that she was not surprised and that I had somehow failed.

A few days later, I got my report on the Pullman Strike back from Sister Mary Mark. She had given me a 95. I lost five points because I hadn't pointed out that the strike was a failure in its original intent. I had pointed out that it showed the power of unified national unions and the rise of Eugene V. Debs as a labor leader and driving force of Socialism in America.

Looking over the report gave me an idea. I was sick to death of doing these drills at 2:30 every day. I lived on the edges of the parish and by the time I got home in these short January days, it was practically dark. I almost always knew the answers and found the drilling repetitive and boring, as did many of my classmates. So that day, as the clock hit three o'clock, I closed up my workbook, put up a sign on my desk, and folded my hands on my desk. The sign was a white piece of paper, folded into three blocks, and then propped up like a nameplate. On it I had written, "*On Strike.*" Slowly, members of the class noticed it. It took a while, since I was in the last seat. As word spread, kids were turning around to see it and reacting, usually with laughter.

Sister Mary Mark soon noticed that something was afoot. Billy Hamberger had the reaction I was hoping for. He immediately closed his books and joined me, putting a sign on his desk, too. Sister Mary Mark was squinting, trying to decipher what the murmuring and laughing was all about. I sat quietly and motionless, with my hands neatly folded on my desk.

"What is going on?" she asked no one in particular.

"Farrell's on strike," said David Dyke with a big smile.

Sister Mary Mark looked back at me, saw the sign, and erupted like a volcano.

"That's it! That is it for you, Mister! Get out of this classroom! Jesus, Mary, and Joseph! Get out!" she screamed.

"I've had it with you! Get out and stay out!"

I wasn't sure what to do, so I started to walk out of the classroom.

"Where are you going?"

"I thought you wanted me to leave."

"Take your desk with you."

"Take my desk?"

"You take your desk and chair and sit in the hall. You're not going to Catholic high school anyway, so I don't care if you do the drills or not. If there was any doubt about my recommending you for a decent high school, you just removed it."

As I slid my desk and chair out into the hallway, she yelled, "Don't set foot in this classroom again! You sit out there and rot and anyone who wants to join him can join him."

Billy Hamberger got up and started pushing his desk toward the door.

"Sit down, Mr. Hamberger!"

"But, Sister, you said . . ."

"You can rot right where you are."

"Sister, I'm not going to Catholic high school anyway, so why do I have to do the drills?"

"Mary, Mother of Jesus," she said through clenched teeth, "sit down and shut up or I'll send you to Monsignor!"

I suppose my strike had similarities to the Pullman Strike. Just as Eugene Debs had gotten a lot of fame and notoriety from the Pullman Strike, so too had I from my brief strike, as word spread to other eighth grade classes. Many of them were disgusted with this extended school day and repetitive drilling too. Even Peter Ross heard about it and told me it was a great move. Guys I only slightly knew, like Glenn Judson, Bill Landers, Dennis Geoghan, and Billy Kelly all expressed their unsolicited admiration.

Just as the Pullman Strike demonstrated the potential power of national unions, Sister Mary Mark certainly understood the potential of my little prank and just as the government had moved swiftly to crush the Pullman Strike, Sister Mary Mark had moved to crush me. Finally, just as the Pullman Strike had failed to meet its original goals, so too did my strike fail. I was kicked out of the classroom and apparently had a snowball's chance in hell of getting into a Catholic high school. Those who do not learn from the mistakes of History are destined to repeat them.

CHAPTER FIVE

◆ ◆ ◆ ◆ ◆

"DIVINE INTERVENTION"

I was open to pain and crossed by the rain
And I walked on a crooked crutch.
I strolled all alone through a fallout zone.
And came out with my soul untouched.

Bruce Springsteen ~ "Growin' Up"

As 8B began, things looked pretty glum for me. I was not allowed in my classroom and was seemingly destined for Flushing High School with its gangs, pagans, hoodlums, and split sessions. Although the details were unclear to me, at that time Flushing High School was so overcrowded that students either went to school from 8:30 to 12 or 12:30 to four. or some such version of that. My mental image of Flushing High was that it was controlled by knife-wielding gangs with greasy hair and leather jackets who hated Catholics. Images of "Rebel Without a Cause" and "West Side Story" came to mind. These images were formed largely from and reinforced by the nuns as well as my parents and relatives.

The only good thing I knew about Flushing High was Elaine Fumo, a beautiful sophomore cheerleader who lived on my block. She was the Natalie Wood of Flushing High, I figured. Occasionally I would see guys come to her house and I would always check them out. Sure enough, they always looked like "Sharks" from head to toe. Lots of hair, usually greasy, pulled down in their faces. Lots of tight-fitting black clothes, leather jackets, and pointy-toed black shoes that rose up above the ankle bone that usually had zippers and chains on them. If I was going to win Elaine Fumo's heart, it was going to take a carefully designed and well-executed plan or more likely a miracle.

The only good news was that Sister Mary Mark hadn't told my parents about my exile from the classroom and the fact that I wouldn't be going to Catholic high school; and I had gotten excellent grades once again. It must have pained Sister Mary Mark to give me all those 90s and 95s, but there wasn't much she could do. She did, however, give me a "U" (Unsatisfactory) in Conduct and an "S" (Satisfactory) in Effort.

Although Satisfactory sounds like it wasn't too bad, it was. Almost everybody got "A"s in Conduct and Effort. An "S" indicated that a serious problem existed and was usually accompanied by a call for a parent conference. A "U" was rare and indicated you were wasting the parish's money being in St. Andrew's as more than likely you were going to hell. She also told me I wouldn't be staying in to do my homework over anymore. If it was sloppy or incomplete, I would get a zero and lose a point on my final grade. I wanted to argue about my Conduct and Effort grade, but it was hard to get called on from out in the hallway.

I had gotten a "U" in Conduct before, in seventh grade, but almost always got an "S." "S" was fine with me and after being summoned time after time, my mother had gotten used to it. I had convinced my parents that the Effort grades were a sham. If I got grades at the top of the class and made the Honor Roll with such a sub par effort, then there is something wrong with the school, I would argue.

The "U"s in seventh grade were caused chiefly by the Stations of the Cross episode in the final marking period and an unusual episode with Mrs. McDonald, our Art teacher, in the second marking period.

Art wasn't taken very seriously at St. Andrew's, but I think because it was a state requirement, we had an Art period every few weeks. Mrs. McDonald was hired part-time by the school to come in periodically and conduct these sessions. Art and Music were not major subjects and although grades were given, they did not count toward your average. Our report cards had all the major subjects on the top half and then a special box below the major subjects for the average. The bottom half had minor subjects like Art, Music and Health and then a section for Conduct and Effort, for which we got "A," "S" or "U" and then Attendance figures at the very bottom.

Our first session with Mrs. McDonald was in early September and the assignment was to draw in crayon something to do with your summer. I wasn't good at drawing, in fact, I was bad at drawing. So I didn't much enjoy Art period. Mrs. McDonald would then go up and down the aisles of the room, offering her advice and commenting on each student's drawing. When she got to me, she saw that I was drawing a baseball field. She didn't say anything and at the end of the period, I handed it in. A few weeks later, in early October, Mrs. McDonald returned and said to draw something that had to do with Fall. I drew a baseball field.

When she came to my desk, she asked what it had to do with Fall. I told her the World Series was called the "Fall Classic" and that it had just ended. She remembered that I had done a baseball field previously and said that I couldn't hand in the same thing twice. So I added a tree with brown leaves in deep left field and handed it in.

Our next Art period was in late October and Mrs. McDonald instructed us that we should draw something for Halloween. The class seemed to like this assignment and went right to work. I took a moment to think and looked around for ideas. The kids around me were drawing pumpkins and bats and houses with pumpkins outside, and even devils. As Mrs. McDonald walked around visiting each desk, I caught Eddie's eye and nodded for him to show me what he was doing. Eddie held up a portrait of an ugly witch and mouthed, "Charlie Horse." I couldn't really think of anything that seemed different than the usual trite Halloween things, so I drew a baseball field with pumpkins for bases. Mrs. McDonald didn't seem to value my creation.

"Is this your idea of a joke or is something wrong with you?" she said loudly and sharply.

"What's wrong with it?" I asked. "The bases are pumpkins."

"If you hand that in, you'll get a low grade. You've already done a baseball field and it's not a Halloween theme," she scolded me as she walked away.

I wanted to say, "Who cares? Art grades don't count!" but I was afraid she'd tell Sister Charles Marie and then I'd be in real trouble. Eddie's portrait of Sister Charles Marie went over fine with Mrs. McDonald, since she didn't know who it was supposed to be.

In November, of course, the theme was Thanksgiving. I thought about doing a football field, but I really didn't like Mrs. McDonald's attitude. I felt if I changed now, she would think her public chastisement of me had worked. I did a baseball field with an ugly turkey at first base. The turkey was not very good, I admit.

Mrs. McDonald didn't seem to care for it. She got loud again. She asked me if there was something wrong with me and then asked those around me if there was something wrong with me. Most of those around me smiled or laughed. Claire Burns shook her head indicating yes.

"I think you're a coward, mister. I think you're afraid to follow the directions. You're afraid of trying something new. Hand that in and you'll get a big fat zero!"

I was a little embarrassed. I think I was getting red because my ears felt hot. As I looked around, Mrs. McDonald was bent over in the aisle talking with the student directly across and one up from me. Cathy Garity and Kathy Lynch were laughing and shaking their heads as if to say, we can't believe you did it again. Eddie and Joe Heaney were laughing and calling me a coward and flapping their elbows in a chicken gesture.

I had a plastic ruler in my hand that I had used to draw the foul lines on my baseball field. In an impulse that still mystifies me to this day, I pulled the top of the ruler back and let it go! It slapped Mrs. McDonald in the ass! Even I couldn't believe what I had done! Of course, she went ballistic and kicked me out of class. She ordered me to wait outside the classroom for Sister Charles Marie to return, which she did in about a half hour.

"What are we doing out here, Mr. Farrell?"

"Mrs. McDonald told me to wait here until Art was over."

"And why is that?"

"She doesn't like my drawing."

Then Mrs. McDonald sees Sister Charles Marie through the window of the door and comes out. She tells her what happened and Sister Charles Marie, without a moment's hesitation, slaps me across the face!

"Maybe that will knock some sense into him," she says to Mrs. McDonald. "I'm very embarrassed and I apologize for his behavior. He'll get a "U" in Conduct for this!"

"Do you have anything to say to Mrs. McDonald?"

"I apologize, Mrs. McDonald," I said, hoping that was what Sister Charles Marie wanted.

Mrs. McDonald seemed stunned by the violence she had just witnessed.

"Well, I accept your apology, Joseph. I just want you to try harder in Art and follow directions," she said meekly. All of her anger seemed to dissipate when she saw how much trouble I was in.

I did indeed get a "U" in Conduct for that marking period. In December, of course, the theme was Christmas and I felt torn between continuing with my Baseball Field series or moving on. I did a baseball field with a Christmas tree in center field. When Mrs. McDonald came around, she glanced at my paper, shook her head "No" and kept going. The next month I switched to a battleship and did a battleship each time for the rest of the year. Mrs. McDonald never really commented on my drawings, but I thought my drawing skills improved each time.

Since we were getting close to the Cooperative Exam, or the Co-Op Exam, it was time to choose which high schools each student would select to receive their scores. We were given literature to take home and discuss with our parents and get their signature on our selections. Each student was allowed to apply to four schools. We were told that it mattered in what order you listed them. It supposedly meant a lot to a school to be a student's first choice. Many schools would admit a student who selects them as his/her first choice over a student with a better score who made them a second, third or fourth choice. Many schools would not generally take anyone who listed them third or fourth. Each school would respond by accepting, rejecting, or wait listing each applicant.

For me, the choice was simple. I wanted to go to Holy Cross High School. Holy Cross was about one-and-a-half miles from my house and their football games were played at Memorial Field, which was three blocks from my house. I had been going to Holy Cross football games for years. The team was good, I loved their uniforms, my cousin Pat Nash went there, and that's where I wanted to go. Holy Cross was my first choice. Monsignor McClancy, in Jackson Heights, was my second choice. That was a new school and, because of that, they were willing to take kids who didn't put them in as their first choice.

My third choice was a reach—St. Mary's in Manhasset. It was a classy school outside the New York City limits and was rumored to be unlikely to take anyone listing it as third choice. My safety school was St. Helena's in the South Bronx. St. Helena's was in a bad neighborhood and was likely to take anyone with a good score. All of this assumed that a student got the parish's recommendation. But as I had been told many times, without it there would be no acceptance and I was not getting it. It was with a heavy heart that I handed in my application slip.

Holy Cross seemed like Nirvana to me as I sat in the hallway and thought about it. A modern, well-equipped building, terrific athletic teams, not having to wear dorky uniforms, no nuns, study halls to do your homework, pep rallies, dances and record hops in the gym. Just the idea of getting a ten-minute break between classes where I could move around, talk, go to the bathroom and get a drink of water, seemed too good to be true! The idea of a study hall built into your daily schedule seemed beyond belief, but Pat Nash verified it for me. He told me, in fact, that he had *two* free periods every day!

Pat also told me that, although he had to wear a sports coat and tie every day to school, no uniform existed, and he wore white socks and loafers to school. White socks and loafers were cool. That's what all the cool guys were wearing. I don't know where or how that style started, but girls liked guys who wore white socks and loafers. I don't to this day know how things like that get started, but both my sisters confirmed it. The clincher was that many of the guys and even some of the performers on "American Bandstand" were wearing white socks.

This was a problem for the cool guys at St. Andrew's because we wore uniforms and that did not include white socks. Girls wore pleated green jumpers over white blouses buttoned to the top and green bowtie-type things that are hard to describe. The one-inch-wide ribbon could either be looped into a bow or worn flat and criss-crossed over each end. Green knee socks with brown shoes and green berets with SAS embroidered on them completed the outfit. Boys wore brown pants and tan shirts with a brown tie (SAS was optional on the tie), brown shoes and brown socks.

The uniform code was strictly enforced. We all hated our uniforms. Girls' hats and bowties were removed immediately upon leaving school property. Boys who wore white socks to school were either sent home for brown socks or given punishment assignments.

Looking back, it seems very curious that for seven grades, each class at St. Andrew's kept so much to itself. Maybe it was because the classes were so big. I did not hang out with kids in the other classes, even though many lived near me. Even when we had parties, kids from other classes were generally not invited. It seems odd, considering that we shared school, church, neighborhoods, playgrounds, etc. We even went to Mass together on Sundays. The nine o'clock mass at St. Andrew's was for the elementary school. Each class would line up outside the church and the nuns would march us in about 8:45. Boys sat on one side, girls on the other.

Nuns enforced the same kind of rules at nine o'clock mass as they did all week. No talking, no laughing, no looking around. You had to bring your missal along (a book designed to follow along with Mass. This was necessary since Mass was in Latin and virtually unintelligible). You had to appear to follow along and to kneel up straight. If your ass hit the pew while kneeling, even for a few seconds, you'd hear a nun snapping her fingers angrily at you. "Kneel up straight, you big lazy lug!"

This mass was almost always said by Monsignor Oechsler. As head of the parish, he must have felt it was his duty to preach to the youth. That's ironic because Monsignor was very old and very much out of touch with our world. Every Sunday for eight years he gave us a sermon and I can't remember anything he ever said that was useful or memorable in any way, except once. In the sixth grade, shortly after the successful launching of Sputnik by the Soviet Union, he warned us of what a horrible world we faced should Communism prevail. The successful launching of a satellite into earth's orbit seemed to shake our country at its core. The fact that the Russians were able to do something that we could not and that they may be able to use space technology to conquer the world and convert us all to godless Communism was a rude awakening and was to become a big political issue in the years ahead. Monsignor told us that the churches and schools would be closed down under Communist rule and we'd all be put into work camps. He then made a forceful and emotional plea to us to study harder, particularly in science and math, so we could become scientists and engineers, defeat the Communists, and keep the world safe for God and Capitalism. He didn't mention that St. Andrew's had no science facilities or curriculum and that I and the other students had never even seen a scientific experiment performed in school. Obviously, Science ranked below Art at St. Andrew's.

So in the eighth grade, the separation between the classes started to change. We were communicating more with each other and getting to know one another. Being a Patrol Boy, getting thrown off Patrol, and my strike episode, had made me better known in the other two eighth grade classes. My circle of friends expanded rapidly and soon included guys who would be friends a long time after eighth grade.

One day in the spring, the whole eighth grade was abuzz with a story out of 8-1. The story involved Kenny Lewis, who ranked near the bottom on the nuns' list of favorites. 8-1 was taught by Sister Mary Thomas, who we all called M.T.

M.T. was old and losing it. She would frequently forget things and say things that made no sense and then laugh. Tommy Taraci would often have me in stitches, telling Sister Mary Thomas stories and imitating her. One story involved him claiming to have handed in homework he never did and convincing her she had lost it. She had announced that a particular homework assignment would be counted as a quiz and noted that Tommy's was missing, thereby earning him a zero. Tommy told her that in fact he had handed it in and that he had handed it directly to her, instead of passing it up the aisle in the usual way. He told her he at first couldn't find it, but then he did, had brought it up, and handed it to her.

As Sister Mary Thomas reacted with skepticism, Tommy supplied more detail about how after looking at it, she had put it on her desk just as class was being dismissed.

"I can't believe you don't remember, Sister. You were standing over by the door and then you walked over and put it on your desk." Sister Mary Thomas finally bought the story, and after a few days, said she had looked everywhere, couldn't find it, apologized, and gave Tommy full credit.

M.T.'s confidence in her own mental acuity must have been further damaged the day Kenny Lewis wore white socks to school.

In the middle of the afternoon, M.T. noticed Kenny snoozing away, slumped down in his seat, with his feet out in the aisle. According to Tommy Taraci, Kenny Lewis frequently slept in class and M.T. pretended not to notice. Lewis was a hell-raiser and a very poor student who would not be going to Catholic high school, and apparently M.T. preferred he sleep in class, rather than have to put up with his wisecracks and disruptive behavior. She would often say that she prayed to St. Jude for Kenny because "St. Jude is the Patron Saint of Hopeless Causes." He would often say of her, "She's fucking wacko."

Seeing the white socks, however, set off some type of alarm in M.T. and she called to him.

"Mr. Lewis?"

Those nearby roused him.

"Yes, Sister?" he answered, getting to his feet.

"Do you have uniform socks on, Mr. Lewis?"

"Yes, Sister."

"You do?"

"Yes, Sister."

"What color are uniform socks, Mr. Lewis?"

"Brown, Sister."

"What color are your socks, Mr. Lewis?"

"Brown, Sister."

"Oh, really? Why don't you go upstairs and ask Sister Kieran what color your socks are?"

"I'd prefer not to, Sister . . ."

"Go show Sister Kieran your socks!!" M.T. yelled.

Kenny left the classroom and headed for the Principal's office. Unbeknownst to anyone however, Kenny had brown socks in his pocket and changed into them in the hallway before going upstairs. He had been hoping that if M.T. saw the socks, she would send him home for brown ones. Kenny's plan was to then go to the luncheonette on the corner, called Sy's, and have a soda, put the brown socks on and, after an appropriate interval, return to class. When he arrived at Sister Kieran's, she had guests in her office that were strangers to Kenny Lewis.

"Sister Kieran, Sister Mary Thomas wants to know if my socks are okay."

Sister Kieran looks at Kenny's socks and looks at Kenny over the top of her glasses with raised eyebrows.

"What's going on, Mr. Lewis?" she said softly. "As you can see, I'm busy and I don't have time for your nonsense." With that, she takes Kenny outside her office into the hallway and makes him hold up his pants so she can see the socks clearly. She doesn't see anything wrong. Speaking softly in deference to the people in her office, she says, "Go back to class, Mr. Lewis, and whatever is going on, knock it off or so help me, you will be sorry."

"Okay, Sister," Kenny says innocently, "but I'm just doing what Sister Mary Thomas asked me to."

Kenny goes back downstairs and puts the white socks that he had stashed under the stairwell back on. He goes back into the classroom and sits down.

"Well, Mr. Lewis, what did Sister Kieran have to say?"

"She said my socks were all right and that I should return to class."

"You didn't go to Sister Kieran's office, did you, Mr. Lewis?" M.T. yelled.

"Yes. I did."

"You go up to Sister Kieran's office, young man, and have her call me on the P.A. to tell me your socks are okay."

Kenny gets up slowly and, shaking his head in disgust and futility, leaves the classroom again. He goes to the stairwell, puts on the brown socks and goes to Sister Kieran's office. Sister Kieran is heavily involved in conversation with the strangers in her office and when she sees Kenny at the door again, she excuses herself for a moment, and takes him outside into the hallway.

"What now, Mr. Lewis?" she said sternly.

"M.T. doesn't believe . . . I mean Sister Mary Thomas doesn't believe I was here. She wants you to call her on the PA and tell her my socks are okay."

"These people in my office are from the Brooklyn Diocese and I don't have time right now to devote to foolishness. What are Sister Mary Thomas' objections to your socks?"

"I don't have any idea, Sister, she picks on everything I do."

Sister Kieran went into her office and picked up the large metal microphone used for daily announcements. She turned on the switch for Sister Mary Thomas' classroom.

"Sister Mary Thomas?"

"Yes, Sister?"

"I have Kenny Lewis here and his socks seem okay to me."

"Okay, thank you, Sister."

"Mr. Lewis, return to class and I don't want to see you again," she said firmly, but softly.

Kenny put the white socks back on and returned to class. He slumped down with his feet in the aisle and tried to return to sleep. Sister Mary Thomas pretended not to see him or his socks.

The Co-op Exam was over and now came the wait for the results. My anxiety seemed to rise each day. The exam itself seemed rather easy. We were so well-drilled that the test itself seemed anti-climactic. There were a few questions where I wasn't sure, but could eliminate one or two choices and took a guess. Most of it seemed pretty easy.

As February turned into March, Sister Mary Mark made a chart to track each student's choices and outcome of their applications. She went down the list, recording each student's first choice and leaving room to list other acceptances. Ralph Azanza had Regis High School as his first choice. Regis was a prestigious tuition-free Jesuit High School. Eddie had Bishop Laughlin, the Diocesan High School, as his first choice because it was cheap ($10 a month) and Eddie had four older siblings, including a brother Bobby, who was one year ahead of him in Holy Cross High School. Billy Hamberger wasn't going to Catholic high school because his mother couldn't afford it. His older brother, John, was in Public School and so too would he go to public high school.

The girls mostly chose the prestige schools of the Dominican Academy or the Mary Louis Academy (where my older sister Maureen went to high school), St. Vincent Ferrer or St. Agnes. The boys selected mostly Holy Cross, with a few choosing the Jesuit schools of Regis or Brooklyn Prep, Bishop Laughlin, or in the case of LeRoy McNally and Francis Baxter, Cathedral Prep.

As Sister Mary Mark was calling names to record first choices, she skipped me as if I didn't matter. For once, I was glad I was in the hallway, so no one could see my humiliation and disappointment.

As we got replies, Sister Mary Mark asked us to tell her so she could record them to keep Sister Kieran apprised of the results. She was particularly interested in how many were accepted into their first choice and how many got in any Catholic high school, no matter what choice. Being wait listed was good news and usually meant you would be accepted as other students made their choices for attending. Sister Mary Mark announced she would count wait-listing as acceptance.

I was becoming frantic as the day of reckoning approached. Not only would I be embarrassed and humiliated, but my parents would be as well, and they had no idea it was coming! I decided the only chance I had was divine intervention. I began to pray hard and often. I would sit in the hallway and say a rosary. I went to church at lunch break each day and prayed. I visited the statues of St. Joseph, in whose name I was baptized, and the statue of St. Patrick, in whose name I was confirmed. I prayed to them and asked for their intervention, just in case God was too busy to hear my prayers but might listen to them. I went to confession every Saturday and communion every Sunday. I even did my own homework!

EIGHTH GRADE GRADUATION PICTURE
ST. ANDREW AVELLINO 1960

HOW MUCH TROUBLE COULD THIS GUY BE?

Now that we were getting out at three o'clock again and I wasn't being made to stay after school as often, I started walking home with Billy Landers from 8-2. Billy lived about a third of the way home from school and I would walk with him to his house and then the rest of the way alone, praying. I told Billy of the situation I was in and he gave me hope. Although he wanted to go to Brooklyn Prep, he felt I could get in Holy Cross if my parents went to the school and asked. Billy said he knew of a situation where a kid was not accepted, but when his parents contacted the school and met with them to plead their case, he got in.

This advice comforted me a little and realizing that my parents were going to be extremely pissed off and that I might need them to intervene on my behalf, I started being extremely considerate and helpful around the house. For weeks, I was like a model child. I did all my chores, on time, without being asked. I was home on time and went to bed on time. I figured it might go easier on me if they were feeling good about me and by offering it up to God, it might help produce the miracle I needed.

Then one day, the notices started arriving. A few of the girls got into Dominican Academy and Ralph Azanza got into Regis. Then a few more girls got into the Mary Lewis Academy. Eileen Quinn, who sat closest to me, that is closest to the door, and Julianne Fenchak got into St. Vincent Ferrer and Eddie got into Bishop Laughlin.

I was feeling sicker every day. Each morning at the start of class and each afternoon after lunch, Sister Mary Mark would ask if anyone had heard. She would then congratulate them and happily record the news on her chart, keeping a running total of how many had been accepted and how many accepted by their first choice. At first it was only acceptances that were coming, but then, after a while rejections started to trickle in. I went home each day with a knot in my stomach, looking for the mail as soon as I hit the door.

A group of us had started to meet at Sy's after school. It was there that I learned of news from other eighth grades. Tommy Taraci caught the bus to Bayside right on Sy's corner and Landers, Dennis Geoghan, Dickie Abella, Eddie, and I and others, including girls, would meet there and goof off for a while. We would have sodas, flirt, exchange stories and information and wait for the bus with Tommy. Why Tommy lived in Bayside and went to St. Andrew's is still a mystery to me.

The day Billy Landers was accepted by Brooklyn Prep, Tommy offered me some comfort. I was happy for Billy as was everybody, but the mounting anxiety due to the coming disaster was starting to show. Tommy wanted to go to Holy Cross and asked me each day if I had heard anything yet.

"I'm not getting in *any* Catholic high school, so quit asking me!" I snapped.

"Okay, ya' prick, I won't ask."

Billy then told Tommy and some others of my situation.

"Go to Bayside High," said Tommy. It's much better than Flushing. I know some kids that go there and it's not bad."

"How can I do it when I live in Flushing?"

"Use a Bayside address. Hell, you could use my address. If you show up and put down a Bayside address, they have to take you."

Billy confirmed what Tommy said on the walk home. Bayside was a much better situation and if you have a Bayside address where you can receive mail, who's going to check it? I continued to pray and do my homework and sit quietly in the hall, but having a possible Bayside option made me feel much better.

Then one day, I arrived home from school and found a letter for me from St. Mary's High School. No one was home and the mail was still stuck in the mailbox in our front door. I took the St. Mary's letter up to my room. I sat on the bed and stared at the envelope. St. Mary's was my third choice and a good school. Being rejected by St. Mary's wouldn't be unexpected or mean I had no chance. I took a deep breath and opened the envelope. I couldn't believe what I saw. *Accepted*! I checked the name on the slip. It was my name and address and the box beside "accepted" was checked. It was St. Patrick's Day.

That night I decided not to tell anyone yet. It occurred to me that it might be a mistake instead of a miracle. If I told Sister Mary Mark, she might contact St. Mary's and get them to reverse the decision. I figured one of three things had happened. One, it was indeed a mistake. Two, Sister Mary Mark had recommended me after all, or Three, God had answered my prayers. Keeping quiet seemed like the thing to do. I figured the other schools would reply any day. I thanked God that night in my prayers and especially I thanked St. Patrick. The fact that this great gift came to me on St. Patrick's Day was not lost on me. It seemed a clear sign that St. Pat had delivered for me. Grateful as I was, however, I continued to pray for acceptance to Holy Cross. I felt a little sheepish about it, but I really didn't want to go to St. Mary's.

The next day was a Friday and as planned, I said nothing to anyone. It was hard not to tell someone, but I managed to stick to my plan. No one, it appeared, had heard from Holy Cross, but a group of boys had heard from McClancy and were either accepted or wait-listed.

There was no mail on Friday and on Saturday, I was watching hawkishly for the mailman. In the mail was a letter from Monsignor McClancy High School. I raced upstairs to my room where I could open it and be alone. I stared at it and thought about the possibilities. This was my second choice. If I was rejected, it made it more likely that St. Mary's was indeed a mistake. If accepted, then Holy Cross was a real possibility. Again, I took a deep breath and opened it. *Accepted!* The box beside "accepted" was checked and there was a letter enclosed confirming it. The letter was dated March 17, St. Patrick's Day and had arrived on March 19, St. Joseph's Feast Day! I was ecstatic! It was obvious that my prayers had been answered. Either or both St. Patrick and St. Joseph were showing me the power of prayer.

BROTHERS OF THE SACRED HEART
MONSIGNOR McCLANCY MEMORIAL HIGH SCHOOL
(ACCEPTANCE LETTER)

BROTHERS OF THE SACRED HEART
MONSIGNOR McCLANCY MEMORIAL HIGH SCHOOL
71-06 - 31ST AVENUE
JACKSON HEIGHTS 69, NEW YORK

March 17, 1960

Dear Student,

Congratulations! You have been accepted for our Freshman Class of 1960. The enclosed folder gives you the information to decide whether to accept or not. If you accept, you must write me a short note of acceptance which must be in the mail by Midnight, Monday, March 28. Once you accept, you will receive the registration procedure.

Once again congratulations, and may the Sacred Heart bless you and your family in His own wise and loving way.

Yours in the Sacred Heart,

Brother Eric, S.C.

Brother Eric, S.C., Principal

(COOPERATIVE ENTRANCE EXAMINATION PROGRAM FOR HIGH SCHOOLS—1960) NOTIFICATION TO STUDENT

COOPERATIVE ENTRANCE EXAMINATION PROGRAM
FOR HIGH SCHOOLS-1960
NOTIFICATION TO STUDENT

ST. MARY'S HIGH SCHOOL
51 CLAPHAM AVENUE
MANHASSET, N.Y.

INFORMS YOU OF THE FOLLOWING ACTION
CONCERNING YOUR APPLICATION FOR
ADMISSION.

FARRELL JOSEPH
30 25 MURRAY LAN
QUEENS 54 N Y

ACCEPTED ☒

NOT ACCEPTED ☐

ON WAITING LIST ☐

COOPERATIVE ENTRANCE EXAMINATION PROGRAM
FOR HIGH SCHOOLS-1960
NOTIFICATION TO STUDENT

ST. HELENA'S HIGH SCHOOL
925 HUTCHINSON RIVER PARKWAY
BRONX 65, NEW YORK

INFORMS YOU OF THE FOLLOWING ACTION
CONCERNING YOUR APPLICATION FOR
ADMISSION.

FARRELL JOSEPH
30 25 MURRAY LAN
QUEENS 54 N Y

ACCEPTED ☒

NOT ACCEPTED ☐

ON WAITING LIST ☐

COOPERATIVE ENTRANCE EXAMINATION PROGRAM
FOR HIGH SCHOOLS-1960
NOTIFICATION TO STUDENT

HOLY CROSS HIGH SCHOOL
26-20 Francis Lewis Blvd.
FLUSHING 58, NEW YORK

INFORMS YOU OF THE FOLLOWING ACTION
CONCERNING YOUR APPLICATION FOR
ADMISSION.

FARRELL JOSEPH
30 25 MURRAY LAN
QUEENS 54 N Y

ACCEPTED ☒

NOT ACCEPTED ☐

ON WAITING LIST ☐

COOPERATIVE ENTRANCE EXAMINATION PROGRAM
FOR HIGH SCHOOLS-1960
NOTIFICATION TO STUDENT

MONSIGNOR McCLANCY MEMORIAL
HIGH SCHOOL
72-02 31st AVENUE
JACKSON HEIGHTS 70, N.Y.

INFORMS YOU OF THE FOLLOWING ACTION
CONCERNING YOUR APPLICATION FOR
ADMISSION.

FARRELL JOSEPH
30 25 MURRAY LAN
QUEENS 54 N Y

ACCEPTED ☑

NOT ACCEPTED ☐

ON WAITING LIST ☐

85

I was thrilled, but decided to once again say nothing to anyone. Later that day, I went to confession and visited the statues of St. Patrick and St. Joseph. I thanked them for answering my prayers and didn't mention Holy Cross. I felt they had done enough. I did, however, ask God to get me into Holy Cross and asked Mary to intercede with her son. I even lit a little votive candle at Mary's statue.

On Monday, I kept my mouth shut when Sister Mary Mark asked if anyone had heard over the weekend, but I didn't have that sick feeling of dread that I'd had for weeks. When nothing came in Monday's mail, I was disappointed and began to think that I should write to McClancy and accept. I felt that I would be safer if I closed the deal before I told Sister Mary Mark and I didn't know when I'd hear from Holy Cross. I wrote a note of acceptance to McClancy, but before I mailed it, I called Tommy Taraci to see if he'd heard from Holy Cross or knew anyone who had. He told me that he'd called Holy Cross and they said acceptances had been mailed out early that day.

"We should hear tomorrow or Wednesday," Tommy said, "if we're accepted."

When I arrived home Tuesday, there were letters for me from both Holy Cross and St. Helena's. I ripped open St. Helena's and saw "accepted" checked. With growing confidence, I opened Holy Cross and again, "accepted" was checked. I was ecstatic!! I raced up to my room, changed out of my uniform, left all four acceptances on the kitchen table for my mother to see, and headed for Bowne Park, where a group of us were meeting to hang out. Although it was out of my way, I ran, literally, to St. Andrew's and went into church and thanked God for answering my prayers.

When I got to Bowne Park, Billy Landers was there practicing fence climbing. Billy could get over a fence quicker than anyone I ever saw. Most of Bowne Park was open and unfenced, but the playground area, consisting of a basketball court, swings, various gym apparatus and a few picnic tables were enclosed and surrounded by a ten-foot high metal chain link fence. Billy, as I was learning, saw any kind of barrier or restriction as a challenge. He had developed a way of going over a fence that we all had adapted and frequently practiced and raced each other, but Billy was the master. The technique was to run full speed directly at the fence and jump as high as possible onto it, catching your one foot in one of the diamond-shaped holes. Taking a step with your other foot, the top of the fence was now about chest high. At this point, you reach down over the other side of the fence and grab it with your free hand and flip yourself over the top, landing on your feet on the ground and ready to resume running. Your feet never touch the top of the fence or the other side of the fence. We all practiced, but nobody stuck the landing as often as Billy. We all practiced except Tommy Taraci, that is, who tried it a few times, ripped his shirt, declared Billy "nuts" and refused to do it anymore.

"I got in!" I yelled at Billy as he landed on his feet on the other side of the fence.

I was so excited I felt I could hurdle the fence without touching it! I ran full speed, took my steps, flipped over the top and landed hard, too hard, turned my ankle, and went down on the hard, cold ground.

"I assume you mean Holy Cross?" said Billy.

"All four!" I gasped, writhing in pain on the ground.

"So, the little witch recommended you after all."

"What do you mean?" I said as I struggled to my feet and tried to walk.

"She was fucking with you the whole time."

Billy ran and jumped the fence back over to the outside. I was in pain and was trying to walk off the turned ankle. Eddie Haggerty, Jean Reed, Kathy Lynch and Cathy Garity arrived. They saw me hobbling around, wincing inside the fence and asked what was wrong.

"The dumb fuck was so excited about getting into Holy Cross, he hurt himself going over the fence," Billy yelled.

Everyone was happy and burst into cheers and applause. They seemed unconcerned that I couldn't walk or talk. I hobbled to the entrance of the playground and as I was limping out the gatehouse, I encountered the park attendant, who we called "Parky," who was locking up the gate.

"What happened to you?" he said in a nasty tone. "Hurt yourself climbing over the fence? I seen ya's doing it the other day."

I hobbled by and continued toward my friends. The Parky followed me and then began scolding us loudly.

"You kids stay the hell off the fence and stay outta the playground when it's closed."

"Why is it closed?" asked Billy. "Why can't we use it whenever we want?"

"Because I have to be here when it's open!"

"Why?"

"To make sure no one gets hurt."

"And what exactly do you do to prevent someone from getting hurt?"

"Never you mind . . ."

"How does sitting at your desk drinking coffee prevent us from getting hurt?"

"Stay off the fence and outta the playground," the Parky yelled.

Billy ran for the fence, flipped over it, and landed on his feet and holding his arms up triumphantly, said, "or what?"

"I'll call the cops," the Parky threatened.

"What are you gonna tell them? There's a kid playing in the public playground?" Besides, cops can't catch us. Ever see a cop go over a fence that fast?"

The Parky walked away, shaking his head. "I hope you break your fuckin' neck!"

"Hey, hey, nice talk in front of children," yelled Cathy Garity.

He gave us the finger without looking back, holding it high over his head. Once the Parky left, the conversation quickly returned to my acceptances. The consensus was agreement with Billy. Sister Mary Mark must have recommended me and was saying otherwise to punish me and keep me in line. I had trouble connecting with that line of thought. "If I believe she didn't recommend me, how would that keep me in line?" I asked.

"It didn't," said Eddie. "You sit in the hall, in case you haven't noticed."

Everyone laughed and we were all happy. All of us had gotten into our first choices and the girls said they had prayed on Sunday that I would get into Holy Cross. It choked me up that they were all so happy for me. When Kathy Lynch noticed tears welling up in my eyes, I blamed it on the pain in my ankle.

On the slow, painful walk home alone, I thought about what the gang said about Sister Mary Mark. Maybe it wasn't divine intervention after all. Maybe all that praying and worrying and feeling sick was unnecessary and I would have been accepted anyway. I wasn't sure what to think or how I felt about it. Was it nice of Sister Mary Mark to recommend me after all or was it mean of her to lie to me and cause me such anxiety?

I put these thoughts aside when I arrived home and decided to just feel good for a while. My parents didn't share my triumphant feelings. Of course, to be fair, they didn't know the depth of the dread and turmoil I had gone through and the lack of recommendation situation with Sister Mary Mark. They expected me to get accepted.

"Why wouldn't you be accepted? You always get good marks in school? I just hope we can afford it," was all my mother said.

That night I called Tommy Taraci to find out if he had heard anything from Holy Cross and he had been accepted too! We talked about what fun we were going to have in high school. We agreed to work out all summer and try out for freshman football in September. I fell asleep with a big smile on my face or at least it felt that way. I also wondered how Sister Mary Mark would react when I told her.

The next morning, after we said our usual prayers, I scooted my desk and chair into the classroom so that I could raise my hand when Sister Mary Mark asked for news on school applications. Eddie, Cathy, Kathy and Jean had spread the word somewhat, among the kids, and a few had congratulated me.

When Sister Mary Mark asked and I raised my hand, a number of my friends were anticipating my announcement. She called on quite a few kids before me, but eventually acknowledged my hand in the air.

"Yes, Mr. Farrell?"

"I got accepted in all four."

The class erupted in applause and cheers.

"Stop that! Stop It!" Sister Mary Mark yelled at the class.

"You just bring in your acceptance slips, Mr. Farrell. I want to see them," Sister Mary Mark said smugly, as if I was lying. She did not write anything beside my name on her chart. "Now get back out in the hallway!"

Her reaction really pissed me off, but it also puzzled me. If she thought I was lying about being accepted, then she didn't recommend me. If she had recommended me, then this wouldn't be such a shock to her. Indeed, it must have been divine intervention after all.

(Weeks later when telling my cousin, Pat Nash about my ordeal, he claimed a more likely scenario. "With all due respect to "The Big Guy," it might have been prayer, but Brother John, the principal, told me they just pick the smartest kids they can get and don't care what the nuns think.")

The next day, I brought my slips into class, crept into the classroom, and raised my hand.

"What are you doing in here? Get back out in the hall," she said.

"I have my acceptance slips, Sister."

She motioned for me to come forward. I walked up and for dramatic effect handed them to her one at a time. She looked closely at them, then handed them back.

"You'll never last. You'll never last, Mr. Farrell, because you lack self-control."

I walked back to my desk, pushed it out into the hall and sat down. I wanted to tell her how stupid it was to say that. Like I did to Sister Charles Marie before her, I wanted to point out that she doesn't know how many times I want to say things and don't; how many funny things I think and never say; how many times I want to get up and move around but remain in my seat; how many times I wanted to scream with boredom, but didn't. I wanted to tell her all these things, but I didn't. I wanted to smack her for the weeks of constant dread and fear and anxiety she had caused me, but I didn't do any of these things—I had too much self-control.

CHAPTER SIX

◆ ◆ ◆ ◆ ◆

"LAND OF HOPE AND DREAMS"

Grab your ticket and your suitcase
Thunder's rolling down the tracks,
You don't know where you're goin'
But you know you won't be back.
Big wheels rolling through fields
Where the sunlight streams
Meet me in the land of hope and dreams.
Bruce Springsteen ~ "Land of Hopes and Dreams"

Much of the remainder of eighth grade seemed anti-climactic, since admission to Catholic High School had been so much our focus for so long. We did need to take special exams at the end of the year in mid-June called Superintendent Exams. These exams were very important to the parish and to the Diocese of Brooklyn. I cannot remember for certain, but I think these exams were required by the State of New York to demonstrate that we were learning up to state standards. English and Math were no problem, since we had been drilling for seven months, but now Social Studies took center stage and we began drilling on Social Studies, a subject that was largely neglected.

Although we had had Social Studies from fourth grade on, it was often Catholic Social Studies. Our books had approval from the Bishop called an "Imprimatur." This word comes from Latin and means, "Let it be printed." We were taught to always look for the "Imprimatur," which would certify that there was no moral error in the book. It seems only logical that books favoring the Catholic view of the world would be the ones selected by the Diocese for use in its schools.

Our Social Studies books were full of missionaries, Pope's Encyclicals, Catholic heroes, and enemies of the Church. One of our texts even had the Catholic population of each state on the inside of the cover. I can summarize my understanding of world history in eighth grade as follows:

- There are Catholics, Protestants, Jews, and a series of bizarre religions (Islam, Taoism, Buddhism, Shintoism, etc.) that are practiced by ignorant people in undeveloped countries. Jews believe in God and in the Old Testament, but not in Jesus as Savior and God's son. Jews are hated everywhere and came to America for freedom from persecution, but only after it was safe—and there was money to be made. All Protestants were once part of the one, true, holy, and apostolic Roman Catholic Church, but fell away because they were weak and couldn't abide by the Church's teachings.
- King Henry, Martin Luther, John Calvin, John Wesley, it doesn't matter; they didn't like something about the one true church, so they formed their own. Then other Protestants broke from Protestants, such as the Baptists breaking from the Anglicans, and so on and so on. It wasn't important to know what each faction believes, just that Methodists, Lutherans, Presbyterians, etc. all broke from the Catholic Church to suit themselves and throughout history, fought, and persecuted those who didn't believe what they did.
- A brilliant and courageous Italian Catholic, Christopher Columbus, believing the world was round, set out in search of the truth, and funded by Catholic Spain, discovered America in 1492.

- The Spanish established the first city in America, St. Augustine, in Florida. Catholic missionaries, mostly from France and Spain, tried to civilize the savage natives and teach them about Jesus, but the Indians bit their fingers off, tortured, and killed many of them. Meanwhile, America becomes heavily populated by Protestants (pilgrims) seeking religious freedom and trying to get away from one another.
- Protestants brought blacks from Africa to serve as slaves. Catholics opposed slavery and helped slaves as much as they could and taught them about Jesus and the one true church. Resentment builds toward Catholics and Maryland becomes a Catholic haven.
- Colonists become increasingly unhappy with the English and issue a Declaration of Independence. Charles Carroll of Maryland was the only Catholic signer of the Declaration. There was a revolution. We won. George Washington became the first in a long line of Protestant Presidents.
- Mother Elizabeth Ann Seton founded the Sisters of Charity in 1809.
- The Irish, being starved and exploited by the English and forced to go to Protestant schools, started to come to America in large numbers. Resentment toward Catholics grew.
- The mostly Protestant, slave-holding South started the Civil War. Catholics, mostly Irish, fought like hell for the Union and to free the slaves. The Irish Brigade fought at Bull Run, Antietam, Fredericksburg, and Gettysburg, where they withstood Pickett's Charge and saved the Union.
- The Ku Klux Klan sprung up after the Civil War and they hated blacks and Catholics.
- The Irish kept coming, but were discriminated against, and exploited. They were forced to work in mines, on canals, and on railroads.
- The first Vatican Council issued its decree affirming Papal Infallibility. Resentment and distrust of Catholics grows.
- Workers, mostly Catholics, formed unions in defense of exploitation. Terrence Powderly, an Irish-American, formed the Knights of Labor in 1874. In 1877, Irish miners are hung in Pennsylvania by Pinkertons who work for the Reading Railroad.
- Italians start coming to America because it is the land of opportunity. Resentment toward Catholics grows.
- Pope Leo XIII issues *Rerum Novarum*, condemning socialism in 1891.
- World War I starts because someone shot Archduke Francis Ferdinand. We enter the war and save France.

- Alfred E. Smith runs for President in 1928 and loses because he is Catholic.
- The Stock Market crashes in 1929 and causes a depression, which is particularly hard on Catholics.
- On December 7, 1941, a date that will live in infamy, the Japanese, who worship their Emperor Hirohito, launched a sneak attack on a peaceful United States. Since they were in cahoots with Nazi Germany, we declare war on both of them. Nazis hate Catholics.
- United States troops, comprised of a large number of Catholics, liberate France, and save the world.
- Communism becomes the biggest threat to freedom. Communists have a plot to take over the world and they hate Catholics and all religion.
- America defeats the Communists in the Korean War.
- Russia launches a satellite (Sputnik).
- Hawaii and Alaska become states in 1959.
- Khrushchev is head of the Communist world and has warned that "We will bury you."

Now in 8B, we are learning lots of American History for the Exam we must take in June. Every day we drill by going over old Superintendents' Exams. We drilled on matching columns, fill in the blank, true/false, and multiple-choice types of tests. The test, however, will include essay questions and these pose a much tougher problem. Part of the solution is to answer essay questions each night for homework. We would go over the answers each day in class. Names, dates, battles, treaties, provisions, acts, inventions, and amendments were drilled into us every day. I cannot remember the nuns ever showing or urging any interest in politics or political events until right before graduation.

Sometime in the spring, Sister Mary Mark told us that something very important had happened. A U.S. Senator from Massachusetts, John F. Kennedy, was running for President and he was a Catholic. He had seemingly won the Democratic nomination despite his religion being used against him. We should remind our parents and relatives that John Kennedy was Catholic and that we all have a lot at stake in November, she urged us.

As graduation approached, I remember winning the school punch-ball championship. Rubbone, Haggerty, Rusie, Baxter, and I were the "Hotrods" and won the school championship tournament. Punch-ball is something I often wonder about because I never, ever have seen it played anywhere but New York and anytime but my childhood. We played it for hours almost every day all during baseball season. It was played like baseball, only the ball was a pink rubber ball and wasn't pitched to the batter. Instead the ball was thrown up in the air and the batter punched it with his fist.

Usually played in the street with two or three players on a team, punch-ball was exciting, and had some unique rules. Bases were usually drawn on the street, but sometimes a manhole served as home plate or second base. An extremely narrow-playing field led to complicated rules on what was "fair" and what was "foul" territory. However, obstacles like cars, trees, houses, poles, wires, and bushes were in play, meaning that if you caught the ball off a car, house, or tree on a fly, you were out. Bases were far apart so that smart base running was very important.

It wasn't how far you could hit it, because unless hit straight down the street, which was almost always a fly-out, the ball would hit something, carom off, and be in play. It became a game of strategy and defense. Jumping a fence or hedges to catch a ball off the roof of a house or rattling around in the branches of a tree, was common. This, of course, did not go over well with homeowners and often led to conflict. St. Andrew's had a schoolyard that was used for punch-ball. It was small and enclosed by the school in right field and a chain-link fence in center and left. You could blast the ball to right field but if hit too high, the second baseman or first baseman would turn around and catch it off the wall for an out. Over the fence was an automatic out in left and center. A line drive was the best chance for a hit, but was often fielded off the fence and resulted in a force-out with men on base because the bases were far apart.

This game was played by kids in neighborhoods all over New York. The balls were Spaulding or Pennsey Pinkie and cost about fifteen cents. We went through dozens in a season losing them down sewers and in rain gutters of houses in the neighborhood. Often we would climb onto the roof of a house to get balls from the gutters.

One homeowner of German heritage, Mr. Lupkemeier, moved onto my block and immediately erected a fence around his property to keep us off it. Once or twice when a ball went into his yard, he would cut it in half with his hedge clippers and throw the halves back to us. After that, we referred to him as "the Nazi" and gave him a "Heil, Hitler" salute, whenever we were playing and he appeared outside his house.

Although we played punch-ball from fourth grade through eighth, once I entered high school, I never played again. Younger kids still played in the streets and schoolyards, but I and my friends never did.

Another memory of those final weeks of elementary school was Sister Mary Mark freaking out when she noticed a huge amount of dirt on the highly polished floor underneath the Connolly brothers' desks. Mrs. Connolly, in a quest for longer lasting, more economical footwear, had purchased a new type of shoe for the boys called "wedgies." "Wedgies" had large-rippled rubber soles, which looked like saw teeth from the side. They were supposed to last a long time and be comfortable. The Connollys were a big family and all went to Catholic schools. They didn't have a lot of extra money, so long-lasting shoes were a practical thing, even if they were ugly.

On this particular day, the Connolly brothers (and why they were in the same grade I'll never know, since they weren't twins) had been trudging through mud in the schoolyard and it was caked into the wedges of their soles. As the mud dried and hardened, it came out of the wedges and as a result beneath the Connollys' desks looked like a sandbox. It was amazing how much dirt those shoes had held. When Sister Mary Mark saw it, she looked like she had seen a ghost.

"What is that under your desk?" she screamed, more at James than at Kevin.

James pushed back his chair and bent down to take a look, as if he had no idea what Sister Mary Mark was referring to.

"Dirt, Sister," he said, as if he had just answered a Social Studies question.

"How did it get there?" Sister Mary Mark screamed in a rage.

"It was in our shoes, Sister," he answered, holding up one of his feet for her to see.

"Ugh! You disgust me. You pigs! How could you sit there in that filth? Were you going to just leave it there? Look at that floor! It's a mess!"

Sister Mary Mark sent the Connollys outside to get any remaining dirt out of the wedges and left the classroom in search of Henry the janitor. She returned with a dustpan and broom and made the Connollys sweep up all the dirt. As they were sweeping, Henry showed up and Sister Mary Mark showed him the floor and what had happened to his high gloss shine. She apologized profusely to Henry and said that the Connollys would stay after school and do the work, if he would supervise. James started to object, saying something about not being able to stay after school.

"O-o-o-o-h-h-h-h-h-h-h-h-h-h, shut up! I swear I never wanted to smack someone so bad as I do right now!" Henry said that he would take care of it and that it was not necessary for the boys to help.

Sister Mary Mark never actually hit James Connolly, but watching her sneer, snarl, and struggle for control was funny to most of us. A few days later, she showed no such restraint at Joe Rubbone's expense. Eddie and I had recently discovered the Kingston Trio, and as Sister Mary Mark was leading us into class after lunch, Eddie and I were in a goofy mood and had been discussing the album, "From the Hungry I" when the bell rang. As we entered the rectory, Eddie started singing "When the Saints Go Marchin'

In" and I, of course, joined in. It seemed like an appropriate song to sing as we were marching into school.

As we went down the stairway into the basement, now that we were inside an enclosed stairwell our singing became louder,. Sister Mary Mark heard something, but she couldn't tell what. As she entered the hallway, at the bottom of the stairs, she asked someone at the front of the line what the noise was. The kid answered that it sounded like singing at the back of the line.

Sister Mary Mark raced toward the back of the line. Eddie and I were next to each other in the double line and Joe Rubbone and Jimmy McVann were last, behind us. Rubbone had been warning us to stop.

"She's gonna hear you," he warned, "S-h-h-h-h! She's gonna hear you."

"Who's singing back here?" Sister Mary Mark yelled.

"Rubbone, Sister," said Eddie without a moment's hesitation.

Sister Mary Mark promptly slapped a surprised Rubbone hard across the face. I clenched my teeth tightly together, determined not to laugh. As she yelled at a wide-eyed, stunned, and red-faced Rubbone, Eddie burst out laughing. He just couldn't hold it in. The look on Rubbone's face was too much.

"Are you laughing, Mr. Haggerty?"

"No, Sister."

"You better not laugh, Mister, or I'll put five fingers on *your* face!"

"Yes, Sister," Eddie said, regaining momentary control.

Sister Mary Mark turned pivoted and returned to the front of the line, while Joe Rubbone stared open-mouthed at her, with his hand over his stinging cheek. We all burst out laughing then, even Rubbone. This was one time I was glad I sat in the hall. I could sit out there and not have to stifle myself. After I gained control of myself, I carefully scooted my desk into the classroom as I usually did, and told Eileen Quinn what had happened. She knew Rubbone had been smacked, but didn't know why. Eileen cracked up. She laughed so hard that Sister Mary Mark noticed. Typically, Sister saw me in the room, blamed it all on me, and made me move back out into the hall.

This game went on the whole time I sat out in the hall. I would slowly, quietly, creep in and hide behind Eileen Quinn. Sister Mary Mark would eventually see me and start yelling, "Out! Out! Get Out!" She reminded me of Jackie Gleason. The way she would motion and yell, "Out, Oooouuuuuut, get out!" was reminiscent of the Gleason character Ralph Kramden. Sometimes Eileen would actually try to get me kicked out. She would lean to one side, so that I was more easily visible or raise her hand to ask or answer a question in order to draw Sister Mary Mark's attention. Then when I was getting chased back out into the hallway, she would laugh. She was quite funny, that Eileen Quinn! We were starting to grow fond of one another.

The report cards were given out on the last day of school and I was to graduate with honors. Commencement took place on Sunday, June 26, 1960, in St. Andrew's Church. There was a lot of hymn-singing and benediction. When they called the names of those with an eight-year average of over 90 percent, the student was to stand and bow his or her head in acknowledgment, and then sit down.

The eighth grade nuns, Sister Mary Mark, Sister Mary Thomas, and Sister Cleopha were sitting on chairs on the altar, facing the congregation, which included the students. Sister Kieran was also seated on the altar. When my name was called, I stood up in my cap and gown, bowed my head, and sat back down, looking at Sister Mary Mark the whole time. Something inside of me wanted her approval or acknowledgment. I would have never admitted it, but I wanted her to be looking at me and smile or nod her approval, as if to say, "Hey, you were a pain in my butt, but you're all right. Good luck with your future." Or even, "I don't like you, but you got it done." But she wasn't looking at me and our eyes never met.

I didn't stop looking at her until I was distracted by giggles and muffled laughter when Eddie was announced for his bow. Eddie's middle name was Pius and that always made us laugh. Edward Pius Haggerty? It just didn't fit.

After the ceremony, there was an awkward milling around outside the church. Parents and families were waiting to meet up with their graduate and hug and kiss and take pictures. There were lots of good-byes and some were awkward because, in some cases, they really were good-byes. You knew you would see your close friends again, so that was no problem. "Good-bye, see ya', take care," were fine for Eddie, Billy, Tommy, Kathy Lynch, and Cathy Garity.

It was a little awkward, however, when you might not see that person ever again, after eight years of being in the same class. Billy Hamburger actually sought me out and gave me a hug. I was surprised and didn't react well, thinking he was playing some kind of joke on me. He was feeling emotional, I could tell. His brother John yelled for him to know where the rest of the family was waiting.

"Don't let them break your spirit at Holy Cross," he said as he walked away.

"I won't," I laughed.

I don't recall ever seeing Billy Hamberger again.

Vincent DiGilio shook my hand and said, "Good l-l-l-l-luck, F-F-F-F-Farrell.

"You too, Vinnie," I responded.

Michael Scansaroli also was feeling emotional and when he shook my hand, he said, "Thanks for being a friend."

Again, being caught off guard, I responded stupidly, and said, "Don't mention it."

As I walked to the place my family had designated to meet, I passed Laurel Kramer who was with some relatives.

"Good-bye, Joe Farrell," she yelled. "Don't ever change."

I didn't answer. I couldn't think of anything to say. Many of my classmates were feeling sentimental, but I was not. I was glad to be out of there. Looking back, I still feel conflicted about my elementary school experience.

I bear no grudges toward anyone, not even those nuns who repeatedly hit me in the face. I do, however, question the overall tone of the learning environment. In fact, my sister, Ronnie, was so intimidated by the nuns that she routinely threw up before leaving for school.

My mother always tried to get us to eat something before we left for school. Ronnie was too "nervous" to eat and in too much of a hurry to get ready. My mother would often bring orange juice, toast, or an eggnog to her room, so she could eat or drink it while getting ready. For the first six grades, Ronnie would vomit her breakfast about half the time.

In her defense, I would point out that her fifth grade teacher, Sister Mary Daniel, was "nuts." I never had her for a teacher, but I did have run-ins with her. She was nuts in the kind of way that she deserved me in her class. There is no doubt in my mind that we would have had a memorable battle and I believe I would have broken her. Seeing how she frightened and intimidated my sister made me angry. I wanted her to try some of her "act" on me. It was some small consolation, though, that Sister Mary Daniel did have my cousin, Tom Nash, who was two years behind me and he, I am happy to report, almost gave her a stroke.

I left elementary school highly competent in Reading, Math and English and fully prepared for high school in those subjects. I knew little, however, of Rosa Parks, Martin Luther King, or the growing social revolution that was about to envelope us. I never remember a discussion in school or a sermon at mass about civil rights.

I could diagram a sentence with the best of them and I can still recite the linking verbs in alphabetical order, but something was missing. I knew I wasn't feeling the way people thought I should, and maybe the way many of my classmates did. I knew I would never be back to St. Andrew's School and I never was, and I knew I would never miss it and I never did. Why would I? Instead of being told of the wonderful possibilities to discover a cure for cancer, defeat communism, travel to the moon, or lead a social revolution for justice, all of which were possibilities for me at that time, Sister Mary Mark predicted that I would fail both in this life and in the next. I don't see why St. Andrew's would feel that way. In this life, my chances for some type of success were high. I was smart (graduating with an average in the mid-90s), happy, well-liked, responsible, athletic, high energy, motivated, and-except for copying homework-honest.

My biggest weaknesses would today probably be attributed to Attention Deficit Hyperactivity Disorder (ADHD). I was hyperactive and bored. My attention span was short, I loved laughing and making others laugh. Today, my daughter is an experienced, certified teacher. She claims I'm definitely an ADHD-type and she wishes some of her students cared enough to copy their homework! She has never hit a student in the face, although she admits sometimes she has had the urge to do it.

As for success in the next life . . . I did see a possible problem. I was hounded by impure thoughts. Moreover, we were taught that sin was in the will, and I definitely had a will for sex. I prayed for strength. I went to confession every Saturday, and to Mass and communion every Sunday. But I still had a will for sex. I was hoping that the nuns and priests at St. Andrew's were being overly strict in their interpretation of the sixth commandment and that Roman Azanza was right about them telling us a bunch of crap to scare us. I also took some comfort from the fact that I did the nine First Fridays, and would have the opportunity to confess before dying.

So I left St. Andrew's without any separation anxiety. I was confident that I could handle high school academically, believing I had been hit in the face for the last time, and strangely enough, hoping that St. Margaret Alcoque was *not* nuts!

CHAPTER SEVEN

♦ ♦ ♦ ♦ ♦

"RUDE AWAKENINGS"

When I think back on all the crap I've learned in high school,
It's a wonder I can think at all;
Though my lack of education hasn't hurt me much,
I can read the writings on the walls.
Simon and Garfunkel ~ "Kodachrome"

I couldn't have been more excited about starting Holy Cross High School during the summer of 1960. This would be the last summer of unemployment. I played baseball on three different teams and did chores around the house for five dollars a week. I had to keep our small, but annoying lawn looking nice, keep the hedges neatly trimmed, vacuum the entire house once a week, and take care of the garbage and garbage cans—put them out on the curb three days a week and return them to the backyard when emptied. My father threatened to deduct fifty cents every time a can wasn't out for collection, or he saw an empty can still on the curb. He never did it, but he threatened to.

My big passion that summer, however, was preparing to go out for Holy Cross football. Tommy Taraci and I both decided we would try out for football and worked hard all summer to be ready. We each had our own regimen to prepare. I lifted weights every day in my basement. I was too tall to lift a barbell over my head in the basement, so I did military presses on my knees. I kept a log, followed a book on bodybuilding that I got from the library, slowly increasing weights, sets, and the reps for each exercise.

Tommy and I would agree to meet somewhere, often Bowne Park and sometimes Kissena Park where we would run, do calisthenics, and throw a football around. We would practice quick starts from a three-point stance and also running backward as if covering a receiver. We pushed each other to exhaustion three or four times a week. Whenever we could, we got a bunch of guys together and played tackle football without pads. Any even number of guys would be split and rules adjusted as to who was eligible as a receiver and bang! we smashed into each other with reckless abandon.

On weekends and evenings, we began to hang out at a luncheonette on Northern Boulevard called Mueller's. High school kids had been hanging out there for years and since we were about to be high school kids, we would stop in, drink Cokes or egg creams, sit in a booth, play and listen to the jukebox.

Many of the girls from our class were doing the same. A few times that summer, June Hope would invite us over to her house to listen to records. As the summer wore on, a few of us started pairing off. Tommy and June became a couple, as did Billy Landers and Jean Reed and Eileen Quinn and me. We would listen to Frankie Avalon, the Everly Brothers, Bobby Darin, Paul Anka, and Elvis. Tommy started to bring his Platters album so he could slow dance with June to "Smoke Gets in Your Eyes," sometimes over and over again. A few times, June's parents had pizza delivered and offered Cokes to go with it. We were just like an episode of Ozzie and Harriet, munching on pizza, drinking Coke, dancing, singing, and laughing. All we needed was Ricky to show up and sing! We all got along great and it seemed we were always laughing and happy and caring about each other. We loved Rock 'n'

Roll and a number of us carried transistor radios around wherever we went so that, no matter what we were doing or where we were hanging out, there was background music.

We'd argue what station to listen to radio stations like WABC, WINS, or WMCA, and which DJs were the best (Cousin Brucie Morrow, Murray "the K" Kaufmann, Peter Trip—"the curly-haired kid in the third row," or Herb Oscar Anderson) and what songs or artists were our favorites. I didn't know it then, but our close friendships were at their peak. The guys would go on as friends for many years, but the girls would soon start dating older guys and drift away from us.

Even though the summer of 1960 was fun, I couldn't wait for school to start. I felt being in high school was going to be a great adventure. About mid-August, my father went to visit an aunt in Rockaway and returned with a back seat full of clothes.

"Help me bring some stuff in from the car," my father said, motioning me to follow him.

"What stuff?"

"Clothes for you to wear to school."

"What?"

"Come and see."

In the car were six suits and two sport coats and pants that I spent the rest of the evening trying on so my mother could make minor alterations. The clothes were high quality hand-me-downs from my father's cousin named Jimmy Daley. Holy Cross did not have or require uniforms, but did require a coat and tie at all times. My parents had been discussing how they could afford to buy me clothes for school, when my father remembered being offered Jimmy Daley's old clothes by his aunt. To this day, I have never met Jimmy Daley, but I wore his clothes all through high school. I am grateful—he was tall, apparently rich, had good taste, and took good care of his clothes. I went to school dressed in expensive suits, but with white socks and loafers.

Just before Labor Day, Holy Cross had "Book Day." On this day we came to school, obtained our schedule and purchased our books and supplies. We were divided into sections. On the front doors of the school were posted each section, the schedule and roster of who was in each section. What soon become obvious was that we were divided by academic ability or projected academic ability in sections A to J. My guess is that it was by score on the Co-Op Exam. I was in Section C.

There were approximately thirty students from St. Andrew's Class of 1960 attending Holy Cross and twelve from my specific class. Only three were in the top two sections and none of them were from my class. Eight St. Andrew's graduates were in the last two sections, including four from my class. There were forty-eight guys in Section C and about that many in each section. Controlling forty-eight boys pulsing with testosterone would be a challenge. I was hoping Tommy would be in my class, but he was in Section B.

I was thrilled with my schedule. I started with Religion, which, not being a morning person, would give me a chance to wake up. Second period was a Study Hall on Mondays, Wednesdays and Fridays and Gym on Tuesdays and Thursdays. This would give me time to do any homework that I hadn't finished the night before. Next came Latin, followed by half a period of Study Hall and half a period for Lunch. I figured I would do any Religion homework and start my Latin in this study hall. The fifth and sixth periods were Citizenship and English, followed by another Study Hall. I would end my day with Algebra. I remember thinking I wish I could switch Citizenship with Algebra, because I get antsy toward the end of the day and Algebra was important. I was hoping that the break between classes would help me in that regard.

After taking a copy of the schedule, we proceeded to the Cafeteria, which was set up as a huge bookstore. We got the books we needed for each course and golden-colored Holy Cross gym shorts and green and white tee shirts for gym class. None of this was optional. Since my father had given me a signed check with the amount blank, I figured he wouldn't mind if I bought some nice shiny Holy Cross High School book covers. On the way out, we got our locker assignments and combinations.

Tommy Rizzo, who I knew from St. Andrew's, was in my class and had a locker near mine, so I waited for him to finish paying so we could search for our lockers together. His twin brother John was also there, but John was in Section B. The Rizzos were to become good friends over the next few years and, since their older brother was a junior and active in sports, they already knew a lot about the school.

Just as we were leaving the cafeteria with all our stuff, there was some commotion. Some student couldn't pay for his books for some reason—I believe he had forgotten his money. When he realized this, he put his books down on a table and started to leave. A Brother saw this and stopped him by grabbing him by the arm.

"Whoa! Whoa! Where do you think you are going?"

"I'm going to the phone to call . . ."

"You're not going anywhere, Mister!"

The student, who was already upset at just discovering that he couldn't pay, was confused and didn't understand what was wrong.

"I need to call my mother, Brother, so . . ."

The Brother turned the student around and pushed him back.

The student was red-faced and extremely uncomfortable.

"I don't understand," he yelled, "What do you want me to do?"

"Did you find those books in a pile like that?"

"No Brother, but I . . ."

"Where did you find them?"

"Each one was on a different table by subject, but I'm . . ."

"Then you're gonna put them back there or so help me, your blood will be all over them," the Brother screamed.

"But Brother, I'm gonna come back for the books after . . ." his voice almost breaking, trailed off.

"You won't need the books if you don't do what I say right now."

The Rizzos and I left the cafeteria at that point and once out of earshot, I asked rhetorically, "Who the fuck was *that* nut?"

"That's Brother Regis, our Latin teacher," answered Tommy. "He's also in charge of the bookstore. My brother already told me to be very careful if you need to go to the bookstore. If Brother Regis is in a bad mood, he'll bust on you for anything."

"Oh, great," I said. "We have him every day and can't avoid him."

"My brother said to be very careful not to get on his bad side. If you do, Latin class becomes like Hell. He picks on you every day and calls you names in Latin."

What I had just witnessed convinced me that Billy Rizzo had given his brothers good advice. I would be very careful to not alienate Brother Regis.

At Book Day, we got notification that candidates for freshman football should report at 9:00 a.m. the day after Labor Day to the gym, wearing gym clothes. Tommy Taraci and I were there and we were ready. This is what we had been waiting for! We had busted our asses all summer to be ready to show what we could do and to play football for Holy Cross High School. After getting dressed in the locker room, we went out to the gym and signed a sheet of paper, then started stretching and limbering up. A lot of guys seemed to know one another, but Tommy and I knew very few others. The coach, Mr. Close, was a math teacher and there were a few other coaches whose names we did not know.

At first we formed a huge circle around the perimeter of the gym for calisthenics. There were easily fifty guys in the circle as Mr. Close blew his whistle. "We'll start off easy, then we'll pick it up, see who wants to play football and who doesn't."

We began with Jumping Jacks, then deep knee bends, then some stretching. Then things got tougher: push-ups, leg raises, sit-ups, and thrusts. As the intensity and pace picked up, guys were dropping out. On and on it went, as sweat ran off us in the hot stuffy gym. One guy slipped on sweat doing thrusts and hit his face on the floor. One coach took him in the locker room with a towel over his bloody nose.

After what seemed like an eternity, the whistle blew and the coach declared a five-minute break for water. Tommy and I had done pretty well and were grateful for the work we had done all summer. As we were in line for a drink of water, the Rizzo twins came out of the locker room and approached us.

"Pretty rough, huh?" said Tommy Rizzo.

"Yeah," I said, my eyes burning from sweat running into them. "Are you going out for football?"

"No, we're equipment managers," answered John.

"Were you here from the start?" I asked. "I didn't see you before."

"We were in a managers' meeting for the whole football program. It just ended. This must have been rough, because there are a few guys throwing up in the lavatory and a few guys left. Are you guys all right?"

"Yeah." Said Tommy Taraci. "I'm not quitting."

"What comes next?" I asked.

Tommy Rizzo shrugged that he didn't know, but the whistle blew, and we were soon to find out.

"When do we put pads on?" I asked as we moved back to the middle of the gym.

"Not until school starts next week."

We resumed our drills by running laps around the gym. After ten or so laps, a few more guys dropped out, claiming they had drunk too much water. I was curious when the coaches asked "Artie" and "Joe" to lead us in the laps, how they knew their names. After laps, we did sprints the length of the basketball court. Oddly enough, there were four groups now who ran sprints, led by "Artie," "Joe," "KC," and "Kevin."

Tommy and I had no problem with anything they threw at us. We were tired and extremely hot, but not even thinking about quitting. The group was under forty now and shrinking.

We got a half-hour break during which some guys ate fruit or other light snacks that they had brought. The coaches ate sandwiches and Tommy and I went outside and laid in the grass and drank a soda that we got from a vending machine. We could hear the Varsity and JVs doing drills on the field nearby.

When we resumed, the group looked even smaller. We did some stretching while being led by some "candidates" who somehow were known by the coaching staff. Tommy and I were feeling much more comfortable now and were growling during some of the exercises. Soon the coach blew a long blast on his whistle and yelled, "Okay, everybody, listen up. I want the first team offense in center court and second team under the other basket. First team defense at center court and second team under the other basket. The rest of you stand along the bleachers on the side."

I looked at Tommy dumbfounded. He looked at me with disbelief on his face. We slowly walked to the sidelines, while most of the guys ran to their designated places.

Mr. Close told the offense to huddle up and called a play in a low tone so that the guys behind the first team could hear it, but we could not.

"Ready, break," yelled the quarterback and the huddle broke and the defense lined up and the offense ran a play. The play didn't go correctly and the coach yelled, "Harry, what was that call?" The quarterback says something like "Split Right 32 Buck."

"That's right, but where were you?" Run it again."

"What the fuck bullshit is this?" I whispered to Tommy.

"I don't know," he answered, shaking his head and looking really pissed off.

The first team continued to run plays for over an hour, then the second team took over. Some of the first team offense moved to defense, which really depressed us. We were hoping that because there weren't enough guys left for two full teams on both offense and defense, that we would get a chance.

After the second team ran plays for about a half hour, we decided to pack it in. We felt so stupid standing along the sidelines watching with about six other guys. No one said anything to us or directed anything to us, and we couldn't hear the play calls in the huddle. After a brief discussion, we walked into the locker room and began to dress without taking a shower. We were humiliated.

"Don't you want to shower?" I asked Tommy.

"I want to get the fuck out of here as fast as possible. What a crock of holy horse shit! I don't understand. How can there be a motherfucking first and second team? They can blow me if they think I'm gonna stand around."

On and on we cursed in our anger and disappointment as we quickly changed clothes.

Just as I put my last shoe on, I stood up and slammed the locker door shut, and saw a man staring at us with his arms folded. He was short, stocky, dressed like a coach, had a flat top haircut, big flat nose, seemed very angry, and was blocking the way out.

"Excuse me, *girls*," he yelled. "I may be new here, but I think your language violates some rule somewhere. Do you want me to ask Brother John (the principal)?"

"No, sir."

"No, sir."

"Are you *girls* freshmen?"

"Yes, sir."

"Yes, sir."

"Well, then if football is too hard for you *girls,* I suggest you leave now. Quietly—without a word! Or would you rather come outside with me and express your feelings to *me?*" he yelled through clenched teeth while hitting himself in the chest with his fist.

"No, sir."

"No, sir, what?"

"No, sir, we'll leave quietly," I said, declining the coach's invitation.

"That's a wise choice. Maybe you're not as dumb as you look. *Go!* Get out of here! This locker room is no place for quitters!"

We left the locker room and as we hurried out the gym door, John Rizzo came running over to us.

"What did you guys do?"

"Did you hear that?" Tommy asked.

"Yeah, he sure was mad."

"Who was that maniac?" I asked.

"He's the new JV coach. Are you guys quitting?"

"Yeah, what kind of bullshit is this? How can there be a first and second team on the first day of practice?"

Rizzo went on to tell us that most of these guys were recruited from grade schools on Long Island where there were Little League football programs. They have been meeting and working out "informally" all summer. Some of the guys have older brothers who play or played football and they were invited to come also. The quarterback's father was the head coach at C. W. Post College on Long Island and friends with some of our coaches.

This went down hard for Tommy and me. We had never played organized football, knew of no Little League football program and didn't know of anyone who did. John Rizzo was a great guy and he offered good advice. He suggested we stay on the team and that we would be able to catch up. He cited a few names, including his older brother, who made the football team despite not having played before high school.

Tommy and I talked about it on the way home, but considering how we left in a huff and our encounter with the J.V. coach, we decided it would be too difficult to go back.

My first day of high school was memorable, but for different reasons than my first day of elementary school. On my first day of elementary school, I was made to stay after school as punishment. My mother was waiting in the schoolyard for me to be dismissed at three o'clock, but when she saw my teacher, Sister Michael Ann, escorting her class to the dismissal point, I was not in the line. I was still in the classroom crying.

During the day, we were told to take the box out of our desk and open it carefully, which I did. Sister Michael Ann explained that the box contained little square pieces of paper, each with a letter, and invited us to find an "A" and put it on our desk, which I did. Then a "B," then a "C," both of which I did. When this introductory exercise was done, she told us to put the A, B, and C back in the box and put the lid on and put the box away, which I did not. I continued to look for a "D." When Sister Michael Ann saw me, she said I had to obey her and do what she asked. I replied, "No, I don't, you're not my mother."

"Well, you just remain here at three o'clock, young man, and we'll discuss this."

When dismissal arrived, Sister Michael Ann reminded me that I was to "stay in" after school to discuss my disobedience. She told me to remain seated at my desk while she took the rest of the children in line down to the school yard. I started to cry and told her if I missed my mother who was waiting for me, that I didn't know my way home. Sister Michael Ann said I should have thought of that before I disobeyed. I cried even harder as everyone left me alone in the classroom. In a matter of minutes, to my great relief, Sister Michael Ann returned with my mother. She then went on to explain that when in school, she had the same authority as my mother and I was to obey her. My mother confirmed this and then I was allowed to leave. My mother was embarrassed by this episode on my first day of school. My older sister was in the seventh grade and was a model student who had never been any problem. Over the years, as I would embarrass my mother again and again, she would always say that she should have known from Day One that she was in for it.

The first day of high school (September 12, 1960) was memorable because it was cut short by one of the worst storms to ever hit New York, Hurricane Donna. The eye of the storm—one hundred miles wide—crossed Long Island about the middle of the day and we were dismissed. I only got to meet my Religion teacher, Brother Francis Killoy and my Latin teacher, the feared Brother Regis. The next day Brother John announced that, we the class of 1964, would be dubbed the "Hurricane Class."

On Day two, I was excited to get to experience my first whole day of high school and to get to meet the rest of my teachers. When period five rolled around, I got to meet Mr. Trentacoste, my Citizenship teacher. He was a tall, lanky, uncoordinated, young man who spent the whole period outlining the rules for his class. Citizenship sounded like it might be interesting.

Next came English class with a new teacher to Holy Cross by the name of Guido Maiolo. We all were anxious to meet Guido and were laughing about his name when the bell rang. My heart sank when, after a few seconds, Guido Maiolo entered the classroom. He was the football coach who had confronted Tommy Taraci and me in the locker room . . .

I prayed he wouldn't recognize me, but as he was calling roll and arranging our seats to his seating chart, my hopes were dashed.

"We've met, haven't we Mister Farrell?"

"Yes, sir."

"Are you going to quit this class?"

"Excuse me, sir?"

"Are you going to quit English class like you quit football?"

"No, sir."

"Are you sure, Farrell? It might get h-a-a-a-a-r-r-d."

"Yes, sir, I'm sure."

The rest of the class period, I was consumed by two thoughts. I was pissed off that Guido thought I had quit football because it was too hard and that now, thanks to Guido, so did everybody in my section! I considered telling Guido after class why we quit, but I couldn't decide whether to do it or not. On the one hand, I would like him to understand and not think of me as a wimp or a quitter. On the other hand, I could not predict his reaction. He was an intimidator—that was for sure, and might challenge me to go back out for the team. Tommy didn't have Guido for class and probably wouldn't go back and I'd have to go back alone. It wasn't an appealing possibility. If anything, I was further behind now and they were going to be practicing in pads starting that very day.

I couldn't really decide. The bell rang and I got up and walked up the aisle toward Guido, who was standing at his desk. As I reached his desk, a few guys were talking to him about whatever it was he had said during class while I was wrestling with my dilemma. I hesitated at his desk momentarily and then, feeling it not a great opportunity, I left.

After Study Hall, I went to Algebra class and met Brother Carl Winters. He was young and seemed pretty cool. He gave us one of those "it's-all-up-to-you" speeches. If we work hard and get the work done, we can have fun, if not, we will grind it out. It's all up to us.

My first dance opportunity was the "Halloween Hop" on a rainy Friday night in October. Tommy Taraci and I decided to go, so I asked Eileen Quinn to be my date. I was pretty excited about my first official grown-up type date. I put on one of Jimmy Daley's best suits and since it was raining, hopped a bus up to 164th Street, about three blocks from Eileen's house. My plan was for us to walk from the Quinn residence to Holy Cross, which was about ten blocks. Since it was drizzling steadily, I wore a raincoat, but I didn't want to carry an umbrella. I felt an umbrella might not be cool. Plus, I didn't know where I'd put it during the dance or where we hung our coats or how this whole dance thing worked and I didn't want an extra thing to worry about. This was before small, collapsible umbrellas were invented. It wasn't raining very hard, anyway.

When I got to Eileen's house, I was nervous about meeting her parents and family and was hoping it would all go quickly and smoothly. I was actually hoping she might be ready and come right out and spare me the ordeal of meeting everyone and making small talk on my first official date.

Of course, she was not ready and her sister answered the door and invited me in. I met Mrs. Quinn in the living room and was making small talk with her, when Mr. Quinn came in to meet me. After shaking hands, he said, "Don't you have an umbrella?"

"No, I don't think we will need one."

"It's raining, isn't it?"

Not wanting to appear stupid, or have him offer me one of his, I said, "No."

Eileen came downstairs and I told her she looked nice. She and Mrs. Quinn were discussing what coat to wear, when Mr. Quinn said, "Why did you lie?"

He had gone outside and discovered that it was indeed raining.

"It is? It wasn't when I came in."

"That's funny, because there are puddles in the street like it's been raining for a while. You know it's one thing to be stupid, but it's a whole other thing to lie."

I was mortified. I thought once again about explaining the whole story like with Guido and quitting football, but Eileen had her coat on and her mother handed her a clear plastic rain bonnet to keep her hair from getting wet and I took the easy way out and we left. "Be home at eleven," her father yelled out the door at us as we left.

"Your father hates me," I said as we started up the block toward Holy Cross in the rain.

"Who cares?" said Eileen, stopping to put her rain bonnet on as the rain was getting her hair wet. The rain had gotten harder since I left home.

I started to tell Eileen how I didn't want to carry an umbrella and all and she said, "Don't worry about it," but I did. It bothered me that her father thought I was stupid and a liar. I felt even worse when I got to the dance and saw a place had been set up in the cafeteria for checking coats, hats, and umbrellas.

I went to the boys' bathroom and dried my hair with paper towels and combed it. Fortunately, Eileen's rain bonnet had protected hers.

The dance was fine and Tommy and I and our dates had a lot of laughs. Eileen seemed to enjoy it and we kept calling each other by our last names like the nuns had at St. Andrew's.

"Hey, Quinn, want a Coke?"

"Okay, Farrell."

I wanted to make sure she was home on time, but there was a lot of confusion at the coat check table and, as a result, we were late. As we arrived at her house, her father was at the door.

"I was beginning to wonder if I should go look for you."

Eileen said good night and shook her head in disgust at her father's overprotection.

As I walked home in the rain, I felt depressed, disappointed, and wet. I had screwed up my first official date. It was so frustrating to have such a seemingly small thing blow up into such a fiasco. No wonder the girls our age are dating older guys, I thought. Cathy Kain, our classmate from St. Andrew's, had been at the dance with a sophomore named Paul Pugliese. She acted like she didn't know us, and she didn't even know of my blunder.

Chapter Eight

♦ ♦ ♦ ♦ ♦

"Full Consent of the Will"

I hid in the clouded wrath of the crowd,
But when they said, "sit down" I stood up.
Ooh—ooh, growin' up.
                                    Bruce Springsteen—"Growin' Up"

The first six weeks grades had me making the honor roll. My grades ranged from 81 in Latin to 91 in Algebra. We sat alphabetically in every class, sometimes up and down rows and sometimes across. Either way, I sat near Jay Carroll, Ray Frasene, and Pat Kelly and we were rapidly becoming good friends. Jay Carroll was a bright, happy-go-lucky guy who loved to laugh and frequently did. Ray Frasene was a more serious, studious guy, but could be really funny at times. Ray had a lot of self-control and could wait until it was safe to offer a funny remark or observation—something I have always had trouble doing! Pat Kelly was a more complicated, moody guy but who, once you got him laughing, couldn't stop.

Pat thought it was funny to answer "Ba-bye" whenever a teacher called on a guy in our class named Bela Babai. The teacher would call on Babai and Pat would say "Ba-bye" and wave good-bye. A couple of times he picked up his books and made a move as if to leave. It got so that when a teacher called on Babai, a lot of the class would look at Pat for his reaction.

"I swear someday, I'm just gonna walk out and say, well, you said, "Bye-bye," Pat promised.

One day in Mr. Trentacoste's class, he called on Babai and when we look at Pat, he laughs and waves. Mr. Trentacoste's attention is drawn to Pat by all of us looking at him and he doesn't like what he sees. He asks Pat to come up to his desk and slaps him hard in the face and tells him to return to his seat and behave. Pat, stunned, returned to his seat, red-faced and silent.

Later that same day in Algebra, Brother Carl calls on Babai. We sneak a glance at Pat. He smiles, but doesn't wave or make any movement. It may have been the only thing Trentacoste taught us all year.

The four of us developed a good working relationship on homework. We cooperated and worked on different subjects and copied each other's in Study Hall. Ray liked doing Algebra, so if I needed to copy Algebra homework, I could count on Ray to give it to me in seventh period study hall. I knew that when I gave Jay my answers to English essay questions, he would put the answers in his own words so as to avoid possible detection by Guido. It wasn't an organized conspiracy and it didn't always work out. Often we did all our own homework, but generally we would help one another out. If I told Ray in first period that I needed the math, he would try to have it for me to copy by seventh period. I usually spent my second period study hall on Latin.

Brother Regis would call on people at random and depending on his mood, either ridicule them or humiliate them. I tried to keep up to avoid his ire. As a fallback position, when really in trouble, I could almost always count on Tommy Rizzo. He would not only give you his homework, he would help you understand it.

Walking home from school was with a totally different group of friends. Because we were all walking in generally the same direction, the cast of characters was all guys from St. Andrew's. Tommy Taraci lived in Bayside and took a bus home, but Glenn Judson, Dickie Abella, Jeff Baudo, the Rizzo twins and I walked together most days. Peter Heaney and Don Glennon were also frequently along. Those walks home were always fun.

Dickie Abella was a short, slender, always well-dressed guy with a terrific cynical, sarcastic sense of humor. He was very emotional and had wonderful facial expressions and gestures. Just watching Dickie react to things was a riot. One of Dickie's favorite reactions when he heard something he considered shocking or unbelievable, was to suddenly stop walking. We'd all be walking along and Dickie would just stop, sometimes squinting, as if to say, "Please tell me you didn't just say that" or sometimes big-eyed, implying, "What a moron." If you were walking behind Dickie and he did this, you better be alert or you would walk right into him.

One day as we were walking home, I mentioned how lucky I felt that we had had an air-raid drill that day during third period and it cut short Latin. If it had happened during a study hall, I would have been screwed. When an air-raid drill occurred, we left our classrooms and lined up in the hallway along the lockers. We were instructed to stand facing a locker, put our heads down and clasp our hands behind our heads. Why, I don't know. I was just grateful for a break, unless it was Study Hall. Dickie thought the drills were stupid.

"Boy, are those air-raid drills stupid or what?"

"What do you mean?" asked Glenn.

"What are we putting our heads down and our hands behind our heads for? What good will that do?"

"It will protect our heads from flying debris or shrapnel," answers Jeff Baudo. Dickie comes to an abrupt stop.

"Flying debris or shrapnel!" he yells. We're talking about a *nuclear bomb*. If you're anywhere *near* it, the heat and radiation will vaporize you."

We resumed walking, as we had stopped when Dickie stopped.

"A lot of good having your hands behind your head will do," he laughed. "It's ridiculous."

We walked on, discussing the futility of drilling for a nuclear attack. We laughed about how, at St. Andrew's, we were taught to close our eyes and put our heads down on our desks. We agreed that New York was a most likely target and that if a nuclear bomb hit anywhere in New York, we were dead.

"Well, maybe our air-raid drills are for a conventional attack," says Jeff Baudo. Dickie comes to an abrupt stop.

"What section are you in, Baudo?"

"Section E, the same as you!"

114

"Yeah, well you better keep your mouth shut in class or they'll send you down to J. You're an embarrassment to Section E."

As Dickie, and all of us who had stopped in deference to Dickie's stopping, began to walk again, we were at once laughing and stifling laughter because Don Glennon, who was along on that particular day, was in Section J. Dickie didn't seem to realize this as he went on to lecture Jeff.

"What country is gonna bomb us with conventional bombs? Who?"

"The Russians," answered Jeff.

"The Russians? They're gonna fly over from Moscow and drop bombs on New York?" asked Dickie.

"Yeah, and hopefully, one lands on your house! And they don't have to fly from Moscow, they could be launched from aircraft carriers in the Atlantic," responded Jeff.

"Do you really think we would let Russian carriers close enough to our borders to launch an attack on New York?" Dickie went on. "Don't you think we have planes and missiles strategically located all over the place to prevent an attack on our coast, especially New York? We have B-52 bombers in the air twenty-four hours a day. Ever hear of SAC?"

"Well, there must be a reason we have air-raid drills . . . you don't know *every*thing! Maybe the Japanese will sneak attack us again," countered Jeff.

Dickie comes to an abrupt stop.

"Maybe J is too high for you! That is really fuckin' stupid. You need your own section for the incredibly stupid! The people that make us have these drills were probably in that section."

Photo from "The Cross" 1961

115

I actually put the question to Mr. Trentacoste one day during Citizenship class. He was talking about the "Iron Curtain" across Europe and it popped into my mind.

"Mr. Trentacoste, why do we have air-raid drills and put our hands behind our heads, when if a nuclear bomb hit, it wouldn't do any good?"

"Farrell, I wouldn't care if you ran outside and tried to catch it!"

The class erupted in laughter.

"I believe there are guidelines put out by the Defense Department as to what should be done, but like I said, Farrell, you do what you want." Mr. T. was very pleased with himself.

That afternoon on the way home, I told the group what I had done and of Mr. Trentacoste's fun at my expense. Glenn went into a tirade of how he hated Trentacoste and what a prick he was.

"I would never ask that prick anything," he said. "I just sit there and glare at him. His class sucks. If I ever hit a teacher, it will be him."

I told the gang that I was prepared for Trentacoste to ask what I thought we should do, but he never asked.

"What were you gonna say?" asked Glenn.

"That we should put our head between our legs and kiss our ass good-bye."

"Were you really gonna say that?" asked Jeff.

"Yeah, that would've been great," we all agreed.

"I thought air-raid drills were stupid, but how about that announcement today?" said Dickie

"What announcement?"

"The one about 'anyone who wants to be an usher meet in the auditorium tomorrow after school'."

"You got something against ushers?" asked Tommy Rizzo.

"No, I've always wanted to show people to their seats. It's been a secret dream of mine. It's what I want to do after high school. I want to get a job as an usher. In fact, I'm definitely joining the Ushers Club so I can sharpen my skills. I wonder if you get one of those dust mittens so you can wipe the seat off? What moron needs an usher in our auditorium when the rows are lettered and the seats are numbered! Let's see, Row C, seats five and six, that would be the third row and the fifth and sixth seats. Even Baudo finds his seat in Study Hall."

The next day, Pat Kelly told me he was going to join the Ushers Club after school and asked if I was interested.

"No, thanks," I said.

"It can help when applying to college."

"How?" I asked.

"Colleges want guys who participate in extracurricular activities. There's a place on college applications for listing the clubs, sports, and stuff you did in school. They think it builds character."

On the walk home that day, I told the group about this.

"Hey, Dickie, my buddy Pat Kelly's going to the ushers' meeting today. He says it builds character and can help you get into college."

Dickie comes to an abrupt stop.

"*Showing people where their seats are builds character?* I'll tell you what. If a college accepted me because I was an usher, I'd refuse to go there."

"You get a discount on a school blazer," I added.

"Who the fuck wants a school blazer? How about a little flashlight? Do you get a little flashlight? I'd do it for a flashlight."

The truth was, I wanted a school blazer. I asked my parents if I could buy one, but they said 'no' because I had Jimmy Daley's suits and didn't need a blazer.

Pat Kelly (seated lower right) and his colleagues show off their reduced-rate blazers with the Ushers' Club.

♦ ♦ ♦

My weekends were usually spent with the St. Andrew's crowd, which included Billy Landers—who went to Brooklyn Prep—Eddie Haggerty, and Dennis Geoghan, who both went to Bishop Laughlin.

We each had friends from school, but with the exception of Pat Kelly, no one ever became fully integrated into our crowd. We went to all the Holy Cross football games (we were the Knights), all the record hops in the gym following home games, and played a lot of pick-up football. We would play tackle at Bowne or Kissena Park and two-hand touch in the street anywhere. When we played tackle, we played rough, and without equipment.

When we played touch, there were parked cars and moving cars, trees and bushes, curbs and uneven surfaces, bike riders, dog walkers, and pedestrians, each an obstacle and/or hazard. It's amazing that no one ever seriously injured himself, although Jeff Baudo once ran hard into a parked car on his street to make a catch of an ill-thrown pass from Tommy Taraci. He hit the car so hard, the sound alone made us cringe. Jeff rolled around on the ground in serious pain, holding his crotch and breathing in short, shallow gasps. When he finally could get up he did, but remained bent over. Then, when he was able to speak, he said it felt like his balls were bleeding! He walked slowly to his house, still bent over. Jeff's father was a doctor, so we figured he'd be taken care of, but we didn't see Jeff for a couple of days and then he seemed all right. He said his balls were all right and weren't bleeding after all.

I cracked two ribs playing tackle and tried to keep it from my parents who, strangely enough, always got mad at me when I got hurt. The pain was too bad, however, and I worried that something was seriously wrong, since breathing deeply hurt like hell, so I broke down and told them. They got mad at me.

My parents always seemed to have what I considered a strange reaction to my getting sick or injured. If it was an injury, I must have been doing something stupid or something I shouldn't have been doing; if I was sick, it was because I didn't go to bed early enough or dress warmly enough or wear a hat or eat a balanced diet. "You're not going out" and "You're going to bed early" seemed to be my mother's remedy for whatever ailed me. So as a result, I kept most things to myself.

At the record hops, older guys were moving on the girls we knew from St. Andrew's and so most of us would stand around together looking for new girls to meet and trying to work up the courage to ask one to dance. Tommy and I would often work in tandem to find two girls together that we were attracted to and then move in. The first time, we'd walk over and ask them to dance and, when the song was over, return to our group. Of course, we'd wait for a slow song like "Theme from a Summer Place" or "A Thousand Stars" or Tommy's favorite, "Where or When." After the first dance, we'd discuss how we felt about taking another chance. If we decided to, we'd make a plan to stay with them when the song ended and then introduce each other as a way to make conversation.

Sometimes after the first dance, we'd have a hard time deciding whether to risk it a second time. We'd steal glances at the girls to see if they were looking at us or seemed to be discussing us and tried to read their body language. If we picked up negative vibes, we'd move on and keep looking. Sometimes we'd disagree about the vibes and one of us would work on the other one to get them to go for a second dance.

It was an awful, awful feeling to be turned down. It was especially awful when your buddies were all watching. Once Tommy and I made a move after long and careful deliberation, but the girl I asked said 'no' while the girl Tommy asked, her friend, said 'yes.' I walked back to our group humiliated and of course, they had seen the whole thing. Eddie and Dennis began teasing me, saying things like, "What were you thinking? She's out of your league! She's way too good looking for you!" Eddie was threatening to ask her to dance just so that if she accepted, it would make me look bad. Tommy luckily brought an end to this emotional abuse by telling me and the group that she turned me down because she's going steady with some guy from another school.

It was amazing to me how difficult it was to simply tap a girl on the shoulder and say, "Wanna dance?" I used to pace around to work up the courage and tell myself, "What have you got to lose?" Sometimes I'd procrastinate too long and another guy would move in. "Dammit! Grow up and quit being such a chicken!" Sometimes I'd have a back-up girl picked out, so that if I got turned down, I would immediately go and ask the other. Hopefully, this would eliminate that long, painful, humiliating return to wherever you came from, not to mention, the awkward standing around during the actual song. Unless, of course, they *both* said 'no.' Then my plan was to just keep going on out the door and home.

Such excruciating anxiety and suffering, all in the hopes of committing a mortal sin and risking spending eternity in the fires of hell. It wasn't a drive for companionship that made us suffer so and risk our pride, our dignity and our self-esteem. And it certainly wasn't our love of dancing that drew us to this torture.

Brothers were always at these dances and record hops, but unlike the nuns, they didn't react like we were all going to hell. They mostly kept an eye out for alcohol and fights or abuse of school property. They saw a lot of close dancing, hugging, kissing, and making out. When they did, their reaction was more like, "Hey, take it outside" than "You're going to hell," so I was slightly encouraged about avoiding eternal damnation.

Halfway through my first year of high school, I was on the honor roll and felt less sure of going to hell, but unfortunately, had not avoided being hit.

The first incident was with, of all people, Guido, the great intimidator. The little All American lineman from Ithaca College and football coach used his tough-guy image and athletic-build to his advantage—and who could blame him. Getting over forty fourteen-year-olds through "Great Expectations" and "Return of the Native" took some major intervention.

On this particular day, during our weeks of reading and discussing "The Return of the Native" by Thomas Hardy, I had been fooling around in study hall and during lunch, while helping Jay Carroll with his English homework. I was mocking a character named Clym Yeobright and had Jay and Ray Frasene and Pat Kelly and others in stitches.

Every time I would speak of him, I would call him "Clym Not-So-Bright, the Furze Cutter." You see, Clym Yeobright is a furze cutter in the story and we didn't even know what 'furze' was! I don't think Guido did either. I would goof around and with an imitation of Red Skelton doing Clem Kadiddlehopper, I would say, "Ah, hiya, I'm Clym Not-So-Bright and I'm a furze cutter." Everyone would laugh and someone would say, "How's your furze, Clym?" "Me furze is 'urtin," I would answer with a British accent.

When we got to English class, Guido asked something like, "Which character do you like?" or "Who is your favorite character?" and calls on me. I, of course, say, "Clym Yeobright," but there is a lot of giggling and muffled laughter around me and I can't help but smile and suppress a laugh. Guido is not sure what is so funny, but feels compelled to pursue it.

"Stand up, Farrell," he says as he walks slowly toward me. "What is so funny?"

"Nothing, sir."

Then, why did you laugh?"

I wasn't laughing as Guido came face-to-face and glared at me. I thought he might think I was laughing at him, in which case I was in serious jeopardy. Guido wasn't comfortable teaching literature or maybe teaching anything, but he was sensitive about it and had a huge ego. He would often make mistakes, while reading a passage or writing on the board, and if there was laughter, he would go into a rage. He would turn and glare in the direction he thought it came from, with a scowl on his face.

Once when he misspelled a word on the board and he realized it didn't look right, he changed it, but it was still wrong. There were a couple of very audible snickers.

"Who thinks it's funny?" he screamed as he whirled around.

Of course, nobody answered.

"Have some balls and admit it!"

Silence.

"You gutless little girls! Laugh behind my back, but hide when I'm facing you."

His face was all red and he slammed the book down on his desk and stared out the window for about ten minutes and then proceeded to give out a murderous homework assignment.

But now, Guido was staring into my eyes with his jaw set, so close he was actually making contact with his folded arms.

I looked him right in the eyes and knew my answer was crucial to my survival. I couldn't say 'nothing' again because he knew we were laughing and might think it was at him. I calmly and sincerely said, "Just something that happened before class started—nothing to do with this class or assignment or anything."

"Oh, well you're in class now, Farrell, aren't you?"

"Yes, sir."

"And I want your full attention." Guido punched me sharply in the forehead with his right fist, a short, sharp jab right in the middle of my forehead.

"Do I have your undivided attention?"

"Yes, sir."

"Then sit down and get your mind on your work."

He bumped me on purpose with his body as he turned away.

I sat down and kept my eyes straight down on my desk. My head hurt where his college ring had made contact with my skull. It felt like it might be cut, but I didn't touch it or show any signs of pain. All in all, I felt I had gotten off easy.

After class, guys were coming over and saying things like, "That was scary" or "Did you shit in your pants?" Jay Carroll looked at my head and said you could see Ithaca College imprinted in reverse on my forehead. I got so much attention it was like I had done something heroic!

My only comment amidst all this as I walked to study hall was, "Me furze is hurtin'!"

The second incident was somewhat of a surprise to me. Although Algebra was the eighth period, the last class of the day, and seventh was a study hall, there were still times when I did not get all the Algebra homework done.

On this particular day in Algebra class, Brother Carl called on me to give the solution to a problem we had been assigned for homework. The procedure was that when called on, the student stood up, read the problem out loud, gave the answer and if anyone in class didn't understand it, he would ask the student to go to the blackboard and show how he arrived at the answer.

Brother Carl's exams were always made up of problems that were assigned for homework. That made the homework important. Most kids in the class studied their homework when studying for an exam. In many cases, guys got the correct solution on the exam, not because they understood Algebra, but because they could recall the solution.

When I was called on, I stood up, and read the problem out loud as usual:

"If it takes "A" four days to do a job,

And it takes "B" three days;

How long will it take "A" and "B" working together?"

Having not yet gotten to this particular problem, I stood with my partially done homework and some other night's homework in my hands (to make it appear that I had done it), looked puzzled, and said very sincerely, "I didn't get this one, Brother."

"You didn't get it? Why?" asked Brother Carl.

"I couldn't figure out how to . . ."

"You guys are letting story problems throw you. This is simple. Now, let's think it through, Farrell. If it takes "A" four days and "B" three days and you are in charge of getting this job done, what would you do?"

"I'd let "B" do it!" I answered smiling.

The class erupted in laughter and to my surprise, Brother Carl raced down the aisle and slapped me hard across the face! I was so stunned, I couldn't even recall what he said. After class, the guys told me he said something about this not being a school for comedians. I was really shocked that he had reacted so suddenly and so violently. I truly expected him to laugh and send me to the blackboard.

What I had apparently missed, but others told me, was that Brother Carl was in a bad mood to begin with and that a few of the guys he had called on, particularly Sammy Magarelli, had annoyed him even further with their attitudes. I hadn't noticed this because I was furiously trying to finish the homework in case he called on me.

That being a Friday, our next class wasn't until Monday and Brother Carl started off by calling on me for the very first homework problem. I had expected that he would either ignore me from now on and hold a grudge or he would definitely call on me, so I was prepared. I nailed it perfectly, including showing how I arrived at the solution on the blackboard. As I left the blackboard to return to my seat, he said, "Good, Joe, very good."

Good *Joe*? Good *Joe*? I guess he thought hitting me in the face made us friends! I took it as an apology.

The third time you might say I asked for it. If the Holy Cross Handbook were the Ten Commandments, I would have committed a mortal sin. We were always taught that a mortal sin consisted of three elements, all of which must be present. First, it must be a "grievous matter." Second, there must be "sufficient reflection." This means the sinner must realize that he is committing or about to commit a serious sin. Third, "Full Consent of the Will" which means you wanted to do it.

The biggest loophole is "Sufficient Reflection." When the "Examination of Conscience" takes place and a person must decide if they committed a mortal sin, this is where they may find wiggle room. If the act was committed on impulse, then it was easy to think, "I didn't actually say to myself at the time, 'this is a mortal sin' and then decide to go ahead and do it anyway." Therefore, it wasn't a mortal sin. I personally used this rationale many times when impure thoughts and acts were involved.

In the first instance, when Guido punched me in the head, there was no grievous matter. I had, in fact, done nothing wrong. I answered the question truthfully and I smiled. Certainly no grievous matter existed. The second time, when Brother Carl smacked me hard across the face, I would argue it was not a "grievous matter," but even if I conceded that point, there clearly wasn't "sufficient reflection." I had impulsively blurted out "I'd let "B" do it" and never expected Brother Carl's reaction.

This time was different. This was in Mr. Trentacoste's Citizenship class during the second half of the year. I was sick and tired of Trentacoste's boring class. Cuba, blah, blah. Berlin, blah, blah. Iron Curtain, blah, blah. I sat in the row closest to the window and took solace in looking out the window and wishing I were out there.

This particular day, he was droning on and on about how Communism gains a foothold in a country. I was listening, but couldn't stand to look at him. I had my right elbow on my desk and my right cheek propped in the palm of my hand with my head turned toward the window. Trentacoste asked the class, "How do the Communists infiltrate a government? Is it ignorance or apathy?" A number of hands go up and Trentacoste is deciding who to call on.

"Ignorance or apathy?" he repeats. "Mr-r-r-r-r . . . . Farrell."

I know he called on me because he thought I wasn't paying attention, but I was. I had heard the question the first time and was chuckling to myself at what answer popped into my mind. Giving this answer to Mr. T. would be a grievous matter. Perhaps a normal person would laugh at it and move on, but Mr. T. wasn't a normal person.

I slowly stood up and for a good four or five seconds considered my answer. Thus, sufficient reflection was present. I just couldn't pass up this. Was it ignorance or apathy? So with the full consent of my will and the proper inflection in my voice, I said, "I don't know and I don't care!"

It took a moment or two for most of the class to get it. Those who got it right away laughed and explained it to others. I'm not sure if Mr. T. saw the humor or not, but he called me to the front of the room and quickly administered the penance. He slapped me hard on the left side of my face and sent me back to my seat.

By now, what I had said had really sunk in and Jay Carroll and Pat Kelly were in convulsions. Even though my face stung badly from Mr. T.'s powerful slap, I had to keep from looking at them, lest I break out laughing. Pat hid his face in his hands, covering his nose and mouth trying to stifle the laughter and Jay was hiding behind Bela Babai.

There were big smiles on many faces and as Trentacoste tried to resume his lecture, I think he got it. He actually seemed to suppress a smile and a few guys in the class let out audible chuckles. On our walk home that afternoon, this of course, was a hot item. Tommy Rizzo told the story with great glee.

"You didn't? You didn't?" screamed Dickie, coming to an abrupt stop. "Beautiful! B-e-e-e-eau-u-u-u-utiful!"

"That awkward fuck hit you?" said Glenn. "I swear if he ever hits me, I'll hit him back. I hate him. I'll bet he used to get beat up when he was a kid and now it's payback time."

"Well, at least I made him laugh," I said, as I recounted how Mr. T. smiled as he tried to resume class and again asked, "Ignorance or apathy?"

"Yeah, he laughed after he hit you," replied Glenn. "I've seen that evil little smile he has when he thinks he's done or said something funny. I hope somebody decks him one of these days."

"Well, we know it won't be Farrell," chimed in Jeff Baudo. "He had a perfect chance today and he pussied out. You should have decked him, Joe."

"Maybe you'll deck him, Jeff," said Dickie.

"I doubt it since we don't have him for class."

"You'll probably get him next year when you repeat ninth grade, you moron."

CHAPTER NINE

◆ ◆ ◆ ◆ ◆

"SQUIRES AND KNIGHTS, MADMEN AND DOUCHE-BAGS"

While Mona Lisas and Mad Hatters,
Sons of bankers, sons of lawyers,
Turn around and say good morning to the night,
For unless they see the sky
But they can't and that is why
They know not if it's dark outside or light.
　　　　　　Elton John ~ "Mona Lisas and Mad Hatters"

As 1960 turned into 1961, the election and inauguration of John Fitzgerald Kennedy was the huge story. It seems that most of the priests, nuns, and brothers and even lay teachers were shocked that JFK won! America was supposed to be too prejudiced against Catholics and against the Irish to ever allow that to happen. If a Catholic was elected President, the Pope would be making our national policy was the stated fear.

At first there was jubilation at Holy Cross and St. Andrew's. His inauguration was regarded as the biggest event of the century. People who never paid any attention to the news or politics were following every development. Stories that he had stolen the election were summarily dismissed as bigotry and sour grapes. His inaugural speech was quoted and discussed in every classroom and at Mass on Sunday. Quotes from the speech were selected for the front and back inside covers of the Holy Cross Yearbook for 1961.

After a few months however, I sensed a different feeling among most Catholics. Fear! I would sense it when my parents and aunts and uncles talked politics. I could sense it when my teachers talked politics. Basically, the fear was that the world was in a sorry state, teetering on the brink of total disaster, and now a Catholic was the leader of the Free World. Anything that goes wrong in any of the many crisis areas, it would be because he was a Catholic, and Catholics would be set back a hundred years.

The world, according to my sources, was going to hell in a handbasket and *now* a Catholic is President! The Russians had superior technology, which was demonstrated by their being ahead of us in the race to the moon. They had gained the advantage because our youth were lazy, undisciplined, watched too much TV, and listened to rock and roll, which was sure as hell a sign of moral decay.

Communism was spreading like wildfire from Russia and China to Eastern Europe, Southeast Asia, and now to Cuba, a mere ninety miles from our shores. Communists had infiltrated our government and many institutions in our society. Indeed they were even trying to weaken our country through fluoridation of our water! Nuclear holocaust was possible—and even likely—as both superpowers had the capability of destroying each other within hours. Just before the election, the Russians had shot down an American U-2 spy plane over their territory and captured the pilot, Francis Gary Powers, which brought a tremendous increase in tension between the two superpowers. And to top it off just before the inauguration, we broke off diplomatic relations with Cuba.

On the domestic scene, there was labor strife, an economic recession, severe poverty, urban gangs, growing racial conflict, and violence.

In the first few months of 1961, Yuri Gagarin, a Russian cosmonaut, became the first man to travel in space. It was somewhat surreal that a Russian communist was actually orbiting the globe as a first step toward eventually landing on the moon while we back here on earth in the United States listened and danced to "There's a Moon Out Tonight."

Freedom riders were attacked and their bus firebombed in Alabama, the Peace Corps was formed, a CIA-backed military invasion of Cuba was launched and tragically failed, bringing world tensions to a new high. Shortly after that, Alan Shepard became the first American in space and, although his flight was brief, it was an answer to the Russians' challenge and showed indeed that it was a race to the moon and the race was on.

And yet, our Citizenship class continued to suck. Trentacoste droned on and on about Initiative, Referendum, and Recall and the process for amending the Constitution. He didn't seem to have any inkling that we had entered what turned out to be the most tumultuous decade of the century.

In February, Tommy Taraci and I went to our second high school dance, "A Knight Out." We took girls that we had met at a "Squires" dance a few weeks before. The Squires were the Junior Knights of Columbus and they sponsored dances at the Knights of Columbus Hall in Flushing.

Tommy and I would go occasionally, but especially when Tommy's cousin Billy Valerie was playing in the band. Billy was a drummer and a real popular guy, particularly with the girls. When we got to the dance, we'd always get Billy's attention and wave 'hello' and then at the break, we'd go over, and talk to him in the hope that he'd introduce us to some girls. He usually did. "Hey, I do what I can for you; the rest is up to you guys!" he'd say with a mischievous smile. We were grateful for the help and met quite a few girls at these dances.

We both thought the Squires and the Knights were weird organizations but we always acted like we intended to join when approached by members. They'd give us applications, which we'd politely take and promise to fill out and return, but never did.

"A Knight Out" went well. There was no awkwardness of not knowing what to expect or how to look cool, like at the Halloween Hop. My cousin, Pat Nash, who was a junior by now, was there and he teased me about being with a "good-lookin' babe." "If you weren't my cousin, I'd move in on her," he kidded. At least I think he was kidding. It meant a lot to me to get his approval. I looked up to him and having an upperclassman and his friends show anything but contempt for freshmen was unusual and made me look cool in front of my friends and classmates.

When football season ended, I developed a keen interest in basketball. Incredibly, although tall, approaching 6'2" at this point and very interested in sports, I had played very little basketball. St. Andrew's had no gym and no basketball program, so access to a court was difficult. Schoolyard and playground courts were very busy in New York and dominated by older guys who were very good. If you couldn't play well, it was especially difficult, if not impossible, to get into a pick-up game, even if you weren't completely intimidated. Now, for the first time other than in Jimmy McVann's driveway, I was playing real basketball.

Our gym instructor was Mr. Connors who was also the varsity basketball coach. Mr. Connors had zero interest in Physical Education and during Gym class, which was twice a week, he would roll out a tray of basketballs and let us play. I loved it and started to get good. Tommy Rizzo helped me understand the basics and encouraged me to practice. He had played a lot of basketball with his twin John, his older brother, and his friends.

By the time winter rolled around, Tommy invited me to play two nights a week at a new public junior high school, P.S. 189, with his brother John and Glenn Judson and Don Glennon. It was free and it consisted of pick-up games among those who showed up. I was excited, but worried that I wouldn't be able to hold my own and be embarrassed. Indeed, there would be some pressure, he warned, because "loser walks," meaning that if a team loses, it has to sit and wait to play again, while the winning team continues to play. If there are a lot of teams, a loser may sit quite a while, before getting another chance. Since everyone came to play and not sit around, the games were intense, depending on how many guys were there.

When we played half-court, it was an eleven-point game, "winners out"—which meant that after scoring a basket, the team that scores gets the ball back. Of course, there were no refs, which made these games pretty rough. If a guy had an easy lay-up or put-back, he was going to get fouled. The penalty for fouling was the offensive team got the ball back. This never seemed quite fair to me. As one of the taller guys, I would battle inside for a rebound, get it, and go back up with it, usually getting fouled hard. If the ball went in, it counted, and there was no penalty. If I missed—which of course was the intent of the fouls—we got the ball back. We had the ball to begin with! Where's the penalty? I complained about this often, usually as I was getting up off the floor, but the reaction was always the same: 'Shut up and play!'

I grew to love basketball and never missed a chance to play. The first team I ever played on was our Section C intramural team. Holy Cross was an all-boys, inner city school and as a result, had a serious intramural basketball program. We sucked and got beat regularly, but so did most of the freshman teams. I was glad to have been asked to be on the team and to have not made a complete fool of myself.

◆ ◆ ◆

I finished my freshman year with an overall "Honorable Mention" for the year. My highest grade for the year was, ironically, a ninety from Guido. Despite our bad start and his punching me in the forehead with his ring, we grew to respect one another. He took us through what I consider a ridiculous program of English literature that interested none of us and yet I learned a lot. Maybe because he was a macho man football player and coach and appeared to take Miss Havisham and Pip seriously ("Great Expectations"), it made it more palatable for us to take it seriously. Maybe we were just frightened of him. Either way, I vividly remember him explaining that Egdon Heath, which was the setting for "Return of the Native," was a character in the book and escaping Egdon Heath was a theme. Egdon Heath was a driving force in itself, a force that has its own nature. This resonated with me and I began to think of Flushing as my Egdon Heath, a force I felt I had to escape. It was the first time I thought of going away to college as my way to escape Egdon Heath's clutches.

Yes, Guido Maiolo took us through a horrible array of English literature that could have been an educational disaster, but somehow it affected us in a very positive, although subtle way. Guido was a football player and coach and whenever some student or player hesitated with an answer, he would say, "Don't think—react." In football, there is no time for thinking, only reacting. A well-coached team reacts quickly to a blitz or a pulling guard. The purpose of the constant repetition is so that no thought is necessary, only immediate reaction. And yet it was Guido who got many of us to do the most thinking in our first year of high school.

Toward the end of the year, Guido was named Head Varsity Football Coach. On the last day of school, he told me he would like to see me come out for the team in the fall. It caught me totally by surprise and I mumbled something like, "I'll give it some thought."

"Come to the meeting August 1ˢᵗ here at school."

"Okay," I said, smiling to myself, but I was unsure if I would or not.

"I'll be looking for you and some of your buddies," he said as I exited the classroom.

Guido in a good mood.
The Cross - 1961

My next highest grades were Religion and Citizenship, each with an 86. Brother Francis Killoy taught Religion and although it was extremely boring, it was not sin-oriented and Brother Francis was an okay guy. He got along with everybody and everybody got along with him. He covered the history of the Church, the Popes, Encyclicals, Martyrs, Crusades, the Inquisition, and the Reformation at 9:00 a.m. without having to hit anyone or demean anyone or threaten anyone.

Not so Mr. Trentacoste. Pat Kelly and I were far from the only ones to get smacked in the face by Charlie Trentacoste. I openly hoped that someone would deck him. Glenn Judson had threatened to, but Trentacoste hadn't quite pushed him far enough. He was tall with big hands, long arms and big feet, but extremely thin and uncoordinated. Many of us felt we could take him on and kick his ass, but of course that would mean expulsion from school. He took subject matter that should have been interesting to us, certainly it was far more enticing than "Beowulf" or "Great Expectations," but yet we hated his class.

I finished with an 83 in Algebra, but it was an uneven year. For two of the six grading periods, I had gotten a 91 and for two a 74. My feelings about Brother Carl fluctuated as well. He was young and could relate well to the students at times and he knew the subject matter. He could also be a prick. Brother Carl had a Nazi armband and occasionally he would put it on in class and horse around, speaking with a German accent and acting like a Gestapo officer. Although he was clowning around, he had a mean streak in him.

Brother Carl would get physical at times, as he did with me after the "I'd let 'B' do it" incident. One day Sammy Magarelli questioned why he got an answer marked incorrect when another student with the same answer got partial credit. Magarelli was a tough kid and most of the guys liked him a lot. He never looked for trouble, but would never back down from it either. He was quick with a smile, had a great laugh, and spoke up a lot in class when he had something to say. He would challenge anything that he thought was unfair or untrue. Guido grew to like Sammy and would often ask him, after giving an assignment or announcing the details of an exam, if it was all right with him, in a joking manner.

Brother Carl on the other hand, hadn't grown to like Sammy or his challenges to his authority or his judgment of fairness. Sammy didn't like Brother Carl's explanation for the seeming discrepancy in the grading that day and showed it with his body language and his tone. Brother Carl went down the aisle, told Sammy to get up, and smacked him hard across the face.

"I'm sick of you, Magarelli," Brother Carl yelled. "What is your problem? You don't understand my grading system?"

"No, Brother, it's that I *do* understand your grading system."

Another smack in the face.

"Just what are you saying, Magarelli?"

"You know what I'm saying."

Another smack in the face.

I look at Jay, who is wincing, and Pat Kelly who is biting his lower lip with his upper teeth. We would like to rescue Sammy, but we don't know how.

Sammy's nose begins to bleed. Brother Carl suddenly seemed to calm down and backed away.

"Sit down, Magarelli, and if you have a question about your grade, come see me after school, and we'll discuss it."

Sammy sat down with blood trickling down from his nose into his mouth. Brother Carl started to resume class when he glanced at Sammy and asked if he had a handkerchief or tissue.

"Yeah, why?"

"Wipe your nose."

"Why? Are you ashamed of what you did?"

Many in the class gasped and groaned and a low murmur began, believing that Sammy's comment would only escalate the violence. If not for the tone and content of the exchange, then surely for not including 'Brother' in his response, as in "Yeah, why Brother?" or "Why? Are you ashamed of what you did, Brother?" Brother Carl, however, remained calm and merely told Sammy to remain after class and that they'd work it out. When that remark brought snickers from others, Brother Carl yelled, "Knock it off, you big babies!"

After class, there was no more violence. Sammy told us the next morning that they just had a heart-to-heart talk. "I forgave him and he bought me a Coke," said Sammy with a wink and a smile. We all knew that Brother Carl was out of line and although he might have felt bad for losing it, he was also covering his ass in a subtle way by acting concerned about Sammy's feelings and acting like the injured party.

I wouldn't say I held a grudge against Brother Carl, in fact I hardly ever thought of him again. He didn't return to Holy Cross the next year and our paths never crossed again. I did understand Algebra, even if I didn't understand him.

◆ ◆ ◆

My lowest grade of the year was an 81 in Latin, which was a problem because I had to take Latin II next year. I found Latin difficult and didn't see any reason to learn it except to graduate.

It didn't help that Brother Regis was an emotionally unstable madman. Often, very often, he was in a dark mood and you could tell just by looking at him. His voice and mannerisms were different when he was like this. His voice was devoid of emotion and he lacked animation, except that is, to explode in anger at the slightest thing. He would hit guys and throw things and give out punishment assignments. A few times, he would give us a translation to do in the text and just sit at his desk with a scowl on his face. When he wasn't in a deep depression, his technique was to intimidate us and call us dummies and fat heads, often in Latin.

I managed to avoid being the object of his direct wrath but Brother Regis made Latin much more drudgery than it ordinarily would have been. I remember one day after Latin class, as we walked to Study Hall, I asked Jay Carroll what he thought made Brother Regis so nuts all the time.

"Well, he wears a dress and never has sex, for starters."

After a good laugh at Jay's answer, I kiddingly said, "But you never have sex and you're not nuts."

"Oh yes, I do."

"You mean jacking off?" I teased.

"I look at it as sex with someone I love! If Regis tried it, he might not be so pissed off all the time." Jay laughed. We talked about how we hoped we were done with Regis and would get someone else for Latin II.

As we walked home the last day of our freshman year, I talked about going out for football and tried to get everyone to do it. I was excited about Guido's comments. The freshman football team had gone 7-0 and Tommy Taraci and I had gone to all their home games and rooted them on with all our might. Tommy was with us that day and he agreed right away. Most of the other guys were reluctant. Dickie kept saying how he "fucked up" his finals and needed a place to live.

"My mother's going to kill me. I have to find a new place to live. Where can I live?"

"Why do you think you fucked them up?" asked Jeff Baudo.

"Because I put down the wrong answers!"

"Why did you do that?"

"Because I didn't know the right answers, douche-bag! Glenn, can I live at your house?"

"Sure," said Glenn, "but my dad will make you work with him out at the garage like I have to."

"Can't you just treat me like a guest and give me food and a place to sleep?" asked Dickie.

"Afraid not. We'll have to get up at 5:30 and won't get home 'til 6:30 or 7:00 p.m."

"How about your house, Tommy?"

"No way," says Jeff. "You can't have a Spic move in with a Wop. It'll ruin the neighborhood."

"Baudo," says Dickie, coming to an abrupt stop, "you are such a douche-bag."

"Notice how he keeps calling me a douche-bag, but he's the one who fucked up. I'll probably be in a higher section than you next year," Baudo responded.

"Notice that I didn't ask to live with you?" said Dickie.

"You'd love to live at my house. You've got the hots for my sister," answered Baudo.

"I already did your sister," said Dickie. "It's your mother I'm hot for."

"I'm hot for his sister," interjected Tommy. "I'll move in with Jeff and Dickie can move into my house. Problem solved." For the next several blocks, Tommy talked about Jeff's sister, Leslie. How beautiful she was and what he'd like to do to her.

As the guys split off for home, it was just Glenn and I in the final two blocks. We talked about trying out for football and Glenn sounded like he would, but wouldn't be definite about it. He was going to work with his father at his father's gas station out on Long Island and thought he might be too tired to work out at night with Tommy and I as we had planned to do.

I might be working too, I told him. My uncle had told my parents about a possible job at a country club where he worked part time as a waiter. My cousin, Pat Nash, and I were going over there to apply tomorrow.

Although we were unsure about our future as football players and our summer working experiences, we were very happy about one thing: *No more Trentacoste!*

Richard M. Abella   Jeffrey J. Baudo   Simone J.

Dickie, Jeff and Sammy from "The Cross"—1964

CHAPTER TEN

◆ ◆ ◆ ◆ ◆

"PAT AND PADDY"

Early in the morning factory whistle blows,
Man rises from bed and puts on his clothes,
Man takes his lunch, walks out in the morning light,
It's the working, the working, just the working life.
Bruce Springsteen ~ "Factory"

I had always liked and looked up to my cousin, Pat Nash, and the prospect of working with him over the summer was exciting, although I was a little worried about being able to keep up with him. The difference of two years is a lot when you're fourteen and Pat was an unusual sixteen-year-old. He was strong, tough, loud, and full of energy (probably also ADHD). He was also the funniest person I had ever met and still is to this day. We didn't know each other all that well, since most of our contact was at family outings and special occasions. Although we both went to St. Andrew's and now to Holy Cross, Pat hung out with his friends and me with mine. When we were together, I always had a great time, but usually caught hell from my parents for something I did or just for being "out of control."

Pat and Tommy, his brother who was two years behind me, and I seemed to be a bad mix, at least to my parents! I would always be forewarned by my mother not to "run wild" or "do anything you shouldn't do," then get punished for running wild or doing things I shouldn't have done! These occasions when I got to see my cousins were hectic. My mother's two sisters, Marion Nash and Lilly Callahan, both had five children and so there were at least thirteen kids at every picnic or party. At one picnic at Belmont Park on Long Island, Tom, Pat, and I were throwing and hitting a baseball around near the tables, the families had taken for our use. Nearby Pat Nash Sr. (who we called 'Big Pat'), and my father were preparing to do the cooking. My father had started the fire in a large grill and they were putting hamburgers and hot dogs on the fire.

The women were setting the two tables with all the condiments and plates and utensils and tablecloths and napkins and cups. One of us hit a ball that got away from us and rolled toward our fathers. Big Pat picked up the ball and, throwing it back to Tommy, said, "Watch it with that ball, fellas. Move further away." A few minutes later, I hit one harder than I expected I could and it landed hard near Aunt Marion at the table. Aunt Marion was startled, and, gesturing with a hot dog bun in her hand, yelled, "Watch it with that ball! You're gonna hurt someone."

"Yeah, Joey, watch it with the ball," my father yelled.

"Go someplace else if you gotta hit a baseball around. This isn't a ball field!"

A few minutes later, Pat hit a high one that Tommy lost in the sun and, putting his arms and hands over his head, yelled, "Heads up!" to everyone at the tables. There was a moment of frozen silence and the ball landed harmlessly, but bounced toward our fathers.

"Hey, what'd I say about the ball playing," my father yelled.

Big Pat let out a loud whistle (the kind you make with your fingers between your lips) and yelled for Pat and I to hear, "I'm not gonna tell you again. If that ball comes over here again, I'm gonna rap you! Understand?"

"Joey, if that ball comes near here again, I'll break both your legs," my father yelled.

This caused us to have a conference. Pat and I had had a chance to hit, but Tommy hadn't and he wanted to hit. After a brief discussion, I suggested that we reverse our positions and that Tommy hit away from the picnic tables, as prior to this, we were hitting sort of parallel to them.

This seemed like a good idea until Tommy, swinging as hard as he could, unbelievably popped one up that sailed behind him. Pat and I both winced as we hoped for the best and waited for the ball to come down. The best was not to be. The ball landed *on the grill!* It sent meat, sparks, hot coals, and ashes flying everywhere!

Pat was the first to take off, then me, and then Tom. We ran deep into the woods until we knew our dads weren't after us and until we couldn't hear the cursing anymore. We were panting and out of breath when we finally stopped.

"Oh man, are we screwed," I gasped. "What are we gonna do now?"

"I know what I'm *not* gonna do. I'm not going back to that table!" said Pat.

We stood silently, catching our breath and listening carefully for any sound.

"I can't believe you did that, Tom," Pat said.

"Oh yeah, like it was my fault!"

"Whose fault was it? Who hit the ball?"

"I didn't do it on purpose."

"You were supposed to hit it *away* from the table, Tom."

"I told you I didn't do it on purpose."

For about a minute, nobody said anything, as we were all thinking about what to do next.

"Let's slowly move back closer so we can hear or see what's going on," I suggested.

"Okay, quietly," said Pat, holding his index finger to his mouth in a be-quiet gesture.

We slowly start creeping back toward the picnic area. After a few minutes, Pat started laughing quietly.

"What the hell is funny? I asked.

"What are the odds of that ball coming down *on* the grill? Jesus, if we were *trying* to do it, we couldn't!"

Tom and I chuckled.

"Did you see the meat and coals go flying? asked Pat, now laughing hard. "I'll say this, Tom—you scored a direct hit! I don't think you could've done more damage if you walked up to it and kicked it over!"

We made our way to a spot where we could see our party and hear their voices, but not well enough to make out what they were saying. Some were eating, my father was still cooking, having somehow saved or rekindled the fire.

"Dad is gonna kill us," whispered Tom.

"Dad is gonna kill *you*, 'cause I'm not going out there!" Pat answered.

"What are you gonna do? Live in the woods?" asked Tom.

"I'd rather live in the woods than die," answered Pat.

"I think I'd rather die," said Tom, looking around with a disgusted look on his face.

Suddenly we heard Aunt Marion's voice calling, "Pat? Tom? Pat?"

"I'm going back," said Tom.

"Be my guest," answered Pat.

Tom went out and talked to his mother. He pointed to where we were crouched down.

"Come on out, Pat," Marion yelled. "Come and get something to eat."

"Yeah, like Dad won't kill me first."

"Your father won't hurt you, I promise."

Pat thought it over, as a few seconds passed.

"Come on out."

Pat looked at me and said to his mom, "How about Joey?"

"Joey, too. Come back and eat—we've all eaten. What you did was stupid, but it's over and forgotten."

"Forgotten?" asked Pat.

"You heard me," said Aunt Marion as she started to walk away, back toward the tables.

"You can't do much better than forgotten," Pat said, looking at me.

"I'm afraid that when my father sees me, that will jog his memory," I said.

Pat laughed. "You're right. That's something to worry about. But if my mom says it's over, then we're probably all right, at least until we get home. If we don't go back now, we'll probably be in worse trouble."

I certainly wasn't going to stay in the woods alone and I was thrilled that Pat had spoken up for me and gotten me included in the deal. We went back to the picnic and nothing was said for a while. Later on, Pat and Tommy were in an argument about something and Big Pat said, "Hey you guys, knock it off. You're lucky you're still alive, so don't get me mad!"

"I thought that was forgotten," shot back Pat.

"Don't push your luck!" yelled Big Pat.

I didn't hear about it until the ride home. My father called me an "imbecile," in fact, he called the three of us "three imbeciles" and said we were lucky we ran away.

This was a typical story of our family times together. Pat and I would laugh a lot and unconsciously, escalate one another until we were in trouble.

Pat's toughness was a reputation that I'm sure, served him well. I have never actually seen him fight, but I have seen him get in people's faces, seemingly unafraid. When I was in the fifth and sixth grades, I was occasionally bullied by a boy two years older, whose name was Billy—I cannot remember his last name. Two years makes a big difference at that age and, on my walk home from school, I would frequently encounter this guy and he would usually be bothering someone. He would walk up beside the person, almost always a younger kid, and push them into hedges or sticker bushes. He would knock books out of other kids' hands and kick them, grab a hat off a kid's head and throw it up into a tree, or literally kick someone in the ass as he came up behind them.

All the kids who walked in a westerly direction from St. Andrew's knew this bully, and when they saw him coming, would prepare themselves by taking off their hats, clutching their books tightly against themselves and not letting him get behind them.

One time Donnie Faher jumped into a large hedge on purpose, just as the bully reached him and said, "There! I saved you the trouble."

These encounters were never serious enough for someone to raise a big stink and, like me, they just endured it and hoped it wouldn't happen again. Often there were resolutions to punch him the next time, but standing up to a kid two years older in grade school takes a lot of nerve.

One day, in sixth grade, Pat Nash was coming home with me to my house after school. For some reason, I can't fully remember (I believe it had something to do with scouting), Pat needed to come to our house and wait until it was time for a meeting and then go to the meeting. My mother had told me that Pat would be coming home with me and I, of course, was thrilled. We were about halfway home, walking on 35th Avenue, when I saw Billy the Bully up ahead, coming out of a candy store (today, a candy store would be a convenience store with a lunch counter and maybe some tables). I instinctively said, "Uh oh" and slowed down.

Pat looked at me and, seeing a strange look on my face, said, "What? Uh-oh what? Whatever it is, I didn't do it. What's wrong?"

I told Pat that a guy up ahead often gave me a hard time on the way home from school.

"What guy?"

"That guy." I nodded in Billy's direction.

"That guy?" said Pat, pointing at him.

"Yeah."

Pat walked toward him and said, "Hey, Billy, wait a second." He motioned for me to come over and I did.

"This here is me cousin Joey. If I ever hear of you bothering him again, I'll break your head."

"I didn't know he was your cousin," said Billy, apologetically.

"I'll bet you didn't!" Pat laughed. "I would hate to think you would bother *my* cousin *intentionally*."

Billy smiled awkwardly, not sure what to make of Pat's humorous sarcasm.

"Oh, I wouldn't, don't worry."

"I'm not gonna worry, believe me, I'm not gonna worry," he said, laughing. Then the laughter stopped and he said, "But if you do, I'll break your head. Let's go, Joey."

Pat started to walk away and I followed silently. Once we were out of sight, Pat started laughing. "That was great. That was great!" He'll never bother you again. I promise you. He's a punk. He's nothing. He wouldn't say 'boo' to any guy in our class, but he bullies younger guys. I hate that. I'm sure you could kick his ass."

Pat saw the look on my face and added, "I know why you might doubt that, him being two years older, but believe me, he's nothin'."

The rest of the year, whenever Billy the Bully would see me on the way home, he would cross the street to avoid me. If I were with some friends, they would see him and say, 'Uh oh, get ready, here he comes,' and I would say, 'Don't worry, he won't bother us,' and sure enough, when he saw me, he would cross the street! My friends were amazed and impressed and I never explained it to them.

Now the possibility of working with Pat was exciting and comforting. I had never had a paying job before and although I wanted the money, the prospect of taking unfamiliar buses and having a boss and working for money with strangers was unnerving. Having Pat along was a great comfort.

We had made arrangements to meet on the Q16 bus. Pat would go to the bus stop on 32nd Avenue, nearest his house, and if I went to the bus stop near my house a few minutes later and waited for the Q16, Pat should be on it. It worked and we rode the Q16 to Parson's Boulevard and got transfers to the Q12. Pat had talked with our Uncle Ronald and vaguely knew where we were supposed to go. The bus wove its way through Whitestone and finally came to its last stop. The driver told us that this was the last stop and if we wanted to stay on, we had to pay again.

"I guess we get off here," laughed Pat.

"I thought you knew where to go? I thought Uncle Ronald told you."

"Well, he kinda told me. Uncle Ronald was kinda unsure himself. He drives, so he didn't really know where the bus goes. I think he figured if they're too stupid to find it, they're too stupid to work there."

"What exactly are we looking for?" I asked.

"Cresthaven Country Club."

"How do we find it?"

"It's near here and it's by the water. Uncle Ronald said you can see the Throg's Neck Bridge from the clubhouse."

"I never heard of Cresthaven Golf Course," I said quizzically.

"They don't have a golf course," answered Pat.

"No golf course?"

"No, I asked because I thought we could caddy, but there is no golf course."

"What kind of a country club has no golf course?"

"I don't know. I guess the kind that would hire Uncle Ronald."

As we walked toward the waterfront, looking for Cresthaven, Pat told me how this all came about. Uncle Ronald was a New York City fireman who was working at Cresthaven on his off days. Cresthaven was a Catholic country club and scene of a lot of wedding receptions and large parties and banquets. Uncle Ronald worked as a waiter at these events. He wore a very dressy uniform, including a gold-colored vest and bow tie and worked a few hours for what he considered very good money.

I'm sure you didn't have to be a Catholic to be a member, but it seemed almost everyone was. Most of the weddings were from local parishes and the Catholic Youth Organization, (CYO) ran a day camp there in the summer for a few hundred grade school kids. A lot of the dinners were Catholic organizations like the Holy Cross Women's Guild or St. Mel's Mothers Club. For the members, there was a swimming pool and wading pool, tennis courts, two snack bars, locker rooms, a bar and a variety of social events.

Uncle Ronald was, according to him, well liked by the owners Rita and Willie Haff. He was talking to the Haffs and found out that they were planning a lot of work on the grounds and were looking to hire some summer help for the groundskeeper Paddy McTee. Uncle Ronald mentioned that he had some teenaged nephews that might be interested and the Haffs said to send them right over.

We soon stumbled upon the entrance to Cresthaven, found the Office and inquired about the jobs. Rita Haff gave us applications to fill out and said the pay was one dollar an hour and if we wanted the job, it was ours!

"When do we start?" asked Pat.

"I'll take you to Paddy McTee, our groundskeeper, right now if you want and you can start Monday."

"Sounds good."

It's hard to describe Paddy McTee. In fact, his name may have been McTeague, but everyone called him McTee and I never saw his name in writing. Paddy was an Irish immigrant, about 5'2", 120 pounds, and in his fifties. He didn't speak often and for good reason. Until you got used to him, he was very difficult to understand. He spoke very quietly with a mixture of Irish brogue and mumbling until he got excited. Then he screamed in a high-pitched Irish brogue and sounded like a pig that was being strangled!

Rita brought us out to a beat-up old ugly pickup truck and told us Paddy was around here somewhere. "We have a lot of work that needs to be done over the next few years and Paddy can't do it himself." Paddy came walking out of the clubhouse and Rita introduced us and told him we are his summer help and then left.

Paddy had on dark green pants and a matching shirt and an old misshapen baseball cap. The same clothes he would have on every day. He spoke to us for about three solid minutes and then said, "Okay?" and got into his truck.

As Pat and I started walking away, I asked, "What did he say?"

"I have no idea," Pat laughed.

"Well, you asked him what time, so you must have understood him."

"I heard him say 'Mundee marn' and I assumed he meant Monday morning. I think he also wants us to wear boots."

"Why do you think that?"

"Because he looked at our feet and said something like 'boots'."

"I couldn't make out any of it," I said. "Where do we get boots?"

"I guess an Army/Navy store? We need boots and we start 'Mundee marn' at eight. Anything else he said we'll just have to wait and see," Pat said, laughing.

So, we showed up Monday bright and early, with our new work boots on, and began to learn the routine. Our days had a variety to them, but always started with the tennis courts. Cresthaven had six clay courts and every day they were to be swept with a big heavy brush that was pulled behind you, one-half court at a time. Then the courts were rolled with a heavy roller, pushed by hand-up and down the length of the six courts. After that, the white lines were swept with an ordinary broom and the new lines freshly marked with a lining machine that was pushed around over the old lines. It was filled with a white solution. Paddy struggled with both the big brush and especially the roller, so he was glad to have us to do it. The club didn't open to members until 11:00 a.m., so we had three hours to do the courts and clean the pool. Cleaning the pool was easy.

Our other daily chore was garbage detail. Twice a day, we had to pick up every garbage can, put it in the truck and drive to a huge dumpster, dump it and replace it. These cans were the heaviest garbage cans I've ever seen. I believe they were military surplus and donated to the club or to the CYO. The cans weighed a lot more than the garbage. The rest of our duties varied and were assigned daily by Paddy. Frequently they were: grass cutting, weed pulling, painting and watering the flowers and shrubs.

That summer was important in my development as a person. I had to adapt to some things that were new experiences to me. The first of which was hard, dirty work. We punched a time clock and were there around 8:00 every morning and worked hard for one dollar an hour until 5:00 every weekday. It was about a forty-five minute commute on two buses, which added to the day and it was hot and dirty work. I had to get up much earlier for work than I did for school. I started complaining a lot at home about the heat, especially how hot it was in my bedroom.

My bedroom was so small that, when I moved out, my parents made it into a closet! In fact, I have been in closets that were bigger. My room had one window that faced west. The sun beat all afternoon and evening on my window and on the shingles of the roof outside my window. New York can get hot and humid in the summer—the concrete and asphalt hold the heat after sundown and throw it back at you for hours after.

My father had two answers to my complaining about not being able to sleep and spend time in my room: hosing down the outside of the house to cool it and installing an exhaust fan in the attic. Many New Yorkers hosed down their houses and surrounding concrete on a hot night and both, my parents and I often did it for our house. It may have helped some, but not noticeably. The exhaust fan in the attic was a good idea for my parents and sisters, but not so good for me. Both of their bedrooms had two windows on two different walls while I had only one and it was on the hot side of the house. More importantly, the attic door, which had to be open for the fan to suck air out of the house, blocked the door to my room when opened, and severely impeded the cooling effect in my room.

"Why don't we get air-conditioners?" I'd ask.

"Who in the hell do you think I am?" was my father's answer.

"Why don't you get an air conditioner for my room?"

"Who in the hell do you think you are?"

"Whoever I am, I'm *hot*."

"If you're so hot, why do you go play football or whatever in the evening?"

"Because I'm goin' out for football. The problem is sleeping. It's too hot to sleep."

"So, close the attic door part way so the fan can suck the air better," my father suggested.

"I tried that and the fan sucks the door closed," I answered.

"You have to find the right spot where the door stays open, but you get the most air that you can."

So when I went to bed that night, I tried it, and, in the middle of the night, an actual breeze came through the window, blew the door a little bit so the fan could catch it, and *Wham!* It slammed closed and woke everybody up, including my father. The next night, he took the door off its hinges. It was still too hot, in my opinion, despite an improvement in the draw of the fan. My father put a thermometer in my room one night, and then checked it as he was going to bed.

"Oh, it's a lot cooler in here," he says, looking at the thermometer.

"It's hot as hell in here," says I.

"It was 86° in here at eight o'clock and now it's down to 78°."

"I don't care—it's still too hot."

"Well, what do you want me to do about it?" he asked. "I don't control the weather."

"Get air-conditioners." I answered. "I know, I know—who do I think we are?"

I also discovered that summer that people treat you differently if you're dirty. Working at the country club, we were often dirty. We did hot, dirty work and wore work boots and dungarees and tee shirts. Occasionally, we would go to the snack bar in the clubhouse to buy a cold drink and the members and even the employees who worked the snack bar would treat us strangely. Mothers would tell their kids to "come over here."

"Why?" the kid would ask.

"Just come here. I want to talk to you." (Translation: get away from that guy.)

Once the college kid behind the counter even asked if I had any money before he got me a Coke. Another told me, "The snack bar is only for members."

On the bus going home, we were always among the first on, since we boarded where the route both began and ended. It was rush hour and the buses got very crowded. People always seemed to sit or stand away from us, if they could. We tried showering before we left work, but the bus left at 5:15 and was about a ten-minute walk from Cresthaven. If we showered, we missed it, and the next one wasn't until 5:45 and worse, the connection to the Q16 was also a delay. So showering could conceivably cost us an hour of our time, plus, if we decided to do that we had to bring clean clothes and a towel along and carry our dirty clothes home.

So most of the time we punched out and headed for the 5:15, dirty, sweaty, and tired. Pat always offered his seat to a woman, if the seats were all occupied and a woman was forced to stand. I thought that was nice and started to do the same. We always started home sitting, but most of the time, were standing by the time we got off.

One day Pat was standing near where I was sitting, having just given his seat to a woman who was very appreciative, when a beautiful young lady boarded the bus. She was dressed very nicely, about eighteen or nineteen years old, and as she started toward the back of the bus, saw that there were no seats available, and moved back a little toward the front. She stood, holding the metal bars provided for standing. Pat looks at me as I'm looking at her and says, "Whoa, whoa, you lucky guy. Quick, give *me* your seat so I can give it to her."

I was a little slow to move as I was struck with shyness because she was young and beautiful. She was the kind of girl that a high school freshman dreams about. I finally did get up and walked down the aisle toward her. As I approached, she turned her back to me. I tapped on her shoulder. She ignored me. I tapped her again and said, "Miss?" She moved a little, but further away. I was feeling a little embarrassed, so I said as nicely and respectfully as could be, "Miss, you can have my seat," motioning toward it.

"I don't want your seat. Leave me alone!" she said loudly.

As I turned and walked back toward my seat, I felt really embarrassed and I'm sure I was red-faced under the dirt and dried sweat. Pat was laughing hysterically. I didn't know what other passengers on the bus were thinking, but his laughter was only attracting more attention.

"Some guys got it and some don't," he said as he took my seat and covered his mouth and nose with his hand to stifle his laughter. He wasn't trying to embarrass me but he found it too funny to let it go. After a few moments, he started laughing even harder as a thought occurred to him that I feared he was going to share. I stood there, holding onto the overhead bar, tight-lipped with humiliation, when Pat finally got enough control of himself to talk.

"I think you should go back and ask for her phone number."

Laughter.

"I think you should ask her if she'd go out with you."

More laughter—this time, harder and louder.

The woman to whom Pat originally had given his seat to was sitting next to him now, and having heard and seen everything, was laughing at Pat and said, "That would be funny."

"Oh wouldn't it? Don't you think he should do it?" Pat asked the woman.

Before the woman could answer, Pat stood up and offered another woman his seat, a woman who had just gotten on. The woman had two bags in her arms and was quite thankful. "Well, thank you, young man! Thank you very much!"

"See?" said Pat. "Nothin' to it."

The three of us laughed and the woman who had just sat down asked "Did I do something wrong?"

"No," said the first lady. "This young man here (indicating me) offered that seat to that young lady, but she wouldn't take it. Now this young man (pointing at Pat) and I think it would be funny if he asked her out."

"What do you think?" asked Pat.

"I think he should ask her out. Why not?"

"See, we all agree," said Pat to me.

"You seem like a nice boy. Why wouldn't she go out with you?" said the second lady.

"Maybe she thinks she's better than him because he works all day and gets a little dirty," said Pat, egging them on.

"That's not fair of her," responded the first lady.

Now Pat looked around and saw a few other passengers listening to this rather loud conversation and asked, "What do you all think?"

Now people were commenting about what they had heard or what they thought was going on.

"Go ahead—ask her out. She's no better than you."

"The hell with her. Fuhgeddaboudit."

"You can get a girl—don't worry about her."

"Get her phone number, so you can call her, and get to know her."

"Why should she go out with you? She doesn't even know you. You could be a wacko or a pervert."

"He's not wacko," said Pat. "The pervert part I'm not sure about!"

"It seems kinda wacko to ride around on buses asking girls out," one passenger said.

"I didn't ask her out!" I answered.

"Then why are you upset with her?"

"I'm not."

"There. She's getting off! You're gonna miss your chance," said Pat.

Mercifully, the girl got off the bus. By now, about eight passengers were involved in this discussion, much to Pat's delight. I was smiling, and shaking my head, in disbelief at how this had spun so far out of control in the back of the bus.

"Don't let it bother you," said the woman with the bags, who was in my seat.

"Oh, his feelings are hurt," said Pat. "He's just smiling to hide the pain."

Finally, our stop came and we moved to the door to get off when the bus stops.

"See ya', everybody," Pat yelled as we stepped off.

"Bye," answered a chorus of voices.

As we waited for the Q16, Pat was laughing and recounting the story. "I wonder what we can get going on this bus," he said as the Q16 rolled up to the stop.

"You'll have to work quickly, Joey, 'cause this one isn't a very long ride!"

Another thing I had to get used to was Paddy McTee. The first thing was the difficulty in understanding the words he spoke, and then even more than that, his thought processes. After a few weeks though, I grew used to his speech patterns and phrasing and mumbling, and I had little trouble understanding his words. His thought processes took longer. Paddy would yell at me constantly for having my hands in my pockets while working. For instance, I would be watering plants, standing with the hose in one hand and the other hand in my pocket. Or after just digging a hole to plant a bush, I'd be standing with the shovel in one hand, and absent-mindedly put my hand in my pocket while Paddy put mulch in the hole.

"Get your hand out of your pocket," Paddy would say the first few times it happened. I would comply by taking my hand out of my pocket, but didn't understand why he insisted. As time went on, he would shriek, "Get your hand out of your pocket! How many times do I have to tell you?" or "Mother of God, will you keep your hands out of your pockets."

Finally, one day, I was painting a door to the snack bar. As I was painting the upper part, I had the brush going in my left hand and just the fingers of my right hand tucked in my pocket. Paddy sees me and gets really mad.

"Jesus, Mary, and Joseph! Now you're painting with your hands in your pockets! What in hell is wrong with you? I tell you over and over, but you don't listen!" he yelled in exasperation.

Being screamed at made me mad and I finally took Paddy on.

"What is your problem? I work hard. Why are you always screaming at me?" I yelled back.

"I guess you don't want this job," Paddy yelled.

Pat Nash, who was trimming bushes with a hedge clipper, heard us yelling at each other, and came over to see what was wrong.

"I do everything you ask, I do it fast and well, so get off my back!" I said sharply.

"Do you want this job?" Paddy asked.

"Of course I want it. Do you think I come here for the fun?"

"Well, if you stand around with your hands in your pockets, they're gonna take you away from me," Paddy yelled.

"What do you mean?" I asked.

"I mean if you don't look like you're working hard, they'll give you to Frank Towcar on the construction crew," answered Paddy.

"But we are working hard. Look at all we get done in a day," I replied.

"But if you got your hand in your pocket, you're not working hard." Paddy put his hands in his pockets in a gesture to illustrate how it looked.

Pat chimed in now. "But Paddy, we are always workin'. It doesn't take two hands to water the plants."

"I know you work hard, but how does it look to Rita or Willie Haff. It looks like, ho hum, this is no sweat. Frank Towcar wants more help and they won't give it to him. So, keep it up and you'll be working on his crew."

"That's why you keep yelling at me?" I asked with a smile.

"Yup."

"Let me get this straight," said Pat, grinning. "You like us? You like us and you don't want to lose us?"

Paddy didn't answer and started to walk away.

"Am I right, Paddy?" Pat asked softly.

"Whether I like you or not has nothin' to do with it," he yelled over his shoulder.

"But you do like us, don't you?" asked Pat with laughter in his voice.

"Finish what you're doing and meet me up at the shed," Paddy said, then looking at me added "and keep both hands busy."

"He's a talented painter. He's an artist. He only needs one hand," yelled Pat, as Paddy got further away.

In truth, Frank Towcar did think we were good workers and borrowed us from time to time. He got this impression because Pat was so gung-ho. He hated watering or painting, preferring to do the hard stuff. Once, we had a huge shoveling job. Cresthaven had just built big, brick flower-boxes to line the roadway from the street to the clubhouse. They would serve as a barrier between the roadway and the pool-and-lounge area. There were about six of them, each about three feet high, three feet wide, twenty feet long.

Paddy was asked to use us to fill the boxes with dirt. He got the trucks, picks, and shovels and drove us to a place where a huge mound of dirt had been dumped. We were to fill the truck with dirt and then unload the dirt into the flower boxes.

"This will take all week," said Paddy.

"Bullshit," said Pat. "The difficult we do immediately; the impossible takes a little longer."

"Yeah, yeah. I'll be back in a little while, so get started," mumbled Paddy.

"Okay, here's the way I see things," said Pat. "Shoveling is one of the best exercises there is. You use all your muscle groups when you shovel. I read where there are football teams using shoveling sand as a way to keep in shape. All they do is shovel sand back and forth."

"So?"

"So, let's take advantage of the opportunity and let's blow Paddy's mind and shovel our brains out. It will build our bodies up and show Paddy and Frank how hard we can work."

I was too embarrassed to say no, so I went along and we filled the truck as fast as we could. When the truck was brimming with dirt, we had to wait for Paddy to return since he expected us to take much longer. When he returned, he was surprised that we were waiting for him.

"Where the hell you been?" Pat asked. "You're holding us up."

Paddy didn't say anything, but got in the truck, and drove to the first flower box.

"Don't go anywhere, boss. We'll be done in a jiffy," Pat yelled.

"Quit ya foolin' around and don't call me 'boss.'"

"Okay, boss."

We shoveled like mad and emptied the truck in minutes.

Paddy was scratching his head with his thumb while he held his cap in the fingers of the same hand.

"What the hell is up with you guys?" he asked.

"I told you," answered Pat. "The difficult we do immediately; the impossible takes a little longer."

"Get in the truck and stop with that shit."

"Okay, boss."

"And don't call me 'boss,'" he yelled as we jumped into the back of the truck.

We returned to the mound of dirt. Before Paddy could back the truck up to the mound, we were out and shoveling like mad.

"Don't go far, boss," Pat yelled.

"I told you not to call me 'boss.' I'm not a boss. I'm just the groundskeeper."

"You're our boss Paddy, and a good one, too."

"Then, why don't you knock this off?"

"Knock what off?"

"This hurrying."

"I told you we do the difficult immediately; the impossible . . ."

"I know, I know. It makes no sense. When we finish this, there will just be something else, ya' know."

"Good," answered Pat. "Just make it something hard—not watering. Because the difficult we do immediately; the impossible takes a little longer."

This went on for three more days as after we finished our usual morning work on the tennis courts and garbage run, we turned to the flower boxes and shoveled like mad. It kind of became fun to see how fast we could load or unload a truck and we were building up our bodies in the meantime. We sweated like hogs and were filthy on the buses home. On the second day, we started saluting Paddy whenever he would tell us something. On the day we finished, to our delight, Frank Towcar came over to all three of us and expressed surprise at how quickly we did it.

"They're good boys," said Paddy. "The place is looking better and better."

"We're getting there," answered Frank. "We have a long way to go, but we are getting there. You think I could borrow these guys for a few days? I have some trucks that need unloading down at the waterfront."

"Sure, but don't kill 'em, 'cause I need them back," Paddy answered.

"Just a few afternoons Paddy, really. Get done what you need to in the morning and send them over to the barn after lunch."

"You guys are gonna help me out for a few days, okay?" Frank said, turning toward us.

"Right-o," said Pat, enthusiastically.

Actually, I had mixed feelings, but Pat was excited about it. I was worried that working with Frank's crew would not be a good experience. We were around those guys at coffee break time every morning, when a van pulled in with coffee and donuts. They never seemed particularly friendly to us. They were in their twenties or thirties and this was their job and they seemed to look at us like dumb kids working for minimum wage, which is exactly what we were! They had keys to everything and drove all the vehicles while we were keyless and didn't even have driver's licenses. I was not yet fifteen and was apprehensive, but Pat, as usual, was supremely confident.

"We can do anything these guys can do. Just remember our slogan, 'The difficult we do immediately, the impossible takes a little longer.'"

That Monday after lunch we reported to Frank, as Paddy had directed, warning us at the same time: "Don't try to impress him, it's only for a few afternoons."

Frank's office was in an old barn that the construction crew used for headquarters. When we showed up, Frank turned us over to a guy named Jack. "Jack, take these guys down to the waterfront and get them started. I'll be down in a while to see how you're doing." Jack drove us down to the waterfront, asked our names, and got us busy. Pat and I were unloading bags of cement mix for a few hours when Jack called to me and asked me to do him a favor.

"Go up to the barn and ask Dave for the elbow grease."

"The elbow grease?" I asked, skeptically.

"He'll know what you mean. I need it for the drainage pipes we're working on."

Jack seemed quite serious, so I started up to the barn. I didn't know which guy was Dave, so when I got to the barn, I asked the first guy I saw, "Are you Dave?"

"No, what do you need?"

"I'm supposed to get the elbow grease from Dave."

"Oh, right. Dave's over there." He pointed to Dave, smiling.

Feeling even a little more awkward, I tried to be nonchalant and, as I approached Dave, I said, "Hey, Dave (acting familiar), Jack needs the elbow grease."

"Excuse me?"

"Jack needs the elbow grease—he said to ask you for it."

"Oh. I gave it to Skip."

"Who's Skip?"

"Skip is the little guy with the curly hair."

"Where is he?"

"I think he's over at the clubhouse working on a toilet in the women's locker room."

I wandered over to the clubhouse and as I reached the entrance to the women's locker room, I stopped. The locker room was quite busy with camp girls and their teenage counselors going in and out—some wet from swimming in the pool, some in street clothes with wet hair, all talking seemingly at the same time.

I was taken aback by the fact that the locker room was in use while a man was working on a toilet in there. I started in, but noticed a lot of eyes on me.

"Is there a guy working in there?" I asked a group of young girls coming out.

"What?"

"Is there a man fixing a toilet in there?"

More girls came out and they started yelling, "Look out! There's a man in the locker room!"

One young girl turned and ran back in yelling, "There's a man coming in!"

There was high-pitched screaming and yelling when I suddenly saw a teenaged counselor and asked her to check for me if there was a man working on a toilet in the locker room. She seemed suspicious, but agreed to check inside. Just as she returned and told me that there was no one working in the locker room, I saw Frank Towcar walking toward me. At first I feared that Frank was thinking that instead of being hard at work at the waterfront, I was flirting with a counselor outside the women's locker room. Then, I noticed he was carrying a toolbox and figured he was working with Skip.

In my anxiety and embarrassment, I quickly said, "Frank, I'm glad I ran into you. Are you with Skip?"

"What?" answered Frank, looking perplexed. "Why aren't you down at the waterfront?"

"I'm looking for Skip."

"Who the hell is Skip?"

"You know, Skip on our crew."

"There is no Skip on my crew—what are you talking about?"

"I was supposed to find Skip in the women's locker room working on a toilet. I was supposed to get the elbow grease from him."

"Who told you to do that?"

Now I felt like a real jerk. I hesitated to tell Frank. Do I say "Jack?" Do I say "Dave?" Both? I grimaced and took a deep breath.

"There is no Skip, kid," Frank said, "and there is no elbow grease. They're playing with you. I'm glad you didn't go in there. Go back to your job and stop over at the barn at five o'clock."

I went back to the waterfront and told Pat what had just happened. He thought it was hysterical. "Tell me from the beginning. Start over! Tell me exactly what happened!" Pat doubled over laughing.

"Oh, Joey, that is so funny! That is so funny. Can you imagine if you had gone into the locker room and someone had called Rita Haff and you said you were looking for Skip with the elbow grease?"

"I'm glad you think it's funny. Frank didn't. He wants me to report to the barn at five o'clock."

"What for?"

"I don't know. Probably to fire me."

"Why would he fire you? You were only doing what Jack and them said."

"How about for being stupid? Suppose he wants me to tell him who did this? What do I do then? If I rat those guys out, they'll hate me and if I don't, then Frank will hate me."

As five o'clock approached, I told Pat I would say that I screwed up and it was my fault. That I would take any blame, since they were just fooling around and I was so stupid. He agreed it was a good way to go.

"Well, it's five o'clock. You coming with me?" I asked.

"Hell, no!" Pat laughs.

"You're not?"

"No, siree! I don't want nuttin' to do with it! Joey? I don't know any Joey? You mean that dumb guy who's always hanging around the girls' locker room?"

Pat's laughing and joking was good for me because I felt sick to my stomach as I started for the barn. We punched out first and Pat walked me part of the way and said he'd wait for me by the tennis courts. When I got to the barn, Frank and the whole crew were there discussing what he wanted done in the morning. As I approached, Frank saw me and nodded at me to wait a second. He finished what he was saying and then he looked at the crew and said, "I asked this young man (I don't think he knew my name) to come over here this evening so I could publicly apologize to him."

He looks at me and continues. "I want to apologize to you for the behavior of my crew. I hope you will accept my apology."

Totally shocked, I make a motion like "no problem," since I was too nervous to talk.

Turning back to the crew, he says, "These young guys do a hell of a day's work and they deserve your respect, not practical jokes." Now, looking at me again, he said, "I hope there's no hard feelings."

He looks at me and as he waits, I manage to squeeze out a "no."

"Okay, that's it. See you tomorrow."

I turned and hurried away back toward the tennis courts where Pat was waiting. I was so excited I felt like I could fly.

"Wow, that was fast," said Pat as he saw me.

"You're not gonna believe this! This is unbelievable!"

"Tell me! Tell me!"

"I'll tell you on the way to the bus stop, Mr. Gung-Ho, let's get going."

Pat, of course, loved the story and we were giddy on the buses all the way home. Frank's crew treated us normally the rest of the summer. The next time I saw him, Jack mentioned that it was all in fun and he hoped I took had taken it that way.

I tried to make light of it and said, "Sure, but I'm glad Rita didn't catch me in the girls' locker room!"

"Fuck Rita!" was his only response.

But as triumphant and satisfying as that incident was, it wasn't my proudest moment that summer. My proudest moment came on the last day. Pat and I were setting up big banquet tables for a Labor Day party and were hot and sweaty.

"You know it was a long, hot summer for us and we never did swim in that pool. We talked about it, we cleaned it, but we never went in," I lamented.

"Well, you're right," answered Pat. "It was a long, hot summer, but let me tell you something, Joey. They say you never really know someone until you work with them. I think that's true—and there's nobody I'd rather work with than you. You actually made it enjoyable. He paused.

"You know our fathers worked together once," Pat went on.

"No, I never heard that," I said.

"Yeah, I've heard the story many times. It was after the war and my dad needed a job while he was waiting to get on the Fire Department. So, your dad got him a job putting in some big boilers somewhere in Brooklyn."

"No kidding?"

"My dad didn't know anything about oil burners so he was just a laborer, but he said he's never worked with a better man than your father, nor has he ever worked harder in his life. Now I can say the same thing about you."

"As for swimming . . . you know Nana thinks we go swimming all the time. I've heard her tell people how her two grandsons work at the country club and they get to swim in the pool."

"Where did she get that?"

"I don't know. I guess Uncle Ronald told her."

"Why did he tell her that?"

"I have no idea! Maybe he thinks we do. I have no idea where he gets half the things he says."

"But don't you tell Nana the truth?" I asked.

"Joey, I don't know how it is in other families, I've never been a member of another family, but in this family, you have to make a big decision."

"What about?"

"Whether to leave people alone or to break their bubble with the truth. In Nana's case, I've made my decision. If she says we swim, we swim."

Chapter Eleven

◆ ◆ ◆ ◆ ◆

"Dreams Denied"

"Gee, Officer Krupke, we're very upset;
We never had the love that ev'ry child oughta get.
We ain't no delinquents,
We're misunderstood.
Deep down inside us there is good!"
          "Gee, Officer Krupke"—from *West Side Story*

World tensions continued to mount that summer. There was a lot of celebrating when Gus Grissom followed up Alan Shepard in space with another brief rocket flight over the Atlantic, but as if to say, "Oh yeah?" the Russian Titov, within weeks, made seventeen and a half orbits of the globe and clearly established that they were still in the lead in the race to the moon.

In August, the Communists erected a concrete wall in Berlin to keep people from escaping. It showed the desperation of the Communists and to what lengths they would go. It was a tangible symbol of the horrors of a system of government, which had to wall its people in to keep them from fleeing their homeland. Amidst this apocalyptic forecast for our future, Tommy Taraci and I devoted almost all of our free time to football and the pursuit of mortal sin in the form of impure thoughts, actions, wills and deeds.

During the week, Tommy and I would meet usually Jeff Baudo at Bowne Park to work out. Guido had sent me a letter with exercises to do and reminding everyone to be in shape when we reported to practice on August 31. We did the prescribed exercises and more. Actually getting a letter from Guido was a strong incentive for us. We drove ourselves hard, dreaming that we'd be playing on Sundays, wearing the Green and Gold of the Holy Cross Knights. In fact, it's hard to believe we didn't seriously injure ourselves. Each night we would end our workout with a drill we believed would toughen us up and prepare us for the season ahead. Each of us took turns running the ball through the other two guys. We marked out a field of play about ten yards wide. Over and over, we took turns, running the ball, without blockers, and without any protection, into two determined defenders. The impact was high and painful, and I remember Jeff complaining more than once of a headache. Tommy usually ran straight between us, as hard as he could, with knees and elbows flying. Jeff and I mixed things up more, trying jukes, feints, and cuts to the outside, but Tommy came straight at us.70027

Jeff was a good punter and often would practice punting, in hopes of making the team as a kicker, if nothing else. Tommy and I would take turns returning Jeff's punts, again against two defenders.

On weekend nights, we would try to meet girls. We often met at Mueller's and discussed what our options were. They were usually pretty meager. Girls our own age and older were usually dating or hanging out with older guys. It was an awkward age for us. Eighth graders were beneath us and most high school girls were older than us. This situation forced us to roam far from our turf in search of new prospects.

Tommy lived in Bayside and we would often hang out there, walking around on Bell Boulevard, talking to any girl we would see. Tommy was much bolder than I and would take many more risks. One ploy he used to break the ice many times was to go up to a girl who wasn't wearing a watch and ask if she knew what time it was. When she'd say, "No" or "I think it's about," Tommy would look at his watch and tell her the exact time. Hopefully, she'd laugh and then he'd introduce himself and me and we would go from there.

One Saturday night, our desperation took us to the South Bronx. The South Bronx was way out of our turf. We had heard that, in an attempt to keep the kids off the streets, there were dances on Saturday nights in the St. Helena's High School cafeteria. There had been a lot of violence in the neighborhood and thus, the dances were a response to a community need. We were told the dances were a hit and that many, many girls came to them. We were also told to be careful, because it was a rough area.

We were told the truth. The place was packed and the ratio was at least three girls to one guy. The dances were open to anyone and as a result, not just the St. Helena's students were there. *West Side Story* had just recently been released as a movie and our trip to the South Bronx was like a scene from that movie. We were two Jets who had dangerously ventured into Shark territory. Tommy and I had on chinos and loafers and white sox and shirts with button-down collars and sported our short "Princeton Style" regulation haircuts. Most of the other guys at the dance wore all black or black pants with a purple shirt or black jeans and a tee shirt. They had lots of dark hair and looked much older than us.

Although Tommy resembled one of the stars of the movie who was a Shark (George Chakiris), we were obviously Jets. We hadn't given our safety much thought since it was a Catholic high school, and we figured the rigid discipline we were used to would prevail here too. This time, however, it was not a St. Helena's event, but rather an event held at their facility, so the customary garrison of nuns, brothers, and priests was not present. There were some adults stationed at the door, making sure no alcoholic beverage was brought into the dance, but it was obvious that many of the guys had been drinking before they came.

All in all, the environment made me a little uncomfortable, but Tommy and I were good at avoiding trouble, we didn't drink, and we weren't looking for any problems, unless you call looking for someone to violate the sixth and ninth commandments with, looking for trouble.

Tommy was a bright, witty, often sarcastic kid, who had a habit of making a wisecrack under his breath. He couldn't resist saying it, but said it softly, so that those close by could hear him, but not the person it was aimed at. Sometimes he would rub the inside corner of his eye with his index finger so that the rest of his hand shielded his mouth and made it hard to see that he was talking. Teachers described him as smug because, even when in serious trouble, he would have a self-satisfied smirk on his face, either at the wisecrack he had just made or the one he was thinking about making.

That night at St. Helena's, we employed our typical strategy, i.e., trying to find two girls who were friends that we could agree on, and then moving in on them together. Sometimes as part of our routine, one of us would see a girl he was particularly interested in and ask her to dance, while the other would look over her friends and decide which, if any, he would take a chance on. The one who had danced would come back with a report on whatever he could find out—as in, 'she's a sophomore here with some friends; seems interested'; or, 'she's a junior—has a boyfriend, let's move on'; or the worst case scenario, 'she hates me—I'm not going back.'

That night, Tommy saw a girl he really liked and when I balked, he said, "I'll check it out, wait here." He asked her to dance (a slow one, of course) and she agreed. They were talking as they danced and I was checking out her friends. The next thing I notice, Tommy and the girl had stopped dancing and there is a guy talking to Tommy. The guy is about six feet, but stocky, has narrow sideburns, a mustache and goatee. To me, he looks like, ten years older than us. He had on a purple shirt with a black leather vest, even though it was summer and very warm. The conversation didn't look friendly.

The guy yells over to a large group of guys who had apparently just arrived. Tommy turned and walked back toward me. As he approaches, my anxiety is growing. As Tommy reaches me, he puts his index finger to his eye and says, "I think we are in trouble."

"We?" I say. "What was that?"

"What is that guy doing? I don't want to look at him."

"He's talking to a rough-looking bunch of guys. What happened?"

"We gotta get outta here."

"What do you mean? Why?"

"Those guys are all drunk and they're gonna kill us. Let's go."

Reacting quickly, I said, "Okay, but we gotta go past them to get to the door."

Realizing I'm right, Tommy suggests we walk casually toward the boys' bathroom, which is out in the hallway, but away from the door.

As soon as we were out of sight in the hallway, Tommy frantically says, "We gotta find another way outta here. This is a school, there has to be other doors."

We started down a dark hallway almost running and then turned into another dark hallway and another, until finally, we saw a door. We hit the crash bar, which opened the door and it led out to a side street. We quietly closed the door and, so as not to attract any attention, calmly walked out to the street, crossed it and started down the block. Once we turned the corner, we broke into a run and ran for blocks. We stopped running when we noticed that running was attracting attention and proceeded to walk quickly and quietly to the bus stop. After we caught our breath, Tommy started to tell me what had happened.

He had asked her to dance and she had said 'yes.' They were dancing and making small talk, when Tommy noticed the guy and his friends coming into the dance. The guy immediately started staring at him. He asked the girl if she knew the guy staring at them and she said, "Yes, it's my boyfriend."

"That's your boyfriend?"

"Yes."

Just then the guy gets in Tommy's face and says, "Who the fuck are you?"

"What did you say?" I asked.

"I said, 'None of your business!'"

"Holy shit, why did you say that?"

"What was I supposed to say? My name is Tommy—mind if I borrow your girlfriend?"

"What'd he say?"

"He said, 'Oh yeah, well I'm gonna make it my business. This here is my girl!'"

"I saw you waving your hand in front of your face. What were you doing?"

"His breath was horrible! It reeked of booze."

"Oh great! They were drunk?"

"Either that or they used booze for cologne."

"Then what'd you say?"

"I was gonna tell him that his grammar was improper. That 'this here' is redundant and incorrect, but since he was drunk, I figured it'd be a waste of time. I'm sure he wouldn't remember it when he sobered up."

We laughed for the first time.

"Thank God you didn't! What did you say?"

"I said, 'Who knew?'"

"Jesus, Tommy, why were you such a smartass?"

"What was I gonna say, 'Please don't hit me or stab me?'"

"You coulda said, 'I'm sorry, I didn't know.'"

"Fuck him!"

"What'd he say then?"

"He said, 'Now you know, so beat it.'"

"And you said?"

"I just walked away, but he yelled to his friends, 'Some fucking guys are moving in on our girls!'"

The bus pulled up and we got on it, feeling giddy after our narrow escape from death or at least a good beating. Tommy was acting like he wanted to go back now and kick that guy's ass.

"I love her," Tommy said, "and I'm not gonna lose her to that scumbag."

"You love who?" I asked.

"Annette or Lynette or whatever her name was. I didn't quite catch what she said. I think she loves me too. I could sense it by the look of terror in her eyes when she saw her boyfriend staring at us. We gotta get off the bus and go back."

"We're slightly outnumbered."

"Well, let's go get our guys. Let's go get the Jets and have a rumble."

"Yeah, great idea. We could all meet on Northern Boulevard and take two buses to the Bronx together and fight older, tougher guys for no reason. Good plan!"

"I know, we could take cabs! Picture that!"

"Yeah, we could tell the cabs to wait while we rumble and then make a quick getaway!"

"And anyway, what do you mean, no reason—what about love?"

Tommy started singing "Maria" from *West Side Story*, substituting the name Lynette for Maria.

"By the way, did you hear what song was playing when we made our hasty exit?" I asked, certain that he hadn't noticed.

"Yeah—" Runaway "by Del Shannon," he said. "That's where I got the idea! I took it as a message from God."

Tommy slept over at my house that night and we stayed up half the night in my basement, laughing, listening to music (including the sound track of *West Side Story*), and watching some stupid late night horror movie hosted by a wisecracking zombie named Zacherly. We never went back to the South Bronx and, as far as I know, that was the end of the torrid love affair between Tom Taraci and Annette or Lynette or whatever her name was. I'm sure he still thinks about her, but does she ever think of him?

On August 31, Tommy and I reported to football practice. Jeff and Glenn had decided not to, but Tommy and I were determined. It was intimidating. We had never played organized football and hadn't played on the freshman team either. We were behind and we knew it, but we loved football and dreamed of someday playing before a big crowd, wearing the green and gold. The previous year's freshman team had been very good and we figured many sophomores would be moving up to Varsity and we had a chance to make the Junior Varsity. We had no idea about what positions we wanted to play in, but decided defense was our best chance, and defensive linemen seem to have to know the least. We decided that if the squad were split up into offense and defense, we would go with the defense. If they split into linemen, backs, and receivers, we would go with linemen.

The first day went well. We went to a classroom where Guido reviewed a lot of signals, formations, and plays. It wasn't review for us, however, and we wrote like madmen. Fortunately, I understood it pretty well. After the classroom session, we went to the locker room and were issued practice uniforms and pads. We tried everything on and were excited. We tried not to show too much excitement in front of the other guys to whom this was no big deal. We went out to the practice field and limbered up.

The practice uniform was all white, but the helmet was the same as game days. We were pumped up to actually be on the team and wearing a uniform. Tommy kept getting down into a three-point stance and growling. I on the other hand tried not to attract any attention. My plan was to quietly do as I was told and make the team. I didn't have any illusions about playing a big role, just to make the team, and learn.

A whistle sounded and everyone lined up for calisthenics. The Varsity captains were up—front, leading the exercises as directed by Guido. Tommy and I were in the very last row. We didn't have any trouble with the exercises, but I did begin to notice how hot it was with a helmet on. It was a hot and humid, but overcast, day. I was relieved when a long blast on a whistle ended the session and I got to take the helmet off and wipe the sweat off my forehead.

Guido called us all into a circle and explained how he wanted the wind sprints run. We were not going to do any hitting that first day, but be ready for two tough practices tomorrow, he warned. During wind sprints, we lined up in seven lines across the field and on Guido's whistle, ran a forty-yard sprint. As soon as a group finished, Guido would make some disparaging remark toward one or two guys and whistle for the next seven.

Although it wasn't a race, per se, if you were last or near last, Guido would chide you and urge you to do better next time. This went on in the heat for a long time. I managed to avoid getting noticed. I ran hard, but once I realized I wasn't last, I eased up. Finally, Guido announced that the winner of a sprint could go shower, but the other six would continue to run. This led to some spirited sprinting. Now guys would go all out. Many knew this was coming, but I did not. I won a sprint before it became an embarrassment, and Tommy did as well. We left school pretty happy with ourselves, and looking forward to the next day's practice.

Our dreams of playing football for Holy Cross died the next day. As we lined up for tackling and blocking drills in intense heat and humidity, a coach whom we had never seen before, harassed and humiliated us. Over and over, he would yell at me for my stance. My butt was too high, my head too low. I didn't do exercises correctly. I didn't hold the tackling dummy correctly. Five of us would line up to hit a blocking sled and all of them would have to repeat it over and over until I got it right.

It was intensely hot and these were things I'd never been taught before. It was awful to have a coach yelling at me and using me as a whipping boy, but now other kids were getting on me to get it right, so they wouldn't have to repeat the drill over and over.

Sometimes I didn't understand the terminology and was hoping the coach would realize that and explain what he wanted. Instead, he called me stupid and acted disgusted every time I made a mistake. Tommy was getting a similar treatment, although I was so hot and so angry, I didn't notice it much. I actually kept looking for Guido! I felt Guido had invited me out for the team and since he knew I hadn't played freshman football, he would know I didn't know a lot of the technical stuff.

Guido was such an intimidator that most guys on the team tried to stay as far away from him as possible and here I'm looking for him as my savior! I know he didn't invite me out for the team to be the focal point of ridicule and scorn. But Guido was across the field with Varsity quarterbacks and running backs.

Finally, the rest period came between the morning and afternoon sessions. As Tommy and I slumped in the shade, we were very demoralized. Although we were in great physical shape, the heat was unusually intense and the pads and helmet added a dimension we were not used to. I had been dizzy a couple of times during the drills and I so wanted to remove my helmet. The helmet was preventing heat from escaping the top of my head and my head felt like it was in an oven.

For the first few minutes we were silent as if neither of us wanted to be the one who first mentions quitting. After a few minutes with our helmets off in the shade, I felt much better and started to notice things around me. Many guys were sick and being administered to. Some had thrown up and others had blacked out or felt faint. Trainers were wiping guys with cool towels and getting them drinks and fanning them with towels. A few guys had their shoulder pads off as if they were done for the day. Others were sitting with their heads down between their knees with cold towels on the backs of their necks or draped over their head.

"I guess we didn't do as bad as I thought," I said to Tommy, pointing to two guys on crutches, amidst those being treated for the effects of the heat. Tommy gave me a half-hearted smirk that said, 'that's not the issue.'

"Did you feel sick at all?" I asked, trying to broach the subject indirectly.

"No," he frowned. "Who the fuck is that coach?"

"I don't know. I've never noticed him before. I've never seen him in school."

"I hate him. I don't want to be on this team if he's the coach."

Just then, I saw John Rizzo lugging water and called out to him. He gave me a just-a-minute gesture, and after wetting a towel and giving it to a player, came running over.

"How you guys holdin' up?" he asked cheerily. "I saw Lanthrop giving you a hard time."

"Who the fuck *is* that guy?" I asked softly.

"That's Don Lanthrop."

"Is he a new coach?"

"No, he's not really a coach."

"What?" screamed Tommy, getting to his feet, "what do you mean, he's not a coach?"

"He's just a guy who helps out. He's not paid and he's not a teacher. He just hangs around and helps out."

"That's it! That's it! I'm not taking shit from some fuckin' weirdo frustrated Vince Lombardi!"

"Hey, I gotta go," said Rizzo and he ran off.

Neither Tommy nor I were the type of person who would take abuse or subject ourselves to ridicule. We had way too much dignity and self-esteem for that, but I had hopes that things would be different if we stuck it out a little longer. I told Tommy that we shouldn't quit right now. We should return for the afternoon session. I convinced him that if it turned into more of the same, we could walk out, but that maybe Lanthrop would be gone or at least not in charge. Maybe Guido would be working with the linemen in the next session or some other coach would take over and Lanthrop was just filling in. I reminded him of how hard we had worked in pursuit of our dream and he agreed to stay and see what happened, but he warned, "I'm not taking anymore shit from that guy. If it's not any different, I'm walkin'."

"Me, too."

The afternoon session started with laps and stretching and then we broke into groups like the morning and it was Lanthrop again, running the workout for our group. At first he gave George Thorsen a hard time and I thought maybe George would be his whipping boy for the afternoon, but when it was my turn to hit the sled, Lanthrop mocked me as he did before and as I returned to the end of the line, I looked for Tommy and said, "I'm ready."

He didn't hesitate and we jogged off together into the school and then walked into the locker room. As we were taking off our uniforms and pads,

I heard a voice behind me, "Joey Farrell, you're not quitting, are you?" It was Kevin Riley.

Kevin Riley was a junior running back who lived on Murray Street, almost directly behind my house. Our backyards were diagonal. The Riley brothers, (Kevin, Jimmy, and Vincent) and the Smith brothers (Bobby and Jackie), who lived next door to the Rileys and I had played sports together for years. We played tackle football at a lot on the corner of Murray Street and 32nd Avenue for years. The lot belonged to an elderly lady who lived there alone, Mrs. Mellare. She was nice to us and actually allowed us to play on her property. We loved her for it and never cursed if she was around and were careful not to damage any bushes or flowers on her property.

Kevin Riley occasionally shoveled snow from her walk for free without being asked. I helped him once. That was typical of Kevin Riley. He was a great guy. Now he was in the locker room with his pads off, but his uniform pants still on. He apparently had been practicing, but was sitting out the afternoon session.

"Afraid so," I answered, with a frown.

"Why?"

"Don Lanthrop."

"Oh, he's an asshole—don't let him bother you," he said with a big smile.

"Hang in there for a few days until school starts. This stuff is just bullshit—the real part begins when school starts. A lot of the guys aren't even here.

"Why is that?"

"They're away somewhere until Labor Day or have jobs they can't quit or so they say. I'm staying in here for this session. I told them I had back spasms."

"Well, I don't think I can do this . . ." I started to explain.

"It's no tougher than our games in Mrs. Mellare's lot. These drills are bullshit—believe me you can do it."

"Thanks, Kev," I said, dejectedly as he walked away. To this day, I wish I had listened to Kevin Riley, but instead Tommy and I got dressed and got out as quickly as we could. Our dreams of playing football for Holy Cross were dashed.

For the second year in a row, we were quitting on a dream. We were depressed and angry and didn't know where to go. We decided to walk to Mueller's for a Coke and a burger. We knew we'd have to tell our friends we'd quit again, but that wasn't really a problem. Tommy, of course, had me laughing soon as he heaped hatred on Lanthrop.

"I hate how he kept calling me 'son,'" Tommy raged. "I wanted to kick him in the nuts and say, 'Oops, sorry Dad. Let's try that again. Let's all line up and kick Lanthrop in the balls and if I don't like how you kicked him, I'll blow the whistle and you kick him again and when we finally kick his balls off, we feed them to wild dogs.'"

Tommy's humor and sarcasm was a welcome tonic for my depression. It had truly taken a lot of guts and desire to go out for the JV after not playing freshman football. I can't remember anyone else doing it. We had worked really hard to prepare, were both over six feet tall, ran well, and were athletic and stronger than most kids our age. We were also smart and good students, and we both dreamed of wearing the green and gold of Holy Cross.

I still have a grudge against Don Lanthrop. Who was he to humiliate and belittle students who wanted to be part of their school team? If we didn't know enough, teach us. If we didn't have enough talent, quietly call us aside and say you appreciate our effort, but you can't afford to carry us. We're too far behind, or we're too stupid to learn, or no matter what, we'd never be able to play because we lack speed or strength or stamina or desire. None of that was true, in my opinion, and yet we were run out of the program twice. I don't believe Guido ever would have let this happen had he seen us that day.

None of our parents were involved in the politics of Holy Cross and both of our mothers were against us playing football, so we had no recourse through those channels. In some circles, that's what would have happened. The kid would have been contacted and told to please come back out and the coaches would have worked diligently with the kid or the kid would have never been treated that way to begin with. We were not in that stratum. No one would ever know except our friends and so our dream was dead. I still believe that Holy Cross lost something that day.

When Registration Day rolled around, I was ready for school to begin. I was tired of the heat and tired of Cresthaven and missed some of the guys. I stopped at Glenn's house and we walked up to Holy Cross together. The class schedule and rosters were posted outside the main door. As I arrived at the door, my eyes quickly searched for my name. I started at Section C-2, figuring I would probably stay in C. I was correct. Just two names down was Glenn's name.

"Hey, Glenn, you're in C with me!"

Glenn was looking at Section D, where he was last year.

I started looking over the whole section roster, anxiously hoping for Tommy Taraci. Nope, no Tommy. Jay Carroll? Yes! Pat Kelly? No. There was a Kevin Kelly, but no Pat. I really wanted Tommy and Pat in my class, but getting Glenn was good and with mixed feelings, I began to scan the schedule.

New, unknown teachers for Math and World History, then "Brother Regis for Latin," I groaned. I was so hoping to not have him again. Brother Arthur O'Brien for Religion and Mr. Dolce for Biology were both rumored to be okay, but eighth period English sent my spirits crashing. I at first couldn't believe it and rechecked to make sure I wasn't reading off the wrong paper.

"Trentacoste for English?" I said in disbelief.

"You're shittin' me!" Glenn responded with a smile as if I was.

"Read it and weep," I said, pointing to it on the door.

"Oh my God."

The smile was gone now. Glenn had a pencil in his mouth and was shaking his head 'no' in utter futility.

"I can't put up with that fuck for another year."

"Another year of Regis too," I added with disgust.

"And we're paying for this? How much worse could public school be? My family can't afford this. This is a disgrace."

I was particularly interested in the Math teacher, but couldn't find out anything about him. I was interested because I had spent some time over the summer thinking about the future. In all likelihood I didn't have much of a future or at least one that I could plan for. The odds seemed very high that I would die soon in a nuclear holocaust. Either that or the Russians would reach the moon and use it as a ballistic missile base and force our surrender. In that case, a labor camp was my likely fate.

I tried to get an adult to say that I was being silly and that things weren't nearly that precarious, but no one ever did.

The more I thought about going away to college, the more I liked the possibility. On the remote chance that I would actually survive high school, I began to think and talk about college. I discovered that in college you needed to pick a subject to major in. I talked to my father about what I should major in and he said, "Be an engineer."

As my father described the world, engineers were responsible for everything good in life. Roads, cars, bridges, airplanes, weapons, space flight, electronics, and appliances were all improving our lives and all were the creation of engineers. Employers would be waiting with offers when you walk out the door with an Engineering degree, he told me.

"What does it take to go to college for Engineering?" I asked.

"You have to be good at math and science."

So I began tenth grade with a renewed interest in math and science, although I had still never had a science class, if you can believe it.

The first day of tenth grade was a memorable one, and this time not because of the weather. When we reached eighth period English, Glenn started ranting about how pissed off he was about having Mr. Trentacoste again.

"Do you believe it?" What rotten luck!" Some of the class hadn't had him in ninth grade and Glenn was telling them what a boring prick he was.

"I can't even stand to look at him. He has a smug smile and little teeth and he's gawky like Farrell."

"Fuck you, I'm not gawky!"

"You are gawky. He's tall and uncoordinated, with big feet, long arms, big hands, and he walks like a gorilla."

"I have small hands," I said, holding them up.

"Other than that, you could be his son," laughed Glenn. As I was vehemently objecting, the bell rang. "You lousy bastard," I whispered, "I don't look anything like him."

Trentacoste usually liked to make an entrance. He waited thirty seconds or so after the bell to come into the classroom and when he did, he expected everyone to be in their seat and completely silent. Glenn and I were in our seats, next to each other, and there was complete silence as Trentacoste walked in. He walked across the front of the room to the desk with his usual long stride, big feet, long dangling arms, sort of like a monkey on stilts with big feet on the ends. I looked at Glenn and he looked at me and we burst out laughing! Trentacoste saw us and called us to the front of the room.

"Farrell, Judson, come up here! We might as well get off to a good start," he said to the class as he swung his big hand and slapped Glenn hard across the face. I knew I was next, so I steeled myself. I noticed Glenn staring right at Trentacoste and his hands were clenched in fists although at his sides.

For an instant, I thought Glenn was going to punch Trentacoste and I'm sure he would have, had Trentacoste taken another swing at him, but instead he swung and hit me. I was looking down, perhaps anticipating it a little, because he caught some of my left ear. It hurt like hell and I couldn't hear normally for a while. I acted like I didn't feel a thing. I didn't want Trentacoste to think he could hurt me and I didn't want the rest of the class, many of whom didn't know me, to think I wasn't tough.

"Return to your seats," said Trentacoste without emotion, as if this happened every class.

I couldn't see how I looked, but Glenn was beet red. He wasn't just red where he had been hit, he was red all over. During class, I kept thinking what would have happened had Glenn punched him back. Glenn was my friend and I didn't want him kicked out of Holy Cross, but something in me wanted him to pop him. I wondered what I would've done. Would I have restrained Glenn or taken a shot at Trentacoste too or stepped aside and watched and rooted for Glenn to kick his ass? I couldn't decide, but it made the class go by quickly.

On the way home with our group of friends, the Trentacoste incident was the major discussion.

"I'm really proud of you two young men," said Dickie. "Getting smacked in the face on the first day is no small accomplishment! Well done, boys!"

"And I'm proud of you, too, Dickie," piped up Jeff.

"Oh, this ought to be good. Why are you proud of me, Jeff? As if I give a shit."

"You went all the way down to Section H, from Section E. Now, that's quite an accomplishment." (Dickie came to a sudden stop.)

"And you, sir, are still a douche bag, whatever section you may be in." (Resumes walking.)

"If you go one section lower, you'll be in shop class all day, making ashtrays, and tie racks."

"So?"

"So, I'm proud of you for not lying."

"What? What are you *talking* about?"

"You said you fucked up your finals and you really did! A lot of guys say they fucked up exams, but then it turns out they really didn't. I hate that!"

"Don't you think there's something seriously wrong with you?"

"No, why, well . . . maybe. Why do you ask?"

"Because you say and do weird things."

"Like what?"

"Like the crack about shop class and guys in lower sections."

"I'm just saying that you need to do better or you'll be screwed in the future. You worry me, Dickie."

"Well, first of all, we're probably all gonna die in a nuclear war, so you're wasting your time worrying."

"But suppose we don't? Suppose the Russian missiles misfire and we win?"

"Then I'll sell ashtrays and tie racks in the day and I'll be an usher in the evenings. I told you last year I wanted to be an usher."

"Okay! I didn't know you had a plan! Now I feel better."

"But why do you think there might be something wrong with you," I asked Jeff. "What do you mean? You said, 'maybe' when Dickie asked if you think there's something seriously wrong with you."

"Perhaps it's that he goes to the movies alone all the time," laughed Dickie.

"What's wrong with that?" yelled Jeff.

"It's fuckin' weird!"

Jeff proceeded to explain that he had found a way to sneak into the Roosevelt Theater and in fact, often did so. The Roosevelt was near Jeff's house and when he felt like it, he walked to the theater and entered through an exit door in the back that didn't lock. Apparently the locking mechanism attached to the crash bar didn't work properly and the strictly enforced New York City fire laws did not permit it to be locked, so it could be pried open. Jeff had discovered this somehow and began to see a lot of movies for free.

"So what's so weird about catching some flicks for free?"

"It is weird," answered Dickie. "I've rarely seen, if ever seen, people in the movies sitting alone."

"Well, I have—plenty of times," responded Jeff.

"And I bet they're weirdos," said Dickie.

"Why?"

"Because they go to the movies alone!"

We all laugh at the beauty of Dickie's logic, as Jeff shakes his head in frustration and tries to come back with something clever, but cannot.

"I still didn't hear your answer to my question, Jeff," I finally said.

"Which was?"

"Why did you say 'maybe'"?

"Oh that. I guess it's because I'm so horny all the time."

"You think it's weird to be horny?" asked Glenn.

"I told you he's fucked up!" laughed Dickie.

"Wait! Wait!," yelled Tommy Taraci. "I want to hear this."

"Go ahead, Jeff, I sense there's more."

"Well, I don't know . . . I just feel real horny all the time. Last night, my sister had some of her friends over and I just wanted to grab them and start humping. (Dickie stops again.)

"Boy friends or girl friends?" asked Dickie.

"Girl friends, you asshole!"

"Just checking," says Dickie and resumes walking.

"So, did you hump anyone?" I asked.

"No. But I thought about it all night and again today in class."

"What class?" I asked, as if that was critical information.

"English, Math, Religion, Study Hall, History . . . Lunch . . ."

"Religion class? You thought about humping in Religion class?" I asked in mock horror.

"Actually, I thought about it the entire class. I'm lucky I didn't get called and have to stand up, 'cause I had a big boner. Can you imagine standing up in Religion class with a big hard-on?"

We all laugh and Jeff then asks, "So, that's why I said maybe. Is there something wrong with me?"

"Oh, there's definitely something wrong with you," answered Tommy without hesitation, "but that's not it."

"That's not it?"

"Nope."

"It's okay to think about humping all the time . . . even in Religion class?"

"I wish you hadn't told me this story, Jeff."

"Why?"

"'Cause now I'm gonna think about humping your sister during Religion class."

"That's disgusting!"

"Oh, like you never think about it?"

"Ugh! You are going to hell, Tommy. Do I ever talk about your sister in such an impure way?"

"My sister is eleven years old, so I would hope not."

"You're the one who's going to hell," I interjected, looking at Jeff.

"Me? Why?"

"'Impure Thoughts' is a mortal sin."

"Oh yeah. I worry about that. I go to confession every Saturday."

"You better hope the bomb doesn't drop on New York before then or you'll go straight to hell."

"I'm serious. I do worry about that."

"Did you try to get rid of these humping thoughts?"

"What do you mean?"

"Well, did you try thinking about Jesus hanging on the cross or did you start saying the Rosary or the "Act of Contrition" to get those thoughts out of your mind?"

"No."

"Then you're on the Hell Express!"

"Hey, when you get to the gates of Hell, Jeff, you can tell them you're in Section D," yelled Dickie. "I'm sure that will make a difference."

"Oh, that reminds me," said Jeff, ignoring Dickie's sarcasm.

"There is a Triduum coming to St. Andrew's soon."

"A what?" I asked.

"A Triduum. It's a three-night service in church."

"And why would we care?"

"It ends with a papal blessing which carries a Plenary Indulgence."

We all knew that a Plenary Indulgence removed all the punishment due your soul for any sins committed up to that point.

"That's great! We can hump away until the Triduum and then have it all forgiven," said Tommy.

"But you have to be sorry," reminded Glenn.

"Oh, I'll *be* sorry," responded Tommy.

"Me, too," added Jeff.

Dickie comes to a sudden stop. "I almost forgot to tell you guys! Guess who's in my class?"

"The village idiot?" laughs Jeff.

"Fuck you, Baudo! Why are you so judgmental?"

"I'm not judgmental."

"You're condescending," interjected Tommy.

"Yeah," says Dickie, "condescending . . . that's a real Section B word. We don't use them big words in Section H. We'd say judgmental."

"You'd say . . . 'Duh,'" said Jeff.

"There you go again, you prick."

"Okay, tell us who's in your class."

"Eddie Hodges."

"Eddie Hodges, the actor?"

"Eddie Hodges, the movie star, singer, and star of Broadway!"

"No shit," said Tommy, "The kid who was in "*A Hole in the Head*" with Frank Sinatra?"

"Yep, and "*Huckleberry Finn*" and "*The Music Man*" on Broadway and he even has a hit record right now."

"Now that's pretty hard to believe," exclaimed Jeff.

"Why? Why is that hard to believe? You don't think I'm making it up, do you? Why would I do that?"

"Oh no, I believe he's in your class," explained Jeff. "It's just hard to believe he's that dumb!"

"You know you should be more careful, Jeff. If I accidentally push you in front of a speeding bus, you'd go straight to hell."

Shortly after school started, the Soviet Union exploded a fifty-megaton bomb. It was the biggest explosion in the history of man. We knew deep down, if it would be used, it would be used on New York.

CHAPTER TWELVE

♦ ♦ ♦ ♦ ♦

"LEADER OF THE PACK"

We busted out of class, had to get away from those fools,
We learned more from a three-minute record,
Than we ever learned in school.
                    Bruce Springsteen—"No Surrender"

The fall of 1961 brought lots of changes. It brought a new principal, Brother Josaphat Chmielewski and a new Dean of Men, Brother Richard McDonald. These two men acted as if they were in a hypnotic trance and programmed not to ever laugh or smile. They introduced themselves to us at a dour assembly in the auditorium. If their intent was to scare us and make us want to avoid them at all costs, then they accomplished their goal. Those guys could sure light up a room.

Bro. Josaphatt stresses the importance of getting good grades to Seniors and Juniors while Bro. Richard watches their reactions.

That fall also brought some new friends, especially a friend of Jay Carroll's, named Paul Falabella. Jay had told me about Paul, but since we were in different classes within the same grade, I hadn't gotten to know him. Now not only was he in our class, but he would sit in front of me or beside me in every class. Every teacher sat us alphabetically, some up and down, some across, and I was always between Ray Frasene and Paul and Jay was always nearby.

I quickly saw why Jay and Paul were friends. We liked each other instantly and became good friends. We shared homework and worked together to help each other out when in a jam. The five of us, Glenn, Jay, Ray, Paul and I, often split up homework assignments and then copied each other's. More often, however, I was in need of someone's homework and Ray and Paul were the most reliable suppliers.

Our after-school routine changed too, in that we began to meet at Mueller's after school. The Holy Cross crowd of me, Tommy, Dickie, Glenn, and Jeff would usually walk to Mueller's after school and meet up with Dennis Geoghan and Eddie Haggerty, who went to Bishop Laughlin, and Billy Landers, who went to Brooklyn Prep. Typically, we'd drink sodas and egg creams, play music, talk to girls, and then head for home, each in our own direction, around five or five-thirty.

It was typical in those days in New York for groups of teenagers to hang around a candy store or a pizza parlor. It was a place to hang out, socialize, meet and listen to music. Mueller's was a good place for us, since it was centrally located near the church and on a bus line. Eddie, Dennis, and Billy and many of the girls rode buses to and from school and Tommy had to catch a bus home from Mueller's. Our crowd, however, shared Mueller's with another group of our finest youth. The place was split right down the middle by the two groups.

The other crowd was mostly high school dropouts. Most of them were a little older than us, had a lot of hair, smoked, acted and dressed tough, didn't play sports, and in fact, a few had done time in a juvenile facility. Thus, we called them the Mafia. They called us the "Sorority Boys" because we went to school and church, often wore suits and ties, played sports and, as a result of going to Catholic high school, all had short hair. They sat in booths on their side and we on our side. The counter stools were neutral turf, open to anyone. We hardly ever talked to each other, but both respected the unspoken arrangement. If our booths were filled, we would sit at the counter before we would sit on their side. The jukebox was right in the middle and was equally popular between the two groups, although the Mafia seemed to play "Leader of the Pack" quite a bit, whereas we never did. Interestingly, one of the first lines from this classic song was, "I met him at the candy store."

This candy store served as both groups' home base, yet we remained two distinct and separate groups for the most part. We never fought with each other, just co-existed in two separate worlds, which met at Mueller's. I'm sure this would have made a good social work study for some graduate student.

That fall also saw the beginning of my lifetime love affair with alcohol. It began at Billy Landers house, when his parents weren't home. He invited me to try some liquor from his parents' liquor cabinet and I did. Each time we would take a sip or two from a bottle, Billy would add water to the bottle so that his parents wouldn't detect any missing. We sampled Scotch and Irish whiskey, gin, vodka, Jack Daniels and I don't know what else. I don't remember anything past being in Billy's kitchen, watching him carefully pour water into the bottles. I'm told I was very funny and Billy and the guys made sure I got home okay.

I don't remember how I got past my parents and got to bed, but I do remember waking up with a whopping hangover and swearing never to do that again. In a few weeks, however, I was giving money to older guys to buy me a half pint of Seagrams 7. The legal drinking age in New York at this time was eighteen, as was the legal age for driving. At first thought, this might seem like a deeply regrettable public policy. The notion of being a new inexperienced driver while simultaneously having the first alcohol experience would not appear to be a wise one, in theory. But, on further review, it seemed a wise policy in reality. Most of us were experienced drinkers by the time we were of legal age and obtaining our drivers' licenses. The fascination or experimenting phases of drinking were over.

We started by finding someone to buy liquor for us. There were plenty of seniors that were 18 or soon to be 18 and we would pay them to get us our order. This was unreliable, so we started paying careful attention to what liquor stores were actually asking for proof of age and which weren't. It seemed to us that the liquor store on Murray Lane, just off Northern Boulevard, was rather lax at asking for ID. Two of the clerks never seemed to ask and we decided we should try it ourselves. Unfortunately for me, I was judged to look the oldest, since I was over six feet, three inches tall.

We arrived outside the store and saw that one of the clerks who had never asked for proof was on duty. I was very nervous. I refused to buy any more than three items and insisted they be of different things so that it didn't look like I was buying for others. If the clerk asked for proof, I would tell him I didn't have my wallet with me and offer to go get it in the car and then leave. If he asked me questions, I was prepared to say my name was Joe and if pressed for a last name, Joe Heaney. I lived on 157th Street and I was a freshman at St. John's University. Eddie and Billy helped me rehearse and stay calm.

"You shouldn't be nervous," counseled Eddie. "After all the trouble you've been in, this should be easy. Pretend it's Sister Mary Mark behind the counter."

"You can get in a lot more trouble at Stations of the Cross than doing this," offered Billy. "They're not supposed to sell to minors, but there is no harm in you trying to buy it. If they say 'no,' it's okay, we go to Plan B."

"What's Plan B?" I asked.

"Getting older guys to get it for us. But this is better, if it works."

"That's right," said Eddie, "it's all part of growing up."

"What is?" I asked. "Buying booze illegally?"

"Becoming independent," answered Eddie, "not relying on others for everything. It's all part of becoming a mature adult."

"That's correct," chimed in Dickie. "This is the right way, the mature way. Some day when you're eighteen and some fifteen-year-olds approach you to buy them booze, you can guide them in the right direction and tell them to buy their own, like you did."

I was still laughing as Eddie pushed me toward the liquor store entrance. "Now get in there before it's too late!"

I went in and looked the elderly clerk right in the eye and calmly asked for a pint of Seagrams 7, a pint of Southern Comfort and a pint of Fleishman's vodka. He put them on the counter, rang them up, bagged them, and took the bills off the counter, where I had counted them out. I was hoping my hand wasn't shaking when he held out the change for me to accept. I picked up the bag of booze and exited to a hero's reception in the parking lot outside.

"Sister Mary Mark would be proud of you tonight," chuckled Eddie as he took a slug from the Seagrams 7 he and I were sharing. "Imagine her saying you'd never amount to anything."

"Maybe we should pay her a visit tonight," suggested Billy, who was sharing the vodka with Dennis Geoghan. "If only it were snowing, we could throw snowballs at the bedroom windows of the Convent and wake them all up. Wouldn't that be great?"

Having no place to go, we'd wander around, drinking in the streets. Sometimes, we'd wind up in Bowne Park, sometimes Mueller's. Sometimes at somebody's house whose parents weren't home, but mostly we'd wander around, looking for girls or a party somewhere that we could crash.

After a few weeks of me being the buyer, it was time to initiate someone else. The group preferred half pints to pints because they were concealed much easier and fit into pockets better as well as not having to stay close to whoever you were sharing a pint with. I was getting nervous about buying six or eight or even ten half pints at a time. I now knew two of the clerks at the store, but didn't want to be the one always taking the chance. How these clerks didn't get suspicious was beyond me. We decided one Friday night that I would take Tommy in with me, and both order. It worked. Now Tommy and I were splitting the duty of buying the booze. Soon Dickie, armed with his older brother's draft card, tried the liquor store on 162nd Street and wasn't asked for ID. The next week, Dennis tried the same store, was asked for proof, didn't have any, and was turned down.

"God damn! I can't believe it!" said Dennis in disgust. "Do I look younger than Dickie?"

"Yes!" we all answered in unison.

Dennis moved to get next to Dickie, who is quite a bit shorter than Dennis, and asks again, "I look younger than Dickie?"

"Yes," we all answer in unison again.

"Dickie looks older than me?"

"Yes," again, in unison.

"Damn," said Dennis as he took a swig of his lime-flavored vodka that Dickie had gotten for him. He then moved to the outside of the sidewalk and walked, looking in the street, shaking his head as if he was disgusted with us for hurting his feelings.

"You're better looking though," said Glenn, seeing Dennis pretending to sulk.

"Damn straight!" said Dennis.

"Fuck the both of you," said Dickie.

We soon found ourselves to be at Bowne Park, sitting and standing around in the playground, in the cold, drinking liquor.

"Is it safe to be doing this here?" asked Jeff.

"What do you mean, 'safe'"? answered Dickie.

"Will someone see us or hear us and call the cops?"

"Who in hell would be in the middle of the park in the dark on a cold night like this?" answered Dennis.

"Someone walking his dog."

"Would you walk your dog into the middle of the park after dark in this weather?"

"I might."

"Then you're fucked in the head."

"See," says Dickie, smiling from ear to ear. "I told you you're fucked up, Baudo."

"Let them call the cops," yelled Billy, tossing off his coat and handing me his bottle. He ran full speed at the fence and landed on the other side, almost as fast as if he had run through it. In another few seconds, Billy was back over the fence, putting on his coat and reclaiming his half-pint.

"Do you think the cops will just drive away and leave us alone after they see that?" asked Glenn, laughing. "Is that the idea, Billy?"

"Well, if that doesn't work, for sure they won't chase us down a manhole." Billy had been lifting manhole covers and exploring the sewers and underground infrastructure of Flushing over the past few months. He would put his fingers in the holes of a cover and lift it off the hole, go down, pull it back, and travel for blocks underneath the street. Various guys had gone with him, but I refused to do it.

"I'll take my chances with the police," I said.

"Me, too," added Tommy, quickly.

"Hey, that's a good plan Billy," said Dennis. "Let them see you jump the fence like you do and then make sure they see you go down a manhole. I'm sure they'll leave us alone after that."

Jeff finished his half pint and tossed the bottle away. It landed on the concrete walkway near the gatehouse and shattered loudly.

"Jeff, Jeff, what are you doing?" said Tommy, in disbelief.

"Don't worry—it was empty," answers Jeff.

"This is a playground, ass-wipe—kids play here," interjected Billy.

"Oh, yeah, that *was* stupid. Someone help me clean it up."

Dennis, Dickie, and I get up and start helping Jeff pick up glass and put it in a garbage can.

"Why'd you do this?" asked Dennis of Jeff.

"Because I'm drunk."

"We're all just as drunk as you are, but no one else threw his bottle and smashed it to bits."

"*You said* I was fucked in the head."

"Why are you?"

"Why am I what?"

"Why are you fucked in the head?"

"Because I threw the bottle."

"Why did you do *that?*"

"Because I'm fucked in the head!"

"Were you fucked in the head *before* you threw the bottle?"

"Who?"

"You! Who the fuck am I talking to?"

"See what I have to put up with, goin' to school every day with this guy?" said Dickie.

We were finished picking up the glass and we walked back to the rest of the group, sitting and laying on seesaws.

I thought you were worried about noise and someone calling the cops?" I reminded Jeff.

"Who would hear it?"

"You said 'someone walking a dog'."

"Who would walk a dog in the dark in the park?"

"You said *you* would!"

"Nah, my sister walks the dog."

"When? When does Leslie walk the dog?" demanded Tommy, looking at his watch. "Maybe I could happen to be out for a walk myself."

"My sister would never be interested in you, but Buster obviously is."

"Oh my God," laughs Tommy, "did you guys ever see Jeff's dog Buster? He's huge and he's horny. Of course, that probably comes from being around Jeff's sister so much. Tonight when I was sitting in Jeff's house waiting for him, Buster started humping my leg."

"Uh-oh—he is a big dog," says Dickie, "he tried to hump my leg once too."

"Well, Buster starts humping me and I say 'down boy, down' but he doesn't stop. Here I am sitting alone on the couch in Baudo's living room and this big dog has his big face with his big teeth near my crotch and he's straddling my leg and humping me!"

Eddie, who was laying on a seesaw with his head near the middle and his feet on the handgrip, laughed so hard, he fell off. We were all picturing the scene and laughing.

"I finally try to push Buster off me, but he growls at me, and starts humping faster. I thought he was gonna actually come on my leg!"

"Uuugh! So what happened?" asked Dickie. "I just stood up when he tried to hump me and he stopped."

"I started yelling for Jeff."

"I'm upstairs combing my hair and I hear, 'Jeff! Jeff!' Come here quick!" Jeff takes over. "I can't imagine what's going on, so I run downstairs, and you should have seen the look on Tommy's face!"

"Know what Jeff says?" asks Tommy. "He says what are *you* doing to Buster?"

"I never saw Buster so excited. I could barely pull him off Tommy."

The discussion then fragmented as Dennis asked Eddie about a party he had gone to recently with the Bishop Laughlin swimming team. Eddie was on the team and got invited to a party by another team member.

"How were the girls?" asked Dennis.

"Great. I was with a really gorgeous girl. We were makin' out for hours."

Tommy, Dickie, Glenn, and Billy were talking about the upcoming ticker tape parade planned for John Glenn, who had just become an American hero by being the first American to orbit the earth. I had one ear in each conversation.

Dickie didn't understand why it was being made such a big deal. "The Russian guy did over seventeen orbits six months ago and was up there more than a day. Our guy did three orbits in hours. It seems to me we're still way behind."

"*The Sunday New York Times* had an article about some members of Congress fearing the Russians will arm satellites with nuclear weapons and force us to surrender," said Billy.

"We'll never surrender," said Glenn. "Before we'd surrender, we'd probably launch everything we have at the Russians."

"And they'll launch everything they have at us," countered Billy.

Dennis, who had finished his conversation with Eddie, heard the end of the other discussion and chimed in with, "What I want to know is, are we gonna get laid before we die?"

"I am," answered Eddie quickly, "but I doubt you guys will."

"Whoa, whoa—what makes you say that?" yelled Tommy.

"I've been getting close and besides, I'm handsome, and you guys are ugly. Who would do it with you?"

"Hey! You can get your own booze from now on," I said.

"Except for Joe, I was going to say. You didn't let me finish."

"And you can borrow someone else's homework," Dennis quickly added.

"And Dennis. Again, you didn't let me finish."

"Damn straight," said Dennis, proudly.

We spent many nights like this in late 1961 and early 1962. It was very young men bonding—expressing their fears, hopes, dreams, and in a weird way, their affection for each other. I loved it.

Our Varsity Football games were Sunday afternoons and most of us went to every game in a 2-5-1 season. The Junior Varsity went 0 and 7 without Tommy and me. The fact that a whole group of sophomores were playing Varsity was a huge mitigating factor for the bad records. Eddie, Dennis, and Billy usually went to the home games, even though they didn't go to Holy Cross.

The games were good, they drew big crowds, and thus a lot of girls and there was a record hop afterward in the gym for fifty cents. After the games, we would walk to the school from Memorial Field. The Holy Cross Marching Band would march back to school, much to the annoyance of the neighborhood. After the game against Chaminade, we were walking along Bayside Avenue to go to the record hop. Dennis was bitching about how stale and hard the pretzel was that he bought on his way out of the stadium. Just as the band comes marching by, Dennis breaks off a piece of the pretzel and throws it at the tuba, a good fifty feet away. The piece of pretzel hits the tuba and bounces off harmlessly. The tuba player looks in our direction with a puzzled look on his face. Emboldened, Dennis breaks off another piece and tosses it hard, but this time right *into* the tuba! We all crack up laughing until suddenly, from out of nowhere, there is a Holy Cross Brother in Dennis's face!

I recognize this Brother, but don't know who he is. He is small, maybe 5'6" and mean-looking. I kept walking, so as to avoid getting into trouble, but after I am a little bit away and sort of lost in the crowd, I stop and watch.

When the Brother first stopped Dennis, his immediate reaction was contrite and apologetic, but as I watched, he seemed to lose that look and became more aggressive. Suddenly, I heard my name being called.

"Hey, Joe, what did Dennis do?"

It was Dennis Mullaney, another St. Andrew's kid who was now in Holy Cross. Dennis Mullaney was walking by, saw Dennis Geoghan and the Brother engaged in a heated conversation, and then saw me watching.

"Who is that Brother?" I asked Dennis.

"You don't know who *that* is? That's very surprising. That's a surprise-and-a-half, actually."

"Why? Who is it?"

"That's the notorious Brother Thomas Burns, a.k.a. "Mousey." Haven't you heard about him?"

"Actually, no. Why should I have?"

"He's a super-prick and he especially hates big guys, so naturally, I thought *you'd* know him."

"What's he teach?"

"Shop."

"Shop?"

"Oh, I'm so sorry. Industrial Arts is what I should have said. Don't *ever* let him get you down in the Shop classroom. He'll beat the shit out of you and no one will hear you screaming. The shop is soundproof because of all the noise the machines make. He's a prick-and-a-half, I'm tellin' ya! Hey, I gotta go—see ya' later."

In about two minutes or less, Dennis resumes walking, and soon sees me and I join him.

"Do you know that brother?" he asks loudly.

"Shhh," I say quietly, because I don't want any part of this, especially given what Dennis Mullaney had just told me.

"Do you know that brother?" he asked again, quietly.

"I just found out who he is from Mullaney and he's a real prick," I said softly, looking around to make sure he wasn't near us. "What happened?"

"He asked me for my student ID card."

"What'd you say?"

"I said I don't go to Holy Cross."

"Then what?"

"He said, 'I don't believe you, now give me your ID card or you'll only make it harder on yourself.'"

"I told him again, 'I don't go to your school—sorry.'"

"Then he said, 'Where *do* you go to school?'" and I told him, "Bishop Laughlin. Then he really got me mad."

"I saw you looking a little ticked off. Then Mullaney came up to me and I missed what happened next."

"He said, 'I think you're lying. Why would you go to the Holy Cross/Chaminade game?'"

Oh no, I thought, here comes the part where he implicates me. "What'd you say to that?"

"I told him I didn't care what he thought. I told him, 'I like football and it's a public event at a public stadium.' Then he asked me why I threw the pretzel and I told him, 'because it was stale.' He said he didn't like that kind of behavior and Holy Cross wouldn't tolerate it, so I told him I didn't like stale pretzels and wouldn't tolerate being called a liar."

"Ho-o-o-oly shit," I groaned. "Then what?"

"He said, 'Maybe Bishop Laughlin would like to hear about this. What is your name?' I said, 'Maybe, but I don't think so' and I walked away."

"Ho-o-o-oly sh-i-i-i-t," I groaned again. I had images of me being locked in the "Shop" and being tortured with power tools.

"Who was he?" asked Dennis.

"His name is Brother Thomas Burns," I said, rubbing my face with my open hand in anxiety. "They call him "Mousey" and he's a real prick."

"They call him what?" laughed Dennis.

"Mousey."

"Mousey? Why do they call him that?"

"I don't know," I answered, dejectedly.

"I agree with the rodent part, but why not 'Ratso?'"

"I don't know," I said, taking a deep breath and looking all around the thinning crowd, hoping not to see Mousey anywhere.

"It's probably because he's small. You don't look so good. What's wrong?"

"I'm worried that he saw me with you."

"You didn't do anything, so what can he do to you?"

I proceeded to tell Dennis what Mullaney had told me.

"Hey, cheer up. It coulda been a lot worse," he said.

"How?"

"If he had touched me, I was gonna deck him."

We soon caught up to the rest of our group, which had missed the whole episode. When Dennis told the story the guys were in hysterics. Tommy was doubled over with laughter, stumbling around, weak from lack of oxygen. Glenn had heard of Mousey and said he was called that because he was so sneaky and small.

"He likes to hide in the hallways and catch guys doin' something wrong, particularly big guys."

I suggested we not go to the record hop for fear of Mousey being there and seeing us with Dennis, but no one else felt threatened. The girls at the game looked promising and we had already picked out some to try and meet.

At the record hop in the Holy Cross gym, I started jokingly keeping a distance from Dennis, while we were standing around looking over the girls. The rest of the guys picked up on it and Dennis would suddenly find himself standing alone as quietly guys moved away from him. Dennis thought it was funny and suggested that we didn't have to move away if he kept his back to our backs as if we didn't know each other. Throughout most of the record hop, we kept our backs to his back and talked back to back.

◆ ◆ ◆

I toyed briefly with the idea of running for class officer or Student Council after Jay Carroll and Paul Fallabella urged me to do it. I was very flattered, but declined. They pressed me to enter my name.

"Most everybody knows you and likes you, I'm sure you'd win," said Jay.

"I've only known you for a few weeks, but I'd vote for you and talk you up to others. I think you are a natural," added Paul.

"A natural what?" I asked.

"A natural leader."

"I don't think the faculty would like it very much."

"That just makes you more attractive as a candidate," laughed Jay. "Will you do it?"

"I'm too shy," I said, and both Paul and Jay broke up, laughing.

"I *am* shy," I insisted.

They laughed some more and Jay said, "Think it over."

"What do class officers do, anyway?" I asked both of them.

"I don't know," answered Paul, and Jay shrugged his shoulders.

"What did our class officers do last year?"

"I don't know," answered Paul again and Jay shrugged again.

"Who were our class officers last year?"

"I don't know," answered Paul and Jay shrugged again.

"And just why do you think I'd do a good job?"

"I don't know," answered Paul and Jay shrugged.

We all laughed and Glenn Judson walked in the room and Jay told him that they were trying to get me to enter my name for Class Officer.

"You'd be good," agreed Glenn. "I'd vote for you."

"Why?"

"You're a complainer. You can tell them all the things that are wrong and how they should be done. You can tell them all that shit you tell me."

Glenn saw us all laughing.

"I'm serious!"

"He says he's too shy," said Paul.

"Do you think anybody will actually listen?" I asked, looking at Glenn.

"No, but that won't stop you!"

I told them I'd decide by the next day, but I didn't think I would run for an office I didn't really want, with responsibilities I didn't really know about, and with a chance of being embarrassed by a poor showing. Athletes usually won for some reason, probably because they have a network of teammates that cut across all sections of the class or maybe it's name recognition.

On the walk to Mueller's after school, Glenn told the group I was thinking of running for Class Officer, but that I claimed to be shy.

"What's so funny?" Dickie asked, as Glenn was smiling and laughing as he made the announcement.

"Do you think he's shy?" answered Glenn with a tone that indicated *he* did not.

"Well, that's a good question," said Dickie. "I can see a case for each side of that question."

"How can a guy who has never missed a dance and is always pickin' up girls claim to be shy?" theorized Glenn.

"Wait a minute," answered Tommy. "I'm usually with him and he is shy. He's a big chicken. It takes him forever to work up the guts to talk to a girl. I'm usually the one who starts it."

"Well, he always seems to eventually do it. I'd like to go to a dance, but I'm way too chicken," said Glenn.

"Maybe he's shy, but also super-horny and eventually horny wins," said Jeff.

"That's it!" I agreed. "It's really hard for me to ask a girl out or approach a girl. I do it, but it kills me."

"That's a good one, Farrell. It's '*hard*' for him to ask a girl out," interjected Jeff. "Get it? It's '*hard*'."

"We get it, you asshole," answered Dickie.

"When it comes to girls," I said, "it's like the nuns saying I had no self-control. They didn't know how bad I wanted to be and you guys don't know how hard it is for me to approach girls."

"Okay, let's leave girls out of it," offered Dickie. "Where else are you shy?"

"I never join any clubs or organizations, I never want to be the head of anything, run anything, or be the center of attention."

"Never want to be the center of attention! You're in trouble all the time!" yelled Jeff.

"That's different."

"How's it different?"

"I'm provoked."

"You're provoked! You were provoked into saying 'I'd let "B" do it' in Algebra?"

"Yes! He called on me for an answer to a problem I didn't do for homework. I had to say something. Do I ever raise my hand to answer in class?"

"You probably never know any answers," interrupted Glenn.

"Do I ever volunteer for anything?"

"What about, 'I don't know and I don't care'?" asked Jeff.

"Again—provoked! *He* called on *me* and asked me a question."

"The nerve of him!" said Tommy.

"Do I ever ask a question at an assembly or start a cheer at a ballgame or try out for a play?"

As we entered Mueller's, Dickie said I had made interesting points.

"You *might* be shy, Farrell, but you're *definitely* off the wall."

"Off the wall?"

"That's right, off the wall."

Some of the girls who we went to St. Andrew's with were at Mueller's and soon joined in the debate. Cathy Garrity agreed that I was indeed shy, but Jean Reed thought the notion of me being shy was laughable.

"Would a shy person go on strike in eighth grade?" she asked, as if the answer was rhetorical.

Soon Eddie, Dennis, and Billy arrived from Brooklyn and joined in the conversation. Eddie agreed that I was shy and cited an example of me not wanting to go to a party where I didn't know anybody but him. I added that I also didn't want to crash a party that we had crashed some months ago.

"Sounds like shy means you have no balls?" laughed Billy.

"Why are we talking about this?" asked Dennis. "Who gives a fuck?"

"I think it's an interesting question," said Billy. "I think he is shy, but most people would be surprised at that."

"How can he be shy and yet can't keep his mouth shut?" countered Dennis.

"I'm shy and I can't keep my mouth shut," answered Billy.

"You're shy?" Dennis asked, incredulously.

"Yeah, I'm shy."

"I'm getting nauseous," said Dennis. "This is fucked up."

"We already agreed he's off the wall," said Jeff, "even the girls agree with that."

I looked at the girls big-eyed, as if I couldn't believe they would agree, to get their reaction to Jeff's comment.

"You have done some crazy things," said Cathy Garrity, smiling.

"Crazy?" I asked.

"Well, not crazy exactly . . . maybe more like quirky."

"You're a little quirky," added Kathy Lynch, holding her one hand out at arm's length and turning her hand side to side. "But in a nice way."

On the walk home from Mueller's, I reminded Glenn of his remark about being too chicken to go to a dance. "Who would you like to take to a dance?" I asked.

"I was thinking Eugenia Desmond, but I don't know if she'd go."

"Want me to find out?"

"How?"

"I'll ask Cathy Garrity to find out if she'd say yes if you asked her. That will take the risk out of it."

Glenn agreed and a few weeks later, Glenn went on his first date. He was a nervous wreck and the yearbook photographer captured Tommy, Glenn, and I with our dates. We did the stroll, the cha-cha, and the twist, which were all the rage.

Sophomores: J. Farrell, T. Teraci, and G. Judsen seem to be enjoying the Student Council Hop as well as their dates.

As the first half of the school year came to an end, I had an unfocused feeling of mental uneasiness. I had started the year with a newfound motivation to go to college and perhaps be an engineer. I thought I would have a good year, having survived the uncertainty and changes of freshman year.

Instead, my motivation had dissolved and I felt a malaise that was overpowering. My grades were decent, but didn't reflect what was going on. My highest grade, a 90, was ironically, in English, where Mr. Trentacoste had developed a respect for my knowledge of correct usage and grammar. The grade was a reflection on the drilling at St. Andrew's by the nuns and not anything Trentacoste had taught me.

My lowest grade was a 78—in World History. I thought I would like World History. I liked to read. I liked movies about history. I was curious about how things came to be. Jay, Paul, and I joked about our textbook being the fifth and last edition since the world was probably going to end soon.

We started the year with a new teacher, Mr. Boyle. He was a nice enough man, but totally incapable of handling the situation. He wasn't capable or hadn't learned to bully and intimidate kids the way we were used to, and soon things were out of control.

Some of the guys, sensing weakness, took advantage of Mr. Boyle and used the class time to do whatever they wanted. Class became chaos with guys walking around, talking, yelling out windows, throwing paper, listening to transistor radios, and just generally making a fool out of Mr. Boyle. Even though it was a minority of the class, it was completely disruptive.

Within two months, Mr. Boyle was replaced. His replacement was Brother Jerome, who didn't seem to have much of an appreciation for history, but did have a deep appreciation for keeping order.

History class became reviewing the answers to the questions at the end of each chapter. Almost every night we were assigned questions at the end of the chapter and in class we would go over the answers. The great events of the planet were reduced to matching columns and fill-in-the-blank questions. History class was just something to get through every day. I almost never read the chapter. I either copied the homework from Paul or Ray Frasene or did my homework by scanning the chapter for the answers.

Biology was my second highest grade, but not because I was learning anything. Mr. Dolce was a strange man. He lectured every day and covered a lot of material. He even conducted the lab sessions. Yet at the end of the year, he still needed to look at his seating chart to call a student by name. He could have lectured to a painting of a class.

The reason I was doing well was simple. Mr. Dolce gave the same exam to his third period class as he did to us in seventh period. By the time we took the test, we knew what was on it. Most of the time, Jay Carroll would brief me before or during fourth period study hall and I would review the material until seventh period. Jay had a friend in third period Bio. who gave him a note that listed the areas the exam covered. My fifth period class was

Religion with Brother Arthur O'Brien. This was a complete waste of an hour, except that it gave me time to bone up for Biology exams.

Mr. Dolce once remarked while returning exam papers to us that our class did quite well on it, "much better than my morning class." We all laughed. Obviously Jay wasn't the only one who had a friend in the morning class.

My notion of going to college and becoming an engineer was still alive. Brother David Murray was an excellent teacher and I was learning Geometry. Although I only had a 79 for the first half of the year, Brother David was a very tough grader and I was learning it.

I still had a problem with concentrating for long periods of time and often I would have the correct answer, but lose some points for not having shown every step of the process, or for not stating the theorem correctly. Brother David knew I knew the work but he also knew that I lacked discipline. I often complained about my grades on his exams.

After Brother David returned the mid-term exams, I waited around after class to talk to him.

"Brother, you're killing me with your grading," I began. "I want to go to college, but I'm afraid I won't get in because of my grades. Don't you think you're being a little nit-picky?" I held up my paper for him to look at.

"I want you to go to college, Joe. You can definitely do college level work. I grade hard because I want you to work hard so you really learn this stuff. A high SAT score in Math will be a big plus for you."

"SAT score?"

"That's the College Board exam."

"Oh. Can't I do that with higher grades? I am working hard and I know this stuff."

"I know you get it. I know you're always with me in class, but you're sloppy on exams. I want you to earn higher grades by being more disciplined. Geometry is like logic; you can't leave out steps and arrive at the correct conclusion. You must prove your conclusion by showing the logic and defining your terms. Keep working hard and it will become automatic."

"But Brother, in the meantime, these grades are going in my permanent record," I laughed. The nuns had often used the threat on me of putting things in my "Permanent Record," so now I laughed at my using it on Brother David.

"Remember college is a means to an end, not an end in itself," he replied.

"How's that?"

"Going to college is the way to get an education; to learn; to become an educated man. Going to college is the means, not the goal."

"It's my goal right now."

"And I want to help you get there and succeed when you do."

I smiled and said I had to get to my next class, but I acted skeptical about his argument, hoping he would be more charitable about my test grades in the future. When I got out in the hall, Glenn was waiting for me.

"Did he change your grade?" asked Glenn hopefully, since he too had hopes of a better grade.

"Nah."

"I didn't think he would," said Glenn, disappointedly.

"Brother David's cool, though," I said, half to Glenn and half to myself.

"He sure is," answered Glenn. "He really knows what's going on."

In fact, Brother David was having a big impact on me. He was the first teacher at Holy Cross to show an interest in me personally and in my future. I always did my homework and came to his class prepared. I was attentive in class and studied hard for his exams. It was a strange never-felt-before experience. It was almost as if I didn't want to let him down.

CHAPTER THIRTEEN

◆ ◆ ◆ ◆ ◆

"THE DUKES OF EARL"

And you've got to learn to live with what you can't rise above.
Bruce Springsteen—"Tunnel of Love"

My dissatisfaction continued in the second half of the sophomore year as well. A new teacher, Mr. Walsh, replaced Brother Jerome, who had been pressed into duty when Mr. Boyle was fired or quit—we never did find out the truth. Mr. Walsh was a young, good-looking, Irish guy who was pretty cool, and had the potential to be a good teacher. The problem now was he was inexperienced, didn't have time to prepare, was new to Holy Cross, and was told that lack of control of the classroom was what got his predecessor blown out of the job.

It's hard to believe that a teacher could have classroom management problems at Holy Cross. If things like recognition, participation in class, positive reinforcement, parental involvement, lowering of grades or worse, flunking, and having to go to summer school, threatening, verbally abusing, detention, indefinite detention, written punishments, suspensions, and being banned from extracurricular school activities didn't work, there was always physical abuse, and expulsion. If you had a complaint, the answer was almost always, "Then go somewhere else."

We were the largest class ever to hit Holy Cross and the Diocese of Brooklyn, and all the Catholic schools were bursting at the seams. Almost all our parents sent us to and paid for Catholic high school for one main reason—*Discipline* They actually *wanted* us to be brutalized and tortured! They thought it was good for us, and that it was what we deserved. To them, things must have looked bleaker than for us. They had fought in the 'Great' World War, the War to end all Wars, suffered through the Great Depression, wanted, and believed in a better world for their kids.

What they were experiencing was the constant threat of nuclear holocaust and the Russians looking down on us from space and threatening to colonize the moon, gang violence and drugs in our cities, growing racial tension and unrest, girls wearing shorter and tighter clothing, guys letting their hair grow, and the increasing popularity of Rock-and-Roll.

My sisters and I all loved Rock and listened to it constantly on the radio and increasingly, Rock music was invading television as well. Elvis got quite a reaction from my parents when he was on the Ed Sullivan Show. Jerry Lee Lewis even had my father threatening to limit what we were allowed to watch. But the night when he saw Little Richard singing 'Tutti Frutti,' he went into orbit! He jumped out of his chair and snapped off the TV.

"This is my house. I pay the bills and you are not watching that degenerate in my house."

In spite of our protests, he was adamant about it. After he left the room, we all laughed about it, and my sister Ronnie turned the TV back on, knowing Little Richard would be done with his song. My father heard the TV on and yelled down the basement stairs.

"What did I tell you kids?"

"Little Richard's over; can't we watch the other stuff?" Ronnie asked.

"If I see or hear *'that nut'* again, I'll take a tube out of the set and you won't be able to watch anything, you hear me?"

"Yeah, we hear you."

We laughed and resumed watching, but we all dove for the volume knob when Little Richard was brought back later in the show to do "Good Golly, Miss Molly." Ronnie and Maureen watched without volume, while I went upstairs to make sure Dad wasn't around where he could hear it or make a sudden appearance. When I returned, they were laughing hysterically at what Dad's reaction would be to what they were watching. Little Richard was jumping all over the stage, dressed in a sequined cape, and high-heeled leather boots that went to the knee, and wearing a turban with sequins!

"Where's Dad?" whispered Maureen.

"He's up in the bedroom," I answered.

"That's good, because this would give him a heart attack."

Anyway, Mr. Walsh, because of the classroom management issue, overdid the somber, tough-guy routine and History became just another boring, uninspiring class.

Much worse, however, was that Brother David was also replaced for some unknown reason. His replacement was Brother Francis Ellis. Brother Francis was a large, muscular, slope-shouldered, homely man who moved awkwardly. I don't know what was wrong with him, but he moved as if he had a permanently stiff neck, and spoke—usually a mumble—out of the side of his mouth, with a light lisp. He often grunted and stared blankly out the window or at the class when waiting for a response. It wasn't long before he was dubbed 'Quasimodo.'

It was hard for me to accept the fact that the best teacher I had known up to that time, and the only one who ever mentioned my future without a scowl or a reference to eternal damnation, was suddenly gone, and replaced by The Missing Link.

Quasi's teaching skills were not finely honed, and he had a few classroom management problems. At the slightest provocation, he would charge down the aisle, making snorting noises, and pummel whoever had made him angry. We sat in what we called student chairs. They were movable metal chairs with an arm on the right hand side and a desktop anchored to the arm. One day Charlie Skupeen and Rob Sikorski were laughing about something in class. Quasimodo saw them and got ticked off. He suddenly bolted down the aisle, snorting and grunting, and grabbed the front of Skupeen's desktop with both hands and lifted. Charlie screamed, "Jesus!" as he crashed on his back, still in his desk.

"Jesus Christ! Are you nuts?" yelled a stunned Skupeen, as he rolled out of his chair, and scrambled to his feet, rubbing his head, which had hit the floor hard. Quasi just glared at him—expressionless for a moment, then pointed at the door. Skupeen left. The rest of the class period went very smoothly.

After class, when we met up with Skupeen, he was furious.

"That fuckin' guy is *nuts*! I could have fractured my skull."

"You're right," said Glenn. "That was outrageous. You should sue him."

"Ya' know, I thought about that while I was waiting in the lavatory for class to be over. If he was a lay teacher I would, but since he's a Brother and doesn't have anything, there is nothing I can win. I'd get kicked out of school and even if I won the suit, there is nothing I can gain."

"Then sue the school," responded Glenn.

"That's suing the Catholic Church. Let's see—Charlie Skupeen vs. The Catholic Church . . . that'll work."

As upset as I was at losing Brother David as my teacher, I realized the importance of geometry, kept working hard at it, and miraculously managed to avoid being the object of one of Quasimodo's rages.

Not so with Brother Regis, however. Latin had been really wearing me down in the final months of my Latin 'experience.' Two years was all that was required and *all* that *I* would be taking. Not only did I find foreign language very difficult in general, but Latin specifically seemed to be a complete waste of time and effort. "Shouldn't we be learning Russian?" I would often say, half in jest and half serious. "It might be helpful when the Communists take over and put us in work camps." My friends would laugh, but I was sick and tired of Latin and sick and tired of Brother Regis's mood swings and abuse.

Tommy Taraci also hated Latin and was sick of the time and effort it took. He had been lucky enough to avoid Brother Regis for two consecutive years. His Latin teacher was Brother John Capistran. Brother John was a very slightly built, small, soft-spoken, pious man, who always seemed to be under a lot of stress. He was the faculty sponsor of the Photography Club and, I'm sure, was more comfortable in the woods alone taking pictures, than in a classroom teaching.

He was particularly inept at dealing with a smart-ass like Tommy. Capistran knew Tommy was always making smart remarks under his breath or with his hand to his mouth, but he seldom caught him. He knew Tommy rarely knew the answers in class, but always did okay on the exams. Tommy was always copying someone else's homework in study hall, and after an exam would say, "Thank God for George Trampler!" who sat next to him in class and helped him on exams. One day when Capistran was giving back exam papers, he handed back Tommy's and, as he did, said, "You would do better, Mr. Taraci, if you kept up with the work daily and didn't *cram* for exams."

As Tommy turned to come back to his seat, his back was to Capistran and, just as he reached his desk, he said, just loud enough for those around him to hear, "and *you* would do better if you *crammed* this up your ass." Of course, the group who heard it broke up laughing and Capistran was upset. He made Tommy stay after class and demanded to know what Tommy had said to make everyone around him laugh. Tommy insisted that he had said nothing, and that they must have been looking at the face he made when he saw his grade.

"What kind of face did you make, Taraci?"

"I think I kinda winced in shock, Brother."

Capistran let him go, unpunished, but once again was suspicious and unable to catch Tommy. He was becoming increasingly frustrated.

One of Brother Capistran's frustrations with Tommy was that he was late almost every day. Tommy had Latin first period and took a strange bus route—I believe it was the Q48, one that was often behind schedule. It didn't matter much to the city, because it lost most of its time around Bayside High School and only had two stops left. Tommy got off at the last stop and still had to walk a few blocks to school.

There were very few Holy Cross guys on the bus and every time it was late, they went to the principal's office for a late pass. Normally, being late meant detention after school, but in the case of this chronic bus problem, Brother Josephat gave them passes without requiring detention. This had become so routine by spring that Tommy would stop at the Office, get his late pass, and rather than go to Latin class, he would wait until it was almost over. He would then go to class, give Brother Capistran his late slip, and miss all but a few minutes of class. He particularly did this when he didn't have his homework. Capistran would collect the previous night's homework at the beginning of class and when Tommy wasn't there, Capistran would often forget to ask him for it or would tell him to hand it in at the end of class and Tommy would just leave and Capistran would forget.

On a few occasions, Capistran would remember that he forgot to ask Tommy for the previous day's homework. Tommy would swear that he handed it in, just as he did in eighth grade. He would be so adamant about it that Capistran would let it go and mutter stuff to himself in frustration. We all loved hearing about Tommy's antics in Latin class, and his prediction that someday, Capistran would have a stroke.

Then one day Tommy was late, as usual, and he hadn't done his homework, so he went outside to wait until Latin class was almost over before going to class. A few times in recent weeks, Tommy had done this and when outside, he would go to where he could be seen from the classroom and wave at Ritchie Capone, who sat by the window. Capone would get a big kick out of seeing

Tommy outside waiting for class to be near the end. Tommy stood far enough down the block that you couldn't see him unless you were facing forward like Capone, and thus, it was unlikely Capistran would see him.

On this day, however, as Tommy was waving to Capone, Capone didn't wave back. Tommy waved again, this time with more enthusiasm, thinking Capone hadn't seen him. Capone had seen him and wasn't responding because Capistran was in the back of the room watching some student working on the blackboard in the front. Tommy started waving and jumping around gleefully trying to get Capone's attention and instead, gets Capistran's.

The next thing Tommy saw was Capistran at the window, motioning with his index finger for Tommy to come into class. Tommy hurried to the classroom, figuring his prank was discovered, and he was royally screwed. When he got in the building, he found Capistran out in the hallway looking for him. "Don't you dare go to the office, Mister!" Capistran yelled, when he saw Tommy coming.

"Excuse me, Brother?"

"Don't you dare go get a late pass," answered Capistran, red-faced and obviously agitated. "Get into this classroom *now*!" he yelled, pointing to the door.

As Tommy walked past Brother Capistran, he yelled, "I'll see you in detention tonight, Taraci!"

It was then that Tommy realized that he wasn't as screwed as he thought. Capistran obviously thought that Tommy was just arriving at school and hadn't gone to the office for a late pass, when in fact, he had gotten a late pass a good half hour ago. If Brother Josephat, the principal, discovered what Tommy had been doing, he would have crucified him outside the main entrance, so we could all see him hanging there as we left school. Now Tommy saw a chance to avoid involving Brother Josephat.

"Okay, Brother," he said in a conciliatory tone, "I'm sorry."

"Sorry doesn't cut it, mister. I'm so sick and tired of you and your smart-aleck attitude. You think I'm a fool, don't you, Mr. Taraci?"

"No, Brother."

"Yes, you do! You think this class is a joke and I'm a fool and I'm sick and tired of it. You're always making smart remarks in class and mocking me, aren't you, Taraci?"

"No, Brother."

"Don't deny it! I know it's true! Don't play me for a fool, Taraci!"

"I'm sorry, Brother."

"You're sorry? You're sorry?"

"Yes, Brother."

"What are you sorry for?"

"I'm sorry you feel that way."

"Give me your homework!"

Tommy started fumbling around in his books, looking for non-existent homework, and Capistran continued to rant, while the class sat stunned by Brother John Capistran's fit of rage.

"Give me your homework!"

Tommy figured there was no point in continuing the charade and confessed.

"I don't have it, Brother."

"Give me your homework!"

"I don't have it, Brother," Tommy repeats softly.

"*Give . . . it . . . to . . . me . . . Taraci*," Brother Capistran said slowly through clenched teeth.

Tommy was unsure what to do now. He wanted to avoid any escalation of hostility and obviously Capistran was seriously upset. He fumbled around in his books, pretending to look, while Capistran stood over him, all red-faced, and with his eyes bugging out. Tommy knew not to make eye contact with any of the other guys in class for fear he would laugh. Capone was doing his best not to break up. He had his elbow on his desk and his mouth in the palm of his hand, stifling his laughter.

"Give it to me!" Brother Capistran insisted.

"If I had it, I'd give it to you," said Tommy in a reassuring tone, not knowing what else to say.

"What?" answered Capistran, as if he hadn't been paying attention.

"*If I had it*, I would give it to you, Brother."

Ritchie Capone finally breaks down completely, as do many others, and the bell rings signifying the end of class.

The bell seems to snap Capistran out of a trance, and he tells Tommy he would mark him down as not having done his homework and walks back to his desk. The class leaves and Tommy leaves with them. He is greatly relieved that he apparently avoided disaster, but he is worried about Capistran's comment about seeing him in detention. Tommy is worried that Capistran will check on detention or try to find him in detention and Tommy wouldn't be there, since his lateness was excused. He finally decided to be late for his seventh period class on purpose, so that he would get detention and be there in case Capistran is there or checks up on him. He knew he couldn't just show up for detention and tell whatever Brother, usually Brother Richard McDonald, that although he wasn't on the detention list, he *wanted* detention. So, after school, Tommy went to detention for about an hour, but there was no sign of Capistran.

The next day, Tommy was on time for Latin class, but Brother Capistran was not. Capistran missed class that day and the next and the next, until Brother Franciscus Willet took over the class permanently. We never did find out why Capistran was suddenly replaced, but Tommy gladly accepted credit for it and his already-pronounced swagger got even bigger.

My Latin problem however, didn't turn out as well. One day in early spring, Brother Regis, whose full name was Brother Francis Regis Crowley, called on me in class, and I didn't know the answer. The question had something to do with the pluperfect tense, which I never really understood. After not giving the correct answer, Brother Regis began calling me a *pinguay caput*.

"You're a *pinguay caput*, Farrell, a *pinguay caput*, a real fathead. You understand?"

I just looked at him silently, hoping he would move on, but he didn't.

"Do they call you Fathead Farrell? Huh? Do they? Do your friends call you Fathead Farrell? When they see you coming, do they say, 'here comes Fathead Farrell'? They ought to."

Brother Regis was so moody that I didn't know how to react. If I laughed it off, which was my instinct, he might think I'm being flippant and go into a rage, which he frequently did. So I just sat there quietly and expressionless and he continued to rant and mock me.

"Does your family call you Fathead, Farrell? Huh? Do they?"

"No, Brother."

"Well, maybe they should. Maybe we all should. I think we should all call you Fathead from now on. That's what I'm gonna do from now on. I'm gonna call you Fathead Farrell from now on."

Brother Regis finally looked away and called on someone else, but as he did, I muttered softly, "and I'll call you 'Fucked up Francis.'" Paul Falabella and Jay Carroll heard it and were laughing and stifling laughter when Brother Regis saw them. He knew something had happened and flew into a rage at Paul.

"Something funny, Falabella?" he screamed.

"No, Brother."

"You're laughing at nothing, you moron?"

"Yes, Brother."

"Don't 'Yes, Brother' me. You tell me what you're laughing at or you'll be very sorry."

Regis had a scowl on his face and I had a sick feeling inside. I kept thinking that Paul should say he called me 'fathead' and maybe Regis would let it go. But Paul was frozen in fear.

"You better start talking, boy, or you're gonna feel the wrath of God come down on you."

"I didn't say anything, Brother," Paul answered.

"What were you laughing at? Mr. Carroll was laughing too, so someone said something funny and I want to hear it."

Now Jay's face was reddening and a terrible look of doom was starting to show up on his face.

"I didn't say anything, Brother," answered Paul firmly, as if that was all he was going to say and the matter was closed.

"How about you, Carroll? Are you the comedian?"

"Me, Brother?" answered Jay, acting shocked.

"Don't pull that bullshit on me!" screamed Regis.

"It was me, Brother," I suddenly said resolutely.

"Oh, well isn't that nice, Farrell. What did you say that made these geniuses laugh?"

"I made a smart remark about being a fathead."

"Tell us all what you said. We all like to laugh."

"I don't remember what it was, Brother."

"You remember. You're just a coward. You're gutless. See me after class, Farrell. I'll take care of you."

After class, Brother Regis gave me a book that the third year Latin class was using. It was a story about the Gaullic Wars. He told me to translate the entire story for homework. If I failed to complete the assignment by class time tomorrow, I would get an 'F' for the marking period. It was basically an impossible assignment.

When I left class and arrived at study hall, I told the guys what had happened. Jay Carroll, Paul Falabella, and Ray Frasene all offered to help me, but I was disconsolate. It was obvious I couldn't do it myself, and if others helped me, Brother Regis would probably suspect I had help. Jay had already figured out that each of the guys would have to translate certain parts and I would have to recopy it in my own handwriting.

I thought about it during the rest of our half-period study hall and we talked again during lunch, but Latin class was third period and there wouldn't be enough time to even copy what the guys had translated for me. I told them I appreciated their offers, but now I was trying to decide whether to spend any time at all on it or just not do any of it. If it was impossible to complete or even nearly complete, than what would be gained by wasting time on a small part of it?

During my sixth period study hall, I worked on homework for the next day while I tried to decide about the punishment. Just before the bell rang,

Paul had asked to see the book Regis had assigned, and I had given it to him. After study hall, he gave me a translation of the first pages of the story.

"You saved my ass," said Paul. "I want to help you out if I can."

"I didn't *save* your ass, I actually *got* you in trouble!"

"You could have let me hang out there. I was prepared to take whatever that lunatic dished out."

"I know you were. Thanks."

Paul and Jay and Ray all felt bad for me and were sincere in their offers to help me. It made me feel really good, despite an overlay of depression. I would much rather have gotten smacked or have gotten detention than to have something hanging over me like this.

After school, I went straight home and started on the punishment. I recopied what Paul had done and then started to translate on my own. It was difficult for me, but I didn't care much about accuracy. I tried to follow the story and made up some of the lines, based on what I thought was happening. Even so, it was a slow process, and I would never be able to finish it, or even come close to finishing it. What kept me going was the belief that if I had a decent number of pages to hand in, Brother Regis would be placated and this episode would blow over. I was sure he wouldn't really give me an 'F' for the marking period as long as I didn't antagonize him and didn't get in any further trouble.

At dinner, my mother sensed something was wrong and started in on me. She had obviously told my father that I had come home directly from school, which was unusual in and of itself, and that I had been doing schoolwork ever since, which is even *more* unusual.

"So, what's going on with you? You in some kind of trouble?" she asked me as I started to eat.

"No. Why?"

"How come you came right home from school?"

"I just have a lot of homework."

"You better be telling the truth or you'll be sorry. You won't see the light of day if you bring a bad report card home."

"Don't worry about it."

"*I'm* not gonna worry about it. *You* better worry about it. We spend good money to send you to Holy Cross. Money we don't have. You and Ronnie cost us over $60 a month in tuition. Your father goes without lunch sometimes to make ends meet."

"You go without lunch?" I asked, looking at my father.

"It's okay. I need to lose some weight," he answered, as if he didn't want in on this argument.

"Well, what do you want from me? Why are you on my ass? Because I came home from school and did homework?" I asked, incredulously.

"Well, all of a sudden, you have homework? We never see you with a book. You play basketball two nights a week; you don't come home from Mueller's 'til six o'clock, you watch television every night . . ."

"So what?"

"So you better not bring home a bad report card or be in some trouble of some kind. I know something's up and I'm just warning you."

Ronnie changed the subject by returning to the issue of my dad not eating lunch. She was deeply upset at the thought of our father being deprived of lunch.

"I eat lunch," said my father. "I just cut back some."

"What do you eat?" pressed Ronnie.

"I have a bowl of soup."

"Is that all?"

"That's plenty. I need to lose some weight."

"You do not."

"Look, Ronnie, if I wanted more, I'd eat it. All I ask is that you kids do well in school. *That's* the point—not my lunch."

While Ronnie and I did the dishes and cleaned up after dinner, Ronnie asked me quietly if I was in some kind of trouble. I explained to her what had happened and she expressed her shock and sympathy.

"You shouldn't react to Brother Regis that way."

"Yeah, yeah, yeah, I know," I answered quickly, dismissively.

When I went back to my room, I was angry. I was angry at myself, at Brother Regis, and at my mother. How did I get in such a mess? I hit the Latin assignment with renewed intensity, which waned after an hour or so because of the futility of it. I wrote large and tried to fill up as many sheets of paper as I could. I was looking up key words and making up the translation as best I could.

The next day when Latin began, I didn't bring the punishment up and neither did Brother Regis. At the end of class, I approached him with the punishment papers in my hand. He held his hand straight out to receive them. He turned, and holding them at arm's length, asked, without looking at me, if I finished the whole story.

"No, Brother. I tried, but I couldn't get it all done."

The second I answered, he opened his hand over the wastepaper can in the corner of the room and dropped the papers into it.

There was an awkward silence as Brother Regis blew his nose and I stood there dumbfounded. Finally, I asked if he wanted me to continue to work on it.

"Sorry, Farrell, you know the consequences."

"But, Brother, it was impossible . . ."

"If I were you, I'd leave now!"

I did leave and for over two weeks, I sweated out the possibility that Brother Regis would flunk me. During that period I caused no more trouble and did my homework (or at least copied it) and paid attention in class. I really believed that if I gave him no further reason, he would forget about his threat.

I took the exam at the end of the marking period and waited for report cards to be mailed out. Brother Regis never brought it up again and I certainly wasn't going to remind him. Then one day when I arrived home, I saw my report card lying on the dining room table. When I took a look at it, I felt like I was a character in the Hitchcock movie, "*Vertigo.*" All I saw was the 'F.'

A large, spinning F. My breath was short, I had tunnel vision, I became lightheaded, and went momentarily deaf. My mother was suddenly there and her mouth was moving and making noises, but I didn't hear what she said. I walked slowly upstairs to my room and fell onto my bed. I laid there in the dark, and cursed out Brother Regis, until Ronnie came to tell me dinner was ready.

"Boy, are you in trouble."

"Yeah, I know. Is Dad upset?"

"Mom's getting him upset."

"I hate her."

"Well, you can't expect them to not be upset at an F on a report card."

"Yeah, well, I'll be down in a minute."

SOPHOMORES-C.P.	1	2	3	1	2	3	SM AV	SM AV	YR AV	CR	E			1	2	3	1	2	3	SM AV	SM AV	YR AV	CR
RELIGION 2					78							ART											
ENGLISH 2					90							BAND											
WORLD HISTORY					82							GLEE CLUB											
MATH. 10					73							TYPING											
LATIN 2					F							GYM											
BIOLOGY					91																		

FARRELL, JOSEPH W.   8-19-46-64
MR. JOSEPH FARRELL   VERONICA
30-25 MURRAY LANE   FL-9-5756
FLUSHING 54, N. Y.   ST.AND.AV.

DAYS ABSENT

TIMES TARDY

HOLY CROSS HIGH SCHOOL — 26-20 Francis Lewis Blvd., Flushing 58, New York — Tel: IN 1-7900

Exhibit 'A'—Spring 1962

I went down to dinner, and within minutes, they started in on me. No more basketball on school nights, no television on school nights, and I

201

was to come straight home from school every day from now on and do my homework.

"Are you gonna check it to see if it's correct?" I asked, sarcastically, knowing they would have no idea.

"Keep being a smart ass and we'll make it worse!"

"Yeah, well, I don't deserve this punishment and I'm not gonna take it."

"What do you mean?" asked my dad.

"I didn't get the F because I didn't know the work. I got it for a wisecrack I made in class."

"What kind of wisecrack?"

"Brother Regis called me a fathead and I made a wisecrack and he told me I'd get an F for it. It's not because I didn't know the work or didn't do my homework."

"So what? You got an F for whatever the reason," chimed in my mother.

"That's right! Don't be such a smart-ass in school," added Dad.

"What about him calling me a fathead and mocking me in class?"

"He's the teacher!" yelled Mom. "He can do whatever he wants. *You*'re the student. You do what you're told to."

"Okay, I'm not arguing that! I'm . . ."

"Lower your voice when you talk to your mother," my dad said, somberly.

"I'm just saying that it's not that I need to study more or because I didn't do my homework," I said softly.

"So?"

"So, I shouldn't have to forfeit basketball and TV and come directly home after school."

"You got an F!" screamed Mom. "You think you can get an F and just prance around unfazed?"

"You could use more time to devote to school, after all these grades aren't so hot," Dad said.

"I got two 90s!"

"And two 70s. One in Religion. How hard can that be?"

I was getting frustrated and tried a different approach to my dad.

"I'm supposed to go to school all day, come straight home, do schoolwork and then no television. I get no fun at all, all week?"

"Yeah, what fun do I get?"

"Any fun you want!"

Ronnie tried to come to my aid, but my mother shut her down quickly.

"You butt out, ducky, or you'll be included; only it'll be no *telephone* for you."

That was enough for Ronnie. "Well, I think you're being unfair," she said, ending her involvement.

"See? Even Ronnie agrees," I said, smiling, trying to lighten up the situation. "It's not fair."

"It's fair," said Dad. "This will give you time to work on getting your grades up with fewer distractions."

"You can't make me study!"

"No, but I can make you wish you did."

"It will give you more time to think about your lousy attitude, you snot nose," Mom chimed in loudly. "You need to be taken down a peg or two. You've got *some* nerve, arguing with us after getting an F on your report card!"

"I'm trying to explain it to you, but . . ."

"Lower your voice when you talk to your mother," Dad warned again.

"Who do you think you are?" Mom screamed. "You lousy bastard. No wonder Brother flunked you. You stink!"

"Okay, let's all calm down," Dad said, raising his hands, palms out. "Joey, you screwed up and you have to accept your punishment. End of discussion!"

"I know I screwed up and the F *was* my punishment and even that was unfair!"

"Well, that might have been the *school's* punishment, but now *we're* punishing you too. That's it! I don't need this shit. I work like a dog all day."

"I won't do it!" I yelled, my anger and frustration escalating.

"You son-of-a-bitch!" Mom screamed, shaking her fist at me. "You'll do it all right! So help me God, you'll do it!"

"We'll see," I said as I got up and stomped out of the kitchen and back to my room. I laid on the bed in the dark in a rage. I could hear my heart beating through the mattress as I laid on my side. "I'm not accepting this" was all I could think of. "I will not accept this punishment." I stayed there all night. The next day was Friday and since it wasn't a school night, the normal routine wasn't disrupted. In the morning, I avoided any contact with my mother and left for school without speaking to her.

At dinner Friday night, I didn't say much. My parents were involved in conversation and I ate quickly—macaroni, cheese, and fish sticks—and got ready to go out. The usual gang was meeting at Mueller's. When I arrived there, Tommy, Dennis, Jeff, and Dickie were outside on the sidewalk singing "The Duke of Earl," the Gene Chandler hit that was surging up the charts. Tommy was singing the lead and the others were arguing and struggling to get the backup part correct.

I stood watching and laughing for a minute or two, when Tommy said, "Joe, come on, we need your help—these fools keep messing up."

"Nah, I'm too depressed to sing. I'll go get the booze. Give me your money and your order."

"We got ours," answered Dennis, "but wait for Eddie, he probably will want some.

"Okay, I'll wait for him."

"Why are you depressed?" Dennis inquired.

"I got an F on my report card. Didn't these guys tell you?"

"No. You got an F?" In what?"

"Latin."

"Oh! From Fucking Francis? I remember now!"

"Fucked *up* Francis," I corrected.

"He gave you an F. That's fucked up. I'm glad I don't go there. Did your mother go nuts?"

"Yeah."

"I figured."

"Why?"

"'Cause I know your mom and she's the type to go nuts."

"Wouldn't your mom?"

"Nah. She would if my sister got an F, but not me. That's part of your problem. You need to lower your parents' expectations. Sorta like Dickie did."

"I did what?" perked up Dickie, hearing his name mentioned.

"You lowered your family's expectations last year."

"Fuck you, Geoghan!"

"Hey, I'm just trying to help out Joe. His mom went nuts."

"What'd she do?" asked Dickie.

"She ranted and raved and screamed and carried on."

"Big deal."

"And I can't go to Mueller's after school, can't go to basketball on school nights and no television on school nights."

"Okay, that *is* a big deal."

"I'm not doing it," I said, as if reassuring myself.

"Well, I'm proud of you, my man," proclaimed Dickie. "Keep it up and soon you'll be with me in Section H. You could be a *star* in Section H. We got Sammy Magarelli and Eddie Hodges? You could dazzle everyone with your *superior* intellect. We'd love to have you. The teachers don't expect much either, down in Section H. It's like the 'Ghetto of Holy Cross.'"

Just then, Eddie arrives and I tell him I'm ready for a visit to the liquor store and ask what he wants me to get him.

"Get me a half pint of Fleishman's Whiskey," he said, handing me some money, "but wait a minute."

"Hey Eddie, Joe got an F on his report card," yelled Dennis, laughing.

"Did you?" asked Eddie, looking at me with a big smile.

"Yeah."

"No shit! An F on your permanent record?"

"Yeah," I shrugged. "I don't see the humor."

"Your parents go nuts?"

"Yeah, wouldn't yours?"

"My mom would, but not my dad."

"Let's talk on the move," I said, indicating I was anxious to get to the liquor store.

"Just a second. Hey you guys!" Eddie yelled to get everyone's attention. "My parents went out and nobody's home for a while. Wanna go to my house and hang around in the basement?"

Everyone thought it was a good idea and since the liquor story was on the way, we all started walking down 162nd Street, toward Eddie's house. As we are walking, Tommy, Dickie, Jeff, and Dennis are still working on "Duke of Earl."

> *Duke, Duke, Duke, Duke of Earl, Duke, Duke, Duke of Earl,*
> *Duke, Duke, Duke of Earl, Duke, Duke, Duke of Earl,*
> *Duke, Duke, Duke of Earl, Duke, Duke, Duke of Earl,*
> *Duke, Duke, Duke of Earl, Duke, Duke, Duke of Earl, (continues throughout song)*
>
> *As I-I-I-I walk through this world*
> *Nothing can stop, the Duke of Ear-ear-earl!*
> *And no one can hurt you, oh no-o*
>
> *Yes-a, I . . . oh I'm gonna love you, oh, hoh*
> *Come on let me hold you darling*
> *'Cause I'm the Duke of Ear-ear-earl*
> *And-a yay-yay-yay-yay, yeah-eah*

This was as far as they got because the background singing got complicated and whoever was supposed to do bom, bom duh duh, in a low bass voice, followed by ba ba bom, ba ba bum, ba ba baba bum, always screwed up and they'd argue over it and argue over who could do it correctly. As depressed as I was, it cracked me up.

Jeff would screw it up and Dickie would argue to let him do it and Jeff would insist he did it right. Dickie would try it and leave out a ba ba, and everyone would laugh. Jeff got another shot and swore he got it right, but all the others would say his timing was off. Dennis is yelling, "I was in the choir at St. Andrew's—I can do it!"

"I got it, I got it," insisted Dickie. "Let's go right now."

Tommy started over, but as the complicated part arrived, everybody broke up laughing at the look on Dickie's face.

"I had it, but I lost it because Jeff distracted me!"

"How?" asked Jeff.

"You're singing too loud, asshole. You're supposed to blend in the background with Dennis and me."

We made slow progress, but eventually arrived at the liquor store.

"Hey, what about Billy?" I suddenly remembered that Billy was going to be late and that we were supposed to leave word at Mueller's as to where he could find us.

"I'll run back and tell Marge where we're going, while you buy the booze," offered Eddie.

"What about something for him to drink?"

"Get another half of something and if he doesn't want it, I'll drink it, or we'll split it."

When I came out of the liquor store, Tommy was expressing his frustration to Jeff, who had apparently just screwed up the opening line of the song by leaving out one "Duke."

"It's four 'Dukes' Jeff, then *three*. I can't believe you screwed that up! We're getting worse instead of better. I'd like to get past the first verse, for Chrissake!"

"Four 'Dukes,' then three 'Dukes.' I got it. Three each time?"

"Yes. Each time. You had it before."

"Yeah, before I started drinking."

Just then Eddie returned and had Billy with him. Everybody greets Billy and we started walking to Eddie's house."

"You're not as late as you thought you'd be," I said. "I got you a half pint of Fleishman's."

"No, I made my parents hurry up through dinner so I could get out. I had just walked into Mueller's and asked Marge where you guys were. She said 'they were outside singing a few minutes ago.' Just then, Eddie came in. Thanks for the Fleishman's."

The "Duke of Earl" chorus began again and a nice-looking girl turned the corner and walked toward us. When Tommy saw her, he got down on one knee, and sang to her as she approached. The girl smiled, but abruptly crossed the street, rather than walk past us. We all laughed at Tommy.

"Hey," Tommy yells at the girl, "is that any way to treat a guy on bended knee?"

She laughed, but kept walking.

We soon reached Eddie's house, but before we went in, Tommy wanted to try the song one more time. Billy, Eddie, and I watched as Tommy gave instructions as to who is gonna do the deep bass part and reviewed a few cues, including reminding Jeff of the "four Dukes, then three Dukes. As they started up again, Jeff counted the Dukes on his fingers with a dumb look on his face and everyone cracked up.

Once we get inside to Eddie's basement, we all started drinking our liquor and Jeff proposed a toast to me.

"Let's have a toast to Joe's F."

"What's he talking about?" asked Billy.

"Joe got an F on his report card," answered Dennis, as if it was something to celebrate.

"No shit? In what?"

"Latin," answered Dennis. "From Fucking Francis or Fucked Up Francis or whatever."

"Okay, everybody," yells Jeff, holding up his half pint of Southern Comfort. I hear the first one's the toughest. They'll be easier to accept from now on, right Dickie?"

"I swear, if you start on me, Jeff, I'll break this bottle on your head," answers Dickie.

"Empty or full?" asks Jeff.

"Wait and see, asshole!"

"I don't want you to waste any booze. I'll help you empty it first."

"Hey, everybody, listen up," Eddie suddenly calls for everyone's attention. "Don't go in the back room, please. My father has stuff in there that he doesn't allow anyone near. So stay outta there."

"Hey, Eddie, aren't you glad we don't go to Holy Cross? Holy Cross is fucked up. That's fucked up giving Joe an F and all. You got Fucked Up Francis and that guy Mousey who called *me* a liar."

"You *are* a liar," interjects Billy.

"*He* doesn't know that."

Eddie responds by listing some names of Bishop Laughlin teachers and administrators.

"Yeah, I guess you're right. Laughlin's no better, but at least we never got an F."

Billy looks at me and asks, "You got an F because you didn't do a punishment assignment right?"

"Yeah, sort of."

"So, it's a one-time thing, not because you're having trouble with Latin?"

"I'm sick and tired of Latin. I don't understand the latest shit, Pluperfect Tense . . . I just can't take it much longer."

"If you think you got it bad, try Greek!"

"Greek?" screamed Dennis. "You take Greek?"

"And Latin."

"Are you nuts or somethin'?"

"It's required at Brooklyn Prep."

"What the fuck for?" said Dennis. Of what use is Greek? That's stupid."

"It trains and develops your mind."

"You got a trained and developed mind?"

"Yeah, I do. We read the classics like the *Iliad* in Greek."

"Then why are you drinking cheap booze with us in Eddie's basement?"

Eddie put on the Duane Eddy album, "*Have Twangy Guitar, Will Travel*" and started jumping around and playing air guitar.

"Let's go get some girls and bring them back here," suggested Tommy.

"Okay, where?" I responded.

"If we knew where to find girls, we wouldn't be *here*" said Dickie.

"Eddie!" yelled Dennis.

"What?"

"Where can we find some girls to get over here?"

"We can't bring girls here. My parents will be home early. We should be out of here in an hour or so. I told them I might have a few guys over to listen to music. They said, 'no girls' and 'no drinking.'"

"So, what's the problem?" laughed Dennis, taking a sip from his bottle.

"If they came home right now, we could all leave quickly and I could deny we were drinking, but if they see girls, what can I say?"

"You can say they stopped by unexpectedly."

"Okay, then find some girls."

"Hey, Eddie," interrupted Dickie, "Jeff's in the back room."

"Hey, Baudo, get out of there, I'm serious!"

"What's so secret?" asked Jeff, as he came out of the back room.

"It's not a secret. It's my father's drawings and equipment."

"Drawings? Your father draws pictures?"

"Hey, yeah, Eddie—tell them about your dad," laughed Dennis. "Wait 'til you hear this!"

"My dad's studying for the Architect exam. That's where he studies and he has drawings and books and instruments laid out back there and he doesn't want anyone touching anything. That's all."

"Ask him if his dad ever took it before," prodded Dennis.

"Did your dad ever take it before?" asked Jeff.

"Thirteen times," answered Eddie, laughing.

"Thirteen times!"

"That's why I told Joe my mom would be mad if I ever got an F, but not my dad. My dad would understand."

"Thirteen times and he's still trying? Holy shit! He got thirteen Fs? I don't want to drive over any bridges he designs! Hey, Farrell, ya hear this?"

"Yeah?"

"Didn't your dad ever get an F?"

"I don't know—he never finished high school."

"*He never finished high school!*"

"Not everybody's dad could be a doctor, Jeff," interjected Tommy.

"What's your dad do, Tommy?"

"He's a healer."

"A healer," Jeff burst out laughing.

We all laugh, partly at Tommy's answer, but mostly at Jeff, who is holding his stomach, and gasping for air from laughing so hard. Tommy tried to look insulted, but couldn't help but laugh at Jeff and Dennis—who had a sip of whiskey in his mouth when Tommy answered, and is now red-faced from laughing, coughing, and trying to swallow, all at the same time.

"Does he heal cripples or what?" Jeff finally managed to ask, when he could breathe again.

"He heels shoes. He puts the heels on shoes in a factory, you creep!"

"Oh, I thought you meant he healed the sick."

"My father's dead, Jeff," chimed in Dickie. "That ought to give you a big laugh."

"I'm sorry, but I thought he meant his father was a faith healer."

Eddie cracked up as just then he realized why everybody else was laughing so hard.

"Hey, does he need to know Latin for that?" Dickie asked Tommy.

"No."

"There you go, Joe, you can be a heeler," adds Dennis.

"What does your father do?" I asked, looking at Dennis.

"He runs a package delivery service in Manhattan, called PDQ."

"A package delivery service? What does PDQ stand for?"

"Pretty Damn Quick."

"Are you kiddin'?"

"No, I'm not kiddin'!"

"That's the real name?"

"That's the name. My father knows Latin pretty good though, Joe. He was gonna call it "Veni, Vidi, Vici," but decided against it. You'd have a better shot with being a heeler."

"Or a healer," added Eddie, quickly.

"A better shot at what?" I asked, laughing.

"At . . . whaddayacallit . . . success!"

"I don't want to be a heeler, or deliver packages."

"What do you want to be?"

"I don't know—maybe an engineer."

"You don't need Latin to drive a train," said Jeff with a big smile, looking around, anticipating a big laugh.

"You do in Gaul," answered Tommy, trying to top Jeff's remark.

"All the train signals in Gaul are in Latin, as are the schedules. I just thought I'd point that out."

"Thank you, Tom, but . . ."

"So are the signs at the train stations."

"What signs?" asked Jeff.

"You know, 'Arrivals,' 'Departures,' 'Restrooms,' 'Danger—High Voltage'. All your basic signs."

"What were you saying, Joe?" asked Dennis.

"That's not the kind of engineer I meant."

"Also, the trains are named in Latin," continued Tommy.

"'Ave, Caesar' now arriving on Track Unus."

"I meant the kind of engineer that builds and designs things."

"Like Eddie's dad," said Dennis. "Hey Eddie, does your dad know Latin?"

"Actually, yeah," answered Eddie.

"Uh, oh, you're screwed," laughed Dennis.

"Wait a minute! You guys keep thinking that I don't know Latin, but that's not true! I got an F because I didn't do a punishment."

"Well, that's a whole other problem completely," responded Dennis.

"A much bigger problem," added Jeff.

"Why?"

"That's a mental problem. That's much more serious," said Dennis.

"You have an Authority Problem."

"Okay. Now we're getting somewhere," jumped in Dickie. "Your problem isn't Latin, it's *authority!*"

"I think you're right," added Jeff. "He's always resisting authority."

Tommy had a big smile on his face and said, "Maybe you can't drive a train, after all. You do have to *obey* the signals, ya know."

"You should talk," I said to Tommy. "You gave Capistran a stroke!"

"Now, wait a minute! We don't know that for sure. I'd like to take credit, but in all honesty . . ."

"I don't have an authority problem—I'm just sick of Brother Regis, 'cause he's nuts!" I replied, sharply.

"Is he?" asked Dennis, assuming the role of fact-finder. "Is Brother Regis nuts? Jeff, do you have Brother Regis?"

"No."

"Dickie, do you?"

"No."

"Tommy, do you?"

"No, but I'd like to get back to discussing important things."

"This *is* important. Don't you think Joe's mental problems are important?" asked Dennis.

"No," answered Tommy.

"What's more important?"

"How about where are we gonna find some girls?"

"My sister said that some of her friends were going to Mueller's after their sorority meeting," I offered. At that time in New York, high school girls often belonged to junior sororities. They had a pledging process and Greek names (Theta Beta Phi Zeta was my sister's) and met every other Friday at the house of a member.

"Let's go," said Eddie.

Eddie made sure we left with our empty whiskey bottles so his parents wouldn't find them and we started to make our way back to Mueller's. We weren't far before it started again: *Duke, Duke, Duke, Duke of Earl, Duke, Duke, Duke of Earl.*

CHAPTER FOURTEEN

♦ ♦ ♦ ♦ ♦

"IN MY ROOM"

Do my dreaming and my scheming
Lie awake and pray
Do my crying and my sighing
Laugh at yesterday.
The Beach Boys—"In My Room"

As luck would have it, the first week of my punishment, there was a Triduum at St. Andrew's. A Triduum is three consecutive nights of prayer and ceremony and a plenary indulgence is attached. A plenary indulgence meant that all of the temporal punishment due your soul was removed. Temporal punishment meant time in Purgatory. This was a glorious thing! If we attended the ceremony all three nights and went to Confession and Communion within seven days, all the punishment for all our sins was wiped clean. Since we were all heavily into mortal sin of the impure type, and all worried about the horrible suffering in the fires of Purgatory as a result, we were all going to the Triduum.

Although we worried mostly about going to hell for dying with an unforgiven mortal sin on our soul, it was entirely possible that a merciful and just God might not send us to hell for kissing and touching girls or more often, for *wanting* to kiss and touch them. It seemed so natural to want to. We wondered why God would give us such urges and then condemn us to the fires of hell for an eternity if we indulged them, *even* in thought! Most of us, like me, went to confession weekly and received Communion every Sunday. We had recently begun to joke about whoever went to Communion on Sunday had had a bad Saturday night, meaning he had struck out or come up empty in the pursuit of love. I would always point out that sin was in the will, as we were taught, and whether 'you got any' or not, it was just as much a sin to 'want any.'

So if we believed we had a chance of not going to hell, we knew the time in Purgatory was going to be substantial. Confession removed the sin from your soul and kept you out of hell, but did not remove the punishment due you for your sins. A plenary indulgence would wipe your soul clean of punishment. If you died after a plenary indulgence, you would go straight to heaven. And with the world teetering on the brink of nuclear war, that could easily happen. So this was indeed a golden opportunity, not merely to wipe clean all the punishment due to the mortal sins, but also due to the many venial sins as well—all the lying, cheating, and cursing.

Even my parents wouldn't deny me that opportunity. My mom wanted to go and tried to get my dad to go with her.

"I'm not going, but I'll run you and Ronnie down to church," offered my dad.

"You should go, Joe," countered Mom. "It's a plenary indulgence at the end."

"By the time I get home, eat and clean up, it'll be too late. Besides, I work in a boiler room all day—I'm not afraid of Purgatory."

"Very funny! Do you understand a plenary indulgence? All the punishment is removed from your soul."

"I'll be damn surprised if I have any punishment coming. I can't imagine what for! All I do is work like a dog, sit in traffic and hand money out to everybody. I'm getting punished enough right here. I can't even get in my own bathroom. Get Maureen to go, too, then I'll lock myself in the bathroom and read the paper."

So, the first week of my punishment went easily. I was out with my friends three nights of the week. I stopped on my way to St. Andrew's to call for Billy and we met Eddie, Dennis, Jeff and Dickie in front of the church. Even Tommy came from Bayside!

On the afternoon of the final day of the Triduum, our class had what was called an assembly during seventh period. This meant that, instead of our usual seventh period class, all sophomores went to the auditorium for a discussion. This assembly was to tell us about a closed retreat being offered to the students of Holy Cross. The retreat was going to be at St. Joseph's Retreat House in rural Valatie, New York (near Albany), beginning on a Friday and ending on a Sunday.

A retreat is a withdrawal from ordinary activities to commune with God in prayer and work and reflection, we were told. The weekend would consist of rising at 5:30 a.m. for prayers, chores, silence, prayers and praying, followed by prayers, Mass, silent reflection, Benediction and ending with a Papal Blessing, which carries with it a plenary indulgence. The retreat would be run by a group of Holy Cross brothers and a Holy Cross priest ("The Retreat Master"), exclusively for us Holy Cross boys. Silence would be observed from Friday afternoon, when the bus left, until Sunday, when the bus returned. Valatie was also where the Novitiates (young men preparing to become Brothers) were living and studying.

I was delighted to be at the assembly. It got me out of Biology class. Jeff was ticked off, however, because he had a study hall seventh period.

As we started our walk home from school, Jeff started in, "Boy—that assembly pissed me off. Now I have homework to do tonight that I would have gotten done in study hall."

"Yeah, but it sure was worth it to hear about that wonderful Retreat opportunity!" responded Glenn.

"Oh, c'mon!" yelled Jeff. "The Triduum is a much better deal. Tonight we get a plenary indulgence and we didn't have to give up a weekend and pray all day."

"I'm *kidding*," said Glenn, looking at Jeff like he was stupid for taking his remark seriously.

"Wait a minute," said Dickie, coming to an abrupt stop. "You don't want to spend a weekend in the woods, praying with a bunch of celibate men who wear dresses?" he asked, looking at Glenn.

"No, thanks."

"In silence?" I added, as we resumed walking.

"Nope."

"With novitiates?" chimed in Tommy.

"Nope."

"Just what kind of guy are you?" asked Jeff. "You haven't gone to the Triduum either, have you?"

"Nope."

"Maybe your parents are wasting their money on you. Maybe you should go to public school with the heathens."

"Why haven't you gone to the Triduum?" asked Dickie.

"I think it's all bullshit."

Dickie comes to an abrupt stop. "You think what's bullshit?"

"Praying and church and indulgences . . ."

"Oh, me too," Dickie answered, matter-of-factly, as he resumed walking.

"Whoa! You think *praying* is *bullshit*?" asked Jeff, incredulously.

"Don't you?" answered Glenn. "Do you believe God answers your prayers?"

"Uhhhh . . . I'm not sure."

"I do," offered Tommy, smiling.

"Really?" pressed Glenn.

"Yeah, if I get what I prayed for, God did it, and if I don't, then it wasn't good for me. Great system, huh?"

"Well, that's good enough for me," I said, laughing.

"What do you pray for?" asked Glenn to no one in particular.

"I pray for the strength and patience not to kill Regis," I answered with a big smile. "And *so far*, it worked."

"Seriously," said Glenn. "What do you pray for?"

"Although I do have fantasies about killing him," I continued.

"I pray for forgiveness," answered Tommy.

"And do you get it?" asked Glenn.

"I don't know! I cer-tain-ly hope so!" answered Tommy, pronouncing each syllable distinctly, mimicking Oliver Hardy.

"And, are you *really* sorry for your sins?"

"Yeah."

Dickie comes to a sudden stop. "*You're* sorry for your sins?"

"I certainly am."

"Then, why are you always planning new ones?"

"Who are you, all of a sudden, St. Richard of Abella?"

"No, but I'm not a phony. I'm not gonna pretend to be sorry if I'm not," stated Dickie emphatically, as he resumed walking.

"Oh, so you're not sorry for your sins?"

"Not for things that I don't think are wrong."

"Well, I'm not sorry for things I don't think are wrong, either," yelled Tommy, in frustration. "I'm sorry for my sins which I *do* think are wrong."

"Which are?"

"I'm not discussing my sins with you, Abella."

"Well, Taraci, you don't seem to be sorry."

"You don't either!"

"I'm not, I already said that!"

"Don't you think anything is wrong?" I asked Dickie.

"Yeah, I think it's wrong to kill somebody or rape somebody."

"That's all?"

"No, I think a lot of things are wrong, like stealing or hurting somebody, but I don't do any of those things, so I have nothing to be sorry for."

"Then, why are you doing the Triduum?" asked Glenn.

"In case."

"In case what?"

"In case this shit they teach us is true! Why do you go to Mass on Sundays?"

It takes a while for Glenn to answer, because we are all laughing at Dickie's answer.

"Well? Why do you go to Mass?"

"Habit, mostly."

"Habit?"

"Yeah, I was brought up to go to church on Sunday and if I didn't, I would probably feel bad, and for sure, it would upset my mother."

"Do you think it's a sin if you don't?"

"No."

"That's where you're wrong," chimed in Jeff. "The church says it's a sin. You don't get to decide."

"Well, that's where I have a problem," said Glenn. "Isn't a sin supposed to be a grievous matter?"

"A mortal sin, yeah."

"Well, what's grievous about missing church on Sunday? Who does it hurt?"

"It's one of the Commandments, 'Remember to Keep Holy the Lord's Day.'"

"So is 'Thou shalt not take the name of the Lord thy God in vain,' but you don't go to hell for it."

"It's a sin, though. A venial sin, but still a sin. You'll get punished in Purgatory," Jeff said, with a warning tone in his voice.

"Yeah, how much time for cursing?"

"Thirty days!" I yell.

"How much time off for a Hail Mary?"

"Thirty days," I yell again.

"How much time for an ejaculation?" interjects Tommy.

"Ten days," I answer.

"Wrong!" yells Tommy. "An ejaculation could get you eternity."

We all groan.

"All I'm saying is that it's all a bunch of bull," continued Glenn. "Live a good life and God will reward you. All this shit about indulgences, venial sins, purgatory, and Easter Duty is bull."

That night, I finished the Triduum and, having gone to Confession and Communion within the seven days, I believed I had received a plenary indulgence. Outside the church after the service, Jeff was telling Eddie, Dennis, and Billy about how Dickie didn't really believe, but he was taking no chances, and how Glenn didn't come at all because he thinks it's all bull.

"I have some questions about this stuff myself," said Eddie.

"Like what?" asked Jeff.

"Like, what about all the prayers I've said up to this point? Each of those prayers had indulgences attached. Do I have time in the bank now?"

"I don't get your question."

"Let's say I had X amount of time off from purgatory for all the prayers I've said, correct?"

"Yeah?"

"So what happens to all the indulgences I gained? Are they all gone or do I have credit?"

"They're all gone, I bet."

"That sucks! All the rosaries and prayers were all a waste of time?"

"How can you complain? You should be happy. I'm happy, knowing that if I died right now, I'd go straight to heaven."

"Maybe I can help you with that!" Eddie grabbed Jeff and started to push him into the speeding traffic on Northern Boulevard. Come on, guys, let's push Jeff in front of a bus so he can go to heaven."

A group of us grabbed Jeff and acted like we were going to throw him in front of a speeding bus. Jeff resisted quite strongly.

"Why are you resisting, Baudo?" yelled Eddie. "Don't you want to go to heaven? Don't you want to see God in Paradise? This might be your best chance."

As a bus neared, Jeff struggled as hard as he could to get free of our clutches and push back from the curb. As the bus went by, we let Jeff go, but Eddie admonished him for his lack of faith. "If you really believed all that stuff, you wouldn't have fought us, you would have welcomed death," said Eddie. "I don't think you really have faith, Jeff."

"You sure don't have faith in us," laughed Billy. "Did you really think we'd throw you in front of a bus?"

"Some of you would!"

"Who would?"

"Taraci would."

"Hey, Tommy—would you actually have thrown Jeff in front of a bus?" Billy asked.

"No," replied Tommy. "A car maybe, but not a bus."

"Why is that?"

"Too many innocent people could have gotten hurt if the bus driver tried to avoid Jeff."

"Do you think *I* would throw you in front of a bus?" asked Dickie.

"No, you wouldn't."

"See—you don't know me. You think you know me, but you don't know me. Do you want to stand on the curb and wait for the next bus and see if I'll do it?"

"Boy, these emotional religious experiences sure bring out the best in us, don't they?" I said to the group, laughing. "Eddie bitches about indulgences being wasted and suggests we kill Jeff. We consider killing Jeff and now Dickie wants another chance. It must be all that sanctifying grace. Maybe we're not used to it."

All that week, I was supposedly being punished for my F, and although I came home from school instead of going to Mueller's, I only felt the loss of TV one night. The other three, I was out at the Triduum and that broke things up. The whole time I was hoping that my parents would forget about the whole punishment thing so I never brought it up.

The next Monday evening, I was quietly and casually watching TV, when my mother noticed and started demanding that I turn it off. I argued that I hadn't watched any TV during the previous week and when that failed, I argued that I had done my homework before dinner, since I had come home directly after school. She didn't buy it, and when my father backed her up, I went to my room in a rage. I laid on my bed in the dark and listened to the radio until just before I fell asleep. This was repeated each night that week.

This was not so very unusual for me. I loved rock 'n' roll and always spent a lot of time listening to the radio in my room. There were four stations that I listened to: WMCA, WMGM, WINS and, of course, the mother station, WABC. The DJs, like Alan Freed, Dan Ingram, Scott Muni, and Harry Harrison were like friends to me. I started every day with Herb Oscar Anderson ("The Morning Mayor") and if I was home in the late afternoon,

I listened to Peter Tripp ("The Curly-Headed Kid in the Third Row") do *Your Hits of the Week*, which was a countdown of the Top 40. Ronnie and I would root for certain songs and often bet on which song would be Number One. I would often have a list of songs I particularly liked, what place they were in last week and an arrow indicating whether they had moved up or down that week.

In the evening, it was a battle between Murray the K and the Swinging Soiree on WINS, Cousin Brucie Morrow or Dan Ingram on WABC, and Scott Muni or Harry Harrison on WMCA. I usually would leave it on one station until they played a song I didn't like and then switch, unless there was one song I liked so much that I would listen until they played it, then switch, hoping to hear it again on another station. If the station I was listening to played something I hated, like 'Wolverton Mountain' (Claude King) or 'Alley-Oop' (Hollywood Argyles), I would skip them one time in the rotation. And if they played 'Peppermint Twist' (Joey Dee and the Starliters) or 'Poison Ivy' (the Coasters) or 'Pink Shoelaces' (Dodie Stevens) or 'Along Came Jones' (again, the Coasters), I wouldn't return to that station for the rest of the night.

Ronnie would also often be listening to the radio in the kitchen or in her bedroom and when something she knew I particularly liked came on, like the Ronettes, the Shirelles, or Ricky Nelson, to name a few, she would yell down the hall or up the stairs to alert me in case I had on a different station. "Hey Joey, Ricky Nelson's on ABC" or "The Ronettes are on WINS."

When I graduated from St. Andrew's, I received as a gift from my parents, a Wollensak reel-to-reel tape recorder. My father loved electronics and knowing I loved music, thought it would make a nice gift. He was right—I loved it. I taped songs I liked, off the radio, and had many hours of music I liked on tape to listen to at my pleasure. I would often fall asleep at night with a tape running and after the tape ran out, one reel would continue to spin until someone stopped it. Often in the morning when I woke up, it was still spinning.

After about a year, the recorder broke. I don't know why. My father, after checking on repair fees, decided he could probably fix it himself. He took it apart, found a blown tube, searched high and low for a replacement, and after finally finding one, couldn't get the recorder back together. After a few weeks of missing my music machine, I asked Dad about it.

"Hey Pop, what's up with my tape recorder?"

"Aw, forget about it," he said, sheepishly. "That thing's more trouble than it's worth."

Even my mom laughed at this. "Don't tell me Joe Farrell finally found something he couldn't fix," she chided.

"I thought the Germans made good stuff, but it turns out it's crap," he answered. It was back to the radio for me.

Every day for the rest of that week, I would go straight home, go to my room, put the radio on, and lie around thinking. Occasionally, I would do some homework or reading, but tried to avoid that from being discovered. If they thought that I was benefiting from this, it would be harder to get them to relinquish. I would leave my room for dinner when called, eat quickly and without talking, and return to my room. I thought a lot about hating Latin, hating Brother Regis and hating having an F on my record. I wondered what effect it might have on getting into college. Going away to college seemed more and more attractive to me. *I had to get out of this house!*

I missed "The Rifleman," "Dr. Kildare," "Ozzie and Harriet," "Dobie Gillis" and a few other favorites on TV, but I also missed Community Center basketball on Tuesday and Thursday nights.

That week, I created my own fantasy basketball game in the hall outside my room. I used a balled-up pair of socks as a basketball and used the "V" created by my door as the basket. The folding door my father had installed because of the attic fan fiasco, formed a nice "V" when opened halfway. It was just a little bigger than a pair of socks. I would see how many jump shots, hook shots, set shots, and bank shots I could hit out of ten or how many consecutive shots I could hit. I wasted hours playing "doorball" in the hall with the radio on. My creation endured, long after my grounding.

When the weekend rolled around, I decided to continue to not speak, unless spoken to. I was getting increasingly intolerant of the routine and was absolutely not going to abide by it. I knew not speaking to them was getting to them. I heard my mother comment to my father about it, but I couldn't hear exactly what she said. I did hear his response, which was, "What the hell do I care? He thinks he's hurting me, but I don't care if he ever speaks to me again."

Mom brought it up over the weekend, when I finished eating and was putting my plate in the sink.

"What do you think you're accomplishing by your attitude? Do you think you are hurting us?"

I didn't answer her or even look at her. I just left the kitchen and went to my room. Later, when I was leaving the house to meet my friends, she remarked again, "You better get over it, you son of a bitch, you're only hurting yourself! You be in this house by eleven o'clock or you won't be allowed to go out at all."

"We'll see," I said as I left.

Sunday night didn't really count as a school night, but I didn't want to be with them in the basement where they were watching TV. I spent it in my room except for sneaking in and watching '*Have Gun, Will Travel*' on the small TV in my parents' bedroom.

On Tuesday, I missed Community Center basketball again and I fumed about it. Basketball was a big thing to me now. I was almost six feet four inches tall and had improved tremendously. I was respected on our local courts and our intramural team had just finished the season, and we had done well for sophomores. St. Andrew's had just built a new addition with a gym and was going to enter a team in the CYO (Catholic Youth Organization) league. We all expected to try out for that and the Rizzo twins knew that the 111th Precinct was looking for players for their PAL (Police Athletic League) team too.

Although I dreamed of playing for Holy Cross, I knew that was probably never going to happen. I had gotten a late start in basketball and we were a very good and highly competitive New York team. The varsity had, in fact, just finished their season, a season that saw an eighteen-game winning streak and a trip to the playoffs. In the playoffs, we had beaten Power Memorial, which had one very prominent seven-footer and another player that was 6'11". Our tallest guy was 6'5". The seven-footer was Lew Alcindor, who later became known as Kareem Abdul-Jabbar!

Our victory over Power was a huge upset in the media, but not in our minds. The game was played before a sold-out crowd at St. John's University. We went completely nuts! We went to every home game and some of the away games, but this was huge and Tommy and I were both hoarse after the game. Power Memorial went on to win its next eighty-eight games. Unfortunately, we lost to LaSalle in the final, but it was a great year and a historical win over Lew Alcindor.

That night, I decided while laying on my bed in my room that I wouldn't miss another Community Center basketball night. On Thursday, I would go—no matter what. "What could they do to me?" I thought. The worst thing would be a physical encounter with my father, which I figured to be highly unlikely. He hadn't actually hit me since eighth grade. He was strong, but not prone to physical violence. As I lay there, I remembered that in the summer between eighth and ninth grades, when my mom first noticed that I was taller than Dad. She made us stand back-to-back and then stood on the stairs to see who was taller.

"My God, Joe! I think he's taller than you," she exclaimed.

"I'm not surprised," he answered. "He's been growing like a weed. If he eats any more, I'll have to get a second job!"

I was all smiles about being bigger than my dad and turned around behind him and put my arm around his neck and locked my hands together in a headlock.

"Pretty soon, I'll be the boss," I declared, playfully.

In an uncharacteristic move, Dad reached behind my head with his right hand and flipped me over his right shoulder! I was caught completely by surprise and hit the floor with a rattling thud.

"Pretty soon," Dad said, smiling at me on the floor, "but not yet."

Since that time, I had grown almost four inches and gotten a lot stronger. The prospect of fighting with my dad shook me up, and I had no desire to, but I felt I could get away from him if he started after me.

Other than that, I couldn't see what they could do to me. I got $5 a week allowance for doing chores. I had money in the bank from my summer job, which was supposed to be for college, but I could use it and I had money, over $100 hidden in my room from shoveling snow, which they didn't even know about. It was enough to last me until summer. If they cut off my allowance, I could easily survive and I wouldn't do the chores.

The more I thought about it, the more I decided that this bullshit was over! The next day, Wednesday, I didn't go to Mueller's after school, but I did get involved in a pick-up basketball game after school in the gym. I was about an hour and a half later getting home than I had been. This worked in my favor, I thought. If confronted, I would announce that I was no longer abiding by the grounding and that I intended to go to basketball on Thursday night.

When I got home, my mom didn't say anything as I passed her on the way to my room and also didn't mention it at supper. That night, I got nervous when I was in my room thinking about the coming confrontation when I would walk out of the house to go to basketball the next night. I got so nervous that I wanted to get it over with, so I went down to the basement and started to watch some television, expecting to provoke a confrontation, at which point I could announce that I was going to basketball the next night.

Either they didn't particularly notice, or didn't particularly care, but nothing was said! The next day, I came straight home from school and went to my room. At dinnertime, I went down and discovered that right after dinner, Mom and Dad were going to a neighbor's house to watch Perry Como in color. The Ghizzonis (Laura and Charlie) had a color TV and raved about it. Charlie was a TV repairman and got a good deal on a console model. I had only seen color TV in department stores. My parents and the Ghizzonis loved Perry Como, star of the Kraft Music Hall, and thus were invited over to watch it in living color.

"Beautiful," I thought. "As soon as they leave, I leave."

My parents left after dinner and I left right behind them. I told Ronnie, who thought this was a big mistake, where I was going.

"What do I tell Mom and Dad if they get home before you?"

"Tell them the truth," was my only answer.

"They'll probably go nuts."

"Too bad. It's them or me."

"Yeah, but whenever you get them pissed off, I always suffer somehow. They take it out on me as well."

"I'm truly sorry about that, but I can't let this go on any longer."

I left and went to P.S. 189. When I arrived, I was greeted with enthusiasm by most of the guys playing. They were glad to see me because in the sessions I had missed, Danny Sullivan had been dominating and now I would be matched up against him. Danny was a junior at Holy Cross and was at least six feet six inches, maybe even 6'7". Whenever we were both there, we always had to play against each other because we were the tallest.

He was big and he was strong and, like me, had gone to St. Andrew's, which didn't have a basketball program and subsequently, he had gotten a late start in basketball, too. He was a hard worker and had improved a lot since I knew him. He was much better under the basket than I was, but I was much better outside and quicker than him. He would always try to post me up and shoot hooks and short jumpers over me. I would move outside and if he didn't cover me, shoot midrange jumpers and if he did come out on me, I would drive to the basket. We battled hard underneath for rebounds, but Danny used his big body well and usually outdid me.

On this occasion, Danny had some good news. Mr. O'Meara had asked Danny to be on the Varsity. Danny hadn't played freshman or JV ball at Holy Cross, only intramurals, so it was unusual to jump to the Varsity. Apparently, O'Meara needed some size and saw Danny playing intramurals and asked him to join the team. In talking to Danny about this, he told me O'Meara had once before recruited a guy named Jerry Frain from intramurals.

I don't know if it was the incentive of playing against a Varsity player or the anxiety of defying my parents, but I played great that night and everybody noticed.

"Maybe O'Meara should've seen *you* tonight," John Rizzo said to me as we were leaving.

"You need to learn to use your right hand," offered Danny. "I overplay you to your left because I know you can't go to your right. Work on that."

"Yeah, thanks Danny," I said, but my mind was on returning home and how to handle whatever fate awaited me."

When I arrived home, my parents were drinking coffee in the kitchen. We always used the side door to our house, which entered into the kitchen, so I had to walk past them to get to my room. I tried to look nonchalant as I came in and went to the refrigerator and looked inside for something to drink.

"Who said you could go out?" asked Mom.

"No one," I answered, getting a glass out of the cupboard and running the tap water for it to get cold.

"Why isn't there anything to drink in this house?"

I don't know why I said that. I guess it was a mixture of being nervous and wanting to change the subject.

"There's plenty of tap water," answered my dad. "Good old New York City tap water. The best water in the country."

'Good,' I thought. 'He doesn't seem pissed off.'

"Did you drink the last of the orange juice last night?" he asked in an accusatory manner.

"I don't know," I said thoughtfully, "I don't remember." It *was* me, I remembered, as I chugged a glass of water.

"Look, there's plenty of orange juice in the cans in the freezer. All I ask is, if you drink the last in the fridge, make another pitcher. Is that too much to ask? When I come down in the morning, all I want is a glass of juice and a cup of coffee on my way out the door, and there's *no* juice."

"Sorry," I said. "Next time I'll make more."

"See that you do."

I nodded in agreement and started for my room.

"You got some nerve going out when you're grounded," said Mom loudly as I walked through the door.

I turned back and looked at her and said, softly, but firmly, "That's over."

"Did you hear that?" she said to Dad. "Did you hear what he just said?"

As I walked away, I heard him say, "Yeah, I heard him, Vera. There's nothing I can do about it. It's his funeral. If he wants to screw up his life, there's nothing we can do. We did the best we could."

I waited out of sight, but within earshot, to hear if anything else was said. Mom muttered something about me thinking I'm a big shot and the hell with me.

I was ecstatic as I went to my room and snapped on the radio. It was a watershed event. They were right. It *was* up to me. They no longer had control over me. They could influence me, but not control me. I felt like our worlds were far apart, but at least we had gotten something cleared up. Something changed that night, if only in my mind. *I* was responsible for me. They didn't and couldn't *make* me study, pray, eat, sleep, or work. My successes and failures were because of me, not a result of their control of me, and now maybe they realized that.

I spent the rest of that evening in my room, because I *wanted* to. I had a lot of feelings and thoughts to sort through. I listened to music and to a new phenomenon—the New York Mets. On April 11, the Mets had made their anxiously awaited debut. Former Dodger and Giant fans had a team again. The team colors were even a combination of Dodger and Giant colors. They played in the old Polo Grounds, which was the Giants old stadium, but a new stadium was being built for them in, of all places, Flushing! I was extremely excited about this development. The Mets lost their first nine games and basically sucked, but they were my team and I loved them. It was wonderful to have baseball back in my life.

As I lay there on my bed, listening to the end of the game and thinking about what had just transpired, Ronnie came to my room. "That Everly Brothers song you like is on ABC," she said.

"Thanks, Ron," I said, switching the station from the Mets to hear it.

"What happened when you got home?"

"Nothin'."

"What do you mean, nothing? They had to say *some*thing."

"I just told them it was over. Dad even admits it."

"You are lucky! You get away with a lot because you're a boy."

"Ronnie, you have choices, too. They can't make you do stuff."

"Yeah, maybe so, but I don't want to live with the consequences."

"Which are?"

"Either them pissed off at me or Mom pissed off at Dad, because that's what happens, you know."

"Yeah, well, I'm not playing that game. They can be pissed off all they want, as far as I'm concerned."

Ronnie left and I switched back to the Mets. I lay there feeling a strange mixture of happiness and sadness. I was happy that some breakthrough had occurred or some precedent had been set, but I was saddened by how it was done. 'Why couldn't they talk to me calmly and rationally?' I thought. 'Why do they make everything so difficult?'

CHAPTER FIFTEEN

♦ ♦ ♦ ♦ ♦

"PANIC ATTACKS"

Don't you understand what I'm tryin' to say
And can't you feel the fears I'm feeling today
If the button is pushed, there's no running away
There'll be no one to save
With the whole world in a grave
Take a look around you boy
It's bound to scare you boy.

Barry McGuire—"Eve of Destruction"

As the summer of 1962 approached, the world and my life seemed to be spinning wildly out of control. There were sharp ups and downs, and it seemed, a great deal of doubt as to the outcome.

In April, Scott Carpenter was sent into space and established a new record of three revolutions around the earth and was in space for almost five hours, making him a new American hero. The celebrating had hardly subsided, when the Russians shattered his record with a four-day space flight, again establishing their superiority in space. And, as if to rub our noses in it, in August, they put two men in space simultaneously in two different spacecrafts—Vostok 3 and Vostok 4.

This, of course, was seen as a severe threat to our existence. The only purpose of linking up two vehicles in space was to perform some hostile act, such as re-arming a weapon or building a large space station to man weapons, or, as a place to travel to in order to outwait the radioactive fallout of a nuclear war, or to serve as a safe place from which to conduct a nuclear war.

In early May, the United States fired the first nuclear warhead from a submarine underwater. The test was near, of all places, Christmas Island, and was a demonstration that the then undetectable Polaris submarine could fire a nuclear missile while on patrol and without ever surfacing. On the evening news, it was reported as good news, because we could launch nuclear missiles at the USSR from the sea just off their coast and dramatically reduce their warning time. In the Sunday paper however, it wasn't reported as quite such a good thing, since the Soviets would feel threatened by this development and it made an all-out first strike more appealing and more likely, lest they lose their missiles to our sudden strike.

The story spoke of the theory of Mutual Assured Destruction, whereby if one side launched missiles, the other side would detect it and proceed to launch its own missiles. Knowing that no one would survive was what prevented either side from launching. If arming Polaris submarines with nuclear missiles upset that balance by giving us an edge so that the Soviets might not have time to respond, then it actually made the world more dangerous, not safer. Some sources reported that this test might provoke a nuclear attack by the Soviets and that such an attack was under active consideration by the Kremlin. This type of news story made studying for finals seem like a waste of time.

Just before finals, the Israelis hung Adolph Eichmann for 'crimes against humanity' in World War II. His defense, that he was just following the orders of his superiors, was rejected and he was sentenced to death. This lesson was not lost on our generation, which would be demonstrated in the years ahead.

In the last few days of school, we received the results of the National Educational Development Tests, which we had taken in early spring. This test measured "educational skills and compared them with other students of the same grade across the nation." The test gave percentile scores in five areas, and a composite or overall score. My overall score was in the 91st percentile, which meant I was in the top 10 percent of tenth graders in the nation. I scored in the 94th percentile in Math and in Science and in the 81st percentile in English usage.

I also got in the 90th percentile in Social Studies. A few days later, I got my final grades for the year. My highest grade was a 91 in English. I got a 79 in Geometry, despite working hard at it or should I say, hard for me. Not only did my grades contradict the NED Tests, they also didn't reflect reality and just made the picture more bizarre and uncertain.

I was always good at English and the grade from Trentacoste really reflected the background from the nuns at St. Andrew's. They had drilled correct usage and grammar and punctuation into us with a vengeance. The second half of the year was literature and I had always loved reading. I was happy with the 91, especially from a guy who didn't like me or at least didn't like me at the beginning of the year. I wondered what Trentacoste thought of my performance in his class. He gave me a 98 in one marking period. I wondered if he thought I was maturing as a student, taking school work more seriously, and that he was part of all that. Glenn, who had also done well, and I had discussed it one day on the way to school.

"That big-nosed, uncoordinated fuck probably takes credit for our grades," Glenn mused.

"I'm sure he does," I replied. "Doesn't that just burn you up?"

"Yeah, it does. He didn't teach us a thing."

"He probably thinks smacking us in the face made us shape up and work hard in his class."

"Ugh. It just kills me to think about it. I wish I'd have decked him. I've been hoping he would hit Charlie Skupeen."

"Why?"

"Charlie told me if Mr. T. ever hit him, he would punch him out and I believe it. Charlie would do it."

My next highest grade was an 87 in Biology. This, however, did not reflect my NEDT score in Science, but was totally a function of cheating. Glenn, Jay, Paul and I and a few others knew the test questions after third period and had two study halls and Religion class to look up the answers.

My lowest grade was a 75 in Latin, which I was thrilled to be done with. The only significance in that, I thought, was that it showed my low tolerance for bullshit. World History and Religion were in between and both courses had been a complete waste of time and proved nothing.

So, based on the NEDT scores, I thought the idea of being an engineer was still viable, but it troubled me. I was worried that despite trying as hard as I had ever tried, I only got a 79 in Geometry. I also felt uncomfortable about the fact that I really didn't know what an engineer did. It was easy to say they build things or design things, but what they did on a day-to-day basis was very unclear to me.

I took some consolation in being pretty confident that, should we avoid nuclear annihilation, I was capable of going to college. I was, after all, in Section C, and A through G were supposed to be college prep sections. I feared I might slip down a little when the class rosters came out for next year, but felt I could do well without Latin and Brother Regis to deal with. I had to continue with a language, but it would be a fresh start in an easier language. I had selected Spanish, which Dickie Abella assured me was a lot easier than Latin.

Just before school was out for the summer, I got a call from Pat Nash. "They want us back," said Pat. "Please say 'yes'."

"Who wants us back?" I asked.

"Cresthaven! Who the hell else could want us back?"

"Oh, right, yeah," I stammered. "Well, maybe St. Andrew's?"

"They *don't*! Believe me!"

"Well, okay, yeah, I don't have anything better. Did they say what the pay was?"

"Yeah, a dollar an hour. I told them I need money for college and Rita said maybe I could work some weddings and banquets for extra money. I don't think you're old enough, but you could ask her."

"I ain't askin'. I'm not even old enough to work on Paddy's crew for God's sake."

"Well, if you think you can get more money, then don't take the job," Pat chided.

"No, I'll take it."

"Why don't you tell Rita a dollar an hour is beneath you, that it's an insult, that you're fed up with the Irish being exploited! In fact, now that I think about it, I'll tell her myself. I'll say, 'I'll take it, but Joe's pissed off . . . He says to shove the dollar an hour.'"

"When do we start?" I asked, laughing.

"Monday, or as Paddy would say, 'Mundy morn'."

"Jeez, I don't even get a break."

"Hey, you've been on a break! Get in the real world. I don't know about you, but I haven't done a thing in weeks."

"Yeah, but you're graduating. My future's still in doubt. I've been taking finals all week."

"Hey, takin' them is easy."

"Easy?"

"Yeah, passing 'em is hard, but takin' 'em is easy."

I was happy to be working with Pat again, but I was looking forward to sleeping in and had planned to delay looking for a job or at least, starting one until after a week off.

We started on Monday and Paddy was delighted to see us back.

"We got a lot to do this summer," he mumbled unintelligibly.

Being around Paddy got us used to his mumbling brogue, but after not seeing him for almost ten months, we were out of practice.

"What?" I said.

"We gotta lotta work to do this summer." "What?" I said again, looking at Pat for help, which wasn't forthcoming.

"We gotta lotta work to do this summer," he yelled. "What the hell is wrong with your ears, goddammit."

"Well, that's what we're here for," started Pat. "The difficult we do immediately, the impossible . . ."

"Don't start that shit again," Paddy cut him off, yelling and holding up his hands.

" . . . takes a little longer," Pat finished.

"I told Rita we need more help. Do you know anybody who wants to work?"

"Yeah, my brother," answered Pat.

"Your brother?"

"Yeah, me brother."

"Is he a good worker?"

"Well, let's put it this way, 'The difficult he does immediately.'"

"I'll go talk to Rita," Paddy said, cutting him off. "You guys get started on the tennis courts."

A few minutes later, Rita came out and asked about Tommy. Pat acted like Tommy was older than he was, by stating that he went to Holy Cross, which was where Tommy would *start* in September. Rita asked if he was old enough (meaning sixteen) and if he wanted the job. Pat said, "yes," to both questions. I wasn't sixteen yet and had never returned the forms required by the state that Rita had given me *last* summer to fill out! She asked me once about them and I told her I had turned them in at the office.

Tommy was fourteen, but was a boy in a man's body. He was big, six feet two inches, strong as an ox and super fast. In the next few months, Tommy would go out for freshman football, get moved up to junior varsity, where he would dominate and break three freshman track records in one day. After setting records in the 100- and 220-yard dashes, the coach needed someone to throw the shot put. The guy that was supposed to, was sick and had missed school that day. The coach asked Tommy if he could fill in.

"You mean just throw it as far as I can?"

"Yeah, but stay in the circle. You can't step outside the circle."

"Yeah, I've seen them doing it."

"Can you do it?"

"Yeah, I guess. I don't know how far, but I'll try."

He did it and broke the freshman record.

Rita said that Tommy could start as soon as he wanted and gave Pat an application for Tommy to fill out.

At lunch break, I mentioned to Pat how nice it was going to be to have Tommy working with us.

"Yeah, I guess it will be nice. I just wish I didn't have to lie about it."

"Hey, don't worry—I'm not sixteen yet and nobody suspects it and Tommy looks older than me."

"I'm not talkin' about *that* lie, I'm talkin' about the one where I said Tommy wants the job," Pat says, laughing! "He'll be real pissed off when I tell him this."

"Really? Then, why'd you do it?"

My parents want him to work, but I swear to God, he is the laziest lug I've ever known."

"Really? I've heard your dad say that, but I thought he was just kidding."

"The only reason Tommy gets out of bed is to eat."

"Still, you did the right thing. If Tommy won't take it, you can tell Rita he got a better job."

"Oh, he'll take it. My parents will make him take it. They'll be thrilled and Nana will be ecstatic. Tommy will act like I kicked him in the nuts; like how could you do this to your brother?"

Tommy did take the job and, having him working with us added a lot to the daily experience. Tommy was much different than Pat. He wasn't "gung-ho" at all and frequently thought Pat was nuts. He would often look to me for confirmation or validation that Pat, and not him, was the crazy one. Having Tommy around and resisting Pat's eagerness for hard work only made Pat more eager and more insistent that Tommy was lazy.

Pat hated watering flowers and bushes and weeding. He felt they were demeaning, or at least, demeaning to him. It just wasn't hard enough. He told Paddy that Tommy loved to water and pull weeds and Paddy believed him. In fact, Tommy didn't mind watering, but he did hate pulling weeds.

Tommy, being the youngest, and the new guy, and this being his first job, didn't complain to Paddy, but he did complain to us.

"Why do I always get the weeding and watering?" he would ask.

"Don't know," Pat would answer. "Maybe because you're the junior member of the crew?"

"That sucks. I hate pulling weeds."

"You don't mind watering, do you?"

"No, watering is okay."

"You lazy lug! You better not tell Paddy or he'll get mad."

So, every morning at the beginning of the summer, I would start by doing the tennis courts, Pat would paint and Tommy would weed. When done with the tennis courts, I would join Pat painting the locker rooms and Tommy would weed. Every morning, about mid-morning, a truck would drive into Cresthaven for coffee break. The truck had coffee, sodas, bagels and donuts for sale and we would stop working for a while and take some refreshment with Paddy. We would take as long as Paddy would allow. Often, in an attempt to extend our break, Pat would try to get Paddy talking.

"Tell us about Ireland," Pat would ask or he would provoke Paddy by asking, "Is it true it rains all the time in Ireland?" Or, "Do they have indoor plumbing in Ireland?" Or "Why didn't Ireland help us during World War II?" Paddy would laugh and often tell a long, rambling, hard-to-understand story, but we didn't care. We just wanted to keep him talking. When break was over, Paddy would say, "Joe, you finish the courts, Pat you go back to painting and Joe will be in to help you, Tom . . ."

"I know, I know, keep weeding," Tommy would say with increasing disgust.

Later, I would finish the courts and join Pat in the girls' locker room. The idea was to paint the girls' locker room each morning before the club opened and then stop just before noon when the locker room would be needed. This made the task take weeks. It was hard work. The locker rooms were not air-conditioned and most of the painting was overhead and it was mostly done with brushes and standing on a ladder. I would wonder why Tommy was annoyed at weeding and watering.

"This ain't no picnic," I would say.

"He just thinks he's missing something. He wants to be with us, that's all. But I have a plan," Pat answered.

"What's your plan?"

"Well, we're almost done in here and I'm getting sick of painting. When we start on the boy's locker room, I'm gonna tell Paddy that Tommy loves to paint!"

One day near noon, an early arrival walked into the locker room while we were painting.

"Can I change in here?" asked the girl about sixteen years old.

"You certainly can," answered Pat, who continued painting as if nothing had happened.

The girl moved to a locker and put her stuff down and waited. Pat and I kept painting as if no one was there, occasionally glancing at her.

"Well?" she finally said.

"Well what?" Pat asked.

"Well, I'm not changing in front of you."

"Go ahead," said Pat, playfully. "We won't look."

I put my palm over my eyes and then spread my fingers so I could see between them. The girl blushed, but insisted that she would not change while we were there.

"Okay. We'll call it quits for today," Pat said, "but the reason this job is taking so long is prudish girls like you."

On the very next day, another pretty young lady arrived a little early and also was surprised to see us and asked, "Can I change in here?"

"You certainly can," responded Pat, "and don't worry, we won't look."

"Oh, I don't care, thanks," she replied and started to open a locker and kick off her shoes.

"All right!" whispered Pat to me. "This is what I've been hoping for."

Unfortunately, the girl already had her bathing suit on under her clothes and ruined our few minutes of fantasy.

Painting the boys' locker room was not as much fun and we didn't have to quit at noon, so we finished it much more quickly. Pat did tell Paddy that Tommy loved to paint and soon all three of us were painting the boys' locker room. While painting it, we found a number of swimming trunks in a box marked 'Lost and Found.'

"This is great," said Pat. "We can use these to go for a swim after work."

"Great idea," I said. "We always talked about it, but we never did it."

"What about towels?" asked Tommy. "And I'm not too keen on wearing somebody else's swim trunks."

"Don't be silly, Tom," Pat said. "The chlorine will kill anything harmful."

"There are towels in here too," I said, looking in the box. "And they look clean."

That day, we decide would be the day Nana's story about us swimming at the club would come true. We were going in the pool.

At five o'clock, we punched out and headed for the locker room, put swim trunks on, showered and headed for the pool. While looking in 'Lost and Found' I came across a black Panama hat with a colorful band and a small feather. I wore that down to the pool, calling it a "chick magnet." I tried to keep it on in the pool, but it came off frequently. It was a hot humid day and the pool felt great. The hat did get the attention of a few young girls and luckily there weren't many other people at the pool at that time of day.

A lot of the adult members, who came on a weekday (mostly women) left as the dinner hour approached, and those who worked during the day weren't there yet. The pool area was sparsely populated with mostly teenagers. We didn't have much time to enjoy the pool as we wanted to catch the six fifteen bus, but the idea was to cool off and clean up for the ride home. We jumped off the high diving board a few times, me holding onto my hat, and we were ready to go. We decided on a quick shower before getting dressed, even though we had only dirty clothes to put back on. ("A lot of little kids pee in the pool," Pat warned.) As we were in the shower, Rita Haff suddenly appeared at the shower room door and started yelling at us.

"Hey, don't you know you're not allowed in the pool?"

We were shocked to see a woman in the shower doorway and Pat immediately covered his loins with his hands. I, fortunately, had my hat on, and quickly took it off my head, and held it in front of my loins. When I looked at Tommy, who had exclaimed, "Geez," he had turned around and was facing the shower wall.

"No! We didn't know," I answered, laughing at the embarrassing poses we all struck.

"Well, I just got a complaint that 'the help' was in the pool and I figured it was you guys."

"We thought we could as long as we were clocked out," I explained loudly, so as to be heard over the running showers.

"No, not anymore," said Rita. "We used to allow it, but we got complaints from members, so we don't allow it anymore."

"Oh, well, we must have been operating under the old policy," explained Pat.

"We didn't get the memo," I added sarcastically.

"Well, someone should have told you. Didn't anyone tell you?"

"No one told me," I answered. "Anyone tell you, Tom?"

"Can we discuss this some other time?" yelled Tom over his shoulder, shaking his head in disbelief.

"Okay, well now you know," said Rita as she left.

We put our dirty clothes on and caught the bus home, grumbling about the complaint and amazed that Rita came in after us.

Tommy was convinced that the complainant was a teenage boy who didn't want us flirting with the girls. Pat blamed it on me wearing a hat and attracting too much attention.

"You think my hat was too flamboyant?" I asked, playfully.

"I don't know about that, but I think it attracted too much attention." Pat laughed. "the chick magnet did us in."

"It's a good thing I had it on in the shower or I'd have been naked when Rita came in."

"'The help' is in the pool," Pat muttered disgustedly as we rode the bus. "Maybe 'the help' should kick some ass."

While we did our work around the grounds, Paddy drove an old blue pick-up truck. Being almost sixteen, driving was something I loved. At that time in New York, one had to be eighteen to get a driver's license, but we were all chomping at the bit to drive. I begged Paddy to let me drive around the grounds, but he wouldn't let me. He did, however, leave the keys in the truck as a matter of routine. He often left the truck with us to load and unload or with tools or fertilizer that we needed on it. When he did this, I would practice my driving by moving the truck a little closer or just moving it and putting it back. I needed practice on letting the clutch up slowly and giving it just the right amount of gas, as any new driver would. I often had it in the wrong gear and it would stall.

One morning, Paddy left us with the truck on the tennis courts to pull all the weeds and grass that was sprouting up near the fence that surrounded the courts. Pat and I were doing it (Tommy was watering) and were just about finished, when I decided to hone my driving skills by trying to back the truck up to the fence as close as possible.

"I'll try to put it six inches from the fence," I told Pat as I searched for reverse. I put it a little too close and hit the fence lightly.

"Hold it! Hold it! Don't move!" yelled Pat. "You hooked the fence with the bumper."

I carefully took the truck out of gear, put the emergency brake on and got out for a look.

"Oh, shit!" I exclaimed. "Paddy is goin' to be mad when he sees this!" One end of the bumper had hooked the fence.

"Don't panic," said Pat. "All you have to do is back it up a little bit while turning the wheel and little bit and it will unhook. I'll watch and tell you when to pull away. Don't panic."

I got back in the truck, found reverse and very carefully eased the clutch up until I edged back into the fence, turning the wheel to the left.

"Okay, pull up," yelled Pat. "It's unhooked."

I put it in what I prayed was first gear and tried to ease forward, but the truck bucked, jumped forward and pulled the fence down!

"Now panic!" yelled Pat. "*Now* you can panic."

Paddy, knowing that we should be about finished with this particular job, was headed back to the tennis courts to check our progress when he saw what had happened. When he did, he made a noise like I never heard before or since. It started like a high-pitched squeal and ended in a deep groan. He ran over to me, threw his hat down on the ground, stomped on it, then kicked it. This behavior struck Pat as funny and he started to laugh.

"Don't panic, Paddy," Pat said, laughing, and I started laughing as well.

"Jesus Christ Almighty, how many times did I tell you to stay out of the truck?" Paddy screamed hoarsely, as if the noise he had made had strained his vocal cords. "What the feck is so funny?"

"I think you're panicking," replied Pat. "Stay calm and let's think our way out of this mess."

"Calm? Calm? You pulled down the feckin' fence!"

"Now, Paddy, that's in the past. You can't live in the past! Joe, go get Tommy, we're gonna need him."

I got Tommy and we fixed the fence and no one else found out about it. Fortunately, the fence was erected cheaply and the actual fencing had just pulled off the wooden beams that held it. The rest of the summer, whenever we needed a laugh, Pat would ask Paddy, "When are you gonna let Joe drive?" Paddy would always react violently. A few times, when Paddy would give us an assignment, I would pretend to throw my hat down, stomp on it, and then kick it, like Paddy had, and we'd all laugh. Once I actually asked Paddy for his hat, which he gave to me and I stomped on it and kicked it. Paddy laughed harder than anyone.

There was one antic that even Paddy never found out about. Some nursery in Whitestone had donated a large load of small flowers to Cresthaven and Paddy had assigned us to plant them. We were to plant each one individually and there were about forty or fifty cases of twenty-four plants each on the back of the pickup. We were planting for a week and getting pretty sick of it. Especially Pat. We planted them in all the huge flower boxes from the street to the clubhouse and then in the flower boxes all around the clubhouse. And still there were more. Plenty more.

Pat was losing his patience and while expressing his frustration to me, I made a sarcastic remark that we ought to just bury them. Pat thought it was brilliant! So, while we were planting them along the outside of the locker room building, we dug a big hole, threw in two cases of flowers, buried them, and then did it again and again. When we ran out of flowers, we told Paddy we were done. He seemed amazed and stood scratching his head with his thumb while holding his hat in his fingers.

"You planted them all?"

"Yep."

"I thought there was more than that left."

"Nope."

"Are you sure you did them all?"

"Paddy," said Pat, holding up his right hand as if taking an oath. "I swear to you they are all in the ground."

The most memorable Cresthaven story occurred that summer in July in preparation for the annual Strawberry Festival. Willie Haff personally ran this event and it was held outdoors on the large patio in front of the locker rooms. He showed up just after noon on the day of the festival in his big white Cadillac and started barking out orders. We had just begun our lunch break and he told us to hurry up and finish because *we* had a lot to do that afternoon. We ignored him, figuring we were on our lunch hour and Paddy would deal with him. About three minutes later, Willie told us to follow him. We got up and carrying our lunches and drinks, followed him to the patio. When we caught up with him on the patio, he said, "Lunch break is over—get rid of that stuff."

We looked around for Paddy, but realized that he was so intimidated by Willie that he wouldn't be any help. Willie was a big barrel-chested, arrogant guy who was feared and hated by most of the employees. The waiters, kitchen staff and janitors quaked in fear whenever he was around. Fortunately for us, he was hardly ever around when we were working.

"Two of you need to go set up tables on the patio. We need sixteen banquet tables and eight chairs for each brought over from the storeroom and set up here, like so." Willie then showed us how he wanted the tables and chairs configured on the patio.

"The other guy I need to help me with the decorations. Are any of you good with a hammer?"

"Tom is," answered Pat, pointing at Tom.

Tom shot Pat a look of extreme contempt.

"Okay, you two go start on the tables, he said, looking at us, "and you stay here with me," he said to Tommy.

Pat and I went to the storeroom and found Paddy there. He had already unlocked it and was counting tables and chairs for us to take to the patio.

"Hey Paddy, this sucks," I said.

"What?"

"This *sucks*. We didn't even get a lunch break. Who does he think he is?"

"I guess he thinks he's the boss," answered Paddy softly.

He pointed out the sixteen tables and the chairs that we were to use. I was feeling angry about Willie's rude and inconsiderate treatment and was balking at doing what was asked.

"I think I'll wait until my lunch hour is over."

"Come on, Joe," replied Paddy, nicely. "Let's just get this done and he'll leave us alone."

"That's no way to treat people," I insisted.

"Joe, Joe, Joe," Paddy said, scratching his head with his thumb. "He's a son of a bitch, but it's best to just get this party set up and he'll leave us alone. Once it's set up, he'll go back to yelling at the waiters and kitchen staff."

"Well, someone ought to tell him off."

"Yeah, someone who doesn't need the work," Paddy mumbled softly.

Pat and I began carrying the large banquet tables to the patio and setting them up as directed. Tommy was working with Willie erecting some wooden supports on the far side of the patio. Then the plan was to hang strings of colored decorations and strings of lights from the roof across the patio to temporary supports that Tommy and Willie were working on. After about our eighth trip in the hot sun of July, Pat decided we should get a cold drink.

"Good idea," I said and, reaching into my pocket for money, I yelled at Tommy and Willie, "Hey, you guys want a soda?"

"No sodas," yelled Willie. "We don't have time. How many tables do you have set up?"

"Eight," I answered.

"Eight? Come on, will ya'?" Carry two at a time. What the hell is wrong with you? A couple of *girls* could carry one at a time!"

Pat and I started back to the storeroom, muttering under our breath.

"What a prick," Pat said softly as we were walking away.

"I can't believe that motherfucker," I replied. "He should be buying *us* sodas! I offer to buy *him* a soda and he bites my head off.?"

"What a prick!," Pat said louder. "We should get him a drink and piss in it."

"We gotta hurt this guy," I continued. "He can't get away with this!"

As we made more trips with two tables, we were fantasizing about ways to teach Willie a lesson. As we came back with the last of the tables, Tommy and Willie were on the roof of the locker room. Tommy was trying to hold a big nail and a board with one hand and drive the nail in with the other in a precise location, while leaning over the edge of the roof. Apparently, Tommy was taking too long and not getting it quite where Willie wanted it and Willie yelled," Come on, will ya—we don't have all day!"

Pat and I look up, thinking he was talking to us, but he grabs the board and nail from Tommy, positions it where he wants it, and says, "Right here—hit it."

Tommy hit the nail with the hammer, but since Willie was holding the nail and Tommy was kneeling on the roof of the locker room, and bending over the roof swinging down, he was cautious. As a result, he didn't drive the nail in far enough. Willie was also bent over the roof and after Tommy hit the nail a few times, he almost lost his balance, and fell off.

"Goddammit! Will you hit the damn nail?" Willie said, as he reset himself and repositioned both the board and the nail.

"Come on, *hit it*," he yelled.

Tommy hit it again, but it still didn't go in very far.

"Come *on*, you big lug. Put some muscle into it! We need to get this done!"

Tommy swung hard and hit—Willie's thumb.

"Aaaaaaooooooowwwww! J-e-s-u-s-s-s-s C-h-r-r-r-r-r-i-s-t," Willie screamed, holding his bloody thumb. "You stupid ass, you're *fired*."

Willie was writhing in pain, and blood had splattered onto his shirt and pants.

"Get out of here *now—*you're *fired*."

Tommy climbed down the ladder and went into the locker room building. Pat and I hurriedly finished positioning the last table we were working on and went after Tommy. Once out of sight, Pat and I went nuts.

"Holy shit!" I said, laughing uncontrollably.

"Do you believe it?" asked Pat, bursting into laughter.

We didn't see Tom around, so we assumed he went into the men's locker room and so we headed in there after him. When we indeed saw him sitting on a bench, he was visibly upset.

"Are you all right?" I asked.

"Yeah, I'm *fine*. I don't have a job anymore, but I feel *fine*."

Pat and I cracked up again.

"I'm glad you think it's so funny," said Tom, annoyed at our reaction. "What do I tell Mom and Dad?"

"Tell them you hit the owner with a hammer," I responded, as we cracked up again.

"They tend to frown on that," Pat added, when he could catch his breath enough to speak.

Just then, Paddy came in looking for us.

"What happened to Willie?" he asks.

"Why do you ask?" shot back Pat quickly.

"He just walked past me cursing and holding his hand."

"Now, don't panic, Paddy," said Pat. "Tommy hit him with a hammer . . ."

"What?" said Paddy, looking at Tommy like he couldn't believe his ears.

"I didn't do it on purpose," Tommy said, looking at Paddy contritely.

"H-o-o-o-o-o-l-y shit!"

"His thumb was bleeding," I said.

"Jesus, Mary, and Joseph," Paddy whispered softly in his Irish accent.

"He had blood on his shirt and pants," Pat added.

"Oooh, Jesus, Mary, and Joseph."

"I think you're panicking," said Pat.

Pat and I started to tell Paddy the details while we were laughing. We told him how Willie had been browbeating us and hurrying us, made us carry two tables at a time, and not allowing us to have a soda, "even though I offered to buy!" We told him how he was yelling at Tom to hit the nail hard, while Tommy was on his knees and trying not to lose his balance and fall off the roof. We told Paddy that we had just been discussing how to teach that prick a lesson when suddenly we heard him screaming in pain and saw him clutching his bloody thumb.

"It was as if Tommy heard Joe and I talking and decided to make our wishes come true," said Pat. "It was like a miracle."

Now, even Paddy was laughing. I wasn't sure if he was laughing at the story or at us laughing so hard.

As it turned out, Willie got some guys from Frank's crew to finish stringing the lights and decorations and the Strawberry Festival was held without a problem, although Willie's thumb was bandaged. Paddy said that Tommy wasn't fired and to forget about it, but suggested he avoid Willie, if possible.

"Don't worry, if I see him coming, I'll run the other way," answered Tommy.

"Good," agrees Paddy, "because if he sees you, he may remember he fired you, and you may have to go. But for now, you're safe."

That summer had other memorable events. It was the first season of the Amazin' New York Mets. The Mets of 1962 compiled the worst record in baseball history, winning only forty games and losing 120, but we loved them. I was elated to have a team, after years of being in baseball limbo. They were a mixture of kids, who should have still been in the minor leagues, and old-timers, who should have been retired. I watched the games on television almost every night and on weekends. Former Giants and Dodgers fans embraced these inept losers, managed by seventy-two-year-old Casey Stengel, whom most of the players admitted they couldn't understand when he spoke.

Casey was a baseball old-timer and former Yankees manager, which made him a well-known commodity in New York. When the season had just started, he was quoted as saying "The secret of managing is to keep the guys who hate you, away from the guys who are undecided." He also said, "The Mets are gonna be amazing," and that stuck as the year went on and proved to be true, as the Mets adopted the name, "The Amazin' Mets," in their ads.

During this year that set a new standard for futility, Casey was also quoted as saying, "Good pitching will always stop good hitting and vice versa" and he wasn't joking! As frustration and losses mounted, he was quoted as saying, "Been in this game one hundred years, but I see new ways to lose 'em I never knew existed before," and "Mister, that boy couldn't hit the ground if he fell out of an airplane."

Once when asked if the problem was a lack of discipline on the team, he replied: "The trouble is not that players have sex the night before a game, it's that they stay out all night looking for it. I got players with bad watches—they can't tell midnight from noon." Perhaps what became his best-known quote was uttered and overheard in the dugout during one particularly horrendous game, "Can't anybody here play this game?"

Watching baseball facilitated another change that summer. We started drinking beer. Cold beer and baseball just seemed to go together and if the parents were out, mine, Glenn's, or Eddie's, we would get beer and watch the Mets. I didn't actually like beer at the start of that summer, but by the end of it, I had acquired a taste for it. Beer also had other advantages. It was available at grocery stores, beer distributors and delis. This was much more convenient, but more importantly, we were much less likely to be asked for "proof of age" than in a liquor store.

Gradually, most of us became beer drinkers and our days of wandering around drinking whiskey from the bottle were behind us, for the most part. Except, of course, special events like dances or record hops, where concealment was a crucial factor and carrying around large amounts of beer was impractical.

One of my tricks was when my parents actually sent me to the grocery store or the deli, I would get the stuff they sent me for, like bread, milk, cigarettes, butter, coffee, cold cuts, potato salad, and oh yeah, "a six-pack of Rheingold." They never asked me for "proof," which in those days in New York was a draft card. While the clerk was ringing up the order and bagging it, I would cast ballots in the annual Miss Rheingold contest. When I got home, I would hide the beer until I needed it.

We had plenty of debates and arguments about who should be Miss Rheingold as we drank beer and watched the Mets. Dennis and I agreed on our favorite and one night at Eddie's house, Dennis showed up with a whole pad of ballots he took from a deli. We filled them out for our favorite while we watched the game, and on our way home stopped in the deli and stuffed them all in the ballot box. Our choice did win, and Dennis, of course, took the credit. "It's a sign from God," he would say. "We were meant to be together. Now, if I could just find her!"

On Friday and Saturday nights we would search desperately for girls. We went to any local dance that was held and to any party that we heard about, invited or not. Often, there were fights or near fights and occasionally, the police were called, but we always evaded serious trouble. Once, the cops gave us a ride home from a party, just to make sure we didn't go back! With school out, the opportunities to meet girls were sadly fewer. Work took more time than school, was much more draining physically, and there were many fewer social events. We sure tried, though.

I remember three world events that we talked about that summer. The first was the Supreme Court ruling that prayer in public schools was unconstitutional. This seemed like a victory for the godless Communists and the pagan forces of evil. "We're lucky we went to Catholic schools," we told each other. We also agreed that our daily religion class was a numbingly boring waste of time and that, when we actually did pray in school, we mindlessly mumbled the customary prayer in response to being prompted by a Brother.

The second was the abject failure of Mariner 1, which flew erratically for several minutes and had to be destroyed without ever leaving the atmosphere. This seemed to reinforce the notion that the Russians remained far ahead of us in the space race and that their nuclear missile technology might also be superior.

The third and for me, the most shocking, was the killing of an eighteen-year-old German man by an East German border guard, captured on film. The East German and a friend were trying to cross the border from East to West Berlin. One made it over, but the other one was shot in the back. He bled to death as he lay at the foot of the wall for nearly an hour. There were pictures of this horrible scene on television and in newspapers the day before I turned sixteen. The newspaper story said it was, in fact, the fiftieth person killed in that year trying to escape East Berlin. The man was unarmed, eighteen and just wanted to leave. 'Would they have shot him if he were sixteen? fourteen? ten?,' we wondered. Was this our destiny as well, or was it nuclear annihilation? Was all the horrible stuff we were being told about Communism actually true?

We talked about these things in the final days of summer in 1962. We were sixteen and the world seemed like a very scary place. Racial tensions and violence were growing internally and Communism seemed to be a real threat that could take over the world. A group of nuclear scientists issued a warning about how close we were to what they called "doomsday." They had created a graphic and called it the "Doomsday Clock" with midnight representing the end of the world. They showed the present threat as being five minutes to midnight. It was hard to care about the future, about getting into college or the upcoming SATs, or even the Mets. Little did we know that, in less than two months, we'd be literally on the brink of doomsday.

CHAPTER SIXTEEN

◆ ◆ ◆ ◆ ◆

"ON THE BRINK"

I've learned to hate Russians
All through my whole life
If another war starts
It's them we must fight.
To hate them and fear them
To run and to hide
And accept it all bravely
With God on my side.
> Bob Dylan—"With God on Our Side"

As the start of school approached, Holy Cross held its annual Book Day, where we would visit the school and see our section and schedule and buy our books. The letter sent home told us of some changes Holy Cross had made. No longer would we have six grading periods, but instead we would have four. No longer would our sections be designated by letters, but rather by numbers. The first change was good, as far as we were concerned—two fewer report cards was a good thing, we all agreed.

The second change was silly. We were still theoretically grouped by ability or at least by performance, although none of us knew the criteria or the method used for moving a student up or down. It was another thing we were asked to take on faith. Now, instead of being in Section C or D, you were in Section 32 or 33. What this accomplished, none of us understood.

The schedules and section rosters were taped to the front door of the school. Glenn and I arrived together and we began nervously looking over the Junior Class rosters.

"Here you are in Section 32," said Glenn and then a moment later, "... so am I and so is Pat Kelly." I quickly began to scroll the roster of Section 32, feeling relieved that I hadn't dropped any since last year's less than stellar performance. I was soon delighted to see Paul Falabella and Ray Frasene in my section and then, near the bottom, to see Tommy Taraci.

Tommy, Pat, Glenn and I all in the same section struck me as a terrific break. I was ecstatic! In didn't know any of my teachers nor had I heard anything about them. I viewed a fresh start as a good thing.

Just before school started, I tried on Jimmy Daley's clothes again and found the pants to be too short. I showed my mom and she told me to pile them up on the couch and she would see what she could do to let them down. She told me I could finally get a school blazer if I wanted, but I no longer wanted one.

"Can't I just buy some clothes, like normal people do?" I asked sarcastically.

"No, we're not normal people," Mom answered. "Who's 'normal' people?"

"People who buy new clothes when they need them!"

"Yeah, well, are they paying two tuitions?"

"I look like a jerk most of the time," I pointed out, pleadingly.

"These are beautiful, high-quality clothes!"

"Maybe they *were* beautiful, high-quality clothes. Now they don't fit, they're worn out and out of style. I've been wearing this stuff every day for two years."

"Well, we can't afford new clothes. Who do you think we are? Maybe for Christmas, we can get you a suit or a sports coat. I'll keep an eye out for sales. Gertz had a sale on suits with two pairs of pants. That would be good. You could wear one pair to school and keep the other pair nice."

Walking to Mueller's after the first day of school, Dickie, Tommy, Jeff, Glenn and I were all feeling upbeat about the year ahead.

"Hey, Joe, Jay Carroll is in my section," said Jeff. "Didn't you tell me he's a good guy?"

"Oh, yeah, Jay's a great guy. I wish he was in my section. You can have a lot of laughs with Jay."

"Jeff's been having too much fun, apparently," chimed in Dickie.

"What?" answered Jeff.

"You dropped a section . . ."

"Yes, I did, but I'm *still* ahead of you, asshole."

"B-u-u-u-t, I came up two sections."

"B-u-u-u-u-u-t, and this is the important part, *I'm still ahead of you!*"

"B-u-u-u-u-t I'll pass you this year and *finish* ahead of you."

"Bullshit! You'll never catch me."

Dickie came to an abrupt stop. "If you piss me off, Jeff, I'll switch from French to Spanish and I'll pass you by so fast, I'll be a blur."

"They won't let you take Spanish."

"Why not?"

"'Cause Spanish is your native language!"

"So what . . . There's no rule about that. How do they know you don't speak French?"

"Why would I speak French, I'm not French."

"How do they know? You could be 'Jahfree Bauduoo' at home," said Dickie with a pronounced French accent. "Come to think of it, Baudo is a weird name. Come to think of it, you're a weird guy."

Jeff was at a loss of things to say and so he changed the subject. "You three are all in the same class, huh? That's cool!"

"Yeah," I answered. "Pat Kelly, too."

"Did Tommy tell you about Billy Regan," Glenn asked, looking at me.

"No, what about him?"

"He's not playing varsity this year."

"Why not?"

"He said it's too much trouble for the little playing time he'd get."

"So? What's the big deal?"

"Intramurals, knucklehead."

"Oh, shit yeah! He can play intramurals."

"We should be awesome," chimed in Tommy.

"We have three Varsity players in our section," added Glenn. "Maybe we can get one of them to coach us."

We visited with the rest of the guys at Mueller's and exchanged first day of school stories and then Glenn and I started for home. On the way, we discussed how this was going to be an important year for us.

"You realize a year from now, we'll be applying to colleges," I pointed out. "Do you have any idea where you want to go?"

"No, I guess it depends on what we can afford, which is not much."

"I'm gonna start sending for catalogs."

"Good, let me see them when you're done."

"I'm really gonna knuckle down this year, starting right now. Our teachers seem okay."

"I'm not so sure, but after Regis and Trentacoste, I know what you mean."

After Glenn broke off at his house, I continued on alone. It was a beautiful late summer evening, and I felt unusually optimistic. Just the day before, JFK had declared that the United States would put a man on the moon by the end of the decade. If *he* was planning for the end of the decade, maybe there *would* be one after all. I was an upperclassman, I had some of my best buddies in my class, no Latin, a clean slate with new teachers, a potentially good intramural basketball team, and maybe some new clothes for Christmas. My dream of going to college seemed reachable, just like going to the moon. I was determined to do what it would take to make it happen.

Shortly after school started, a news story caught my attention. A young man named James Meredith tried to enroll as a student at the University of Mississippi, but was barred from entering. Local officials and state police, acting on orders from the Governor, did not allow him to enroll. In the next few days, Federal troops and U.S. Marshals assembled in Oxford, Mississippi, to enforce the law and allow him to enroll in classes. The television news showed troops and marshals in Army trucks, taking over the Administration Building. A riot broke out and two people were killed and over seventy-five troops and marshals were injured. Ole Miss students were jeering and waving the Confederate Flag. Meredith, dressed in a suit and looking very afraid, was escorted into the building by the United States Assistant Attorney General, registered, and was escorted out. The whole scene was very unsettling to me. Why couldn't a black man go to a public college? Why would it provoke such violence? Was this a Communist conspiracy to divide us and weaken us as a nation?

This incident was the subject of some discussion on a subsequent Saturday night. Pat Kelly claimed to have found a neat place for us to drink beer. We were too young for bars and walking the streets with large amounts of beer was looking for trouble. We liked going to someone's house if his or her parents weren't home, but often, we had no place to safely drink. Pat recently had discovered a place just a few minutes' walk from Mueller's that was secluded and quiet and lonely at night. It was a wall near the Long Island Railroad station that was shielded from view from the street by hedges and overgrown brush and was dark and quiet at night. It was actually on residential property, but far from the house.

One Saturday night in early October, he suggested we get some beer and he'd show us his discovery. Dennis and I agreed and Dennis volunteered to get the beer, since he had his brother's draft card in his wallet in case he was asked for proof of age. We walked to the deli and Dennis got two six-packs and we walked to what became known as "the wall."

"Isn't this cool?" asked Pat as he sat down and held out his hand for a can of beer.

"Yeah, this is nice," responded Dennis, reaching in the bag and pulling a can out of the cardboard wrapper that held six cans of beer. He gave one to Pat and started pulling at another for me. Pat put his other hand out and Dennis looked at him quizzically.

"You got one," Dennis said, handing a beer to me and reaching into the bag for one for himself.

"The key?" said Pat, his hand still outstretched.

"The what?"

"The 'church key'?"

"The what?"

"The can opener?"

"Don't *you* have an opener?"

"No. Do you think I walk around all the time with a can opener?"

"Actually, I did. You always had an opener when I've been drinking with you."

"That's because it comes with the beer if you ask for one."

"Really?"

"Yeah, you just ask for a key and he puts it in the bag."

"No shit?"

"No shit."

"I suppose you don't have an opener, either," said Dennis, looking at me with disappointment in his voice.

"Uh-h-h-h, no," I answered. "I left my opener in my school pants."

"Jesus Christ, I don't want to go all the way back for an opener."

"I knew we shouldn't have sent kid to do a man's job," said Pat to me, smiling broadly and chuckling.

"Yeah, yeah, fuck you," said Dennis, getting to his feet and starting to walk away.

"Want me to go with you?" I asked.

Without answering my question, Dennis broke into a run, leaving us puzzled, but confident he would be back. He was back in about three minutes!

"I'm a fucking genius," he proclaimed, holding up a piece of concrete a little bigger than his hand.

"What? We're gonna smash the cans with a rock?" asked Pat.

"If you *were* a genius, or even of average intelligence, you would have asked for an opener," I added.

Dennis held up his other hand to reveal a nail.

"Did you notice the construction site down the block?"

He grabbed a can of beer and punched a hole in it and sucked some out. He handed the can to Pat and punched a hole in another and began drinking.

"Hey, what about me?" I asked.

"Mary, Mary, quite contrary—what?"

"What about me?"

"I'm not letting you use my nail or my rock until you apologize."

"For what?"

"For your remark about my intelligence."

"Come on, give me the nail or open me a beer."

"That hoit my feelins," Dennis said, looking down at the ground, shyly.

"Come on—open me up one."

"The boadayous hoit my feelins."

"What?" said Pat, giggling.

"The boadayous," Dennis repeated, pointing at both of us.

"Why me?" Pat laughed. "I didn't say anything about your intelligence."

"What about the boy and the man crack? Youse think I got no feelin's?"

"Okay, I'm sorry," I said.

"You're just sayin' that, 'cause you want my nail."

"No, honestly, I mean it—I'm sorry," I said again, faking contriteness.

"I oughtta make you find your own nail," Dennis said as he handed me the nail and the rock.

I punched two holes next to each other and took a sip.

"Give me those," Pat said, holding out his hand for the rock and nail. He punched a second hole directly across the top of the can from the first hole and took a big slug.

"That was better!" he proclaimed.

"Why?" said Dennis. "Something wrong with the way *I* did it?"

"It has something to do with equalizing pressure," I offered. "We haven't gotten that far yet in Physics."

""Hey, that would be a good question for Houlihan," said Pat, laughing. "Why does beer pour quicker with two holes in the top, even if you're only drinkin' out of one?"

"Mary, Mary, quite contrary—who is Houlihan?" asked Dennis.

"He's our Physics teacher," I answered.

"Physics? Physics sucks," Dennis proclaimed. "I'm ready for another beer."

He held out his hand for the nail and rock.

"I'll open it for you," offered Pat, reaching into the bag for a beer can."

"That's all right, you've done enough already," answered Dennis, feigning hurt feelings.

"You *are* kidding, right?" asked Pat, suddenly not so sure.

Dennis turned his head away and looked up toward the sky. Pat punched holes in the beer can and held it out to Dennis.

"Dennis, you're kidding, right?"

Dennis took the beer and said, "yeah" while he shook his head no. We all broke up laughing.

"Of course I'm kiddin'. You two morons can't hurt my feelings."

"Speaking of being morons, we have the PSAT this week, do you?" I asked Dennis.

"Of course we do. It's a national test."

"Did you see that guy in Mississippi enrolling at the university?" I asked both guys.

"Yeah, that was something," said Dennis. "That poor guy."

"I couldn't believe the hostility and anger. The poor guy's just trying to better himself. They should be helping him, not trying to stop him," I offered.

"My father says it's all about jobs," answered Dennis. "They're afraid if the Negroes get an education, they'll be taking jobs from whites."

"Hmm, that's interesting," said Pat. "I hadn't thought of that. I thought it was that they didn't want Negroes marrying whites."

"This guy's just trying to go to school, not get married," responded Dennis.

"Yeah, but if the Negroes are allowed to go to school with whites they probably will becomes friends and socialize . . ."

"So?" asked Dennis.

"You didn't let me finish, I was taking a sip of beer. Once they start socializing, they'll start dating and eventually marrying."

"Are you finished *now*?" asked Dennis, sarcastically.

"Yeah."

"*So?*"

"What do you mean 'so'?"

"So what? What's the big deal?"

"Well, obviously, it *is* a big deal. Those were *federal troops* that were called in."

"Yeah . . . unbelievable. Federal troops and rioting, just to *register* one Negro? How is he gonna go to class? Is he gonna have bodyguards?"

"That's a good question!"

"Mary, Mary, quite contrary, how does your . . ."

"Hey, let's put the empties back in the bag and throw them away somewhere. We don't want to make a mess here and have cops checking this place out," Pat suggested, reaching for a fresh beer.

"What do you think, Joe?" asked Pat, punching holes in a new beer.

"I agree, we don't want to ruin this place."

"No, I meant about the Mississippi stuff."

"Oh, well, it really upsets me."

"Why?"

"I just can't believe the way those people were acting."

"Who?" asked Dennis. "The Mississippi—ites? Or is it Mississippians?"

"It's Mississippians . . . yeah, them," I answered. "The level of violence and hostility was unreal."

"Why do you think that was?" asked Pat.

"Well, it makes me mighty suspicious."

"Suspicious of what?"

"It *could* be Mississippites," chimed in Dennis.

"That it was Communist-inspired," I answered, ignoring Dennis. "I think that the Communists might have incited the whites to get them all riled up."

"Why?" asked Pat.

"To divide us as a nation and make us look bad to the world."

"I don't think it's Mississippiers," said Dennis. "That doesn't sound right . . ."

"Bad to the world?" asked Pat.

"Yeah, whenever there is trouble in this country, the Communists use it as propaganda."

"Yeah, I can understand that," said Pat thoughtfully, "but who are you talking about inciting the violence?"

"I really don't know, but they always seem to mention outside agitators whenever there is trouble."

"Who does?" asked Dennis, with a big smile on his face, "the Mississippiers?"

We all broke up laughing again.

"I think I'm gonna put an end to this controversy," Dennis declared, looking in the bag for a fresh beer.

"What controversy?" I asked.

"About what to call the people from Mississippi," Dennis answered.

"There's a controversy about that?" I asked, laughing and looking at Pat.

"What do you think I've been wracking my brain about over here all this time?" answered Dennis.

Pat was just swallowing some beer and almost choked at Dennis' answer. "Jesus Christ, are you trying to kill me?" Pat asked, once he regained the ability to speak. He blew his nose in his handkerchief. "I got beer up my nose, for God's sake!"

"Mary, Mary, quite contrary—I'm gonna call them the 'People from Mississippi,'" Dennis announced quite proudly. "That way we will avoid any hard feelings."

"Hard feelings from who?" asked Pat, laughing.

"*From the People from Mississippi!* Haven't you been listening?"

We laughed hard and Pat kept coughing and trying to clear his windpipe.

"I'm glad you're not in our school," laughed Pat to Dennis, still trying to catch his breath.

"Oh yeah, why is that?"

"Because you're fucked in the brain."

"*I'm* fucked in the brain?"

"Yeah, and it's hard enough now to be serious in school with Joe and Tommy and Glenn and Dickie and Jeff."

"How many are left?" I asked Dennis, holding out an empty can.

"Well, I've never been there, but I'd say . . . oh . . . a lot."

"What?"

"How many what are left? Beers?"

"Oh, three . . . I thought you meant people from Mississippi."

"You *are* fucked in the brain," I said, grabbing a new beer and putting my empty in the bag.

"You guys get mean when you drink, did you know that?" Dennis asked.

Pat finished the beer he was drinking and reached for the last two. He handed one to Dennis and asked, "So, what do you think of my discovery? This will do in the pinch, won't it?"

"You mean this place?" I asked.

"Yeah."

"I think it's great."

"How about you, Dennis?"

Dennis was taking a leak on some bushes with his back to us. "I think it's great, too," he answered over his shoulder.

"You're not pissin' where it'll run over to here, are you Dennis?" Pat asked.

"Of course not! Do you think I'm fucked in the brain?"

"I think we clearly decided that, didn't we?" said Pat, looking at me.

"Mary, Mary, quite contrary, how does your garden grow?"

"And why do you keep saying that over and over?" I asked Dennis.

"Oh, it's just a little ditty I heard and I can't get it out of my mind."

"Your alleged mind, you mean."

"Ha! Ha! Very funny."

"How's it go?" asked Pat.

"Mary, Mary, quite contrary, how does your garden grow? With blue bells and cockle shells and one fuckin' petunia."

This time, *I* was swallowing and almost choked.

With the beer gone, we started back to Mueller's with the empties, which we threw away in the trashcan at the Long Island Railroad Station.

"That was fun," said Pat. "I really enjoyed that. I like sitting around and talking and thinking about serious stuff."

"Me too," I answered.

"Me three," said Dennis.

"We ought to do it more often."

"Okay we'll call it 'Philosophy Club,'" I suggested.

"Why can't we call it drinkin' and talkin'?" asked Dennis.

"We can if you like," I answered.

"You always want to give things names, did you know that?"

"No, I didn't."

"Well, it's true. You better be careful or people will start thinkin' you're fucked in the brain."

That Monday, after a brief, but strong lecture about the importance of this test in determining our future, we took the PSAT exam.

Ironically, as we sat at our desks, poring over questions and nervously and quickly checking and rechecking our answers, (we were instructed to pass over things we had no idea of—to return to later after answering all that we thought we knew), the prospect of there even being a future was in serious doubt. The world was on the brink of humanity's worst nightmare, nuclear war. We didn't know it, but four U.S. tactical squadrons were ordered to prepare for air strikes on Cuba as a result of the discovery of Soviet missile bases under construction in Cuba.

Two days later, President Kennedy addressed the nation on TV. Kennedy announced that the Soviet Union was nearing completion of missile installations that were capable of carrying nuclear warheads that could easily hit American cities. He announced a "strict quarantine" on Cuba and solemnly promised a "full retaliatory response upon the Soviet Union" if any missile was launched. The Strategic Air Command had earlier in the day begun a massive alert of B-52 nuclear bombers that kept one-eighth of the force airborne at all times.

After this special announcement, I went to my room to deal with my own personal crisis. The next day it was my turn to read my composition to my English class. Brother Arthur had given us the assignment about two or three weeks before this and each day one of us read his to the class. We were progressing alphabetically and it was my turn. Six guys had gone before me and typically, I hadn't really started on mine until that day. The others had been pretty dull, I thought, and Brother Arthur had stressed that good writing should grab the readers' interest and hold it.

"Write about something you care about! Write about something you believe in! If it's not interesting to you, why would it be to others?" he implored us.

Fifty percent of our grade would be grammar, spelling and punctuation, and the other fifty, content and delivery. He emphasized holding the readers' or listeners' attention, being logical and organized in our presentation, and reading with the proper emotion, inflection and tone.

The only thing I could think of to write about, that would be of interest to all of us . . . Holy Cross High School.

I wrote a composition about how Holy Cross could be made a better school. I first made a few notes and then began writing. As I did, I actually started to enjoy doing it. I felt the issues I would discuss would definitely hold everyone's attention and it was something I cared about and believed in. I worked on putting them in a logical order and checked grammar and punctuation. I actually regretted waiting so long to start the assignment, since English was first period and I needed time to practice reading it out loud.

As class began, I was nervous, but also excited. I thought I was going to score big with this. Glenn and Paul and Pat asked me what it was about, but I told them they'd have to wait and see. A few minutes after class began and before I had begun my presentation, the alarm for an air raid drill sounded. We all filed into the hallway and stood facing the wall, with our arms behind our heads. After a few minutes, Brother Josephat walked past quickly with a stopwatch in his hand.

"I want absolute silence during a drill!" he yelled as he passed and turned the corner.

"I guess he wants us to hear the bomb explode," whispered Paul.

"That's not funny," answered Anthony Fontanelli, who was on the other side of me. "Did you hear the President last night?"

"Shhhh," said Ray Frasene, who was on the other side of Fontanelli.

Paul, Ray and I all laughed. Normally, Fontanelli would never, ever break a rule or not obey an instruction or talk when he wasn't supposed to, so Ray shushing him struck us all as funny.

After the drill, Brother Josephat came over the Public Address system with a report on the drill. He said things generally went well, but there was some confusion in certain places and he discussed those areas that needed clarification and again expressed the desire for absolute silence. Ray mimicked the sound of a bomb exploding, in an attempt to unnerve Fontanelli, but I couldn't safely turn around to catch his reaction. Never had an air raid drill been taken so seriously. When Brother Josephat was finished, it was too late for my presentation and Brother Arthur postponed it until the next day.

I was happy with the unexpected reprieve and that night, I took extra time to check grammar and punctuation and practiced reading it in my room a few times.

That night, the news on TV was grim. Soviet ships were heading for Cuba and were believed to have submarine escorts. What would happen if they failed to stop and honor the quarantine? If American ships took action, would the Soviets retaliate? Would the Soviets launch their nuclear missiles, fearing we would first and afraid if they didn't, that they would lose their ability to? The first Soviet ships were due to reach the quarantine line the next day, Friday, said Walter Cronkite, in a deadly serious tone.

In the morning, Glenn, Don Glennon and I talked about the crisis on our way to school.

"Anyone hear any news broadcasts this morning?" I asked.

"The Russian ships are near the line and still coming," responded Glenn.

"Maybe we shouldn't go to school," I offered. "If this is our last day on earth, why spend it in school?"

"Oh, that's bull," said Don.

"What's bull?" asked Glenn.

"Nothin's gonna happen."

"Why do you say that?" I asked.

"The Russians will back down! They don't want to die!"

"That's probably what they are saying about us," I answered. "Let's cut school."

"And do what? Everybody else is in school. You just want to get out of reading your composition! I just realized that," laughed Glenn.

"Not true," I responded. "I'm ready."

"What's it about?" asked Don.

"He won't tell anyone," said Glenn, mockingly. "It's a secret."

"Why's it a secret?" asked Don, looking at me.

"It's not that it's a secret," I answered. "It's just that I had a good idea and think it would work best if guys don't already know what's coming."

"Well, I'm not in your class so tell me."

"It's about how to improve Holy Cross."

"Okay. Well, how?" asked Don.

"Through the Student Council."

"Sounds boring. The Student Council doesn't do anything."

"That's my point!"

"That's what you wouldn't tell us?" asked Glenn, shaking his head in disbelief. "I'm sorry you ruined it for me now," he added sarcastically.

Speaking in front of a group was an anxiety-producing situation, but although nervous, I also had confidence in my composition being better than those that had gone before me.

After a few minutes of class, Brother Arthur announced it was time for my reading. I began by saying that this composition is about making Holy Cross a better school. I pointed out that each section elected a member to the Student Council and in addition, we as a class, elected four class officers. But, I stated, "the Student Council seems to have no role in the school other than to sponsor one dance each year. If the Student Council was to have any importance, shouldn't it have some say in the rules and policies that affect the students?" I asked rhetorically. I glanced up at the class and I seemed to have everyone's attention. "Good, this is going well," I thought.

I went on to propose that the Student Council could be given a more important role and had suggestions into what specific areas they needed to address. I could tell by the reaction of the class that this was going well. I noticed heads nodding in agreement and Tommy Taraci with a big smile on his face. When I sneaked a quick glance at Brother Arthur, he was sitting at his desk with his chin in the palm of his hand and fingers over his mouth. I could not really tell his reaction, but it seemed okay.

The first area I suggested for Student Council to deal with was the dress code. As soon as I mentioned it, the class reacted. There were murmurs and "yeses" and nervous giggles. "What is gained," I asked, "by us being uncomfortable and hot while in class?" I went on to talk about the heat in the school during May, June, September, and even October. Windows were rarely ever opened because of street noise and the southern side of the building baked all day in the sun. I argued that consideration should be give to allowing us to remove our jackets in class or leave them in our lockers on hot days and allowing us to loosen our ties and open our collars when appropriately warm. I even proposed that the requirement of jackets be scrapped completely. "One teacher," I read, "when he heard our complaining about the heat, suggested we offer it up as penance for our sins. We are not here to do penance; we are here to learn!"

I felt I had delivered that line well and by the class reaction, I knew I had achieved many of the objectives Brother Arthur had been speaking about. I went on to the requirement of a "Princeton-type haircut." No one seemed to know precisely what a Princeton cut was, but we knew the policy enforced meant short and we knew it meant no facial hair of any sort. Guys were constantly being harassed and warned about their hair being too long or them needing to stand closer to the razor or get the fuzz off their upper lip. Occasionally, someone would be sent home and told not to return until in compliance with the code.

"It's *our* hair. It grows on *our* bodies. Why is it anybody else's business? What does it have to do with learning? The military has a similar requirement for various reasons, but we are not in the military. At least not yet."

That line, I imagined, would get some laughs, but went largely unnoticed due to the strong reaction to the lines before it.

When I glanced again at Brother Arthur, he was glaring at the class with a stern look on his face. I took it to mean he didn't like some of the class reaction, but not as a sign of displeasure with me.

I went on to raise an issue that was not often discussed, but one which I thought had a lot of merit and one that had been discussed within our group on our walk home a few times: student evaluation of teachers. As soon as I got the words out of my mouth, there were cheers and applause.

"Be still!" yelled Brother Arthur at the class.

"Cool," I thought. "This is the best composition so far." I paused a moment and went on. I stated that no harm could come from teachers seeing what their students thought of them and from considering suggestions for how things could be done better. I also suggested that the Principal and Dean of Men see the evaluations so they would know how students felt. I then made what I thought was one of the best points in my whole composition.

"The administration probably thinks that the student body would rate easy teachers high and the more demanding teachers low," I exclaimed. "This, I believe, is not true. I believe that many of the demanding teachers, like Brother David Murray who many of us had for Geometry last year, would be rated very high and many of the less-demanding teachers who we've had for Religion or Social Studies would be rated low." I felt it was okay to use Brother David's name, since he was no longer at Holy Cross.

The class reacted again in a positive, enthusiastic way, to my delight. I glanced at Brother Arthur, but his reaction wasn't exactly what I was hoping for. Now he was glaring at *me* with a scowl on his face. Although my stomach tightened and my heart sank, I had no alternative but to continue.

Lunch was my next target. I argued that our lunch period was too short. The total time allotted for lunch was half a period, i.e. twenty-five minutes. The long lines to get food and pay the cashier could easily take ten of those minutes or more, thus forcing us to wolf down our food. The prices were too high and rising. The most popular item was French fries, which had gone from ten cents to fifteen cents to twenty cents in three years. Pizza had also gone up and was too infrequently on the menu. I had just mentioned that the fish sticks on Friday were horrible and that's what led to a French fry shortage on most Fridays when Brother Arthur stopped me.

"You're finished!" Brother Arthur said, and motioned for me to approach him.

Unfortunately, I was reading the composition and thought he said, "*are* you finished?"

"No, Brother," I answered. "I have more."

Suddenly, Brother Arthur was in my face. He grabbed my shirt and tie at about my chest level in his hand and sneered, "Do you think you're funny, Farrell?"

"No, Brother," I said, in a tone that conveyed confusion, like, 'why would you think that?'

"I said you're finished."

"Oh! I thought you *asked* if I was finished."

Brother Arthur let go of me and snatched the composition out of my hand. He went to his desk, wrote a big red zero on the top of the paper and underlined it.

"Here, Farrell," he said, as he held it out for me to take. "What do you think of that?"

I looked at the zero for a few seconds, as if I couldn't believe it and said, "I don't think that's fair."

"Well, I do! That was inappropriate content!"

"What about the 50 percent for grammar and punctuation?" I asked.

I was feeling desperate since the grade on the composition was to be a large part of the first quarter grade. Unfortunately, the class thought my question was funny and laughed. That didn't help my cause.

"You go ask Brother Josephat if he thinks it's fair," Brother Arthur answered.

I turned and meekly headed back to my seat when Brother Arthur yelled, "Did you hear me, Farrell? I want you to go show your composition to Brother Josephat and ask him if your grade is fair."

I was speechless and groping for something to say, "Go! Now! And let me know his answer," Brother Arthur yelled.

I turned around and left the classroom in disgust. I walked down the hall and turned the corner toward the Principal's Office. Once out of sight, I headed into the boys' bathroom. I needed time to think!

I paced around the bathroom and rubbed my face nervously, trying to figure out what to do. I had never spoken to Brother Josephat and would have preferred to keep it that way. I avoided him and Brother Richard McDonald, the Dean of Men, like they had the plague. Now my heart was beating loudly in my chest and I felt short of breath and completely disgusted.

I really thought my composition was good and would get a good grade. I wasn't looking for trouble. And here I was, in possibly the worst trouble of my life, and I didn't *intend* to do anything wrong. My mind was racing and I thought maybe Brother Josephat wasn't in and I would catch a break. I decided to walk past his office and see if he was there, hoping against hope, he wasn't. Of course he was. Not only was he in, but he saw me looking in his office.

"What do you want, Farrell?" he yelled as I ducked behind the outer wall of his office.

'Oh, my God, he knows who I am,' I thought, panicking. As I backed up so he could see me, I said, "I need to talk to you, Brother Josephat," I answered meekly, "if you're not busy. If you are, I could come back later."

"Wait right there and I'll be with you in a minute," he answered.

I sat down in a chair outside his office, feeling sick. "*Now* would be a great time for the Russians to attack," I thought. It was the only chance I had. I started *hoping* to hear air raid sirens.

But, of course, I wouldn't be that lucky. During the wait I thought, 'Going to Flushing High wouldn't be so bad.' Now, I wasn't intimidated by the public school scene like I was in eighth grade. I thought that maybe I should just walk out of here now, go to my locker and get my stuff and leave Holy Cross. My parents would go completely nuts, but maybe that was inevitable. I clung to the hope that Brother Josephat would not see this as a big deal and feel that a zero was punishment enough. Maybe there was even a chance my parents wouldn't be brought into this. So I stayed and hoped for a Russian attack.

"Okay, Mr. Farrell, what can I do for you?" Brother Josephat called out.

"Brother Arthur wanted me to show this to you," I answered, holding out my composition.

Brother Josephat took it from me and began reading it.

"Is this an assignment?"

"Yes, Brother. Each student has to write a composition . . ." My voice trailed off as he was reading it intently.

"Well, Mr. Farrell, let me ask you something. Why do you come here to school? Why don't you go somewhere else?"

"I like it here, Brother."

"You like it here?"

"Yes, Brother."

"From reading this, I wouldn't think so."

"I like it here, Brother, but it could be better. That was my point."

"Is this Brother Arthur's zero?"

"Yes, Brother."

"I guess he didn't like your point?"

"No, Brother."

"So he sent you to *me* for a punishment?"

"No, Brother."

"No?"

"No, Brother, I didn't think the grade was fair and so he said to see what you thought."

At this point, I was feeling relieved. Brother Josephat was calm and didn't seem angry. He seemed amused, if anything.

"Is there anything you're not telling me that I ought to know about this?"

"Uh, just that we read our compositions to the class."

"Oh, I see! You read this in class aloud?"

"Yes, Brother."

"Wait here a minute," Brother Josephat said, as he suddenly got up and left. When he returned, he told me to step next door and see Brother Richard.

"I have another appointment to attend to, Mr. Farrell. I want you to get Brother Richard's opinion. He's reading it now."

I slowly walked to the office of the "Dean of Men" and, as I entered, I saw Brother Richard reading my composition. He looked at me menacingly and motioned for me to sit down. As he was reading it, I was struck by the contrast between the two. Brother Josephat, the principal, was tall and manly with a strong deep voice and a tough demeanor, yet the Dean of Men, who was in charge of discipline in a school with 1,100 teenage boys, was short, effeminate and spoke softly and distinctly. He had also recently been named the Faculty moderator for the annual musical Holy Cross put on each year.

When he finished reading it, he glared at me and asked, "So Brother Arthur Hanaway gave you a zero?"

"Yes, Brother."

"What is your problem? You went to Brother Josephat to get your grade changed?"

"No, Brother. I was *sent* to Brother Josephat."

"Why?"

"Because I told Brother Arthur that I didn't think my grade was fair."

"Fair, huh? You don't think it was fair?"

"No, I don't, Brother. The punctuation and grammar alone are supposed to be worth 50 points."

"Do you think it was fair that Jesus suffered and died for your sins?"

"Uh . . . no, Brother."

"Yet you have the arrogance and gall to demand fairness when Jesus did not?"

"I just can't afford a zero, Brother."

"Perhaps you should have thought of that earlier, Mr. Farrell. Have your parents seen what you've written?"

"Uh . . . no, Brother."

"I bet they haven't. They spend good money to send you here and, perhaps they are wasting it."

Brother Richard started writing a note. When he finished, he folded the note and handed it to me. "This is for Brother Arthur. Make sure you give it to him. As for the grade, like Pontius Pilate, I wash my hands of this matter. It's up to Brother Arthur. Good day, Mr. Farrell."

I started back to class and once again, darted into the bathroom to read the note. It said, "Brother Arthur, let's make sure Mr. and Mrs. Farrell know about this. Have them sign the composition."

"Son of a bitch," I whispered quietly to myself. I couldn't *not* show Brother Arthur the note because I knew they would talk to each other. I had to give it to him and face the music at home or just leave school now. I kept thinking how innocently I had arrived in such a mess. I just couldn't believe it. As I left the bathroom and headed back to class, I thought to myself, 'I'm not going to the musical this year—I hope nobody goes!'

Just as I entered class, the bell rang, signaling the end of class. Brother Arthur motioned for me to stay as the rest of the class filed out.

"Well, Farrell, what did Brother Josephat think?"

I quickly told him what happened and handed him the note from Brother Richard. I was getting concerned about being late for my next class.

"Excellent idea," Brother Arthur said after reading Brother Richard's note. "I want your parents to sign this and return it to me on Monday."

"Okay, Brother," I said, and started for the door.

"Hold it, Farrell! Who said you were dismissed?"

"Brother, I'm going to be late for math!"

"Oh, that would be such a shame, wouldn't it? Maybe that's another item for your composition. No detention. Come to class whenever you want."

The bell signaling the start of second period rang.

"Oh, too bad, Farrell. You can go now."

As if I wasn't already having a terrible day, now I had detention on a Friday afternoon.

After math class and all the rest of the day, I was the major topic of discussion in the hallways. Word spread quickly and guys were congratulating me and expressing how unfairly they thought I was being treated. It did little to ease the sick feeling in the pit of my stomach.

While I was sitting in detention, I decided on what I was going to do. I would forge my parents' signatures. I just couldn't stand the thought of their (mostly my mother's) rantings and ravings and carrying on. I was pretty sure I had copies of other things they had signed and I would forge their signatures.

When I arrived at Mueller's, the whole crowd was there and had been talking about the composition episode. Some of the girls from our St. Andrew's group were there and they were saying how much worse they had it than us. Kathy Lynch was demonstrating how, as soon as they were out of sight of the nuns at their high school, they took off their hats and bow ties, opened their blouses at the neck and rolled up their pleated skirts at the waist until they were considerably higher than regulations allowed.

"At least you don't have to wear hideous uniforms," she exclaimed.

I told everybody that I was going to forge my parents' signatures. Jeff Baudo reminded me that the business office had signature cards available to teachers for the exact purpose of checking signatures.

"You better do a good job," said Jeff. "If you get caught, you get suspended!"

That weekend, the world came the closest it's ever come to nuclear disaster. Some of the missiles in Cuba became operational and an American reconnaissance plane was shot down and the pilot killed. Military Rules of Engagement called for us to retaliate against the Cuban sites that fired on our plane, which almost certainly would cause them to defend themselves and the whole thing would spiral out of control and escalate into a nuclear war. I *didn't care one bit*!

I found an old paper my mom had signed, but could not find my dad's signature on anything that I could have so as to use for practice. I practiced duplicating my mom's signature, but I couldn't get it to look right. By Sunday night, I was panicked and asked Ronnie to help me. She was reluctant to do it. She tried to persuade me to confess and face the music. She practiced forging my mom's signature a few times and then made a great suggestion. She suggested that I trace over my mom's signature on the old paper with my composition under it at the appropriate place and press hard. Then I could just follow the impression on my composition.

That's what I did. I tried it and I thought it looked okay. Since I didn't have anything to use to trace my dad's signature, I figured I'd just give it to Brother Arthur with the one signature and hope it would suffice. I was confident that he wouldn't make me take it back for my dad's signature. Confident, but wrong. He did. I couldn't believe it. I told him I had asked my dad to sign it, but he forgot to and had left for work before I realized it.

"Well, take it home tonight and bring it back tomorrow with both signatures," Brother Arthur directed. "I suspect your mother might be protecting you from your dad. I want them both to know how their investment in your education is going. And I'll be checking their signatures, so don't be a fool."

So, just as the Russians blinked and backed down, so did I. Since there wasn't going to be a thermonuclear war, I told my parents the story after dinner. Of course, everything was made worse when they discovered what I had tried to do. I gave the composition to my dad to sign. He read it and as he signed it, he saw the signature I had forged.

"You didn't see this, Vera?" he asked.

"No! What are you talking about?"

"You signed it."

"The hell I did!"

I told them what I had done and now I was not only an idiot and a fool, but a sneak and a liar. She ranted and raved for days.

I turned in the composition with the signatures and started praying that Brother Arthur wouldn't really give me an "F" for the quarter on my report card. The quarter ended in about two weeks and I was a model student in English during that time and I prayed every night that somehow, Brother Arthur would change his mind. There was no way I could pass with a zero. If he gave me a 50, it would hurt my grade, but I would at least pass. Brother Arthur was a pretty good guy and deep down, I believed he would give me a break. My other scores on quizzes were good and I got a 95 on the quarterly exam. It was only supposed to account for 25 percent of our grade, but I thought it was important for Brother Arthur to see that I knew the work and was taking it seriously.

One day after the exam, I stopped in St. Andrew's Church on my way home from Mueller's and lit a candle beneath the statue of Mary. She knew what was in my heart, I reasoned. She knew that I truly thought my composition was good and never intended it to be taken so seriously and get me into such trouble. I was pretty confident, that, since I truly meant no harm and did nothing wrong, it would turn out okay.

When my report card came, I got a *big fat* "F" in English.

JUNIORS-C.P.	1	2	3	4	FIN EX	SM AV	SM AV	YR AV	R		1	2	3	4	FIN EX	SM AV	SM AV	YR AV	R
RELIGION 3	86									SPANISH 1	73								
ENGLISH 3	F									PHYSICS	83								
U. S. HISTORY	86									BOOKKEEPING 1									
MATH 11	71									BUSINESS MANAGEMENT									
INT. ALGEBRA										BUS. LAW									
LATIN 3										TYPING									
FRENCH 1																			

FARRELL, JOSEPH W.   8-19-46-64
MR. JOSEPH FARRELL   VERONICA
30-25 MURRAY LANE   FL-8-5756
FLUSHING 54, N. Y.   ST. AND. AV.

ART | BAND | DAYS ABSENT | TIMES TARDY 1

HOLY CROSS HIGH SCHOOL — 26-20 Francis Lewis Blvd., Flushing 58, New York — Tel: IN 1-7900

My parents went nuts again, even though I told them it was all because of the composition, which they already knew about. It didn't seem to matter.

"You can kiss college good-bye," my mom yelled at me. "They'll never take you now, Mister Bigshot! Mister I'm-Gonna-Go-To-College! When all your friends go off to college and you're left behind working at Cresthaven, then you'll wake up!"

I didn't say anything in response. I couldn't really think of anything to say. I laid on my bed in the dark with the radio on for hours. I could always go in the service, I finally concluded. At least, that would get me out of here.

CHAPTER SEVENTEEN

◆ ◆ ◆ ◆ ◆

"HITTING THE WALL"

Lights out tonight,
Trouble in the heartland
Got a head-on collision
Smashin' in my guts, man
I'm caught in a crossfire
That I don't understand.
            Bruce Springsteen—"Badlands"

That "F" in English had a big effect on my state of mind. I had a hard time getting past it. I had started the year with a good attitude toward school and a determination to do well and go to college. An "F" in a subject that I expected to be one of my best was a serious blow. The way it had come about was frustrating. I didn't know how much it would affect the prospect of college, but given how I was struggling in some other classes, I felt it was a serious setback and I was alternately depressed and angry. From Thanksgiving through the Christmas break, I struggled with despair. I spent a lot of time in my room, laying in the dark listening to music.

One night during the Christmas break, Pat, Jeff, Dickie and I were drinking beer at the wall and I started asking about post-high school plans.

"Any of you guys thinking about the service?" I asked.

"No, why?" asked Jeff.

"'Cause I've been thinking about it."

"You're fuckin' kidding, right?" responded Dickie.

"No, I'm serious. I'm worried about getting into college and I've been thinking about it."

"I think the cold air is shrinking your brain," said Dickie shivering, before taking a big swallow from his beer can.

"Hey! Hey! Wait a minute! What's wrong with the service?" asked Jeff.

"Nothing's wrong with the service, unless you're Farrell."

"What do you mean?"

"Farrell can't do high school! How's he gonna do the military?"

"What do you mean, 'he can't do high school'?" asked Pat.

"He's in trouble all the time. Can you picture him in the Army?" responded Dickie.

Everybody laughed.

"He'd probably give a speech on how Paris Island could be improved," laughed Jeff.

Pat started choking on beer as he was swallowing, when Jeff's remark registered.

"Farrell in the military, a national nightmare," exclaimed Dickie, dramatically.

"Why are you talking about me like I'm not here?" I asked.

"It wouldn't really be a nightmare," said Pat. "They would throw him in the stockade and forget about him."

"Hey! I said 'why are you talking about me like I'm not here?'"

"'Cause it's fun," answered Dickie, finishing a beer and throwing the empty as high and far as he could across the street toward the railroad tracks.

"Hey, Dickie," I yelled plaintively, "this is a good place to drink and we don't want to attract any attention."

"Well, *excuse me!* I hope they throw your ass in the brig and throw away the key."

"The 'brig' is a Navy term," said Jeff.

"Yeah, so what?"

"So, he didn't say he was going in the Navy."

"Well, nobody said you're an asshole, Jeff, but everybody knows it! I'd love to see Baudo in the Army," Dickie answered.

"If I went in the service, I'd do the Marines," said Jeff. "If your gonna do it, do it right. How about those Marines that came to our last assembly in school?"

"What about them?" asked Pat.

"They were fuckin' awesome."

"Well, I'm not going in the Marines," I said with certitude.

"Think of the pussy you could get in that uniform," Jeff added.

"It's gonna take more than a uni-form to get you laid, Jeff," quipped Dickie. "It'll take *chloro*-form."

We all burst out laughing.

"If I was gonna go in the service, and I have thought about it," said Dickie, "I'd definitely do the Air Force."

"Like they'd ever let *you* up in a plane," laughed Jeff.

"I don't *want* to go up in a plane," answered Dickie, "and just *why* wouldn't they let me?"

"Then why the Air Force?" asked Jeff, ignoring Dickie's question.

"Because the Air Force has the best deal. You eat good food, sleep indoors in comfort, stay clean, shit in a toilet and rarely, if ever, have anyone shooting at you."

"What a pussy," taunted Jeff.

Just then Glenn and Dennis arrived with a six-pack each in brown paper bags.

"Hey, good to see you guys," yelled Pat. "We're about out of beer!"

"You ain't gettin' any of *my* beer," answered Dennis.

"Aw, c'mon, just one can?"

"No, sorry."

"Come on, Dennis, don't be selfish."

"You have your own beer."

"Yeah, but I only have one left."

"Ask me when your beer is gone."

"Okay," said Pat, smiling as if he had prevailed.

"You know this is pretty pathetic," offered Glenn.

"What is?" I asked.

"Sitting in the cold, dark bushes, drinking beer—alone."

"What do you mean, 'alone'?" asked Pat.

"Without girls," answered Glenn, taking a swig of his first beer.

"Hey, we're havin' fun," responded Pat. "We're discussing going in the military."

"I agree, we are pathetic," said Dickie. "But I notice you're here now and you didn't bring any girls."

"I'm gonna go find some girls as soon as I finish these off," said Glenn, holding up the beer.

"Hey, you got Schaeffer?" interjected Pat.

"Yeah."

"How about you give me one of those. I love Schaeffer. That's my brand."

"No way. I'm drinkin' these babies."

"What did Dennis get?" asked Pat.

"Rheingold."

"Rheingold tastes like piss. Schaeffer is the best."

"So, why are you guys talking about the service?" Dennis asked.

"Speaking of piss," interrupted Glenn, getting to his feet. "Where do you take a leak around here?"

"You have to piss already?" asked Dennis, incredulously.

"Yeah, why, you wanna hold it?"

"Talk about beer going right through you," quipped Jeff.

"Hey, didn't you pee before you left the house?" asked Dennis.

"No, I didn't."

"Didn't your parents teach you *any*thing? You should always pee before you leave the house."

"So, why are you talking about the service?" Dennis asked again.

"Farrell brought it up 'cause he's worried about getting into college on account of he flunked English," answered Jeff.

"He's such a worrier," said Glenn over his shoulder as he peed along the bushes. "He drives me nuts."

"I'll bet *he* pissed before he left the house," yelled Dennis. Then looking at me, he said, "didn't you?"

"Yes, I did."

"I knew it! Worriers always go before they leave the house."

"Anyhow," continued Jeff, "Dickie says the Air Force is the way to go even though they'll never let him near a plane."

"And Jeff claims that the Marines that came to our school recruiting were awesome," I added.

Jeff looked at me with a confused look on his face. "So, didn't everybody?"

"No, I didn't. I thought they were *nuts*."

"Hey Glenn," yelled Jeff. "What did you think of the Marines that came to our assembly?"

"Well," said Glenn as he returned to his beer, "let's put it this way . . . I'm not signing up."

"Jeff, why do you keep saying they'll never let me near a plane?" asked Dickie with a threatening tone in his voice.

"Because you're a spic! They're not gonna let a spic take one of our planes!"

Dickie shook his head in disgust, took a slug of beer and made a motion as if he was going to throw the can at Jeff. Jeff laughed as he put up his hands and arms and ducked in defense.

"Do you think I'd waste beer on *you*?" asked Dickie. "There are no words to describe what a waste *you* are, Jeff."

"My father says to stay the hell out of the military and if you *are* in the military, don't volunteer for anything," chimed in Dennis.

"But if you *were* going in the Service, which branch would you go into?" asked Pat.

"I said I ain't goin' in."

"But, if you were, which service would you pick?" Pat persisted.

"I dunno . . . probably the Coast Guard."

"The Coast Guard?" yelled Jeff.

"The Coast Guard doesn't count," said Pat. "Pick another one."

"Wait a second, *the Coast Guard doesn't count*?" said Dennis, unbelievingly. "Tell that to our boys guarding our coasts this very night, whilst we partake of our frothy lager!"

"Speaking of which," Pat began, his voice rising to be heard above the laughter, "can I have one of your beers now?"

"You talkin' to me?" asked Dennis.

"Yeah."

"No," answered Dennis, shaking his head 'yes.'

"No?" asked Pat in a confused tone.

"No!" answered Dennis.

"You said to ask you when my beer was gone . . . ?"

"So?"

"So, my beer is gone and I'm askin'."

"And I'm answering you 'No.' Besides, you said Rheingold tastes like piss."

"Well, I'm ready to drink piss."

"Then wait a few minutes and I'll have some for you to drink."

"Hey, where are Eddie and Tommy," I asked, to no one in particular.

"They're trying to meet up with some girls Eddie knows from some swim team party," answered Dennis.

"*Oh, really?*" exclaimed Jeff.

"No, I'm makin' it up," quipped Dennis.

"How come Eddie took Tommy with him and not you?"

Dennis took a long slug from his beer and looked away and didn't offer an answer.

"Did you hear me, Dennis?" Jeff asked.

"Yeah, I heard you Jeff. What's your point?"

"Well, you go to school with him every day—so why didn't he take you to meet these girls?"

"I don't know! Maybe he was afraid they'd all like me better than him."

"Or maybe he thinks Tommy is cooler than you."

"Let's get back to Joe flunkin' English," answered Dennis. "What branch of the service are you goin' into?"

"I don't know. *That's* what we were talking about."

"He's not goin' in the service!" yelled Glenn.

"Why not?" asked Dennis.

"'Cause he's goin' to college. He's just a big worry wart."

"I don't know about that," said Jeff. "He just flunked *English!*"

"Jesus," exclaimed Glenn, "we're in Section 32. If we don't get into college, who will?"

"The real question is," interjected Dickie, laughing, "which branch of the service will Joe get *kicked out of?*"

"Quit worrying and let's figure out where we can find some girls," said Glenn to me. "I saw your sister and Susan Manley and some other girls heading toward Mueller's. Maybe we can talk them into going somewhere."

"Hey, where's Billy?" Dennis yelled suddenly, realizing that Billy wasn't there.

"His brother is home and the family went to dinner somewhere," answered Dickie. "He said he'll find us."

"Dennis, *please* give me a beer?" pleaded Pat.

"Here," said Glenn, holding out an unopened can of cold beer, "You can have mine. I don't need it, I'm high on life."

Pat was delighted. He took the beer, opened it and took a long slug, then offered to share it with me.

"Billy's brother was in the Air Force," said Dickie.

"And we care because . . . ? responded Jeff.

"I'm just sayin', the smart choice would be Air Force."

"The smart choice is college," said Jeff. "Even St. John's is better than the military."

"Hey, there's always St. John's," said Pat, looking at me. "For sure you can get in there."

"I think I'd rather go in the Marines than go to St. John's and live at home."

"The whole thing comes down to the SATs," said Glenn. "So quit worrying and let's get out of here, I'm freezing."

As we started for Mueller's, Pat and I were walking together slowly, finishing the beer Glenn had given us and looking for places to throw away the empty cans.

"It was good to see you laughing tonight," said Pat.

"What do you mean?" I asked.

"I haven't seen you laugh for a while."

"Really?"

"Jay and Paul noticed it too. They asked me what was wrong with you."

"Yeah, well, I'm bummed out about that 'F.' Nice of Jay and Paul, though."

"They admire you."

"They *admire* me?"

"Well, okay, I don't know if 'admire' is the right word, but they care about you and look up to you."

"Wow! Really?"

"Yeah, they're really good guys."

"I agree. We ought to get them to hang around with us."

"They got their own guys in Bayside to hang with."

"So? You're from Bayside and you hang out down here."

"Yeah, that's true . . . but . . . nobody likes me in Bayside."

"Nobody likes you in Flushing either," I kidded, as we arrived at Mueller's.

The rest of the school year, I got along with Brother Arthur, but I must admit, I felt he owed me something. I kept looking for him to give me a break to make up for the injustice, but he never did. My English grade went up each subsequent quarter, but because of the "F," I ended the year with a 76 in English, my second lowest. The lower grade was in math, where I finished the year with a 73 and gave up any hopes of being an engineer. I had always been good at math. I felt it was mostly logic and although I frequently got only mediocre grades in math, I knew the problem was insufficient preparation. I always followed what was going on in class and did enough homework to know I could do the work.

In the spring of 1963, I found myself in trouble in Brother Charles Varnak's math class. Brother Charles was not a good teacher. He was a classic case of someone who could do the work, but not explain how to do it. He was also Athletic Director and was obviously not prepared when he came to class. We were all struggling. The book was called "Fusion Math" and was a new text in its first year of use. It sucked. Between Charlie Varnak's mumbling and stumbling in class and the book's unclear explanations, I was completely lost. Paul was lost too and so were Tommy and Glenn. Just as I was getting over my 'F' in English, I got an 'F' in math on my third quarter Report Card.

When I got home, I saw my report card laying on the dining room table, saw the 'F' and took the report card to my room. I felt indescribably frustrated. The only other grade under 80 was a '76' in English and that was because of Brother Arthur's continuing punishment of me. In Physics, which was the absolute toughest course I had, and one of the toughest of all in the Holy Cross curriculum, I had gotten an '88.' I was pissed at Brother Charles.

In the days since the quarterly marking period had ended, I inquired of my classmates as to how they were getting better grades than I, yet professed to be lost. The answers varied. Paul Falabella and Ray Frasene said they were doing badly, but put down anything to get partial credit.

"Varnak gives credit if you have anything down. Keep working on a problem even if you have no idea," said Ray. "I told Paul I had only one correct answer on the last test, but got partial credit for absolute gibberish on the other four."

Tommy Taraci's answer was simply that he cheated and Glenn said he copied some and bluffed his way to a lot of partial credit. Glenn said that he remembered two of the test questions were former homework assignments and had studied them just before the exam.

A few guys actually knew the stuff and when I expressed surprise, I was told they get help from their fathers. These guys had no idea what a problem they were to the rest of us. The decent test scores they were getting were ruining the curve.

Pat Kelly was lost like me and hated Brother Charles. I can't remember if he got an 'F,' but he got a low grade and was angry about it. "I don't think he cares if we know the work or not," said Pat. "I don't think he cares if we cheat. He just goes through the motions and does his sports duties."

Now, as I lay on my bed in my room, I had two big problems: how to finish the year in math, and how to deal with whatever grief I was going to get from my parents when I went downstairs for dinner.

Surprisingly, their reaction was not what I expected. Apparently, my father had convinced my mother to let him handle it and although she wanted my bloodshed, she agreed that there was little they could do. "I want to talk to you after dinner," my dad said as we sat down to eat.

I was supposed to play basketball that night and knew that Glenn and the Rizzos would be stopping by to get me shortly. I thought about mentioning that to him, but this was highly unusual and I held my tongue. Just as we finished dinner and started clearing the table, the doorbell rang and I ran to answer it. I told the guys to go ahead without me, but that I might be right behind them if things didn't go well.

After dinner, Dad suggested we sit in the living room while Ronnie and my mom cleaned up the kitchen. It was unusual for me and my father to actually sit and talk and it felt awkward. My anxiety was rising and I was tempted to say, "Go ahead—just say what you're gonna say, and let's get this over with," but I held my tongue.

"So, what's your story this time?" opened Dad.

"What do you mean by that?" I answered.

"Well, this is your third 'F'—the second one this year. You always seem to have a story, so let's hear it."

"I don't have a story. I hate Math, I'm lost in this class and I don't want to be an engineer," I blurted out.

"Look, Joey, here's the deal. You don't have to be an engineer, you can do whatever you want, but we're afraid you're screwing up your future."

"How so?"

"You're smart and you're screwing up! You won't be able to get a decent job without an education."

My anxiety level was still high, and being overly defensive, I took a cheap shot which I immediately regretted. "You never even *finished* high school, so you're not one to talk!"

"That was because I had to quit to help the family, not because I didn't try."

"I'm trying!"

"You're trying?"

"Yeah!"

"I swear I never see you open a book, never."

"Bull!"

"Don't tell me 'Bull.' I know what I'm saying."

"A lot of the time I'm in my room I'm doin' school work."

"With the radio on?"

"Yeah, I can study with the radio on."

"I'm sure it doesn't sink in with the radio on, but that's not the point. The point is, times have changed and having an education is the key. Do you want to work in hot, dirty boiler rooms all day, lugging heavy tools and parts, fighting traffic and be dirty and smelly all the time?"

"No, not really," I answered, meekly.

"Well, I don't want that for you either, but if you don't get an education, that's the kind of thing you'll have to do. He paused, looking at me. We know you're smart and can do the work, but we're worried that you're gonna blow your chances at a better life."

I was completely thrown off guard by this rational, caring approach. I couldn't think of anything to say and finally, in desperation to break the silence, I blurted out the thought of going into the armed forces.

"Bad idea, Joey, bad idea," he replied. "If you want to go in the service, go in after college."

"Why?" I asked.

"Well, with a college degree, you can be an officer, otherwise you'd just be a grunt. Officers eat better, sleep in better quarters, get paid better, live in more comfortable conditions and get killed less often. Officers are management, enlisted men are labor and, in both cases, you lose control of your life."

"What do you mean?"

"Well, in either case, you go where you're told and you do what you're told. I don't think you'd like it!" he smiled.

I laughed at the way he said I wouldn't like it. It wasn't condescending. It was almost as if he was proud that I wouldn't like being told where to go and what to do. Our little meeting ended with him asking me to promise to work harder and apply myself to my school work more. I, of course, promised I would.

"I can't make you do it. You're too big for that now. It's up to you. We've done our part to give you a chance—now you have to make your own decisions."

I went to my room and cried. I didn't even know why I was crying. I felt a strange mixture of emotions that I had never felt before. A mixture of anger, fear, pride, love, disappointment, and frustration.

There were no more Fs that year, although things were not as they seemed. I passed Math in quarter four, but it wasn't because I was learning it. A combination of studying homework problems, getting partial credit for complete crap and cheating got me through.

Religion class was a complete waste of an hour every single day, while Brother Renatus droned on and on about things we couldn't care less about. Spanish was very trying for me. I liked Brother Thomas Kane and he liked me, but I hated memorization and that's what Spanish I was all about. The only time we actually spoke Spanish was in the language lab, which was traumatic. The taped voice spoke Spanish very quickly and we were supposed to answer him in Spanish, while Brother Thomas sat at a master switchboard and listened in, at random.

"I do not hear you, Senor Farrell," Brother Thomas would say, after tuning in to me and not hearing me respond to the tape.

"I can't quite catch what he is saying, Brother," I would plea. "He goes too fast!"

"Well, respond as best you can, Senor Farrell, don't just sit there in silence."

At the next question, I would respond, "No entiendo, Senor" (I do not understand, Mister), or "Hablo mas dispacio" (Speak more slowly). Brother Thomas would shake his head in disgust and smile. One day when I was lost in Spanish Lab and not responding, he urged me to try harder and to pretend I am in Spain and no one speaks English and I have to think in Spanish.

"Si, Hermano," I answered. Then I decided to seize the initiative and whatever the man on the tape said, I responded with one of the Spanish phrases I knew.

"Donde esta los banos?" (Where are the bathrooms).

When I glanced at Brother Thomas to get his reaction, he was red-faced and laughing. He shook his head at me and said something in Spanish that, roughly translated, meant that I was a hopeless case. Brother Thomas was cool, though. He urged me to try harder, but he moved on. He didn't hate me for not really caring about Spanish and he didn't want to ruin my life because I didn't like memorizing vocabulary. I finished the year with a 79—a mediocre grade for a mediocre performance. No problem.

Physics was by far, the most demanding and the best course I had. Brother John Houlihan was a great teacher. He was young and energetic and actually gave thought to his classroom lectures. He involved us in his classes and actually cared if we learned! He would bet a Coke that a feather would hit the ground at the same time as a steel ball bearing when dropped from the same height! (He didn't mention the experiment took place in a vacuum.) He would meet after school with any student that was having trouble with any assignment. He checked homework to see if you were having any problems, not to punish you. His exams were extremely tough, always five complicated problems, where all work had to be shown. Cheating was almost impossible. He made his exams hard and curved them with only a small percentage getting in the 90s. Everybody respected Brother John and liked him and worked hard to please him. Which is why getting kicked out of his class was such a bummer.

It seems there is a John Kapchus in every class—some bright, studious kid, who likes to impress adults with his brilliant questions and observations. Kapchus was famous for asking complicated questions, which were designed to impress the teachers. He once even reminded a teacher just as the bell ending class rang, that he had forgotten to assign us homework. Mike Delaney quietly told him after class that if he ever "pulled an asshole stunt like that again, I'll kick the shit out of you" and he meant it.

He had recently been catching a lot of guff from other guys about this, when one day in the spring, he asked Brother John about the purpose of a horizontal stabilizer on an airplane. It was totally unrelated to what was going on in class, but somehow had popped into Kapchus' brain, so he raised his hand and asked it.

Brother John was caught by surprise. He didn't understand Kapchus' question, probably because it was out of context. He hesitated a moment, as if trying to understand, and then shrugged his shoulders and said, "I don't know, John. I'm not sure I understand your question."

This struck me as extremely funny. Kapchus had outdone himself and asked a question so forced that even Brother John was mystified. I looked at Glenn and we broke up laughing. Unfortunately, Brother John saw me laugh and thought for some reason that I was mocking *him*. He exploded at me and then kicked me out of his class. I was stunned and made a feeble attempt to explain, but he was too upset to listen.

"Get out of here and don't come back!" he yelled, all red-faced. "Go to the Dean's Office and tell him I won't allow you in my class. I will not be mocked by you!"

I left, shaken, and stopped in the bathroom to collect myself.

I had been avoiding Brother Richard like Ensign Pulver avoided the Captain in one of my favorite movies, *Mr. Roberts*. If I saw him coming down the hall, I turned around or ducked into a classroom or bathroom. If I heard his voice in a stairway, I would take another stairway. If I saw him at a sporting event, I stayed as far away from him as I could. He was a weird guy and, after the incident with Brother Arthur, I just wanted to stay off his radar screen. Now I'm being sent to him again, and again, under unusual circumstances. I liked Brother John, thought he was the best teacher I'd ever had and was *not mocking him*! 'How do I get into these messes?' I asked myself in the bathroom. 'I can't fucking believe this.' I tried to collect myself and figure out how to tell Brother Richard what had happened. "He'll probably say, 'Jesus was misunderstood, why shouldn't you be?'" I thought.

Feeling frantic, I took a deep breath and left the bathroom for the Dean's Office. I considered waiting for the period to end and trying to square things with Brother John, but he was very upset and if I didn't do what he had told me to do, it might make things worse.

I knocked on the door as Brother Richard was hanging a picture of President Kennedy on his office wall.

"Ah, Farrell, why aren't you in class? I hope it's because you're transferring to another school and you've come to say 'good-bye.' Is that it, Farrell?"

"Uh . . . No, Brother," I answered with a flat serious voice. "Something's happening and I need your help."

"Don't tell me you've been kicked out of class again?"

"Well, actually, yes, I have, Brother."

The smile disappeared from his face. "I'm sure Brother Arthur won't take you back a second time, Farrell."

"It wasn't Brother Arthur, Brother."

Incredulous, he asked, "Who was it this time?"

"Brother John."

"Brother John . . . ?"

"Brother John Houlihan, Brother. It was a big misunderstanding."

"That's what you said last time."

"I know. And it was. And it is again."

"All right, let's hear your story, Mr. Farrell, and it better be the truth, or so help me, you will regret it."

I poured my heart out to Brother Richard. I told him how much I thought of Brother John and how hard I worked in his class. I told him about Kapchus, although I knew that was risky. (My strong sense was, like, Kapchus, Brother Richard McDonald was himself an out-of-the-mainstream guy who I suspect was the object of some ridicule himself, when he was in high school. Although I did consider the possibility that he once liked rock and roll, girls and sports; but that, as he matured, developed a taste for Broadway musicals, celibacy and Romance languages.) I told him the exact truth about what had happened, how Brother John thought I was mocking him and how badly I felt about it. I ended by asking for his help.

"How can I help, Mr. Farrell?"

"You can help me to get Brother John to understand what really happened."

"How can I do that? It seems to me, Farrell, that *you* are the one to do that."

"I tried and I'll try again, but I'm afraid he's so angry, he won't believe me."

Brother Richard sat at his desk with his hands folded on it, pursing his lips as if thinking over his response. Just then, Brother Josephat knocked on the door and said, "Brother Richard, can I see you for a minute?"

"Certainly, Brother," he answered, rising and starting for the door.

As I turned and looked at Brother Josephat, he recognized me and said, "Mr. Farrell, do you still go to school here?"

No answer was necessary as they went into the hall for a private discussion.

"Great." I thought. "Just fucking great. Josephat has to come in here in the middle of this!"

While they were talking in the hallway, I thought about my response if Brother Richard brought up Jesus. Jesus was misunderstood. Jesus suffered and died and had done nothing wrong. As I struggled to come up with an answer, my eyes wandered to the picture of JFK on the wall. It was a duplicate of the one I had seen in the business office when I paid my monthly tuition. 'I'll bet they didn't have Eisenhower's picture up when he was president,' I thought to myself.

I heard the conversation coming to an end in the hallway and thought, "If the Jesus question comes up, my answer would be: 'Jesus wasn't trying to get into college.'"

"Well, Farrell," Brother Richard said, sitting back down behind his desk. "Tell me why I should help you?"

"I can't think of any reason, Brother, except that you know the truth and that should count for something."

"I'm not sure I know the truth, Farrell. You say it's the truth, but that doesn't make it so."

"Have I ever lied to you, Brother?" I said, half in jest.

"Let me ask you something, Mr. Farrell. Are you upset about this because of Brother John's feelings or because of the inconvenience to you and possible effect on your grade if you're not allowed back in class?"

"Both, Brother," I answered, without any hesitation.

"Very well, Mr. Farrell, and let me ask you this: are you sorry for mocking John Kapchus?"

Caught by surprise, I stalled. "I don't understand what you're asking, Brother."

"Are you sorry for mocking another Holy Cross student and classmate and child of God?"

'Oh, great,' I thought, 'a trick question.' "I didn't mock him, Brother. I didn't even look at him. That's why Brother John thought I was mocking *him*." I left out the part about looking at Glenn Judson.

The bell rang, ending the period and I asked Brother Richard what I should do tomorrow at Physics period.

"I guess you should come here and study, unless you hear otherwise," he answered.

The next day, when Physics class came around, I went to Brother Richard's office. I never thought I'd be anxious to see him, but I was. I had had a sick feeling in my stomach all night and all day and was desperately hoping he would have some good news. He did, but he made me wait until the end of the period to tell me. He told me to sit quietly and contemplate my sins and ask God's forgiveness.

"Can I do homework?" I asked.

"Yes, Farrell, I guess so," he answered, shaking his head as if he was disgusted with my rejection of his suggestion.

At the end of the period, he told me to go see Brother John after school in Room 302.

"Will he let me back in class?" I asked, anxiously.

"I don't know, Mr. Farrell, that's up to him. I know I wouldn't."

His answer stung. I originally was encouraged by this development, but now I was panicked. I sat nervously through History and Spanish until eighth period was over and raced to Room 302.

Brother John took me back. He said he would take me at my word. He didn't bring God into it, he didn't demand an apology or further explanation and he didn't hit me. He just said, "Okay, then let's forget about it and get back to work."

I raced to catch up with my friends who were delaying their start to Mueller's so that I might join them. They had decided to wait five or ten minutes and then proceed since there was no way of knowing how long Brother John would keep me. They had gone about half a block when I caught up to them. I told them that I was back in Physics class and that Brother John was nice about it and believed my story. We debated what possible role Brother Richard had played. Most of the guys thought Brother Richard would not have done anything to help me, yet I kind of thought he probably did.

Tommy chided me about getting off easy, claiming he never would have allowed me back in class. At first, I argued with him.

"What do you mean, I got off easy?"

"If you had mocked me, I wouldn't let you come back," Tommy declared. "That's all I'm saying."

"*I didn't* mock him!" I protested.

"Yeah, sure! Likely story."

"Tommy, cut it out. Don't even kid about it," I pleaded.

"Yeah, sure . . . the truth hurts."

"You prick," I said, shaking my head.

"Okay, okay, don't be so uptight. Where's the famous Farrell sense of humor?"

"I left it in Brother Richard's office," I answered.

I got my chance to get back at Tommy a few weeks later. After another incredibly boring Religion class, we were noisily making our way down the hall. Tommy was a few feet behind me and on my left, when I suddenly caught a glimpse of Brother Thomas Burns ("Mousey") heading toward me. Mousey was so short, it was hard to see him amidst all the student traffic in the hallway. I felt a moment of acute anxiety as he passed on my left. Just as I felt my body returning to normal after the anxiety alarm that a Mousey sighting brought on, I heard a loud unusual noise over my left shoulder. It sounded like somebody being slammed up against the lockers which lined the hallways at Holy Cross.

When I turned to see what it was, I saw that indeed, Tommy had been slammed up against the lockers by Mousey! I and all the guys in the hallway started moving double time to get as far away as possible. As I turned left at the end of the hallway, I slowed and looked back down the hall. Mousey had Tommy up against the lockers and was holding the knot of his tie, as if choking him with it, and had his face in Tommy's face. I took another step so that I was out of sight an stopped and listened. I couldn't hear anything because of all the usual noise in the hallway between classes. I decided to take a quick peek around the corner to see what was happening. When I did, I saw Tommy hunched over, his books strewn all over the floor, as Mousey disappeared into the stairwell at the far end of the hall.

As I walked toward Tommy, I saw he was doubled over in pain and gasping, trying to gather his books up off the floor.

"What the hell was that?" I asked. "Are you all right?"

"That motherfucker . . ." Tommy gasped. "Help me get to class."

I picked up a couple of Tommy's books and handed them to him as he slowly made his way down the hall toward our next class. Fortunately, our next class was a study hall where Tommy sat with his head down and recovered and briefly told us what happened. Mousey had grabbed him, much to his surprise, and for no apparent reason, and slammed him against the lockers.

"You're a real wise ass, aren't you?" Mousey said, according to Tommy. When Tommy answered, "No, Brother," Mousey had grabbed his tie and was pushing the knot into his throat when he suddenly kneed Tommy in the balls and said, "I hate big guys" and walked away!

We were aghast at what Mousey had done. The next period was lunch and Tommy, who was a little paranoid about talking about it, repeated the story again quietly to those around him. Most of us had heard stories like this about Mousey and were enraged that he could get away with this kind of behavior. Some thought Tommy must have done something for Mousey to have picked him out for that kind of treatment. Tommy was, after all, the consummate smart ass.

On the way to Mueller's after school, I gave Tommy some of his own medicine.

"You must have done *some*thing for Mousey to do that to you," I began.

"I didn't do *anything!*"

"You must have said something," I continued.

"I didn't. I swear!" Tommy insisted.

"We all know what a smartass you are—you probably said something under your breath and he heard you."

"Jesus Christ! I swear I didn't do or say anything!"

"What do you guys think?" I asked of the rest of the group.

"You *are* a fuckin' smartass," chimed in Dickie. "I'm surprised some teacher hasn't wailed the shit outta you before now."

"Your story *is* hard to believe," added Jeff, piling on like I knew he would.

"He just hates big guys," answered Tommy. "You guys have heard stories about him.

"He walked right past me to get to you," I reminded everyone, laughing. "The question is 'Why?'"

"That *is* a good question," said Glenn. "Why would he pass up Farrell for you?"

"I'm tellin' you I don't know! He's fuckin' nuts! Who can explain a fuckin' nut?"

"I think Mousey knows I wouldn't have taken it," I chided.

"Oh, gimme a break," Tommy whined. "You would have fought back?"

"Damn straight," I said. "If someone attacks me like that for no reason, I'm gonna defend myself. Wouldn't you, Glenn?"

"Absolutely. I would have punched him when he slammed me up against the wall."

"Oh, fuck you guys! Trentacoste smacked the both of you in the face and you didn't do anything."

"That was different," said Glenn.

"Yeah," I added, laughing. "We *knew* what that was for."

"I wish I *had* popped him," said Glenn through clenched teeth.

"You're screwed now," teased Jeff. "Mousey knows he can kick you in the balls and you won't do anything. He's a bully and once he knows he can get away with it, he'll do it again and again."

We kept up the good-natured ball busting and braggadocio for a couple of days. It's just what we did to each other. It was fun and funny. We must have hit a nerve this time, however. A week or two later, on a Friday night, we all met at Mueller's and planned our night. As usual, at that particular point in time, we would start by drinking at "The Wall."

"The Wall" had become our place to talk, to plan, to meet, to drink. It was a dark, lonely, quiet place just hundreds of yards from one of the busiest thoroughfares in Queens. In a short time, we would begin to go to bars and no longer need the "The Wall," but for now, it was our "pub." It had heard our hopes and fears and dreams; our boasting and cursing, our ball busting and supporting of one another, our planning and our thoughts on our parents, school, sex, the military, politics, communism, religion, civil rights, college, and sports.

This Friday night in late spring, we decided to get our beverage of choice and meet at The Wall. It was a beautiful warm night. Tommy seemed unusually animated and when I got to the wall, I discovered why. He had already been drinking at home. His parents were entertaining some friends and Tommy had helped himself to a few "highballs."

He downed a beer quickly and when the discussion turned to what to do or where to go for the rest of the night, Tommy said, "I know what I'm doing. I'm going on a Mouse hunt."

"What are you talking about?" asked Dennis.

"I'm gonna go find Mousey and kick his ass," Tommy answered.

"O-o-o-o-h, that's right," said Dennis, suddenly realizing what Tommy meant. "That guy's nuts! Remember when I had trouble with him at the football game? Fuckin' guy's wacko!"

"You should have taken him out for ush," Tommy slurred.

"Damn straight, I should have," Dennis agreed.

The topic switched back to where to find girls. As we finished our beer, we started back to Mueller's in small groups. We were hoping someone would have a party at their house. Frequently, someone's parents would relent and allow the group to listen to records in their basement or their yard. Even my parents allowed it on a few occasions.

I arrived at Mueller's with Dennis and Pat. A few minutes later, Jeff and Dickie arrived.

"I think we got a problem," said Jeff, looking at me.

"What?" I asked.

"Tommy said he's goin' to Holy Cross to find Mousey and kick his ass," said Jeff.

"Really?" I laughed. "Where is he?" I asked since I hadn't seen him come in.

"We were walking back and he suddenly turned down 162nd St. toward Holy Cross. I yelled 'Tommy, where you goin' and he said, 'to kick Mousey's ass,'" answered Jeff.

"Holy shit! I gotta stop him!" I said as I started out Mueller's door.

"I'll go with you," yelled Dennis as he ran to catch up to me.

We ran across Northern Boulevard and then proceeded down 162nd St., half running.

We alternated walking fast and jogging down 162nd St. to 32nd Ave. and then started up 32nd Ave. toward Holy Cross. We were thinking this was Tommy's most likely route, but we didn't see him anywhere. As we approached the school block, I thought I heard someone yelling.

"Uh-oh, I think I hear something," I said quietly to Dennis. We kept walking but slower and more quietly. Then we heard it again, but couldn't make out what was being said. We continued walking as we were now at the 32nd Ave. side of the high school. As we reached the corner, we heard Tommy very clearly yelling for Mousey to come down and fight like a man. We ran to him, and when we got close in the darkness, we saw a shirtless Tommy, fists clenched, ready to swing at us.

"Tommy, what the hell are you doin'? I asked.

"Oh, shit, it's you guys! What are you doin' here?" he slurred.

"We came to stop you from getting kicked outta school," I answered.

"Fuck shschool," he slurred again. "I'm gonna kick his ass."

"Tommy, it's not worth it! Let's get outta here."

"Where's your shirt?" asked Dennis.

"I took it off."

"I can see that, but why?"

"I don't want to get blood on it. I like that shirt."

"Where is it?"

"It's over there on the grass," Tommy answered, pointing in the direction of a nearby lawn.

"Come on down here, Mousey, you fuck!" Tommy suddenly yelled, looking up at the upper floor of the Holy Cross building where the Brothers lived.

"Holy shit!" I whispered. "I hope nobody heard that or we'll all get screwed."

"Not me," said Dennis. "I don't go to this school."

"Be a man, Mousey," Tommy yelled.

Dennis started chuckling. "Did you hear what he said?"

I had, of course, but was too filled with apprehension to laugh.

"Tommy, let's get out of here," I pleaded.

"I want to kick Mousey's ass," he replied.

"I know you do, but Mousey's not gonna fight you . . ."

"I'll kick his ass. I'll *kill* him!"

"I'm sure you would, but Mousey won't fight fair and instead we'll get kicked outta school. Dennis, get Tommy's shirt and let's get goin'."

"I'm not leaving 'til I fight Mousey, that prick!"

"Come on, Tom," I implored, grabbing his arm. "Getting kicked outta school isn't gonna help even the score. That would be another victory for Mousey."

"He's right, Tommy," chimed in Dennis, who now had Tommy's shirt in his hands. "This is, whatchamacallit . . . a lose—lose situation."

"Ah, fuck!," said Tommy. "I've got to get that little prick somehow. I never should have let him touch me to begin with. I should have decked him as soon as he grabbed me."

"Hey, we were just kidding about that, Tom," I said, thinking of the hard time we had given him about the incident with Mousey. "We were just bustin' your balls."

"Well, *I'm* not kidding," said Tommy. "I'm not taking shit anymore. We are too old for this shit. Anyone who hits me is gonna get hit back. I don't care who the fuck it is."

"I agree with you. I'm with you on that," I said.

"Really? You mean it?"

"I do."

"Me, too," said Dennis, laughing. "If Mousey ever hits me, I'll kick him right in the balls."

I started walking away from the building and was relieved when Tommy started to come along.

"So, you really mean it? We're not taking any more physical abuse from these guys?" Tommy asked. "Cause I'm serious."

"I am too," I answered.

"Wait a minute! Where's my good shirt?"

"I got ya' shirt," answered Dennis. "I don't see what's so hot about it."

"I *love* this shirt," said Tommy as he put it on.

"I think it's ugly," said Dennis, winking at me and smiling, knowing that getting him off the subject of Mousey was a sign the danger had passed.

"Ugly? Ugly? This is a beautiful shirt! Are you shittin' me?"

"I think it's ugly."

"You like that piece of shit *you're* wearing?" he challenged.

"Yeah, I do."

As we walked back to Mueller's, arguing about Tommy's taste in clothes, a great sense of relief increasing as we got further and further from Holy Cross, I thought about what Tommy had said and I had agreed to. Although I had agreed instantly to get Tommy to forget about Mousey and get out of there, I couldn't stop thinking about it. We were approaching seventeen years of age. In most cases, we were bigger, stronger, tougher and smarter than the guys who were smacking us around. 'What gave them the right?' I wondered. 'Tommy is right!' I thought. 'I do mean it! Nobody is gonna hit me again and get a free pass. I'm not going to stand with my hands at my side and get smacked in the face ever again.' As we got near Mueller's, I thought it was safe to bring up the subject again.

"Hey, Tommy, I meant what I said before about not letting anyone hit me."

"You better mean it," he answered, "'cause I fuckin' mean it. Mousey went way too far. That's it for me. Never again." He extended his hand for me to shake. I shook it.

The next day Tommy called me at home and thanked me for saving his ass. "Boy was I smashed," he said. We laughed about it and I reminded him of Dennis calling his shirt ugly and how they argued about it for blocks as we walked to Mueller's.

"Do you remember what we promised each other?" I asked.

"Oh, yes indeed," he answered. "I was smashed, but I meant it. Never again."

"Okay, good. Me too."

Funny, but no one ever tried to abuse us again . . .

Chapter Eighteen

♦ ♦ ♦ ♦

"Dreams Denied, Part Deux"

Talk about a dream
Try to make it real
You wake up in the night
With a fear so real.
Spend your life waiting
For a moment that just don't come
Well, don't waste your time waiting.
Bruce Springsteen—"Badlands"

One of the biggest grudges I have toward a teacher is directed at a surprising source. It's directed at a teacher who never hit me and in whose class I received the highest final, an eighty-four, of any class I had and the highest quarterly grades, ninety-two and ninety, that I received all year. It's hard to imagine having sixteen-year-old boys for American History and boring the living shit out of them while teaching them nothing except to hate history.

It's hard to believe that sixteen-year-old boys wouldn't be interested in how a relatively small group of disorganized farmers and tradesmen humiliated and beat the greatest, most powerful army of the time in the American Revolution or a debate over what a democracy should look like and how to insure its survival. Perhaps an examination of slavery from its introduction in America, the way our Founding Fathers handled it, the horrible civil war that it spawned and the conditions and policies toward African-Americans that were at that point tearing our nation apart, would generate some interest. Or maybe, just maybe, a discussion of the great war our fathers and uncles had just fought to save the world from tyranny would spark our curiosity. But no, Mr. Joseph Lipp spent the entire year preparing us for the State Regents Exams and reduced all of American History to true and false, matching columns, and fill-in-the-blank questions.

We were bored out of our minds. We had an entire book of past State Regents Exams and were supposed to do certain parts for homework and review the answers in class. All of the great events of American History were reduced to matching battles with generals, treaties with dates, presidents with a theme, and constitutional amendments with their subjects.

Mr. Lipp was a tall, lean, thin-lipped man with a big pointy nose and an overbite. He always wore a bow tie and had a weird way of speaking that can best be described, ironically, as a frequent smacking of the lips. When Mr. Lipp opened his mouth, it made noise as if he were chewing on something. I sometimes thought he was in fact, and would watch him carefully to see if he put anything in his mouth or chewed. He never did. He called us 'kiddos' and slowly we began to hate the sound of his voice. He never learned our names and even in June, he had to refer to a seating chart to call on most of us by name.

Thankfully, I sat in the aisle closest to the windows and would look out the window for things to help pass the time. There was a woman who lived in a house across the street from the school who was frequently out gardening or raking leaves or shoveling snow depending on the season. I would fantasize that I was walking by and said hello to her and that she invited me into her house and we had sex. I never saw her from less than about a hundred yards, but in my mind she was a beautiful and sexy lady.

So right in the middle of seventh period History, while drilling for the State Regents Exam, I was quietly committing mortal sins. On Saturday, I would confess it as 'having impure thoughts,' but the next time she was out there while I was in History, I found myself doing it again. At first, I would try to pay attention to Mr. Lipp and get those terrible thoughts out of my mind, but after a while, I gave in. She would always be the winner over a matching column.

Mr. Lipp fortunately never hit me, but he did hit others. We talked about how when he slapped someone in the face, he would close his eyes on impact as if he was the one getting hit. He didn't seem particularly comfortable doing it, but nevertheless he would occasionally feel the need to smack someone in the face. Pat Kelly came close to getting hit. Paul Fallabella sat next to me and Pat behind him. One day, bored almost to tears while Mr. Lipp was taking us through a true/false section of a past Regents Exam, and fighting my thoughts of sex with the woman across the street, I jotted a question of my own on a scrap of paper and handed it to Paul while Lipp wasn't looking. It read: "A guy can die from horniness. True or False?" Paul laughed and circled 'True' as I watched.

Pat had seen me pass the note to Paul and Paul laugh and was wondering what was going on.

"What's so funny?" Pat whispered to Paul.

Paul took the note in his left hand and deftly held it low and behind him for Pat to take. Mr. Lipp was in the center of the classroom at his desk on our right. Pat took it, laughed and leaning forward and looking toward me, whispered, "I think it can lead to suicide." I ignored him, since I, looking to my right, saw Lipp looking toward Pat. Pat, thinking I didn't hear him, repeated his comment, only a little louder and leaning more forward and to his left.

Lipp slammed his hand on his desk, got to his feet and moved quickly toward Pat. He stopped right beside Paul in the aisle and, glaring at Pat and clenching his teeth and breathing heavy through his nose and holding a pencil in his hand, he suddenly snapped the pencil in half.

"Do you have a problem, mister?" Lipp asked through clenched teeth, his lips smacking. A big bit of saliva flew out of his mouth and landed on Pat.

"No, sir," answered Pat, his freckled face now scarlet and trying not to react to the saliva that landed somewhere on his face. Seeing this sent me into a near convulsion. I turned away toward the window, put my right hand over my mouth, chin in the palm of my hand, and clenched my teeth to keep from cracking up. I didn't see what happened next, I couldn't look, but fortunately, Lipp went back to his desk, looked at his seating chart for Pat's name, and called on him to read and answer the next question. Pat, being a little rattled, blew the answer. A fifty-fifty chance to salvage a little dignity and he blew it. There was a small smattering of groans and giggles when Pat gave his answer.

"Try not be ignorant all your life, Mr. Kelly," said Lipp.

On the walk to Mueller's after school, this incident was reenacted loudly and repeatedly with Tommy Taraci doing a brilliant imitation of Lipp.

"I'd rather get hit than spit on," offered Dickie.

"Yeah, or have a pencil snapped at me," added Jeff. Everybody looked at Jeff as if he was crazy.

"What? You don't believe me? That's embarrassing having a pencil snapped at you. Getting hit is honorable."

"Come here, Jeff," snapped Tommy, holding up a clenched fist. "I want to honor you."

Jeff moved quickly away from the group, laughing.

I tried to convey how funny it was to see Pat's face when Lipp's spit landed on him, but I couldn't. The first few times I tried to explain it, I broke down laughing so hard, I couldn't finish. Then when I could control myself, I found I couldn't adequately convey what was so funny about it. It had to be seen. He was staring at Lipp as the pencil was snapped and Lipp started yelling at him. Then he seemed to follow the spittle as it came at him and landed on his face. There was a moment of disbelief followed by a moment of revulsion as if he wanted to wipe it off in disgust and then he realized he better ignore it and refocused back on Lipp, all in about two seconds.

For the next few days, guys would snap pencils at Pat and imitate Lipp between classes or at lunch and I would laugh, but not as hard as when I would think about that look on Pat's face.

I had started the school year with the intention of getting involved in some clubs or school organizations in order to help get into colleges. We were told repeatedly that colleges viewed participation in such things as a big positive. I thought at first I would try out for the Spring Play, but my relationship with Brother Richard was such that I decided at the last minute not to. I felt very nervous about auditioning in the first place and wasn't sure I could work up the courage, but when I realized Brother Richard would be in charge, I felt too vulnerable, even if I made it as a cast member, to do it.

Brother Richard was so strange and my relationship with him so strained that I felt I would be better off with minimal contact with him. I figured he would probably not select me, so the trauma of auditioning would all be for nothing and he might even ridicule me in front of girls who were recruited from other schools for the play. On the other hand, if I did land a role, the more he got to know me, the less he would like me, I feared, and that could lead to trouble somewhere down the line.

My friend Peter Heaney was going to join the Debate Team and had talked me into it too. He convinced me that colleges love applicants that were debaters and since I read a lot and "loved to argue," I would like it and be good at it. Then, when the day came for new interested students to show up after school, I found out that Mr. Lipp was the debate coach!

"Sorry, Peter," I said when I saw him in the hallway between classes.

"Why not?" he asked.

"You failed to tell me that asshole Lipp was in charge."

"I thought you knew that."

"No, I didn't."

"I heard he's not so bad with the debate team," said Peter, trying to convince me to change my mind.

"I can't even stand the sound of his voice and I think he hates me," I responded. "Sorry."

I was pretty much out of options. Spanish Club crossed my mind, but since those guys seemed really into Spanish and I wasn't, and I only knew a few phrases, I rejected that idea. Spanish, to me, was all memorization, and who wanted to be in a club that memorized things. Then came an announcement of a new club being formed that really interested me. A 'Great Books Club' was being formed and anyone interested should sign up on a form on the bulletin board. I loved reading and always was reading a book or two on my own. I went to sign up and, much to my dismay, the form indicated the Club Moderator was Brother Richard McDonald. Again, I was faced with a serious dilemma. I didn't sign up then, but wrestled with the idea until the next day. I thought about the risk of Brother Richard growing to hate me and that he might be hard on me or ridicule me, but I felt I could take it in front of the guys. On the other hand, maybe he could see a side of me he wasn't familiar with. The side that liked to read and discuss ideas.

I decided to take the chance and signed up. Unfortunately, Brother Richard decided *not* to take the chance and told me, unceremoniously, that he didn't want me in the club. He had stopped me in the hallway between classes to tell me. I meekly asked why and he replied that I was not the kind of student he was looking for to join this club.

So it was to be that intramurals would be my only extracurricular activity. When I got to class, I told Pat Kelly, Paul Falabella and Ray Frasene what had just happened and they laughed.

"It's not funny!" I said. "I have nothing to put on a college application except intramural sports."

"You could put 'detention,'" quipped Ray.

"That's an idea," said Paul. "You do it after school so it is 'extra-curricular'!"

"And, you're good at it since you've done it a lot," laughed Ray.

"And, you've done it all three years so far," chimed in Pat.

"Thanks, you guys," I said. "I appreciate your concern. I suppose under my graduation picture in the yearbook, I should list: Detention 1, 2, 3, 4."

Intramurals might not mean anything on college applications, but they meant a lot to me. I received a trophy for winning the hundred-yard dash in the intramural track meet that year, which was exciting, but not nearly as exciting as intramural basketball.

In an all-boys New York City high school, intramural basketball can be very exciting and important. I had had a very good year on a good team. Glenn, Tommy, Pat, former jv'er Billy Regan and a few other guys and I had battled into the playoffs and were to play a senior team in the semifinals on a Saturday afternoon. Varsity players were usually the referees of intramural games until the playoffs. Then it was a varsity player and a coach from the athletic department. The varsity basketball head coach (Mr. O'Meara) would do the final game himself. The day before our playoff game while at lunch, I felt a tap on my shoulder and turned to see the Rizzo twins standing behind me.

"Are you ready for the big game tomorrow, Farrell?"

"Yeah, why?"

"Do you know who the ref is for your game?"

"No, who?"

"Mr. O'Meara."

"No shit! Cool! I thought he only reffed the final?"

"He wants to check you out," said Tommy Rizzo.

"What?" I asked, skeptically.

"He's looking to add some height next year and he wants to check you out."

"Holy shit! Wait a minute—are you guys goofin' on me?"

"Swear to God," answered John Rizzo, holding up his right hand as if he were taking an oath.

"We don't want you to be too nervous, but remember, O'Meara has done this twice before," said Tom. "Jerry Frain two years ago and Danny Sullivan last year."

"H-o-o-o-o-o-l-y shit" was all I could say as they walked back to their table to eat their lunch.

As I sat in my afternoon classes, all I could think about was tomorrow. I had given up hope of ever playing varsity. I had been playing intramurals and for the 111th Precinct in the Police Athletic League. The PAL schedule went way beyond the high school varsity schedule and varsity players from Holy Cross and other schools were added to teams late in the season. Now, in just one day, I would unexpectedly have a chance to make the Holy Cross varsity. A chance I never dreamed of.

Paul Falabella had been sitting next to me at lunch and heard what the Rizzos had said. I hadn't mentioned it to anyone by the end of the day, because I was scared and didn't want anyone to know in case I didn't make it. When the last bell rang, Paul told me that he and Jay would be there and they would be rooting for me.

"Thanks, Paul," I said. "I think I'm gonna be a little nervous, since I have trouble breathing even now when I think about it."

"Don't be nervous. You have nothing to lose. Look at it that way and play your game. See ya' tomorrow!"

As I was getting ready to leave school, I decided to tell Glenn. Our lockers were next to each other and I could tell him without anyone else hearing it.

"Guess what?" I said to Glenn, deciding what books, if any, to take home for the weekend.

"I know, the Rizzos told me," he answered.

"Do a lot of people know?"

"I don't know. I was wondering why you didn't say anything to me," answered Glenn.

"I didn't want everyone to know in case I fuck it up."

"Well, Paul Falabella knows and Pat Kelly knows and I'm sure word is getting around."

"Paul heard the Rizzos tell me about it at lunch. I guess Paul told Pat."

"So, why are you so glum about it? You should be psyched."

"I know, but I'm nervous. I'm afraid I'll screw up tomorrow."

"Oh, here we go! You're gonna worry about it? That's fucked up! Just hit the boards hard and don't try to do anything spectacular. If he picks you, he picks you, if not, no big deal."

I didn't respond as we started out of the building to meet the rest of the guys for the walk to Mueller's, but I thought, 'It is, too, a big deal . . . a *very* big deal for me!'

When we met up with the rest of the guys and started walking to Mueller's, they already knew. Glenn told them all that I was trying to keep it quiet because I was afraid I would choke, "which you probably will," he added, mockingly.

"Nice guy," said Jeff, looking at Glenn. "Why don't ya just kick him in the balls?"

"You guys are on the same team, aren't you?" laughed Dickie. "Is this 'motivation by ridicule' a la Guido?"

"No, I'm just sick of his worrying all the time," answered Glenn.

"Does worrying ever help? Is it gonna do any good? Is it gonna change anything?"

There was a moment of awkward silence as Glenn waited for me to answer and I thought about it.

"I guess not," I finally said.

"You act like we should feel sorry for you. Well, I don't! You *need* a kick in the ass. You have a chance to make the varsity basketball team. Instead of being happy, you get depressed. That's bullshit!"

"I'm not depressed," I said.

"Oh yeah, well then, what are you? Certainly not happy?" asked Glenn.

"I'm worried," I answered. " . . . worried about blowing it."

"What you need to do is put it out of your mind and play like we always do and win," asserted Glenn.

Not much was said about it the rest of the way, as I tried to do as Glenn said and put it out of my mind.

That night, we all started at The Wall and then all but Pat and I went looking for girls.

"How come you're hanging around?" I asked of Pat.

"I figured I'd keep you company," he replied. "I know you're uptight and thought maybe you need to talk."

"Well, I think Glenn's right," I said. "I need to put it out of my mind."

"Then, why didn't you want to go with the guys?"

"Because I can't *get* it out of my mind," I laughed.

"So, what were you gonna do? Sit here and drink alone?" asked Pat.

"I was gonna finish my beer and go home, I guess," I responded, weakly.

"I don't mind talking about it if you want to. I think Glenn was being a little hard on you," said Pat.

"I want this *so* badly," I blurted out, unashamed. "I can't believe this is happening and I just can't blow it. I've got to play the game of my life."

"That's gonna be tough," offered Pat, "these guys we're playing are good, real good, and they don't want to lose to juniors and they're gonna have a big crowd behind them. All the seniors will be rooting for them and against us."

"So, won't all the juniors be rooting for us?"

"No," said Pat, with a big smile.

"No? Why not?"

"Because we beat them and they are jealous. I know a bunch of juniors that hope we get our asses kicked."

Pat and I talked for about an hour and then we went home. I watched a little bit of television and then thought it would be wise to get a lot of sleep. I went to bed but found it hard to sleep.

I don't remember much detail about the game. I remember a senior, Richie Favaro, guarded me and was absolutely determined to keep me off the boards. I really liked Favaro. I had gotten to know him in a study hall where we sat next to each other. He was only about six feet tall, but strong as an ox and had a plan. They had scouted us and decided to be very physical. Favaro would concentrate on keeping me away from the basket and I would get no easy baskets. If I got the ball inside, they would foul me hard and let me shoot foul shots.

I remember going to the line a lot and making only about half of my foul shots.

I remember pulling down a rebound and having it smacked away from me, resulting in a fast break basket for the seniors.

I remember a small guard tying me up and getting a jump ball call after I battled to gain control of another rebound.

I remember playing defense as if my life were on the line.

I remember we lost.

At the end of the game, all I could think about was: would I be asked to be on the varsity? I was in the locker room naked, when Mr. O'Meara suddenly appeared and yelled, "Farrell, see me before you leave."

"Oh my God," I thought. "I must've made it."

He doesn't know that I knew why he reffed our game, so he must want to tell me that he wants me on the team."

"If not, he wouldn't have to tell me anything at all."

I took the quickest shower in recorded history. I didn't use any soap, just stood under the shower water for about fifteen seconds and then toweled off. I went back to my locker to get dressed and found that word was spreading. The Rizzos were there, as was Jay Carroll, Billy Regan and Tommy.

"Is it true?" one of them asked.

"What true? I answered, dressing as fast as I could.

"O'Meara wants to see you?" said Billy Regan.

"Yeah," I said, buttoning my shirt.

"Then it must be about being on the varsity," he concluded. "Congrats."

"All right!" said Jay, excitedly.

As I sat down to put my shoes and socks on, Glenn and Pat came over on their way into the shower.

"Is it true?" asked Pat.

"I haven't talked to him yet," I answered.

"I'm happy for you," said Pat. "We're gonna drink a few cold ones tonight!"

I smiled widely as I stood up to go see Coach O'Meara.

"You don't seem too sad about us losing," said Glenn with a smile. "Tell me you would rather we had won than you making varsity,"

"I wish we had won and I made the varsity," I answered. "Now, if you guys will excuse me, I have to go see Coach O'Meara."

As I walked away, I heard some applause and some 'congrats' and some 'way to go, Joes' as word spread and the area was becoming crowded with well wishers. As I approached the coach's office, I heard someone yell, "Hey, Farrell." I turned and it was Richie Favaro in his underwear. "What's this I hear?" he asked.

"Whaddya mean?"

"Don't play dumb. I heard your gonna be on the varsity," he said, extending his hand.

"No thanks to you," I replied, shaking his hand. "I'm just going to see O'Meara now."

"Well, I'm happy for you," he said. "It makes the victory all that much sweeter."

I knocked on Mr O'Meara's door and saw that he was on the phone. He motioned for me to sit down. As I sat there, I felt a keen sense of excitement. I was thinking about wearing a Holy Cross uniform and running out of the locker room to the cheering of thousands of fans.

O'Meara hung up the phone.

"Mr. Farrell, you know this gym isn't a playground?"

There was an awkward moment of silence as I searched for what Coach O'Meara was trying to tell me. I thought it was a reference to how I had just played.

"I'm not sure what you mean, Mr. O'Meara?" I answered.

"Your language!"

"My *language*?"

"Yeah. Your language could get us both in trouble," he said as he stood up and started putting on his green and gold Holy Cross jacket.

"I'm sorry," I said. "I'll be more careful in the future."

"You better be, mister. If Brother Richard heard you, he'd probably banish you from the gym."

"I didn't realize I was that bad," I said, as Mr. O'Meara came around his desk as if he was going to leave.

"You were," he answered, motioning for me to leave ahead of him. "Take my word for it."

"Is that *all*?" I asked in panic and surprise.

"Yes, and don't take it so lightly if you ever want to play in the gym again."

Mr. O'Meara flicked off the light in his office and disappeared.

I walked slowly through the locker room into the gym and out into the hallway, wishing *I* would disappear.

♦ ♦ ♦

Of course, everyone had a good laugh at my expense and I can't say I could blame them. First the guys at Holy Cross as they told one another, and then the rest of the gang that night at Mueller's. None of it was mean-spirited. Dennis found it particularly funny and throughout the night would comment every time I would use foul language.

"There you go again" or "watch your fuckin' language," Dennis would say anytime I said anything off color. Then after a while, he started chastising everybody, imploring them to clean up their language.

"Jesus Christ, we're not fuckin' morons, ya' know. We oughta be able to express our goddamn selves without resorting to offensive terminology. Remember all those . . . whaddaya call it . . . all those mother fuckin' words the nuns made us memorize? . . . vocabulary words! That was so we could express our feelings without being offensive to others."

"Fuck you, ya prick," Eddie yelled and everybody laughed. "That's what you should have said to the coach," Eddie yelled at me. "You should have gotten up and, as you walked out, said, "Fuck you, ya prick!"

The kidding and laughing helped me get over it and back to my normal life of trying to survive.

Near the end of the school year, we got the results of the National Merit Scholarship Exam that we had taken in March. We had been told that this exam was a good indicator of where you stood academically and how you would do on the SATs. The results were comforting, if not confusing. I got a composite score of 87th percentile. I scored an 89th percentile in both Math and English and an 81st percentile in Social Studies and in Science.

This seemed to indicate that I might indeed be able to get into college, but why, if I was able to score better than 87 percent of high school juniors in the nation, was I doing so poorly in my classes, I thought. My grades were potentially my biggest problem. This fear was further magnified when I flunked three finals in one day.

Mom and Dad had gotten into a terrible and violent argument the night before my final exams in history, physics and math. I was lost in math to begin with, but doing well in physics and getting good grades on the history exams (stupid as they were). I got no studying done at all that night as Ronnie and I tried to referee the argument and get them calmed down. I really got very little sleep either, as the battle raged on late into the night and was very upsetting. I thought I might try to tell my teachers that I wasn't prepared and ask for mercy, but I couldn't bring myself to do it somehow. I had three more the next day and although things were tense at home, I managed a little studying and passed them, but didn't do what you would call well.

One of my worries began to wane in late spring. For some reason, I was led to believe that when applying for college, a student had to know what he wanted to do with his life. Teachers and guidance counselors were always asking and providing us with literature about choosing a career and college applications always wanted you to specify a major. We were even tested for our interests and given a profile of what professions matched our answers. I used to joke that my test showed I should be a shepherd. (I would make a good shepherd.)

Even "College Night," which was an annual event for upperclassmen where representatives from dozens of colleges came to our school to promote their programs, seemed to focus on this question. Various colleges touted their excellent programs in such and such major and gave statistics for admissions to graduate and professional schools, their junior year abroad, their senior year internships and their five-year combined degree programs.

Due to the influence of my father, I had always answered that I wanted to be an engineer. In fact, I knew nothing about what an engineer did day-to-day or what it took to become one. I knew that whatever Brother Charles was talking about in math class was not interesting to me nor did I understand it. Reading the colleges' literature and the courses that Engineering students took made me abandon that idea and I was completely lost about what I wanted to do.

Billy Landers was the only one of our crowd who seemed to know. Billy wanted a pre-Med program. He had good grades at Brooklyn Prep. And knew what he wanted to be and knew he could do it.

One day in May, I was at Eddie Haggerty's house, waiting for Eddie to get ready for a party we were going to. Eddie was running way behind because his brother Robbie had "taken an eternity in the bathroom" and Eddie hadn't showered or shaved. While I waited, I started looking at some books lying around. Two Psychology textbooks caught my eye and I started to page through them. When Eddie was ready, I asked about the books and he told me they were his brother, Charlie's college texts. I asked if I could borrow them and Eddie asked Charlie, who said I could have them.

It was an epiphany. I spent the next few weeks reading two college textbooks cover to cover and then bought more psychology books that summer. I now knew what I wanted to major in. I looked through college catalogs at the courses psych. Majors were offered or required to take and I was fascinated. Finally, I had some notion of what to do in the near future, should there be a future.

The final day of school in my junior year was a half day. Exams were over and we were all passing around our newly distributed yearbooks for autographs. It was fun to write some cute poem or funny saying, although sometimes hard to be original.

As our last class ended, a few of us were signing each other's yearbooks in the hallway and laughing at what others wrote. Jay Carroll showed up and we exchanged books and signed. Jay wrote that it was too bad we weren't in the same section this year, a sentiment I shared completely. Gary Allen wrote that I was really a good friend but should stop cheating on exams. I remember signing Paul Falabella's, but I didn't remember him signing mine.

"Hey Paul, sign my book," I said, offering it to him.

"I already did," he answered.

"You did?"

"Yep!"

"Are you sure? I didn't see it?"

"I'm sure! It's in there," he said as we started off on our separate ways for the summer. "And I mean it too."

"Okay, I'll find it," I yelled. "See ya! Have a good summer."

When I got home, I remembered that I hadn't seen what Paul had written and looked for it. When I found it, I suddenly knew why I hadn't seen it when he wrote it. He must have closed the book when he handed it back to me or passed it to someone else to sign, without calling attention to what he had written.

It read:

> To Joe,
>   *Wherever you go, the sun will rise*
>   *Darkness will shrink back in shame*
>   *And the people will remember you.*
>
>   *Your loyal friend,*
>   *Paul*

◆ ◆ ◆

The summer of 1963 I worked again at Cresthaven, but this time for $1.25 an hour. All summer long Leslie Gore ruled the jukebox in the snack bar. First it was "It's My Party" and then "Judy's Turn to Cry." I hated both of them. Pat Nash was in college and had decided to become a New York City Police Officer and did not return to Cresthaven. Tommy Nash and I did, and to my surprise, Jeff Baudo, the doctor's son, was working there as a garbage man!

Jeff had asked me months before if they were accepting applications at Cresthaven for summer jobs and I had told him I didn't know, but that Pat Nash wasn't returning and maybe he could take his place. I really didn't think he meant it. He told me his father was on his ass about doing nothing all summer. As it turned out, the CYO day camp enrollment had grown to the point where they needed a crew to handle garbage almost all day and Jeff had been hired for that job. We didn't work together on Patty's crew, but saw each other every day at work. Dr. Baudo would drop Jeff off and pick him up every day in a new white convertible and every once in a while, he would offer us a ride, which we gratefully accepted.

When Tommy Nash and I first saw Jeff at work putting garbage cans on the back of a pick-up truck, we talked and Jeff introduced himself to Tommy. As Jeff rode away in the truck, Tommy looked at me and said, "I thought his dad was a doctor?"

"He *is* a doctor," I answered.

"He must be a bad one to make his son work here."

"I don't know about that," I responded. "He just wants Jeff to learn about life and the value of a dollar. I admire both of them for that."

"Not me," answered Tom. "I want my doctor to be so good that he has a summer home he sends his family to. This guy must be a quack."

After meeting Dr. Baudo and being given a few rides home in his fancy convertible, I asked Tommy one day if he still thought Dr. Baudo was a quack.

"Maybe not, but then, why does he torture his son?" he answered, laughing.

Jeff worked hard all summer, lifting heavy duty garbage cans, and flirting with camp counselors. He learned, however, as we had, that being filthy dirty, and doing manual labor in the hot sun is not particularly attractive to the country club set. I did, however, get one charming young club member, Valerie, to go out with me that summer, and got Tommy Taraci to go out with her friend, Jayne. We had a number of dates during the brief fling, including a Holy Cross dance in the fall. They were well-off financially and our age was a disdvantage, meaning they were used to dating older guys with money. They were very good looking, sophisticated, yet were willing to take the bus to the movies with us. One night on the bus on the way home from Valerie's house, after a few hours of making out with Val and Jayne, we were pretty pumped up.

"Man, this is working out pretty good, isn't it?" I said to Tommy.

"Damn straight!" he answered, with a shit-eating grin on his face.

"I wonder what they see in us?" I asked.

"You mean, what they see in *you*?" he answered, running his hand through his hair with a very egotistical flair.

"I'm serious," I said, laughing.

"See here, Mr. Farrell," Tommy said, mimicking The Kingfish from Amos 'n' Andy. "You might be serious, but I *resembles* that remark."

"I don't think this is gonna last," I continued. "I think we are their rebellion, ya know, they find us exciting because we are the bad boys, so to speak."

"Don't start that shit, please."

"What shit?"

"That analyzing shit. Whatever their reason, however long it lasts, let's just take it as far as they will go."

So we did.

I had the added pleasure of seeing some of the guy members jealous and pissed off when Valerie would look for me and flirt with me while I was working. A few times, she went to the snack bar and got me a cold drink. I would usually pretend not to notice the guys staring and shaking their heads in disbelief. One time I mentioned it to her.

"Your friends seem amused that you're talking to me," I said, nodding in their direction. "Particularly the guy in the Villanova shirt."

"Please don't mind them," she answered. "I used to date that guy. He thinks he's God's gift to women."

By the time Thanksgiving rolled around, she was back with "God's gift," and it was over between us. I didn't mind. Tommy quit dating Jayne as well. It was a fun thing and none of us had invested a lot of emotion into it.

What I did invest in was air conditioning. The prospect of another summer struggling to sleep in my tinderbox bedroom prompted me to buy a window air conditioner at the Gertz department store. I saw an ad in the *Long Island Star Journal* for a sale on lightweight, window air-conditioners and bought one for $89 with money I had made shoveling snow. I followed the instructions, installed it in my room, and finally slept in comfort. My parents were amazed and within weeks there were air-conditioners in their room and my sister's room.

Although my bedroom was cooler, the country was not. The threat of nuclear holocaust continued to grow as world tensions remained high. Castro visited the Soviet Union, where he was warmly embraced and there was growing concern about events in some far off place called Vietnam. At home, a civil rights leader in Mississippi, Medgar Evers, was shot and killed in front of his home; four black girls were killed in a church bombing at Birmingham, Alabama; the governor of Alabama, George Wallace, stood in the doorway at the University of Alabama and barred two black Americans, accompanied by Federal law enforcement officials, from enrolling, in defiance of Federal law; and the largest demonstration for human rights in United States history took place in Washington, DC where perhaps the greatest speech *ever* was delivered by the Reverend Martin Luther King. *All* this in one summer.

The march on Washington was of course the leading story on the evening news that night and after the news, there was a special report on it. I watched in awe. I had never heard of Martin Luther King before, but I knew I would be hearing about him in the future. It was truly one of the most stirring and inspiring moments in American history.

After the program, I went to read more psychology in the backyard until it was too dark to read anymore. The speech kept popping into my mind as I lay in a lounge chair with my book.

So Martin Luther King had a dream of a better world. Maybe we won't die in a nuclear war? Maybe we won't be enslaved in work camps by Communists? Maybe we won't be torn apart by hatred and violence? One short year from now, I thought to myself, I'll be out of high school and part of the real world. I'll be working or in the military. It would be nice to be in college studying psychology. It would be nice to be part of Martin Luther King's dream. It would be nice not to go to hell for impure thoughts, deeds, and desires. So far, none of my dreams had come true (except for the 1955 Dodgers and they packed up and left me), so it was hard to believe in new ones, but Martin Luther King and the quarter of a million people with him gave me hope.

CHAPTER NINETEEN

♦ ♦ ♦ ♦ ♦

"HELL FREEZES OVER"

But I would not be convicted
by a jury of my peers . . .
 Paul Simon—"Still Crazy After All These Years"

Senior year began like the others, with a trip to Holy Cross to see our schedules a few days before school began. And like the other times, there were surprises and mixed emotions. The first thing I looked at was the class roster and I was ecstatic at what I saw. Paul, Ray, Glenn, Pat, Tommy, and I all in the same section! I also noticed that Joe Rubbone from St. Andrew's was in our section, Section 4-3. My ecstasy was short-lived however, when I noticed one shocking development. I expected to have Brother Thomas Kane again for Spanish II. I liked him and we got along well, despite my not caring much about Spanish, nor knowing very much about it.

Now, suddenly, I felt sick to my stomach as I stared in disbelief at the schedule on the wall. By some incredible twist of fate, I had drawn Brother Richard McDonald, the Dean of Men, for Spanish II. All the way home I complained of the incredibly bad luck to Glenn and Tommy, who seemed amused by it all. Tommy took French and said he regretted he wouldn't be able to see Brother Richard "torture" me. Glenn said, "Get it out of you system *now*, because I'm not listening to you bitch all year long."

There was, however, a completely different feeling about being a senior. It seemed like we were much older than last year, more detached from the usual high school scene. This "above-it-all" feeling probably came from a number of sudden developments in our lives. In a matter of months I had taken a job, started drinking in bars, had a steady girlfriend, was writing to colleges, and was aged by a tragedy of an unprecedented nature.

The job was a tremendous stroke of luck and the result of a great friendship with Pat Kelly. He had gotten a job rolling coins at an armored car company and at my urging, got them to hire me as well. The company was Cross Armored Carrier, on Northern Boulevard in Bayside, and I could work on any day I wanted after school, and for as long as I wanted. We considered the work easy.

We would set the machine for whatever coin we were to roll that day, empty a bag of loose coins into the hopper, sit, and fill the tubes one at a time. This was achieved by stepping on a pedal, which released the proper number of coins and shot them down into the paper tube. The last step was to stick the open end into a crimper, which closed the end of the tube. When a bag was finished, we returned the now-rolled coin to the bag and sealed it. The bags were placed on a pallet by denomination and later loaded onto an armored truck and delivered to a customer.

We were paid $1.50 an hour, which we viewed as terrific pay. This was new freedom for me. I no longer had to rely on my parents for spending money. I worked an average of three days a week for three or four hours and Saturdays for six or eight hours and had plenty of spending money. Cross Armored loved us. We did a lot of work, cheap. They had a crew of four full-timers, but were always in need of more rolled coins, and we were perfect to supplement the production. We could outroll the regulars any day, but one of our first "real world" lessons occurred when Bill Wallace, the Coin Room supervisor, called us aside and told us to slow down. He gave us each a copy of a note where he had written what was expected for each coin per hour. We were exceeding it by a good bit.

"If you had to do this every day, you'd see that you don't want to set the bar too high," said Bill.

"Okay, we understand," answered Pat.

Often about 4:30 p.m. the permanent crew would be gone and we would be alone in the vault except for the sole guard on duty. We would occasionally roll as fast as we could and sign out, adding an hour to our time, since the production was there to justify it.

It was a maturing experience to have a steady job and not be needing money from Mom and Dad. More often than not, Pat and I would work past our normal family dinnertime, walk to a nearby White Castle, eat hamburgers for dinner before we caught separate buses home. We were very close friends who spent a lot of time talking about our lives and what lay ahead of us. We knew our lives were about to change drastically and had no idea how. We promised we would always remain friends, no matter what happened to us.

Most of us were seventeen at the start of the school year and would be turning eighteen soon. The legal drinking age was eighteen in New York and although we had been drinking for years, we hadn't been going in bars. Now, we would try a place and once we got served, would return, befriend the bartender, leave a tip, and become regulars. Gradually, we were able to drink at Michael's Lounge, the Vinwood, The Depot, the Log Cabin, Tommy's Bar, and the Villa Esquire.

It was a dramatic step up from drinking in the streets or secretly in someone's basement. Sometimes we were carded (asked to show our draft cards as proof of age) the first time, but then not on future visits. Eddie and Dennis would use their brothers' draft cards which they "borrowed" for one night and after they were known, Tommy and I would go to the place with Eddie and Dennis and the bartender would assume since we were friends, that we were legal and so on. Dickie also had an older brother, who fit his general description, and he would sometimes carry his ID just in case.

The steady girlfriend was Sheila Lennon. We met at a party and liked each other and started dating pretty steadily for most of my senior year. It was the first time I had ever dated a girl more than a few times. I introduced one of Sheila's friends, Eileen Fenchak, to Pat and they quickly became a couple and eventually married.

I had started writing to colleges and reading their literature during the summer and when school began I started in earnest to narrow down my focus. I wanted a school that had Psychology as a major, wasn't expensive, and wasn't in New York. I felt I had to get away from home or I'd go nuts. When I told my parents that I was considering going away to college, they told me they couldn't afford it and that St. John's in Queens was my best option.

I told my father about the New York State Higher Education Assistance Agency, which would lend me money for college, but he dismissed it as if I didn't know what I was talking about.

"No bank's gonna loan a kid that kind of money," he told me. "You don't have any collateral and I'm not risking our house for you to go away to school." I told him it didn't work like that, but until I brought home the actual loan application and literature, he didn't believe me. They seemed quite stunned that I indeed could borrow the necessary money without them having any responsibility for it. Stunned and somewhat annoyed. Just exactly why they were annoyed, I can only speculate.

In later years, when I asked about their reaction, they denied it, but I know it was true. Either they thought that somehow this was going to cost them a lot of money, or that I would screw up and flunk out or get kicked out after borrowing a lot of money. More than once, I heard my mom say, "Mr. Big Shot thinks he's going away to college," when talking to my uncles and aunts or the Ghizzonis.

The tragedy was, of course, the murder of our President in broad daylight in front of thousands of people. It was a Friday and we were almost done for the day when Brother Josephat came over the public address system and announced that the President had been shot and badly wounded and that we should go home and pray for the President, his family, and our country. There were no other announcements. Nothing else seemed important. After class, the hallways, which were usually filled with loud talk, laughing, yelling, and locker doors slamming, were quiet. Although filled with students, there was little conversation and those who did speak, spoke softly. Lockers were closed more gently. There was a tremendous sense of sadness.

I decided not to roll coins that day and went home instead. On the way home near Bowne Park, I ran into Dennis Mullaney who was on his way to Mueller's where he had recently started working part-time. Dennis, through a lucky quirk in scheduling, had no classes in the afternoon and was allowed to leave at lunchtime. He knew it was early for me to be out of school and so he asked what was up.

I told him, "Someone shot President Kennedy."

"Goddamn! You're kidding, right?" Dennis asked.

"No, I'm not kidding. They let us out of school."

"Ho-o-o-ly shit," said Dennis as he walked away, shaking his head.

At home I found out that the President was indeed dead. I was glued to the television while I was home. My mom was terribly sad and had been crying. When Ronnie got home from school, she cried as soon as she saw my mom. My dad had been working in an oven at Peter Pan Bakery and didn't hear about it until he was leaving the bakery around five and asked why the employees were all crying.

We ate dinner together in front of the television, but didn't talk much. It seemed like everyone, everywhere, was crying, even Walter Cronkite.

After dinner, I went to meet my friends at Mueller's, but when I arrived, Mueller's was closed. Mueller's was never closed, except on Christmas and Easter, but it was closed now. Apparently, the owner Marge, was so grief-stricken, she closed up and went home crying. Pat Kelly and Jeff were there when I arrived and Dennis and Tommy arrived soon thereafter. We decided to get beer and go to 'The Wall.' It was a strange Friday night. The whole world seemed sad. We drank slowly and talked about how this could happen and who did it and why.

Lee Harvey Oswald had been arrested and was charged with the killing and rumors were that he was a Communist. Speculation was running wild as to what the motive was and what was behind it. Was it the Mafia because of Attorney General Robert Kennedy's vigorous prosecution of Mafia figures? Was it the Russians? Was it the Cubans?

Lee Harvey Oswald would be the key, we all agreed. What he knew and would tell about this earth-shattering event would be monumental. Pat thought it was the Russians and would lead to nuclear war.

"If it turns out to be the Russians, we're fucked," offered Pat. "It'll mean war and the whole world is in danger."

"I think it was the Mafia," said Jeff. "It doesn't make sense for it to be the Russians."

"I agree with Jeff," I said. "The Russians wouldn't risk it."

"Why not?" asked Dennis.

"Maybe they don't think we can trace it to them," answered Pat.

"It would be a big risk just to kill Kennedy. What does that really gain them?" I said.

"Maybe they just hate him because of the whole Cuban missile thing," said Dennis.

"Maybe," said Jeff, "but I don't think they would shoot him in Dallas."

"I hope you guys are right," said Pat, looking at Jeff and me, "'cause if it was the Russians, New York is toast."

"Maybe not," said Tommy. "Maybe they'd target military bases and ships that carry nuclear weapons."

"What do you mean, 'they wouldn't shoot him in *Dallas*,'" yelled Dennis at Jeff. "Why do you say that?"

"I just don't think they would," answered Jeff.

"Oh, I see," said Dennis, sipping on his beer. "I'm glad you clarified that 'cause at first it sounded a little stupid."

We all laughed as we sipped our beers and kept glancing at the sky, hoping not to see anything unusual streaking across the darkness.

The next day, we were all glued to the television as details began to become known. It was revealed that Lee Harvey Oswald had a Russian wife and had actually lived in Russia. The military was on a worldwide alert. Pictures of Jackie Kennedy in her blood-spattered, pink suit boarding Air Force One back to Washington were devastating to the millions of Americans watching.

The networks continually aired clips of Kennedy's inaugural speech, his famous speech in Berlin and his triumphant trip to Ireland, as well as clips of his beautiful young children, now without a father. The whole situation seemed too sad and too shocking to be real.

As bizarre and scary as things seemed that day, on Sunday, things would reach a new dimension of horror. The man assumed to be one of the men who killed our President and had answers to the many questions and mysteries surrounding this catastrophe, was shot and killed in front of millions on live television while being transferred by police.

The gunman, Jack Ruby, was a man with underworld ties who ran a local strip club. The next day, schools were closed as President Kennedy was buried at Arlington National Cemetery in one of the saddest events in our nation's history. The horse-drawn caisson, the riderless horse, the drumbeat, Jackie lighting the eternal flame and John Jr.'s salute of his father's passing coffin were indelibly imprinted on our brains. America wept. It was too sad for words to describe.

For the weeks and months that followed, there was sadness and a tremendous sense of apprehension in the news and in conversation. Was Johnson capable of handling the Russians? Would we all be dead if he had been President during the Missile Crisis? Through all the tension, chaos and uncertainty that seemed to surround us, Kennedy's voice always seemed calm and sure and optimistic and now that lone voice was gone . . .

◆ ◆ ◆

This was the backdrop of my application to college: chaos, despair, sadness and uncertainty. I had been looking at materials for months and trying to find the right place for me to escape to. I wanted to go away but not too far away. I wanted Psychology as a major and the school had to be affordable. I went to our annual College Night and spoke to some representatives from different colleges, but without any real results. One day in study hall, Mr. Cronin saw me looking at a brochure from St. Vincent College and struck up a conversation. Mr. Cronin was one of the coolest teachers we had at Holy Cross. He was young, smart, dressed well, liked rock music and was known to bring dates to school events. I never had him for anything, but study hall, but guys who did have him for class liked him a lot. It turned out Mr. Cronin had gone to St. Vincent and loved it. He strongly recommended it to me. He even thought I could get in, based on being in Section 4-3, as long as my College Board exam scores weren't bad. As it turned out, they weren't.

We had taken the College Board Exam the previous spring and had just gotten the results. My results surprised a lot of people, including me! The total was 1157, which put me on some list of students who did extremely well. I know this because Brother Richard, being Dean of Men as well as my Spanish teacher, had the list and took the opportunity to mock me in class. I had gotten a 698 in the math part of the exam, which put me in the 97th percentile nationally, but as Brother Richard knew, I was flunking math at the time and had been kicked out of math class by Mr. Vinciguerra twice already.

"Let me say this to you, Senor Farrell. I think God reserves special places in hell for people like you who don't use their God-given talent. You have the '*IQ*,' Senor Farrell, but not the '*I Do.*' You have nothing to be proud about."

This was yet another point on which Brother Richard and I disagreed. I *was* proud of my scores. Looking back on it, it really shouldn't have been such a surprise. I had scored very high on each of the National Aptitude and achievement tests we had taken, but that seemed to go unnoticed. I had an impulse to mention his refusal to welcome me to the Great Books Club, but controlled that impulse.

I was feeling pretty confident now that I could get into college and start all over. I applied to St. Vincent College and only St. Vincent, relatively early, hoping I could quit worrying and enjoy the rest of the year. The waiting was painful. Every day, hoping to hear something, only to be disappointed.

Then finally, just before Christmas, I was accepted at St. Vincent College. The letter, however, contained a clause that was to haunt me the rest of the year. It said that I must maintain at least an eighty average for my senior year or my admission could be revoked.

And so, 1964 began with a strong schizophrenic feeling. Our hero and President was dead—murdered by unknown people, his alleged killer gunned down suspiciously. Racial tension escalating throughout the country. Nuclear annihilation possible and talked openly about on any given day. A growing strange controversy over an assassinated leader named Diem in some country called Viet-Nam. Doom and gloom and yet, I had been accepted into a reputable college of my choosing and was happy and hopeful about the future, should there be one.

My strange and complicated relationship with Brother Richard would continue until the bitter end. He started every Spanish class by calling on me.

"Levantense ('stand up'), Senor Farrell," he would say upon entering class and he would proceed to ask me questions in Spanish.

Fortunately, I had a half period study hall immediately before Spanish and spent it anticipating his questions and reviewing my copied homework, so as to be prepared. It was a daily struggle and although Brother Richard frequently exposed my ignorance, I managed to avoid a disaster and finished the year with an 83.

Unfortunately, that wasn't my only daily contact with the Holy Cross Dean of Men. In late October, I had been given a week's detention by Mr. Schiliro, our chemistry teacher, for "disorderliness." That was the technical term for making everyone laugh during chemistry lab. Brother Richard was in charge of detention and so I spent at least an hour under his supervision after school for a week.

Student ...F.A.RR.e.l.l.,.J.u.e...

Section ....7.3.... Date ./0/.3//.63.

Teacher .R.T.SCHILIRO...

MISDEMEANORS

....1. Loitering

....2. Gum Chewing

....3. Cleats on Shoes

....4. No Equipment

....5. Eating Outside Cafe

....10. Offence

....6. Talking Out Of Turn

....7. Talking Repeatedly

✓..8. Disorderliness

....9. Missed late detention.

MISCONDUCT

....1. Truancy

....2. Smoking

....3. Defiance

....4. Defacing Property

....5. ....

D.M.C.

Printed by H.C. Ind. Arts Dept.

Mr. Vinciguerra had twice kicked me out of math class, which meant report to the Dean's Office until you get accepted back. Mr. Vinciguerra was one of the worst teachers I ever had. He was short, hairy, dark-complected, with long arms and no neck. In short, he looked like an ape. Apes, however, have much better personalities. He also had a speech impediment which seemed to be a requirement for employment in the Math Department. Brother Francis Ellis (Quasi Modo) and Brother Charles Varnak, my two prior math teachers both had speech impediments.

Mr. Vinciguerra had a high-pitched voice and a lisp. His appearance and his voice didn't seem to fit. He would come into class with a book bag, put it on his desk, take the textbook out, open it up, and start talking in a high-pitched monotone for fifty minutes. He seemed oblivious to the fact that most of us weren't paying attention and didn't understand what the hell he was doing. He never called on anyone unless they raised their hand with a question and didn't seem to give a damn if you were learning anything or not.

Exam scores were horrible, but he curved them sharply so everyone wouldn't flunk. Once, Ritchie Capone got a 4 percent on an exam! Mr. Vinciguerra was standing in front of his desk calling out names for students to come up to his desk and get their graded exams back. Capone went up and as he started back, he got a shocked look on his face and muttered softly, but audibly, with disbelief, "Four? I got a four? How could I get a four?"

He turned and went back to Mr. Vinciguerra and asked for a zero.

"You want a zero, Capone?" Mr. Vinciguerra asked.

"Yeah! I'd actually prefer a zero."

"Why is that?" asked Vinciguerra, crossing out the four and making a zero at the top of Capone's exam paper.

"Because a zero sounds like you got caught cheating," he responded. "How do you explain a four?"

I sat next to John Herlihy in math. I hadn't even known John until senior year and he was smart and funny and we were becoming good friends. John had a great laugh. It was one of those infectious laughs where everything seemed funnier because of how funny that person thinks it is. My cousin Pat Nash had that kind of laugh. Just watching people like that laugh or hearing them laugh made me laugh. By seventh period math, John and I were both near delirious from boredom and tedium anyway, and we found a lot to laugh about.

The first time I got kicked out of class was when Mr. Vinciguerra was discussing $E = mc^2$ and described "c" as the only constant in the universe, the speed of light. John looked at me and said softly, his hand over his mouth to prevent Mr. V. from hearing him, "How about the speed of darkness? It seems pretty constant to me!"

Then John completely lost it and was laughing himself silly and trying to stifle it at the same time. I don't know which I thought was funnier: John's comment or his enjoyment of his comment, but I lost it, too, and Mr. Vinciguerra of course seemed to notice me.

"Allwight, Fawwell," (I was one of the few students he knew by name which in my case was a bad thing.) he said with a pronounced lisp, "What do you find so funny?"

I was laughing uncontrollably and without even standing up, which was absolutely required when called on in class, I blurted out, "The speed of darkness!"

Nobody laughed! *Especially* Mr. Vinciguerra. Maybe I didn't articulate it properly or maybe it wasn't in the proper context, but to my extreme surprise, no one seemed to think it was as funny as I did.

Mr. Vinciguerra pointed to the door with a glare in his eye and I knew what he meant. I gathered my belongings and headed for the Dean's Office, where I was greeted with a 'I'm not surprised' shrug by Brother Richard.

The second time was a day when Mr. Vinciguerra was having a particularly bad day articulating. He was covering pwobabiwity (probability) and said something that no one seemed to understand. A few hands shot up and he was asked to repeat it, which he did. Still, no one seemed to be able to decipher what he was saying. There was some giggling and murmuring and another request to repeat it. From a few rows away, I heard Tommy Taraci say with his hand in front of his mouth, as if scratching his nose, "I think it has something to do with a cwazy wabbit." Even though I thought that was funny, that wasn't what made me lose it. Herlihy leaned over and said, "Imagine what a meeting of the Math Department must be like."

The mental picture of Brother Francis Ellis, Brother Charles Varnak and Mr. V. talking to each other made me completely lose it. I absolutely lost it! John Herlihy and I both were picturing the same thing and I could not contain myself, nor could John. Mr. Vinciguerra, of course thought we were laughing at his difficulties and erupted in a violent, *"You two get out,"* which we did not have trouble understanding.

We collected our stuff and left the classroom as quickly as we could. We stopped in the boys room on the way to the Dean's office and laughed ourselves sick thinking about a staff meeting of the Math Department. Mr. Vinciguerra let John back in class after one day, but I spent two in the Dean's office before he would take *me* back.

My self-destructive impulses seemed to grow stronger or my tolerance for bullshit shorter as I grew older because, in the spring very near St. Patrick's Day, I was kicked out of Religion class for the duration of the year. My Religion teacher, Brother Joseph Zutelis, was demented. I had experienced many bad teachers which I have mentioned in these stories, but Brother Joseph was unique. He was demented. He was so over-the-top crazy that it took a couple of months just to get over the shock of having such a teacher.

He spoke in a quiet mumbling voice almost like he was talking to some other group of people not present in the room. Most of the class sessions, he was muttering about the Second Vatican Council which had commenced that September and was *very* important to him, but didn't mean a damn thing to us. He would mutter softly for an entire period about Vatican II and always—usually twice a period—say, "Beauty is truth, truth beauty. That is all ye know on earth and all ye need to know."

At first we thought he was trying to test us and this would be an exam question or would be the answer to something big coming up. Then we thought it was funny and would say it to each other and mutter it everywhere as a joke. After a half a school year, it stopped being a source of amusement and we began to understand it for what it was: the ranting of a lunatic.

I had learned to cope with this lunatic who I had for the last period of every day by putting my head down on my books piled on my desk and sleeping. I had grown to have complete contempt for this colossal waste of time and Brother Joseph didn't seem to mind or notice. His exams were questions from the end of each chapter and occasionally one question about Vatican II, so paying attention to his mutterings was not really necessary. I would copy homework if there was anything available to copy, but it was usually too early for someone to have actually done their homework for me to copy.

For some odd reason on a day in March, Brother Joseph, out of the blue, called on me in class. I didn't hear him as my mind was far away. Ray Frasene shook me to alert me and others made me aware that I had been called on. I stood up and being completely caught off guard said, "I'm sorry Brother, I didn't hear the question."

"I'm not surprised," Brother Joseph answered, in his usual quick cadence and soft voice. "I doubt you would have any wisdom to share if you had heard my question." He then made a strange "Hmm" noise that he frequently made between sentences or thoughts.

"So, let me ask you something you may be able to answer, Mister," he said, his voice rising unusually. "Why do you come in here every day and put your head down and sleep during my class?" he yelled, challengingly. Without a thought about the consequences and feeling challenged by someone I regarded as a lunatic, I answered clearly and loudly, "Because this class *blows*."

A smattering of applause broke out and Brother Joseph erupted in rage never before seen by any of us.

"Get out of here . . . and don't ever come back!" he shrieked like a banshee, pointing to the door. I was pissed. I slowly got my books together and slowly walked to the front of the room and walked out. I glared at Brother Joseph until I could no longer make eye contact with him and continue out.

I went slowly, defiantly to the Dean's Office. Even I was sick of this shit! I was ready to tell Brother Richard off, but he was luckily not there. Some brother I didn't know was filling in for him and told me to sit and study until Brother Richard returned. By the next day, I had cooled off and was properly contrite and Brother Richard accepted me as a daily visitor to his office for the rest of the year. Brother Joseph let me take exams and gave me an 83 for the year, which didn't seriously hurt me, but most guys used Religion class to help their overall average grade. That didn't happen for me, as much as I could have used that cushion.

I think we all felt lucky to have Brother John Joseph Donnelly for Senior English. We called him JJ and he knew not only our names, but our hopes and fears as well. He seemed interested in the overall well-being of each of us and that, strange as it may sound, made him unusual and maybe even unique. His class often became a forum for discussing whatever was on our minds. Once, after JJ chaperoned one of our fall dances, I believe it was the Football Frolic, he chided Ritchie Capone in class on Monday for dancing so close with his date. They were dancing slow with both arms around one another which was not uncommon.

"Geez, Capone," JJ said with a smile, "didn't you ever hear of leave room for the Holy Ghost? I was embarrassed just to *look* at you."

Capone got red in the face and started to answer but thought better of it. Finally, he said, "I don't know what to say, Brother. Why are you singling me out?"

"I don't mean to be unfair, but I did notice you and how you were dancing. That's all."

"I don't know why the school even has dances anyway," offers Capone.

"Why do you say that?" asked JJ.

"Because, aren't we supposed to avoid near occasions of sin, Brother?"

"Well, yes, but dancing isn't a sin!"

"Well, Brother, what do you think we're thinking about when we're dancing slow in a dimly lit room?"

There was quite a bit of laughter and reaction to Capone's comment and JJ suddenly felt a little awkward and defensive.

"I don't know," answered JJ, "and I'm not sure I want to know."

"Tell us! Tell us!" yelled Tommy Taraci.

Capone was red-faced now with embarrassment and merely said, "If you saw my date, you'd know what I was thinking."

Those that heard it laughed and some who didn't asked for him to repeat it.

"Don't repeat it!" yelled JJ.

The entire year I never got in trouble with JJ. He actually advised me sometimes on how to handle the trouble I was in. If I seemed unusually quiet or tired or disgusted, he would ask me if I was okay. It was as if he was a happy man who taught high school kids, did it well, and cared about how they were doing in their lives! It was very strange. He never hit anyone or yelled at anyone, got us to do our work, helped us understand why some things were happening, offered himself as a reference for college or jobs and treated us like young men. He must have been regarded as strange in 'Brotherland.'

♦ ♦ ♦

The football team that I never made won the City Catholic School Championship that year, with Tom Nash playing a big role. The basketball team I thought I made went to City Playoffs and lost to Power Memorial. I did, however, receive the honor of being voted onto the Intramural All-Stars, which was a great honor. Each year the All-Stars play a game against the faculty as a fund raiser. Tickets are sold and the gym is practically full. I was really excited about this, but unfortunately, came down with the flu and missed the game.

As graduation approached that spring, the Beatles had exploded onto the scene and had at one point, the top five songs, an unprecedented accomplishment. Jack Ruby was convicted of killing Lee Harvey Oswald and sentenced to death in what seemed like a very short time since the original crime. The New York City World's Fair opened as did Shea Stadium and a group of us skipped school to be at the game. I cannot remember how we got tickets, but we did, and I remember Fat Jack Fisher served up a homerun to a guy named Wilver Stargell as the Mets lost to the Pirates, 4-3.

The World's Fair must have thought a twelve-foot-high fence was security enough to keep out freeloaders, but they were wrong. We climbed over the fence routinely to get in free and spent most of our time at a bar called the Red Garter, drinking beer and trying to pick up girls.

I first remember hearing of Nelson Mandela and Malcolm X around this time and began to hear of Vietnam more and more often.

I was greatly encouraged when both Glenn Judson and Bill Landers chose St. Vincent College. Having friends along on this scary new adventure would be a great relief.

As May came, it would seem like a time for enjoying the end of your high school career. Yearbooks, senior prom, graduation and summer vacation all lay before us, yet it was not to be without its problems for me.

My senior prom was memorable only for how much it sucked. Billy Regan and I had been becoming better and better friends over the last few months, largely I thought, due to playing basketball together on our intramural team. Although Regan had played for the Holy Cross freshman team and JV, he quit as a junior and played intramurals. He was always helpful and supportive of me and seemed happy that I made the All-Star team. He was a rich kid whose father was some kind of big shot with Coca-Cola and had bought Billy a hot rod.

It was a green Chevy (1957 maybe?) that was all souped up with a rake and a four-speed transmission on the floor, white racing stripes and "Grasshopper" stenciled on both front fenders. He started showing up at Mueller's and hanging out with our crowd, offering them and me rides to wherever anyone was going.

I thought it would be cool to go to the prom in the "Grasshopper" and finally suggested to Regan that we double date. He wasn't going to the prom, he told me, and my efforts to get him to go were futile.

As it turned out, Billy Regan had been moving in on my girlfriend and prom date, Sheila Lennon, unbeknownst to me. He had been picking her up after school in the "Grasshopper" and driving around with her showing off. Apparently, they had discussed the prom, but I had asked Sheila weeks before and she didn't want to renege. They had, however, made a date to go to the beach together the morning after the prom.

A week before the prom I found all this out and felt sick about it. I had never been dumped before and this was being dumped for a so-called friend in front of all my friends, male and female. I was humiliated and despondent all week. On the night of the prom, I was angry and quiet. I kept hoping Sheila would say it wasn't true, or that she just liked him as a friend, or that she had been infatuated by a guy with a car, but that she had come to her senses—but she didn't.

I was invited to a few post-prom parties but I declined the invitations. I just wanted the night to be over. I kept thinking Sheila felt the same way. She probably wanted to get to bed early so she could have a full day at the fucking beach with Billy Regan and "The Grasshopper."

About a month before graduation on a beautiful Monday afternoon, I was summoned to Brother Richard's office from study hall. I had no idea whatsoever why Brother Richard would want to see me. I would be seeing him in Spanish class the next period and then again during the last period of the day, which I spent in his office ever since Brother Joseph had kicked me out of *his* class.

When I arrived, his door was open so I knocked on the open door and when he looked up, said, "You wanted to see me, Brother?"

"Oooh, I certainly do, Mr. Farrell, I certainly do. Sit down."

Brother Richard had a strange tone in his voice. It wasn't the angry tone I knew so well, yet it wasn't a good tone either.

"I just got off the phone with the police, Mr. Farrell; do you have any idea why?" he said, calmly.

"No, Brother."

"Do you know a girl by the name of McCarthy? A Margaret McCarthy?"

"Uh, oh, yes, Brother. Margaret Ann McCarthy."

"I sense you know something then about why the *police* are calling me!" he said quietly, yet with an ominous tone.

"No, I don't, Brother."

"Well, it seems that she is missing . . ."

There was a pause that seemed long and awkward,

" . . . and you were the last person known to be with her late Saturday night. Care to explain?"

I went on to tell Brother Richard what I knew . . . that I was at a party Saturday night with our usual gang of friends, including Margaret Ann McCarthy.

After the party a group of us were walking home and Margaret Ann asked which train to take to get to the Bronx. Of course, the question of why was she going to the Bronx came up. She explained that her father had been beating her and that she was not going home. She intended to take the subway to some relative's house in the Bronx. I argued with her that a sixteen-year-old is not safe riding the subway at one o'clock in the morning, but Margaret Ann insisted she was not going home. She claimed her father would be drinking and would be abusive to her and her mother.

I urged her to reconsider for over half an hour, but she was adamant. She said she would feel a lot better if I would accompany her, but I didn't want to die or get beaten up or stabbed, so I declined. As we talked, she really seemed shook up and I felt bad for her. I suggested she sleep at my house and go to the Bronx in the morning. My parents would be asleep I told her, so she could sleep on the couch in the basement and I'd get up early and wake her so she could be gone before anyone was up.

She agreed and this is what happened. When she left the house on Sunday morning, that was the last I had seen her or heard from her.

"Did your parents know about this?" asked Brother Richard.

"No, Brother."

"Well, they do *now*," he said, shaking his head as if in disbelief.

"What do I do now, Brother?" I asked meekly. "I was trying to do a good thing."

"Were you or were you not involved with this girl, Farrell? Your story is difficult to believe."

"We are just friends, Brother. There is nothing romantic going on," I said, emphatically.

"You amaze me, Farrell, you absolutely amaze me. If I were you, I'd leave right now and do whatever it takes to get her back home as soon as humanly possible," he said.

"I can go right now?" I asked, since I had three classes left in the day.

"Yes! Go right now!"

I felt a sudden feeling of elation and gratitude. Brother Richard seemed to understand and seemed to be actually trying to help me!

"Did you say my parents know about this?" I asked as I got to my feet to leave.

"Yes, I spoke with your mother. The poor woman knew nothing about any of this, just as you said. She was very embarrassed."

"Well, like I said, Brother, I was trying to do a good thing. I'll go find Margaret Ann and try to get her to go home."

I started out the door when Brother Richard stuck a dagger in my back.

"Take all your belongings with you," I thought I heard him say.

"Excuse me, Brother?" I said, in disbelief.

"That's right, Farrell, take all of your personal belongings with you because, you see, if I'm contacted by any newspapers about this, I'm referring to you as a *former* Holy Cross student," he said as if he had given it a lot of thought and was proud of the idea.

Stunned by what Brother Richard had just said, I got my belongings together and found I couldn't easily carry all my books and materials, so I left some of my stuff in my locker and started home. 'If I get kicked out of school, I won't need any of that shit anyway,' I told myself as I started for the door. I remember thinking as I walked down the hall past classes in progress that for once, I wish I was in class . . .

I raced home, cursing out Holy Cross, Brother Richard and Margaret Ann. When I arrived home, my mother was near delirium.

"What in hell have you done now?" she shrieked. "I have never been so humiliated in my life! What do I tell the police if they come here?"

I went to my room without answering her, quickly changed clothes, wrote down some phone numbers of Margaret Ann's friends, took some money I had stashed in my sock drawer, and knowing it was too early for any of my friends to be home from school yet, decided to head for Mueller's.

Just before I left I told my mother, "Mom, I don't have time to explain all this, I have to find Margaret Ann and get her home."

"What have you done? What are you mixed up in?" she cried.

"I tried to do a good thing, but I don't have time to discuss it. If anyone calls, write down who it is and where they can be reached."

"Where are you going?" she screamed, as I walked past her and out the door.

"To find Margaret Ann and get her to go home," I said with determination.

"What do I tell the police if they show up here?" she cried. "What do I tell the neighbors?"

"Tell the police I'm looking for her and I don't know where she is."

"Why did you *do* this?"

"I gave her a place to wait 'til morning so she wouldn't take a train to the Bronx in the middle of the night! I don't have time to get into this now."

"What do I tell the neighbors about the police?"

"I don't give two shits what you tell the neighbors. You don't even like any of the neighbors," I yelled at her as I went out the door.

"Yeah, well I hope they take you to jail, you son of a bitch," she screamed out the door at me, apparently not worried what the neighbors would think of that.

I went to Mueller's and waited for some of the girls to arrive from school. When they did, I asked for their help and we eventually tracked down Margaret Ann at her friend's house in Bayside where she had gone on Sunday and stayed on Sunday night. When she heard about all that had happened, she seemed pleased about it all, but agreed, nevertheless, to go home. I got on the phone with her and calmly asked her if she would kindly call her parents and let them know she was all right and was coming home and to please do it immediately.

"Why should I?" she answered. "Let them worry."

"So they tell the police and I don't get kicked out of school!" I screamed into the phone.

"Okay, Okay, I'm sorry," she said.

"Do it right now," I demanded.

"Okay! Good-bye! I'll call right now."

Margaret Ann did go home and I didn't get kicked out of school. I did, however, have to face the ranting and raving of my parents. My mother focused on the embarrassment and humiliation she felt in that others (particularly Brother Richard) would think she didn't know what was going on in her own home. My father focused on the possible legal ramifications if something had happened to Margaret Ann. He felt I had jeopardized their home and their future. I was "too stupid to go to college" and "not getting any help from them." I could "go to hell" because I "didn't care about anybody but myself."

I had decided that if I got kicked out of Holy Cross and wasn't able to graduate, I would immediately enlist in the service and get the hell out of town. I considered it again during the days following this inglorious event. I couldn't understand why nobody seemed to think I did a good thing.

Slowly, this whole mess faded into the background and soon the only thing between me and graduation was finals. I had filed my application to the New York State Higher Education Assistance Agency (NYSHEAA) and gotten approval for a loan covering my room, board and tuition at St. Vincent College.

Final exams were the final hurdle, but not one I could easily clear. I had serious reasons to worry. English was no sweat and as it turned out, the Spanish final was very easy after Brother Richard starting every class by calling on me. I had serious trepidations about Math, but Mr. Vincaguerra practically told us what problems would be on the final and I studied them. Even so, I only got a 74 and a 70 for the year.

Religion wasn't a worry for anybody except me. I felt that since I wasn't allowed in the class for the last three months and had caused Brother Joseph to erupt in a psychotic rage, he might take revenge on me if I screwed up. The exam was mostly questions from the end of the chapters which I had been answering each day in Brother Richard's office and I passed easily.

As the exam schedule worked out, my class had four finals on the Wednesday, Thursday and Friday and one, Chemistry, on Tuesday. I had been getting by in Chem. thanks to Ray Frasene sitting on one side of me and Paul Falabella on the other. They would help me understand some things that I had trouble grasping, tell me what to study for exams, let me copy their homework and even help me on an exam if Mr. Schiliro was distracted.

I was going into the final not in terrible shape. I just needed to pass the final and I would graduate. Although I loved Physics, I hated Chemistry. I didn't care for Mr. Schiliro and he didn't care for me. He knew Chemistry, but I thought he was boring and didn't really care about me. He thought I was an asshole and frequently gave me detention. Sometimes he wouldn't even stop class. He would see me doing something goofy during lab or see everybody laughing around me and without even asking about it, he would suddenly walk over to my desk and hand me a detention slip with his name pre-stamped on it.

We had no exams on Monday and didn't even have to go in to school that day and so I figured I would study Monday for the exam. Mr. Schiliro had made it clear that the final would be multiple choice and cover the second half of the year. It was a lot of material to cover, but at least the exam wouldn't require actually doing equations. I thought this was a break. So when the idea of going to Rockaway Beach on Sunday came up and the whole crowd was going, I figured I could afford to go too, as I had all day Monday and Monday night to study.

What I didn't count on was sunstroke. Pat Kelly and I wound up severely sunburned. By the time I got home in early evening, I had the chills and was nauseous. When my parents saw me, they called the doctor who didn't have much to offer by way of relief. I laid on my bed all night, sleeping only a little between shaking with chills and vomiting.

On Monday, I felt awful. My skin felt like it had shrunk and every movement hurt. I kept slathering Noxema skin cream all over my body in hope that it would help. When I wasn't laying down, I felt dizzy and weak. I was exhausted from not sleeping much and drank water and ate toast since my stomach was unsettled. I tried studying for the final in bed, but fell asleep and woke up at dinner time.

I ate chicken noodle soup and saltines for dinner, moved very slowly and painfully and tried to study. Studying for me was difficult even under the best conditions, but studying when tired and feeling horrible was not working at all. I called Pat Kelly to see how he was doing and to see if he was thinking of skipping the final. He felt horrible as well and hadn't studied, but he thought cutting the final would be a bad move. I thought so too. If Mr. Schiliro wanted to get me, cutting the final would be just the excuse he needed. Pat also speculated that perhaps the make-up test would be oral or worse, balancing equations, which would have totally exposed our ignorance. At least with multiple choice, we had a chance of passing. We agreed we had to go and take the test no matter how painful.

And painful it was. Walking was torturous and slow. I felt miserable and hot. Beads of sweat dropped off my face onto my near blank exam paper. For ease of correcting them, they were all multiple choice with a space for the answer on the left hand side of the paper. It was obvious Mr. Schiliro would just put the correct answers alongside an exam paper and mark the incorrect ones. I knew two or three of them for sure. I was desperate and looked to Paul and Ray, sitting on each side of me, for help. They wanted to help me, but Schiliro was being unusually attentive, sitting at his desk, looking out at the class.

Paul purposely dropped his pen on the floor and as he bent over to pick it up, he told me number one was "B." I was grateful, and put 'B' down, but I was still in desperate straights. I actually started wondering if I would feel well enough to enlist in the service and leave town by the time they notified me I wouldn't graduate.

As the exam period neared an end, Mr. Schiliro announced that when you were finished, you could hand your paper in to him and leave. A number of guys immediately went up to the front and handed their papers to Mr. Schiliro. This created the opportunity and I whispered that I was in trouble. Ray suddenly switched exam papers with me. In Chemistry class, we sat at long tables and switching papers was done in an instant. He wrote about ten answers very lightly and very small on my paper and at the next opportunity, switched them back.

"Those are the ones I'm sure of," he whispered without moving his lips, looking straight ahead. "Write them in with your own writing."

"Ok. Thanks!" I whispered softly.

Ray got up and handed in his paper and left.

Paul checked with me before he handed in his paper. "Are you ok?" he whispered, as more and more guys were handing in their papers and making more and more noise.

"Yeah, thanks," I whispered back.

I waited until near the end to hand my paper in. When I did, I tried to find Ray to thank him. I was lucky to catch him outside the front door waiting for a friend.

"Thanks, Ray," I said. An awful chance you took."

"Yeah, well you took an awful chance going to the beach with that white skin of yours."

"And I'm paying for it, big time!"

"You and Kelly should know better. The beach is no place for Irish guys. Do your drinkin' in the shade!"

I thanked him again and went home and went to bed. For the next few days, I laid around in my room, recuperating. I thought a lot about all that had transpired over the last four years. My feelings were complicated. I was happy it was over, yet everyone kept saying that those were the best years of your life. For sure I would miss the guys like Ray and Jay and Paul, who I rarely saw other than at school or at a school function. I had graduated and gotten into the college of my choice, but yet I didn't feel good about it. I knew something was wrong with me, but I couldn't figure out what. Why was I always in trouble? Why did I do so well in Physics but know no Chemistry? Do well in Algebra and Geometry, but suck at Trigonometry and Calculus? Why couldn't I sit still? I blamed a lot of it on the teachers, but deep down, I knew that some guys learned even from Varnak and Vinciguerra and Dolce.

A lot of guys didn't give a shit about learning. They were going to get jobs or go into the service. There was a lot of talk about the exams for police, fire department and post office jobs. I went through Holy Cross in the third highest section the whole way and didn't feel I knew anything useful. I felt a sense of disappointment. While I admired Brother John Houlihan and Brother David and J.J., I felt Trentacoste, Lipp, Vinciguerra, Regis, Quasimodo and Brother Richard and many others had missed out on something. They had a chance to inspire us and help us prepare for the future if there was going to be one, but they did not. I felt sad and somewhat resentful when on June 14, 1964, I received my diploma from Holy Cross High School. There were 23,300 American military personnel in Vietnam.

CHAPTER TWENTY

◆ ◆ ◆ ◆ ◆

"FREEDOM?"

There's something happening here
What it is ain't exactly clear
There's a man with a gun over there
Telling me I got to beware.
I think it's time to stop, children, what's that sound?
Everybody look what's going down . . .
        Buffalo Springfield—"For What It's Worth"

As soon as I was able I started my summer job at Cross Armored Carrier. We had worked out a deal where I would come in around three and could work as long as I wanted. Although they had plenty of coin to be rolled, particularly in the summer, there was no unused machine until someone left or was on vacation. Pat Kelly, being senior to me, got to work regular daylight hours on the only machine not used by a regular full-time employee. Dennis Geoghan and I were allowed to work any hours that were available. There were four full-time regular coin rollers and each was scheduled for a two or three week vacation which meant Dennis and I frequently got to work the eight to five shift, but otherwise we could start at around three and work until eleven if we liked. Compared to Cresthaven, Cross Armored was heaven. The work was much easier and cleaner, the vault was air-conditioned, the commute was quicker and the pay was much better.

When I worked the early shift, I was home for dinner and out for the evening by seven, feeling great. When I worked late, I enjoyed being with Dennis and talking and laughing while we worked; or working alone listening to music. I brought a transistor radio with me and it was an awesome summer for rock music. The Beatles, the Stones, Roy Orbison, the Supremes, the Four Tops, Four Seasons and the Beach Boys were all on the charts at once that summer.

If I was working alone at night, I couldn't wait until everybody left so I could put my radio on, turn it up loud, and roll coins while I sang along to "Ragdoll," "Where Did Our Love Go?" "Baby, I Need Your Lovin," "Pretty Woman," "Hard Day's Night," and my favorite, "It's Over."

One Friday night while I was working alone, I took the "*Daily News*" into the men's room and took a crap. While I was sitting on the throne, I noticed something that piqued my curiosity. I had never noticed a hole in the wall before, but then again I had never taken a shit before while at Cross Armored. Just as I was getting up, I examined this mysterious hole and mystified as to what it was, probed it with my finger. After a careful and curious exam with my eyes and finger, I returned to my work station, with no inkling of what it was.

Even when I heard sirens, which was not that unusual in Queens, I had no idea. The sirens stopped right outside the vault doors. Then more sirens . . . and more sirens . . . I turned my radio down to get a better idea of what was going on and was startled by the only other person in the vault, a guard, suddenly yelling from a room away, "Hey, kid, are you all right?"

"Yeah," I yelled.

"Come here, kid. I need to talk to you," he yelled back.

I got up from behind my machine and started toward the room where the guard worked. When I looked ahead, I saw him with a drawn gun pointed toward me, but down at the floor.

"What's going on?" I asked, sheepishly.

"I don't know," the guard answered. "Did you hit an alarm?"

"No," I said.

"Everything is okay back there then?"

"Yeah."

"Okay, I'll take care of this," he said.

While the guard went to the entrance I proceeded to the office area where there were windows to see what was going on. I was amazed to see the number of police and other security vehicles that were outside the building and to see roadblocks set up on Northern Boulevard and the Cross Island Parkway.

At first I thought it was cool that something big was happening and I might see it go down. Then I heard a helicopter land on what sounded like the roof or rear parking lot of the building and cops dressed in bullet proof vests and helmets and armed with automatic weapons surrounding the place. Then, still clueless, I began to feel worried that I was in the middle of something scary.

The guard yelled at me to return to my work area and stay away from the window. The phone rang and he answered it as I left the room. In a moment, he was yelling for me to come back into the office area where he was stationed. The police were in force outside and wanted to see me. The guard had told them that I was okay and hadn't set off an alarm, but they wanted to see me and be sure that I was speaking freely and without a gun at my head.

Cross Armored had a security system that used two heavy steel doors that couldn't be opened simultaneously. One door had to be closed securely before the other would open. The guard controlled the process from a bullet-proof glass enclosed area that gave him visual and voice communication with anyone outside or in between the doors. The cops outside asked for me to step between the doors where I would be safe from anyone inside. When I did, they asked me if I was okay, if anyone else was in the vault, if I had set off the alarm and if there was anything wrong or unusual going on. I answered yes, no, no, and no.

The cops were satisfied and told me to come out. I went out and they went in. Soon the place was full of cops and private security guys who worked for the alarm company. After a complete search of the facility, they allowed me back in and I returned to work. In between rolling, while sealing a bag of rolled coins and opening a bag of loose ones, I could hear what was going on. The police were leaving and lifting roadblocks, the helicopter took off and the private security guys were looking for the source of the problem. Soon the president of the company arrived and he came back to where I worked to meet me.

I can't recall his name, but he introduced himself and shook my hand. He was a big man, dressed in a suit without a tie. We had never met but I did recall seeing him around a few times, unaware of who he was.

"You didn't accidentally set off an alarm, did you?" he asked.

"No, sir," I replied.

"I was at a cocktail party getting a buzz on when I got the call. Timing couldn't have been worse, know what I mean?"

"Yes, sir."

"You probably did it just to ruin my Friday night buzz time," he said jokingly.

"No, sir," I said, laughing. "I don't know *how* to set off an alarm."

"Are you serious?" he asked.

"Yeah, I'm serious."

"Nobody ever showed you the alarm system?"

"No, sir."

"Well, that is ridiculous, and that's *my* fault," he said, shaking his head in disgust. "I'll fix that on Monday. Of course the way traffic is backed up out there, I might not make it home 'til Monday."

He started to tell me about how bad traffic was backed up due to the roadblocks, when one of the private security guys came in and announced that the alarm had been set off in the men's room. I suddenly felt sick as the president and the security guy left to talk to the guard.

It wasn't long before the president returned. He sat down on a pile of unrolled bags of coins and asked me to stop working for a moment. He folded his arms across his chest and looked me square in the eye.

"The alarm was set off in the men's room," he began, "and the guard says you were in there shortly before all hell broke loose. Is that correct?"

"Yes."

"Did you set off the alarm in the men's room?"

"I might have done it accidentally," I said.

"Explain what you mean, 'accidentally'?"

"I noticed a hole in the wall that I never noticed before and I did put my finger in it but I didn't know it was an alarm," I replied.

"What did you think it was?" he asked.

I felt terribly embarrassed as I explained that I had no idea but had assumed it was an old light switch or bathroom deodorizer system.

"Well, do you frequently put your finger in mysterious holes," he asked, laughingly.

"No," I said. "I'm sorry!"

"Don't worry, kid, I won't tell the thousands of New Yorkers stuck in traffic that it's all your fault!" he laughed. "I need a drink," he proclaimed, as he walked back toward the office area.

I rolled a few bags of nickels, wondering if they'd be my last, before the president returned. He did indeed have a drink in his hand.

"I'd offer you a drink, kid, but you're still on the clock," he said, playfully. "I'm gonna try to find a way back to my cocktail party, but before I do, I want to talk to you about your problem."

"What problem is that?" I asked, worried that I might get fired.

"Your problem with putting your finger in mysterious holes," he answered, smiling.

I was again embarrassed and muttered something like "It's not a problem" or "I don't have a problem."

"I have some advice for you that I want you to remember and I think it will help. Are you listening to me?"

"Yeah," I said, "but it's not a problem . . ."

"This is good advice for anyone," he interrupted.

"Keep your fingers out of holes unless they have hair on them."

We both laughed heartily. He, because he thought he was so witty and funny; me because I was relieved not to be in trouble and because it *was* a little bit funny.

I left work a little early that night, anxious to find my friends and tell them the story. I went first to Mueller's, but when I saw "The Grasshopper" parked outside, I kept walking and started checking the neighborhood bars until I found Dennis and Tommy. I told them what had happened and Dennis loved it. Tommy seemed kind of drunk and sang quietly along with the jukebox the whole time I was talking. At eleven, I asked the bartender if he would put the news on the television, but he refused.

"You wanna know the news, kid? Buy a paper."

The bartender and a few of the patrons laughed. They were watching the Mets on the one television behind the bar. I was still a few weeks shy of my eighteenth birthday and didn't feel I could press my case. I must have shown my disappointment on my face because a patron looked at me and blurted out for all to hear, "I'll tell you what's new, kid . . . nothin'. Same Shit, Different Day."

I turned away from the television, took a few sips of my beer and started singing along with Tommy.

The next day, I asked my dad if he had watched the news the night before.

"Yeah. What the hell was goin' on up there? They never actually explained, but the traffic was a mess."

When I told him the story, he got a big kick out of it. He told that story for years afterward.

The guy at the bar's comments about nothing being new struck me as ironic because that very week, there were two huge news stories. It was reported that two U.S. destroyers were attacked in the Gulf of Tonkin by

North Vietnamese forces. This alleged incident led within days to the Gulf of Tonkin resolution which allowed the president to wage war in southeast Asia without a formal declaration of war by Congress.

The other incident was the discovery of the bodies of three civil rights workers in Mississippi. Two of three were from New York City, and all three had been hunted down and murdered by the Ku Klux Klan for promoting registration to vote. Both of these events two weeks before I turned eighteen would echo throughout the rest of my life . . . not exactly "Same Shit, Different Day . . ."

A few weeks before the start of college, I received a letter from St. Vincent College (SVC), reviewing things to bring and other important matters. It was then that I started taking inventory of what I needed and would be taking with me. I quickly discovered that I had no trunk or luggage to speak of. The Farrells very rarely went anywhere and trunks or luggage weren't a necessity. I mentioned that I needed such items at dinner one night and my mom offered me a solution. She went to a cupboard in our dining room and produced a big bag full of S & H Green Stamps. I spent the next few nights watching the Mets on TV while I glued Green Stamps into the books they needed to be in for redemption.

A few nights later we made a trip to the S & H Redemption Center and got a trunk and a few suitcases for me to take to college. I was excited and began packing at once. A few weeks later, I was unpacking on the third floor of Aurelius Hall in Latrobe, Pa. It was hard saying good-bye to the guys the night before, but the impact was lessened since Billy and Glenn were going with me. I kept thinking about those walks to Mueller's after school. It was hard to accept that they were over forever. In a similar way, I missed drinking at "the Wall." Drinking in bars had its definite advantages, but in many ways, it wasn't as much fun. There were other people around and involved, including the bartender, in whatever we were talking about, there were women we were eying and trying to impress, television and juke box noise and telephone calls.

Ironically, we had just become legal consumers of alcohol that summer and we found ourselves illegal again in Pennsylvania where the drinking age was twenty-one! And again, in those early days at SVC, we would drink illegally in our dorm rooms or in cars or in some secluded spot outside and talk and solve the world's problems as we did at "the Wall."

We were surprised to learn in our first few days at SVC about the Orientation Program. The program lasted six weeks and during that time, we were told that we had "Rules" to obey. Among those rules were that we had to wear coats and ties everywhere and address all upperclassmen as 'sir.' We also had to wear lapel and back signs (like a small sandwich board) with our name, major and hometown printed on them and little green beanies they called 'Dinks,' with a gold 1968 on the front. Each night after dinner, we had to stand at attention outside our rooms for inspection by members of the Orientation Committee. Social activities for this six-week period were all planned and mandatory.

Here I am dressed for room inspection.

Added to this was a certain degree of hazing. We were expected to carry books for upperclassmen and sit where we were told to sit and allow them in front of us in any sort of line. We disposed of their dirty dishes in the cafeteria and on Saturday mornings reported to the upperclassmen dorms for cleaning and shoe polishing and laundry duty. We had to learn the school cheers and songs and recite them on command.

The social activities were dances and mixers with a number of nearby women's schools, a Pittsburgh Pirates baseball game, a play at the Pittsburgh Playhouse and other assorted cultural events. In each case, we wore dinks and signs and coats and ties, and, if off-campus, rode together in buses.

Some members of the Orientation Committee would be on each bus and lead us in various songs and cheers as we rode. Often they would pick a "frosh" to stand up and recite various things we were supposed to know from the student handbook or sing our high school fight song. They would often ridicule our home towns or states, our high school names, or how we were dressed. I got ridiculed for wearing white socks and discovered that it wasn't viewed as cool everywhere or at least not any longer. Some guys couldn't tie a knot in their tie very well and an Orientation Committee member named

Ken Zanca identified them and held a seminar on tying a tie. Many of the victims, although a little embarrassed, were grateful for the help.

"We're Bearcats," he would scream. "Bearcats wanna look sharp. We're cosmopolitan. We're aware. We don't look like we have shit on our shoes and just fell off the turnip truck. Do you have shit on you shoes, Gorney?" he shouted at freshman Mike Gorney.

"No, sir!" answered Gorney.

"Are you horny, Gorney?" he shouted.

"Yes, sir!" answered Gorney.

"That's good, Gorney, because we're going to a mixer! There will be girls at the mixer, Gorney! Do they have girls where you come from, Gorney?"

"Yes, sir."

"I can't hear you, Gorney."

"Yes, sir!"

"Do you like girls, Gorney?"

"Yes, sir!"

"That's good, Gorney. Especially for your roommate. Do you know how to dance, Gorney?"

"Yes, sir!"

"Good, because if I don't see you dancing, I'll pick someone out for you to dance with! That goes for all of you. If I see you standing around not in the company of a young lady, I'll pick one for you."

These threats made us all nervous, but the pressure to socialize was good for us and we mixed rather well. For the rest of our lives, Mike Gorney would always be 'Horny Gorney' to us. All this regimentation and hazing caught many of us off balance and made many of us angry.

"This is bullshit," said Glenn one night in the first week of Rules. I thought we were men now. I wouldn't have come here if we're going to be treated like children."

Of all my friends, the one most likely to punch out an upperclassman, an Orientation Committee member, or anyone else harassing him, would be Billy Landers, yet Billy was surprisingly philosophical about Rules.

"I think it's good for us," he exclaimed. "We need to be more humble."

"Well, that settles it," answered Glenn. "You're nuts!"

"Why?" asked Billy. "You don't think you have a big ego?"

"I don't think my ego is what this is about," replied Glenn from the top bunk, which I graciously and without argument, agreed to.

Billy lived a few doors down the hall with a guy named Roy Lanz.

Roy thinks we think we're hot shit," said Billy.

"And?" asked Glenn.

"And what?"

"And why do I care what Roy thinks?"

"There you go! That's proof positive. Maybe whoever thought this program up had that in mind."

"What do you think, Joe?" Glenn asked. "You're being awful quiet."

"I think you have a big ego," I chuckled. "That's why you had to have the upper bunk!"

"Shit! If you're gonna bitch about me having the upper bunk all year, I'll switch with you now."

"All right!" I said, getting up to jump up into the top bunk.

"Fuck you," laughed Glenn. "I'm not sleeping down there."

"I'm serious," repeated Billy. "Maybe this program is designed to start us all equal and make us get to know one another and break down cliques. I already know everybody on our floor and a whole lot of others in my classes."

"And you wouldn't know those guys if you hadn't crawled on the floor barking like a dog like they made us do last night?" asked Glenn.

"Maybe not," replied Billy.

"Oh, bullshit," said Glenn.

"I'm serious," countered Billy. "It served as a conversation starter with a couple of guys. Look, I'm not saying it's something I agree with, but if you think about it—and have an open mind—it probably has a worthwhile purpose.

Billy saw a big smile on my face and asked, "Why are you smiling? Do you think I'm crazy?"

"No," I said. "I just think this is fun."

"What part?"

"The part about us living together and experiencing and learning new things. I think it's gonna be fun."

"Yeah, me too," answered Billy. "How about you, Glenn? Aren't you looking forward to new experiences together?"

"Right now I'm looking forward a good night's sleep, so if you two knuckleheads don't mind . . ."

Glenn rolled over on his side toward the wall, indicating he was done with the conversation.

"Okay," said Billy. "Joe and I will go to my room and belittle Roy for a while. C'mon, Joe."

About a week into orientation, all the freshmen were to assemble in the auditorium of John F. Kennedy Hall to meet with the Dean of studies, Father Ronald Gorka. I expected this to be one of those "look at the guys next to you because one of you won't make it" type of talks. I figured he would go over the grading system and requirements for graduation and attendance requirements and tell us we're not children anymore.

Father Ronald didn't do any of that. He wanted to know what was on our minds. He answered questions about grades and Quality Point Averages and changing majors when asked, but didn't seem to think it was very important. He actually told us not to worry so much about grades.

"What do you care about? Why are you here? What do you value?" he kept asking.

Realizing that these must be trick questions, I remained mute, but many others offered their answers. Most of the answers were superficial and trite and politely accepted as valid reasons by Father Ronald, but he continued to probe deeper.

"I'm here to get an education," offered one student.

"What is an education?" asked Father Ronald nicely.

"It's knowledge," replied the student.

"Knowledge of what?" asked Father Ronald.

When the student drew a blank, Father Ronald asked "What makes knowledge so important? So valuable?"

"If you know a lot, you'll have a better life," offered someone.

"Why?" asked Father Ronald.

"You'll have more choices," muttered one of the group.

"Choices? Did I hear choices?"

"Yes, Father."

"Choices of what?" he asked the group as if we were on the brink of the correct answer.

"Jobs," came from someone in the front row.

"A better choice of jobs. More economic freedom. Are these some of the benefits of knowledge?" asked Father Ronald.

When the group seemed to agree with that statement, Father Ronald went further.

"Perhaps freedom is something you value?"

Everyone seemed to agree on "freedom" being valuable. Taking the premise that "freedom" was something we cared about, Father Ronald proceeded to make his point.

"Knowledge *is* freedom," he said. "There are five forces acting on you at all times—determining the length, quality, and nature of your life. The more you know about these forces and how they work and affect you and others, the freer you are. The more you know of these forces, the less you are at their mercy! The less you know, the more they determine your destiny."

Father Ronald went on to name the five forces and give examples of how they were affecting us all as we sat there. He talked about the Political, Economic, Social, Psychological and Physical forces that had brought us together that very night. He used certain guys' haircuts and style of clothing as examples of social and economic influences on our lives.

"I'm not talking about some high-minded intellectual abstracts," he said. "I'm talking about real concrete things that touch your lives. Poverty and hunger are real. Racism is real. Cancer is real. War is real. Communism is real. The more you learn about the forces that control your life, the more *freedom* you will have in your life.

So I urge you to take advantage of this opportunity to learn as much as you can. We view ourselves as a community of scholars in search of the truth. While you are getting a degree so you can get a good job (which was the most common answer to his questions), open yourself up to new ideas and values. Examine what you believe and what you've been taught. Learn *how* to learn so that you can continue to learn long after you've left here. Take advantage of the library and the faculty. Take courses that aren't required. Audit courses for free. Take advantage of the speakers and artists that come to our campus. This is a tremendous opportunity for each of you. Don't leave here an educated yet ignorant man."

On our way back to our dorm after the meeting, Billy asked what I thought of Father Ronald's talk.

"I thought it was terrific," I said. "It made a lot of sense to me. What'd you think?"

"I liked it, too. It sounds kind of silly to say, but these really might be the most important years of our life."

"No doubt," I replied.

"I don't mean just getting a degree. You can have a degree and still be an asshole," Billy added.

"I know," I laughed.

"I'm serious," continued Billy. "Who do you know who has a degree and is an asshole?"

"Most of my teachers at Holy Cross!" I answered, emphatically.

"Good point," laughed Billy.

We talked for quite a while about Father Ronald's message and we both agreed that we would try to learn as much as we could about the forces controlling and shaping our lives. Father Ronald's little talk had made as much sense to me as anything I had ever heard. I just hoped I could do the work. I felt lucky to have Billy to confide in. Someone I could honestly tell how I felt and would honestly respond. Billy was very good at being honest and in my case, he could see where I was, but he also knew where I'd been and that would turn out to be very important to me. I felt like, in the first week, St. Vincent College had already made an impact on my life.

It didn't take long for Billy to be proven correct about "Rules." After the first three weeks, the frosh knew each other pretty well and had learned a lot about SVC, its history and traditions, cultural opportunities in the Pittsburgh area and had met young women at area women's colleges. We also knew many upperclassmen due to wearing signs with our vital information which made it easy for upperclassmen to connect with you because of your major or hometown.

We quickly found out that guys from the New York area had their own club (the Met Club) that worked together on transportation issues and held parties in New York over vacations. More importantly, we had slowly tired of the hazing and room inspection and regimentation and slowly started rebelling. It began to dawn on us that there was nothing behind the "Rules." There were no consequences for non-compliance except the disapproval of the Orientation Committee, which increasingly meant nothing to us. Floor by floor we began to rebel and then fight back.

The week before the Freshman Recognition Dance, we abducted a few members of the Orientation Committee and threw them in Bearcat Lake and in a well-coordinated raid of an upperclassmen dorm in the wee hours of the morning, tied their doorknobs together with rope, thus locking them in their rooms for a time until someone passed by and untied the rope.

The room inspections stopped in the last week because Orientation Committee members felt unsafe in the freshman dorm. This was a triumph for the Orientation committee, for in fact, it was their goal to bond us as a class.

Thanksgiving came quickly, yet it seemed a lot had happened. Glenn, Billy and I took the Met Club bus to Manhattan and Dennis Geoghan met us there to take us home to Flushing. I felt excited to see all the old crowd again. It had only been three months since we left, yet it was the longest I had ever been away from home. I felt really different. I felt I had changed and grown up a lot in a short period of time and wondered if anyone would notice. No one did.

On the long ride back to Latrobe that Sunday night, I felt disappointed or let down in a vague way that I didn't understand. Christmas break was longer and after that break, I had the same sad feeling but a better understanding of why. The old gang had also changed and things were very different. Eddie was hanging around with friends and teammates from St. Francis College where he was on an excellent water polo team. Jeff was involved with new friends at St. John's and Pat spent a lot of time with his girlfriend Eileen Fenchak who was a junior in high school. Tommy Taraci was going to CCNY in Manhattan. The old crowd wasn't spending time together like they used to. I wanted things to be like they were before, but guys had girlfriends to be with, and water polo matches and fraternity parties and jobs. Being home was a big deal to me, but not so much for most of the old gang.

The part about "learning as much as I could" was also sputtering. I had meant it and within days of Father Ronald's talk had subscribed to Newsweek. I didn't have much money to spare, but I felt like this was a way to keep up on world affairs and learn about those forces acting on me. I promised myself I would read it cover to cover every week and I did.

The difficulties were coming in the classroom. Call it ADHD or poor powers of concentration or lack of discipline, but I could not sit still and study for very long. That, plus my academic deficiencies from high school and the normal adjustment to a college environment of learning were causing me a great deal of anxiety.

My biggest problem was math. It was required by the Psych. Department and I found myself behind almost immediately. Mr. Dudzinski was the professor and he went very quickly through the first few chapters because in his opinion, we should have known it all from high school. I paid dearly for my cheating and copying homework. I spent hours staring at my math book, trying to understand functions, limits and asymptotes and cursing Brother Charles Varnak and Mr. Vinceguerra.

After the final, I prayed for Mr. Dudzinski to give me a break. I knew I had a high D average, but hoped he would realize I was a freshman and adjusting to college and take pity and give me a C. Mr. Dudzinski, however, was a mathematician and to him it was all in the numbers. My average for the exams was under 70. I got a D.

My four-credit physics course was going okay after a rocky start. Mr. Gainer was a great teacher who invested a lot in his teaching. I liked physics a lot and Brother John Houlihan's teachings gave me confidence. The difficulty was physics Lab. We didn't have Mr. Gainer for Lab. We had Father Roland. Roland was a pious, humorless Benedictine monk who lived in another world. In our very first lab period, I was partnered with Bob Flynn, another freshman, and it took us over six hours to measure a block of wood. We actually thought we were done in an hour and a half, but when we reported to Father Roland the "mass" of our piece of wood for him to verify, he asked how we knew that we had correctly measured.

"How do you know your measurements are correct?" he asked.

"We were very careful," I answered. "We measured everything three times as instructed."

"Can you prove that your measurements were correct?"

"Well, Father, you are welcome to check it out yourself if you think we're lying," I answered with a laugh.

"Science isn't funny, mister," Father Roland said. "You two think about it for a while and let me know how you prove your measurements."

Bob and I went back to our work station feeling a bit stupid as we sat there stymied by the problem we were facing. Bob started to mimic Father Roland under his breath and we started laughing.

"Science isn't funny, mister," Bob said softly as we stared at each other trying to figure out what our next step should be. Father Roland saw us laughing and came over to us and asked if we had discovered how to prove our measurements.

"Uh, no we haven't, Father," I answered.

"What do you find so funny?" he asked, showing annoyance.

"Nothing, Father," I answered. "Certainly not the science."

My remark struck Bob as extremely funny and set him off laughing. Father Roland walked away silently.

"Now you've done it," said Bob. "You're ruined my whole career in science. However unfunny science was, you've just make it even more unfunny."

"I always thought science was funny," I countered. "Don't you think about science sometimes and just break up or is that just me?"

After a while we started looking at other guys at other work stations who seemed to be making progress and some were finished and leaving. I saw the guys at the closest work station to us getting water from a sink and asked them how we were supposed to prove our measurements. They just looked at me didn't respond. I finally wandered over to Glenn Judson and quietly asked him, as they seemed to be weighing water at a station with a scale and weights.

"It's in the lab manual," he whispered.

"But we don't have lab manuals," I reminded him.

"My partner does," was his answer.

I went back to Bob and told him it was in the lab manual.

"That's fucking great," said Bob. "Now all's we need is a lab manual."

Neither Bob nor I had one since the bookstore was out of them and had ordered more but they hadn't come in yet.

"We need to tell Father Roland," said Bob, "so that he'll know why we are stuck."

"Yeah," I agreed. "We'll teach him what is funny."

We argued about who was going to tell Father Roland for a while but realizing it was getting late, I volunteered to do it.

I went over to Father Roland in a corner of the lab where he was checking some other team's work and told him we didn't have lab manuals and that's why we were stuck.

"Why don't you have manuals?" he asked.

"They're out of them in the bookstore," I answered. "Mr. Gainer knows about it. They ordered more but they haven't come in yet. Perhaps we could borrow someone's lab manual?"

"Yes, perhaps! Perhaps you should come to class prepared. Perhaps you should have borrowed someone's manual before you got here and been prepared for class. Perhaps you'll wait now until I'm finished with these guys and I'll lend you mine."

A few minutes later, Father Roland came over to us with a lab manual which he handed to me, again expressed the opinion that this isn't funny and that we should always come to class prepared.

Now there were only four other guys left in the lab and as Father Roland went to check the work of two of them, Bob and I feverishly looked through the manual to find our next step. We discovered that the next step was to fill a beaker with water, drop the block of wood in the water and catch the water that spills out. It seems that the volume of wood displaces an equal volume of water. Finally we discover that if we weigh the water, we will know the volume of water displaced and thus, the volume of the block of wood! Then if the measurements check out we know we've measured it correctly.

Unfortunately, just before we were about to weigh the water, the last of the other students left and we were alone with Father Roland. He came over to check our progress.

"Have you two made any miraculous discoveries?" he asked sarcastically.

"Yes, Father," I answered, "we are just about to weigh the water that the block of wood displaced and prove our measurements. Just in time, I might add, to make dinner." I looked at my watch to remind Father Roland that the dining hall was soon to close for dinner as it was well past six o'clock.

Just then Bob Flynn blew away any chance of making dinner or of avoiding an F in this lab. I put the beaker of water on one side of the scale and in full view of Father Roland, Bob picked a weight out of the set of weights provided by the lab and put it on the other side of the scale. *Unfortunately, he did it with his bare hand!*

"*What are you doing, you fool?*" Father Roland yelled.

Bob looked a little confused but explained that he was weighing the water.

"Now I have to go to Washington and recalibrate the weights," Father Roland exclaimed. "What do you think those tweezers are for?"

"I *was* wondering what they were for," laughed Bob.

Father Roland carried on for a bit about how oil from our hands would somehow corrupt the weight and thus the need to recalibrate it at the Bureau of Weights and Measures in Washington, DC. He was so upset that he didn't check our results. He just asked us to leave.

We immediately headed for the dining hall, laughing our asses off all the way. Bob Flynn is one of the funniest guys I ever met and his mocking imitation of Father Roland throwing what he called "a shit fit" was hysterical.

I should have thrown the weight right through the window and screamed, 'There! I saved you a trip to Washington!' If he's gonna get hysterical about it, we should get hysterical too. We should have started breaking beakers and text tubes. And what's this about the oil on my hands corrupting the weight? How does he know I'm half Italian? Wait till my mom hears this. She'll teach him what's not funny. If he thinks science isn't funny, wait until he gets a load of my mom. She'll leave oil from her hands on his neck!"

We got an 'F' for the lab and couldn't stop laughing. Although I liked physics and was well prepared, the rocky start with Father Roland hurt my overall grade and I got a C.

In English Composition, I also salvaged a rocky start. In our first major assignment, we were to pick a topic from a list provided and write a convincing essay promoting a particular point of view. I chose Communism. I cleverly titled my paper, "Better Dead Than Red" and argued that being under Communist rule was worse than death. There was no freedom under Communist rule and life without freedom would be torture to the human spirit and not worth the effort. I got a D from Mr. Scofield. He made a few comments about sentence structure and changing tenses and active and passive voice, but also commented that my argument was one of the dumbest he had read in quite some time. 'Freedom?' he wrote, 'What is freedom? Who is free?' Mr. Scofield was a good man and a good teacher. He pushed me to improve and encourage me to apply myself. He also gave me a C.

World History and Theology were classes that were true "college" experiences. Chuck Manoli was the World History professor and the textbook was "The Rise of the West," a huge 600+ page award-winning book. Manoli, however, never talked about World History in class unless there were questions and never brought the book to class. Most of the discussion was about current world events or recently published books.

The upperclassmen dominated the discussion and many cut class regularly. After a few weeks I quit lugging the book around but wondered just what the hell was going on. Finally, Jude Dippold, another freshman, asked Manoli about what was expected and why we needed the book.

Manoli very calmly explained that the exams would be on the content of the book. He doesn't bring it to class because he's already read it. Class time is to learn from each other by sharing thoughts and observations and questions about history. 'Wow,' I thought. 'That's pretty cool. Now if only

I had some observations, thoughts or questions about history.' All I knew were dates and treaties. When exam time came, I read the book and felt I did pretty well on the exam. I got a 'C' for the semester.

In Theology, the professor was Mr. Ryer. I thought it was strange to be at a Catholic college and have a layman teach Theology. I thought Ryer was even stranger. He came to class with a rock. There was no text book. He put the rock on his desk and asked the same question every day. He told us it was the only question of the course and would be the only question on the only exam at the end of the semester. The question was, "How do you differ from the rock?"

The class was all freshmen and as far as I could tell, we all thought this was ridiculous. At least at first we did. Slowly we realized that Ryer was trying to make us think about things we never thought about and to make us think in new ways. Each time a student would offer an answer that appeared obvious like, "I can think" or "I can feel" or "I can move," Mr. Ryer would counter with "And how do you know the rock can't?"

I struggled with this new exercise, but figured it was better than learning about vestments and Encyclicals. At exam time, I answered the question as best I could and was grateful I didn't have to study for it. I got a 'C.'

I was thrilled with my choice of major as I loved Psychology. My professor for General Psych. was Father Bernard Pagano. Father Pagano was a big, tough maverick priest who was not a Benedictine monk, which is who ran St. Vincent, but for some reason, was teaching there. Father Pagano was interesting and friendly and ironically included discussion of the reliability of eye witness testimony and of the reliability of lie detectors, both of which he was skeptical about. I say ironically because a few years later, Father Pagano was arrested in Delaware and accused of being the "Gentleman Bandit."

The "Gentleman Bandit" was accused of committing nine robberies in Delaware and Pennsylvania in which a polite, middle-aged man pulled a gun on store clerks and demanded money. He used a chrome-plated pistol, was dressed well, wore a fedora and treated his victims with elaborate courtesy. Father Pagano was picked out of lineups seven times by victims and failed a lie detector test. At the time, he was working at St. Mary's Refuge of Sinners Church in Cambridge, Maryland.

During his trial in 1979, a string of witnesses testified he was the one who robbed them when in a dramatic turn of events, a man from Philadelphia came forward and confessed to the crimes. Prosecutors dropped the charges and the Philadelphia man went to jail. The story was made into a movie ("The Gentleman Bandit") in 1980 with Ralph Waite playing Father Pagano.

Father Pagano gave me a 'B' in General Psych. which saved me from being on Academic Probation.

My grades arrived while I was home on semester break. Although Father Ronald had told us not to worry so much about grades, I had just managed a 2.0 GPA and avoided probation. All of my courses except General Psych. were two semester courses so I faced pretty much the same hurdles in second semester except for a different Psych course and professor. Eighteen credits, probably a little more difficult (particularly the math) and an unknown Psych. professor, was something that gave me considerable anxiety. I did get an unexpected break however, when George Dixon replaced Bob Bush as our student prefect on our floor. George was an excellent student and great guy who took an interest in my fate, made a quick diagnosis of my problem, and helped me at a crucial time in my life.

"Maybe part of the problem is that every time I go by your room, there's something going on in there," George said. "You can't concentrate with a lot of noise and with people going and coming constantly. If you want help, I'll help you."

I agreed to try what George prescribed. Each night after dinner, George would tell me to prioritize my assignments, lock my door and begin. He would keep people away from me for a couple of hours and then I could take a break. If I needed help with something, he would help.

"The power of concentration is like a muscle," he would say. "The more you use it, the stronger it becomes. In your case, it's extremely underdeveloped."

Night after night, I would spend hours alone in my room studying or at least trying to. Occasionally, I would hear George telling someone heading for my room to leave me alone. After a few hours, George would tell me it was time for a break and ask how I was doing. George was an English major yet he could do the math and the Physics if I was stuck. He even had ideas on how we differed from Ryer's rock. Slowly, my ability to sit still improved. It was still bad, but better than it was, just like George had said. I got better at concentrating and better organized. I started having some success in English, Physics and Psychology and that helped my confidence and reinforced my work habits.

The only television I watched that year was football. The only actual television set was in the student lounge and the only time I was in there was for football games. I continued to read my Newsweek cover to cover and was becoming more and more familiar with a place that just a short time ago I had never heard of . . . Vietnam.

In February, the U.S. had announced a bombing campaign against North Vietnam. It was called Operation Rolling Thunder and its purpose was to destroy the will of the North Vietnamese to fight. In March, U.S. Marines were sent to DaNang to protect a U.S. airfield and a group called the Students for a Democratic Society held a teach-in against the Vietnam war at the University of Michigan.

We talked about these events in Manoli's class. He seemed very skeptical about the bombing being successful. He said history showed that bombing might be effective in cutting industrial output or supply lines in a conventional war and that the Vietnamese people had been fighting a long time for their independence against the Japanese and the French and wouldn't be easily demoralized.

I thought heavy daily bombing of an area about the size of New Jersey would bring an end to resistance in a matter of weeks. Also during this time, Malcolm X was assassinated in New York and there was mystery and confusion about who was responsible and a series of marches from Selma to Montgomery, Alabama, organized to publicize voting rights took place. The first one ended after a brief march with demonstrators being attacked and badly beaten by state police and local law enforcement officers. This became known as Bloody Sunday and pictures of this bloody beating of peaceful marchers were everywhere.

We talked about these events as well and the irony of these events wasn't lost on us. We were waging a war on the other side of the globe to bring democracy to South Vietnam, yet our own law enforcement officers were pummeling and killing American citizens for peacefully marching to support the right to vote.

As we packed to go home for the summer, I was anxious to see what my grades would be, and anxious to see what kind for job I could get for the summer.

There were over sixty-five thousand American military troops in Vietnam . . .

Chapter Twenty-One

◆ ◆ ◆ ◆ ◆

"Please, Sorry, Thanks"

Well, now the years have gone and I've grown
From that seed you've sown
But I didn't think there'd be so many steps
I'd have to learn on my own.
                    Bruce Springsteen—"Walk Like a Man"

When I arrived home that summer in 1965, I had three things on my mind: my grades, which I expected to show improvement, a job for the summer, and getting my driver's license. The driver's license issue was complicated. I had turned eighteen (the New York age requirement) just two weeks before leaving for St. Vincent and hadn't had time to practice and take the exam. To complicate the issue further was the fact that I could not use the family car. Our car was owned by my father's company Oscher & Reisss Fuel Oil and he was the only one authorized to drive it and the only one insured.

This was a giant issue to me. I bitched and bitched about it on a regular basis. I was in college now and felt I could no longer take out girls on the bus. While I was home on Spring break, I had taken the written test and gotten my Learner's Permit, but now I wanted my license ASAP. All of my friends were driving now and it was embarrassing not to have a license. I even made the argument that I might need a license to get a job.

As soon as I arrived home I started in on my father showing him the documents that explain that when practicing with a licensed driver, the student driver is covered by the insurance of the licensed driver. My mother was listening to the conversation and chimed in.

"Did you tell him the good news, Joe?" she prompted Dad.

"What?" I asked. "What good news?"

"I have something I want to talk to you about as soon as you have a minute," Dad said.

I immediately thought it was about a car. Either we were getting a car or I was getting a car or something to help this situation.

"I've got time right now," I said emphatically. "Tell me the good news."

"I got you a job," he said, gesturing for me to sit down.

"A job? I thought you were gonna say a car."

"A car! What are you, nuts?" he asked, laughing.

"No, I'm not nuts! I can't live without a car to drive."

"Oh, I think you can," he said. "In fact, I'll bet you can!"

"What's the job?" I asked in disgust.

"Working with me," he said proudly.

"With you?"

"Yeah, me or sometimes Vinny."

"What am I gonna do? I don't know anything about oil burners and who's Vinny?"

"Vinny is the company mechanic. He keeps all the trucks and cars running. When he needs help, you'll work with him . . . otherwise, you'll work with me. We'll show you what to do."

There was a long, awkward silence. I was thinking, 'Oh, shit, this is gonna suck big time' but I had no other options and Dad seemed so proud of getting me this job. Things were slow at Cross Armored and they weren't taking on any summer help.

"You can start on Monday and it pays $70 a week. You can ride with me so you won't have any transportation costs or problems," he said, breaking the silence.

"Let me get this straight," I answered. "I work in boiler rooms and under trucks and I have no car to drive all summer."

"If you can get something better, do it," Dad answered. "I was trying to help you out. I thought you'd be pleased."

"Can I at least do some driving so I can get my license?" I asked, plaintively. "I'm gonna be nineteen years old and I don't have a driver's license? You don't seem to realize how ridiculous that is."

"I don't see why it's such a big deal when you don't have a car to drive anyway and you don't seem to realize how expensive cars are to maintain and insure," Dad said.

"I'm the only one I know who doesn't have a license," I yelled, and then after a moment added more softly, rolling my eyes, "except for Mom and Aunt Marion and Nana. Maureen said I could use her car sometimes."

"Oh yeah well, what about insurance?" Dad asked.

"She says her insurance covers any driver who uses her car," I answered smartly.

"That's property damage, but not personal injury, I bet. If you hurt someone in an accident, they'll sue you for everything you're worth."

"If I was worth anything, I'd have my own car and insurance," I yelled. "Let 'em sue me!"

"Okay, okay," Dad finally relented. "I'll help you get your license. Do you want the job?"

"I guess so," I answered, half-heartedly, buoyed somewhat by the idea of driving.

I started that Monday and my grades came that week also. I had indeed improved. In psych. I got my first 'A,' rose to a 'B' in physics and in literature, but still got a 'D' in math.

My instincts about the job proved to be correct. It sucked! Dad woke me up every morning, always happy and raring to go. The time varied between six thirty and seven forty-five. The variance had to do with the fact that Dad only did "emergency" calls. On most mornings, he slept until the office called him with an emergency. If there weren't any, he would get a call about seven forty-five and be on the road by eight fifteen. The phone would ring and a short time later, he would be in my room, in his green uniform with "Joe" scripted on the pocket and "Oscher and Riess Fuel Oil DI-6-6000" on the back. He would say things like "Let's go, Schmoe" or "Up and at 'em" while I stared silently at him like he was nuts.

I would slowly, painfully, get dressed in jeans, work boots and a tee shirt, comb my hair and go down to the kitchen where he was hurriedly downing a cup of coffee. I usually had a glass of orange juice and went to the car where I went back to sleep. All the way to our first stop, I slept. Often it was Brooklyn. Even by the end of summer, I didn't know my way to the office since I was always sleeping when we went there from home.

Up to this point in my life I had little knowledge of what Dad's work day was like. All I knew was that he worked on oil burners and came home filthy dirty and tired. What was there to know?

One of the first things I learned was that he got all of the "emergency" calls. In his line of work, an emergency means some company has a problem that is costing them money. Big money. In the first week, my understanding of emergency and of oil burners changed drastically.

The companies involved were huge companies, mass producing products for huge markets and could not tolerate 'down' time. There were a number of bakeries like California Pie which baked thousands of pies for restaurants and diners all over the New York metropolitan area and like Peter Pan, a chain of bakeries all over New York. If their ovens didn't work properly, they had no pies and baked goods to sell and were losing money. Losses that couldn't be made up. They burned oil to heat their huge ovens.

Kentile had ovens too, but instead of cakes or pies, they baked floor tile. The nation's biggest floor tile manufacturer with a huge plant in Brooklyn burned oil to generate steam to heat ovens. Kirsch Beverages in the Williamsburg section of Brooklyn, a huge bottler of soda including the first sugar-free soft drink ("No Cal") used oil for steam as did French's Mustard.

These plants and many others were Oscher & Reisss' big customers. They burned enormous quantities of oil and down time was expensive. Most of these companies had full-time mechanical crews and even engineers to keep them running, but yet there were problems only Dad seemed to understand.

When we would arrive at one of these places, people always seemed to be anxiously awaiting our arrival. They seemed happy and relieved to see Dad and began anxiously telling him what was wrong. It occurred to me that in some ways it was like Dad was a doctor and the oven or steam generator was the patient and the plants' managers were the concerned family!

They were happy to see Dad arrive, nervously told him the symptoms while walking to the location of the patient. Dad would then start asking questions as he began his examination with his flashlight. When did it quit working? Was there an attempt to restart? Was there ignition? What color was the fire? How long after ignition did the problem become noticeable? What was the temperature when it shut down? What was the oil pressure when running? What else is affected?

After hearing all the symptoms, Dad would usually remove the covers to some control boxes and start testing the controls with his meter. Like a doctor with a stethoscope, he would carefully and quietly take readings at various places while the management people stood quietly and anxiously nearby waiting for a diagnosis.

Most of the time, he had one within an hour.

"You got a faulty relay," he would say, or "The safety didn't reset" or "The ignition switch is shot" or "You need a new oil pump." Whatever it was that he announced, there was usually great relief and always one question, "How long 'til we're back?"

Realizing there was a lot riding on his answer, he usually hesitated before giving an estimate. He sometimes checked the car to see if he had the needed parts and when he didn't, where he could get them quickly. In some cases, the customer would send an employee for them so Dad could start working immediately on removing the old ones.

Sometimes another service man from Oscher and Riess would be dispatched to pick up and deliver the parts. In either case, Dad would call the suppliers (usually Honeywell or Johnson) and carefully order the needed parts. He didn't trust anyone else to do it correctly. He knew the parts people and would often have instructions for them as to exactly what he wanted.

Once he gave his estimate as to when service would be restored, the word spread quickly and the mood changed from tense to jovial. Nobody seemed to have any doubts that it would be fixed when he said it would be.

The next part is when the job would really suck. We would go to the car and get the tools we would need. He would point them out and I would carry them to where we would be working. It was always someplace intensely hot and sometimes extremely noisy, usually both. Dad would tell me what to do and I'd do it.

It wasn't that the actual work was hard (I had worked harder at Cresthaven), but the conditions were horrible and scary. It seemed we were always either squatting or working over our heads, either near steam lines or an oven, dimly lit and always so noisy you couldn't hear yourself think. It was so hot that when Dad would send me to the car for a tool or a part (he would have to yell in my ear what he wanted), it felt like air conditioning to step out into the 90° New York heat and humidity.

I was afraid of the jungle of pipes and wires that surrounded us. There were often flashes of fire when a steam generator or boiler would ignite and sometimes arcing of an electrical control when turning on.

Sometimes we'd be working on the installation of a boiler and there would be welding going on nearby. Welding scared the hell out of me. The welders were all protected with asbestos suits and face masks, but I was just walking past or working nearby and worried about an accident as sparks were flying and intense heat being applied to steel.

Dad would often see the fear on my face and laugh. Afterward, I would tell him what caused my anxiety and how much I hated these places and he would always say, "Just keep your head in the books, my boy, because without an education, this is what's waiting for you!"

"Don't worry, I will," I would answer and then repeat it quietly to myself.

At the end of the service call there would always be a talk with the manager or VP of the company about the situation and dad would introduce me, "This is my son, Joe," he would say. Almost always to my surprise, the response would be, "The college boy?" or "The one who's in college?"

"Yeah," Dad would say, "This is the one."

Then, almost invariable, they would say it was nice to meet me and that if I wanted to get in the oil business, Dad was the guy to learn from.

"He is the best in the business," I heard over and over and more than a few times that Dad was the only one they'd let touch their equipment. One plant manager told me that dad had saved his job once by covering up that he had screwed up and caused a complete shutdown.

"Your dad explained it to the bosses in a way that sounded like it wasn't my fault," he told me. "He's a helluva guy."

Time and again at plant after plant, customer after customer, I heard testimony to Dad's competence and character. Even Dad's only residential customer, Mrs. Greene, raved about Dad and gave us iced tea and cookies. Mrs. Greene told me how she learned over twenty years ago that Joe Farrell was the man to get if you want good honest service and she insisted on him doing her annual cleaning and inspection and so every summer they scheduled Dad for a stop at Mrs. Greene's house. I was completely unaware of this aspect of Dad's life and although surprised, it wasn't my only surprise.

On about half the days we never made it to the office. We were radio-dispatched so Dad often got a telephone call with our first job or we got called in the car on our way to the office. Some days we'd get sent from job to job and never got to the office. Some days we would get to the office after handling some calls and some days we'd go to the office before handling any calls.

On the days we went straight to the office, it was because I was supposed to help Vinnie the automotive mechanic. Vinnie was a wonderful Italian man who spoke broken English and kept the fleet of cars and trucks running.

Whenever things would get backed up, he would ask for help and I was dropped off to provide that help. At first, I had trouble understanding his broken English, but once I got used to his pronunciation and cursing, I was able to understand what he wanted me to do. I hated it.

The first time Dad dropped me off to work with Vinnie, he said, "He's not much for working with his hands, Vinnie . . . do the best you can with him." This pissed me off but also made me want to do well to prove Dad wrong. I was determined to impress Vinnie and have Dad eat his words. At first, there was the language problem, but like I said, I got used to it and we conversed quite well after that. We'd have long talks over lunch break that were really enjoyable. I would ask a lot of questions about coming to America without a job, speaking no English, about Italy, learning his trade, various jobs he had held and his views on politics, unions and Oscher and Riess. I found his opinions to be wise and fascinating. One day when he was reminiscing fondly about Italy, I asked him if he ever wanted to go back. "No fucka way, man, no fucka way," was his immediate and final answer.

There was no lift in the garage to get underneath a car or truck, but rather a pit that vehicles were pulled over. This sucked. I was six feet four inches tall and had to stoop all the time while working in the pit. I couldn't count the number of times I hit my head on something. It was also impossible to catch a breeze in the pit and although it wasn't a boiler room, it was plenty hot. I worked hard doing oil changes, brake jobs, replacing spark plugs and mufflers and always tried to impress Vinnie by working fast.

One day when washing our hands at the end of the day, I asked Vinnie how I was doing.

"You doin-a beautiful," he answered. "You-a big-a help to me. I tol'a your fadda if notta for you, I be way behind."

"Oh," I said, "I'll bet he was surprised."

"Notta so much," said Vinnie. "I tol'a him you learn'a very fast but why you wanna learn this-a shit, eh? You keepa study hard. You don'a wanna learn this-a shit."

On the days I worked with Vinnie I frequently got to meet and interact with the other service men of the company who came and went all day long. There were the Swartz brothers Izzy and Artie, Duke, Wade and Tony, who everybody called "Boccagallupe." Vinnie would introduce me usually by calling me Giuseppi. They would always seem really interested in meeting me, always knew I was in college and always mention how much they thought of my dad. When I met Preston Wade, who everybody called Wade, he said, "It's an honor to meet you, young man. Your father and I go back a long way and he is the greatest guy in the business or any business, for that matter."

"That's what he tells me," I joked.

"Your studying to be a headshrinker, aren't you?" he went on.

"Well, I'm majoring in Psychology," I answered.

"Yeah, that's right . . . a headshrinker. We can sure use you around here," he yelled loud enough for the guys who were there to hear.

"Oh, really?" I said.

"Yeah, we got some bona fide, first-class, freakin' nut jobs workin' here!"

This caused a big uproar, much to Wade's delight.

"Look who's talkin'," someone yelled. "You're the number one nut job, ya fuckin' nut, ya."

"Did you hear that?" Wade asked me.

"Yeah," I answered, laughing.

"Did you see who said it?"

"No," I answered, truthfully.

"It was Boccagaluppe. Have you met Boccagaluppe?" he asked.

"Is that Tony?" I replied.

"Yeah," said Wade. "Have you met him?"

"Yes, I have."

"I rest my case," he laughed, throwing his arms up above his head for emphasis.

All the guys treated me great and obviously like and respected Dad. One Friday as Vinnie and I were cleaning up at the end of the day, I noticed all the servicemen were hanging around. All except Dad. I was anxious to get going home since it was Friday and I was going out. I asked Vinnie why everyone was here and my heart sank when he told me they were waiting for Dad so they could have a union meeting.

'Shit,' I thought. 'How long is this gonna take?'

I walked over to Izzy Swartz and tried to find out.

"Having a meeting?" I asked.

"Yeah," Izzy replied, "as soon as your Dad gets here."

"Is it gonna take long?" I asked, getting right to the point.

"I hope not," Izzy said. "I want to get the hell home."

"Can't you start without him?" I asked.

"Hell no, he's the shop steward!" Izzy answered.

"I didn't know that," I said.

"Oh yeah, he's always been shop steward. Every year we vote and it's always unanimous. He basically hired us all, he trained us all, he covers our ass when we fuck up, and we all trust him completely, so why would anyone else be steward."

The meeting was short. They all voted to let Dad represent them in Negotiations and signed something that gave him their proxy vote.

On the way home I asked Dad about a number of things I had been thinking about.

"I didn't know you were shop steward." I said. "I guess that's quite an honor?"

"Not really," he answered. "I've just been around the longest."

"Izzy told me you hired and trained everyone?"

"Well, Joe Reiss doesn't know anything about being a mechanic, so he always asks me to choose the new guy."

"How can you tell if a guy is a good oil burner mechanic?"

"You can't," Dad answered. "Anybody can call themselves a mechanic. That's one of the problems."

"So, how do you decide who gets the job?"

"Hire someone with a good attitude and I'll teach them the rest, is what I always say."

"So you taught each one of them?"

"More or less," Dad explained. "Wade was a mechanic in the Navy and he's good. I taught him some stuff about wiring and electricity and he does well. You only have to show Wade something once."

"I bet I know who's the worst," I offered.

"Who?"

"Boccagaluppe," I answered, laughing.

"Tony's (he never called him 'Boccagaluppe.') the weakest of the bunch right now, but he tries hard and he's getting better. He needs to stay calm and think before he does something. He gets so anxious to fix the problem, he just starts changing parts until he gets the right one."

"What's wrong with that?" I asked.

"It's a waste of time and money. I tell him all the time, 'Tony, you can't learn anything if your talkin'. Empty barrels make the most noise."

I laughed at that expression.

"Haven't you heard that expression?" Dad asked.

"Yeah, but I never thought of it like that," I answered.

"It's true! You cannot learn if you're talking."

"I always thought of it as 'stupid people say a lot of stupid stuff' but never that talking a lot was why they are stupid," I said, laughing again.

"Well, think about it," Dad said, smiling.

"How come everybody I meet knows about me being in college?" I said, switching subjects.

"I'm proud that you're going to college and I guess I mention it more than I realize," he answered. You're the first Farrell to ever go to college, you know?"

"No, I didn't realize that," I said.

"Well, that's the truth and it's something I'm proud of." Then, after a brief moment of silence, he added, "at least I will be if you graduate."

"I'll graduate," I said.

For the next few days on the ride home, I would ask about the family tree and Dad would tell me all he knew.

It seems that James Farrell was my great, great grandfather, and living in Longford, Ireland when his land was taken from him by the British in 1846. Five years later, after surviving the potato famine, he came to America as a stowaway on a boat named the "Urgent." He settled in Saratoga, New York, where he worked on a farm and married a woman named Bridget Hickey. (Records show Bridget Hickey arrived from Ireland in 1852 aboard the ship "Balmoral" from Limerick.) My great grandfather, also named James but called Will as a young man, was their eldest son.

James Sr. died in 1891 and is buried in St. Peter's Cemetery in Saratoga. James Jr. married my great grandmother Esther Ulton, who was born Alton but had her name changed as a result of immigration through Ellis Island. She was the first female telegraph operator in the United States. They met in Saratoga when Esther was assigned temporarily to Saratoga to telegraph horse racing results. James left the farm for New York shortly thereafter and found work as a carpenter.

I never knew my great grandfather, as he died in 1939, but I do remember Esther who lived until 1960. She was wonderful and funny even into her early 90s. I can't say the same for my grandfather Charles however, and for the first time I understood why.

My only memories of my grandfather Farrell were of him sitting at his kitchen table in Rockaway drinking beer, smoking and staring out the window. He seemed like a loser to me. But in fact, he had been quite a success for a while. A hard worker, he had learned the construction trades working with his father and had started buying property and building houses himself. He married Josephine Gallagher and had four children, Dad and his three sisters. By the time my father was born in 1916, Charles and Josephine were rich. They lived in a big house in Rockaway which my grandfather had built.

When the stock market crashed in 1929, my grandfather felt very smart. He never trusted the stock market and kept all his money in the bank. In 1931 when the banks failed, he lost $860,000 and his heart. He took to the drink and except for a brief period, never worked again. It was so bad, in fact, that Dad had to quit high school and get a job to help support the family.

Charles had three brothers: Jim, Bill, and Ed Farrell. All three were talented skilled workers. All three had problems with alcohol. My Dad never drank alcohol and now I knew why.

"It isn't worth the chance," he said. "If it gets a hold of you, it wrecks your life."

I wondered if he knew I had been drinking for years.

My father was named Joseph after a cousin Joseph Coleman who fought and died in World War I as a result of a mustard gas attack. I had heard parts of this family history before, but never in an organized, detailed way. I knew Dad had never finished high school, but it never quite registered *why* he quit and how difficult life had been for him as a teen and young man.

A lot of things I never realized before started to resonate that summer and I talked to Pat Kelly about it a number of times. That summer, Pat spent a lot of time at Eileen Fenchak's house, which was just a few blocks from my house. Many nights after work, I was too tired to do anything except read and listen to music.

On nights when I wasn't too exhausted and was restless, I would set out on foot for a bar called Michael's Lounge on 162nd. I would always walk past Fenchak's house and if Pat was there, we'd talk. If he wasn't there, I'd continue on past Mueller's and stop in there to see if Pat and Eileen were there.

Eileen was still in high school and she and her friends still hung around in Mueller's, often with Pat. If he wasn't in either of these places, he was at Michael's Lounge which he called "The Rock" for a reason I never understood.

In any event, we'd talk and I remember telling him about Dad. I told him about Dad being rich and then having to quit school to help support his family and how all the other workers at Oscher and Reisss looked up to him. I told him how the customers big and small all praised him and told stories about how good he was at his job. I told him how Dad never used the "F" word and rarely said anything worse than "shit" or "goddamn," which was noticeable in that environment.

Pat listened patiently as a good friend would and I know he sensed that I was thinking out loud about my new awareness of Dad as a man separate and apart than as my father. I remember one night after Pat and I had a few beers, using the word 'dignity' to describe Dad. It struck me funny to describe an oil burner service man as dignified, but that's the term that best applied. He conducted himself with *dignity*.

On Thursday nights most of the time, I went to Club 21 in Whitestone. They had a disc jockey and it was ladies night which meant cheap drinks for the ladies. Although I had to get up early the next morning and shaving and cleaning up, particularly scrubbing the grime from my hands and fingernails was a bother, lots of drunk young women was a powerful draw. I would splash on some Canoe and beg someone (Dennis Geoghan, Eddie, Glenn, Don Glennon) to pick me up. It was a great summer for rock 'n' roll with the Beach Boys, Bob Dylan, the Byrds, the Righteous Brothers, the Four Tops and Sonny and Cher all in their prime and all having big hits but no song was played more in clubs than 'Satisfaction' by the Rolling Stones. Club 21 was no exception. They played it multiple times a night and always ended the night with it.

Friday mornings were tough if I had gone out Thursday night which was most of the time. Friday nights almost always started at Michael's Lounge. Whatever happened after that was totally unpredictable. Eddie, Dennis, Glenn, Tommy, Pat, Mice Mullaney, Don Glennon, Robert Dunn, Billy, Jimmy McAleer, Dickie, and Jeff Baudo may or may not show up on any given Friday night and the group may stay together or split up, based on what was going on and what options were available. As much as I wanted everybody to stay together and do things together like the old days, that just wasn't going to happen very often.

Sometimes someone knew of a party where we would be welcome and a group of us would go. Sometimes clubs like the Club 21 or the Straw Hat out further on Long Island were our choice of the night, but the group usually had many things going on and split up for most of the night. Often we would meet late after the bars closed at a diner on Northern Boulevard and eat and exchange stories about our night. Those were enjoyable endings to our Friday nights. Very funny guys were all tuned up and had stories to tell about parties, ball games, dates, dances or whatever had transpired that night or that week. The banter and ridicule back and forth was hysterical.

One night Dennis and Glenn claimed to have saved my life and in retrospect it was probably true. We were at a party in Flushing that one of our group was invited to and told to bring some friends. At the party I met a nice girl whose former boyfriend was drunk and jealous and pushed me beyond my limit. I avoided fights very successfully almost always, but this guy was obnoxious and I was drunk enough to snap. Dennis had seen this situation building and told Glenn they had to get me out of there.

Apparently the guy who I had just angrily confronted was the younger brother of a 'made' man in the Mafia. His name was Joey Farina and I knew nothing about him or his family. Just as we scuffled in the basement, the host's older sister, Kathy Fisher, came to the basement stairs and announced the party was over and everybody was to leave immediately.

I recognized Kathy Fisher as a friend of my older sister Maureen and she recognized me. Joey Farina and I had agreed to fight outside and presumably he was waiting for me as Kathy and I exchanged pleasantries. Dennis and

Glenn asked about another way out of the house and Kathy helped them get me out the back and out of the area. Drunk as I was, I felt badly than my friends seemed to lack confidence in my ability to take this obnoxious, drunk asshole.

A few hours later at the diner, Dennis loved telling everyone what had happened. By his account, he saved my ass from a thumping. Either Joey Farina would kick my ass or worse, I would kick his ass and his 'family' could come after me to settle the score.

"I saved your ass big time," Dennis said, laughing. "You owe me."

"I'm not so sure about that," I said, trying to defend myself. "I could have kicked Joey's ass and laid low until I go back to school."

"That's nuts!" Dennis said.

"Why?"

"Why? I'll tell you why. They park outside your house and wait for you to come out *and* if you go back to school, you think they can't go to Pennsylvania?"

"Okay," I said. "I owe you," hoping to put an end to this particular subject.

"Fuckin' A. Big Time!"

"How big?" I asked.

"I need to think about that," Dennis said. "I'll get back to you on that, but it'll be *big!*"

"Tell me about your driver's license test," I asked, totally changing the subject.

"Why?" he asked.

"'Cause I'm takin' mine this week and I want to know what to expect," I answered.

There was some laughing and snickering from a number of the guys.

"Yeah, Dennis, tell him about your driver's test," Jimmy McAleer challenged.

"Most guys fail the first time," Dennis replied.

There was more snickering and laughing.

"It's true! Jimmy, you know that's true," Dennis insisted.

"All right, that is true," Jimmy laughed, "and you were no exception."

"I take it you failed your first time?" I asked.

"That's correct," Dennis said with a straight face, studying the menu and acting like the conversation was over.

"What were the reasons?" I asked.

"What?" Dennis asked, absentmindedly.

"What were the reasons?" I asked again, louder.

"I forget the exact reason," answered Dennis, trying to keep a straight face. It had something to do with an accident and a bus."

"You had an *accident* on your driver's exam!"

I cracked up laughing along with everyone else.

"*With a bus?*"

"That's what they said," Dennis replied.

"What do you mean, '*they*' said?" I pressed. "You were there! Did you hit a bus?"

"No," said Dennis, shaking his head yes. "Anyway, good luck with your exam but odds are you'll flunk it."

Dennis was wrong, fortunately. I passed my driver's exam and immediately started borrowing my sister's car for dates.

Although it dramatically improved my situation to be able to ask a girl out and be able to pick her up, my sister's old dark dull blue Dodge station wagon with a push button transmission didn't score many points for me. It was the ugliest, most uncool car imaginable, but the radio worked and I was grateful to have the use of it on certain nights. Maureen and Brian Guidera, my brother-in-law, lived on Northern Boulevard about ten blocks away. The Dodge was their second car and often they didn't need it on weekends.

Sometime in the beginning of August, I received a letter from St. Vincent saying I had been selected to serve on the Orientation Committee. It was a big honor to be selected and I sensed George Dixon had a lot to do with it. I called George in Pittsburgh and, of course, he already knew. I told him about my grades and thanked him again for all the help he'd been and for recommending me for the Orientation Committee.

"The way to thank me is to pass it on," he said. "The Orientation Committee is a good opportunity to get to know some freshmen and help them get started in the right direction."

"I'll try," I said, "but I'm not sure I'm out of the woods yet."

All summer the airwaves were filled with news stories of an escalating war in Vietnam and racial violence in America. Rioting in the Watts section of Los Angeles left thirty-four dead and over a thousand injured including many firemen and police. Watching the evening news was an anxiety-producing experience.

In July, LBJ announced the government would be drafting thirty-five thousand men a month. One night on the way home from work after hearing the news on the radio, I expressed some anxiety about the war to Dad.

"Don't worry about it," he told me. "It will be over soon. These are peasants in rice paddies. They can't stand up to the best-trained, best-equipped military force on the planet."

"If they're just peasants in rice paddies, then why are we there? Why are we bombing rice paddies?" I asked.

"'Cause the Communists want to take over," he answered.

"So what?" I asked.

"So we have to stop them somewhere," he answered.

It was then I asked how come he wasn't in the military during World War II like my uncles and learned that the Defense Department gave him an occupational deferment.

"Just about every factory and plant was producing something for the war," he told me. "Somebody had to keep them running and that somebody was me."

This summer of bonding had one memorable bump in the road toward the end. It was a Friday and I had an actual date to meet a girl at the Straw Hat in Mineola. We were on our way home on the Interboro Parkway when a call for Dad came over the radio. Boccagaluppe was at some plant in Brooklyn where he had been all day and could not get the boiler running. Would Dad go there and see what the problem was. Of course he said yes and we turned off the Parkway and headed for the Williamsburg section of Brooklyn.

I was pissed off and moaned and groaned. The more I thought about it, the more pissed off I got. I had to get home, get clean, put on some Canoe, eat, walk to Maureen's house to get the car and drive out to Mineola. Now all of this was going to be delayed indefinitely while we bailed out someone who couldn't do their job correctly! If this took too long, it might be too late to go at all. Maybe my date would think I stood her up and leave or worse, would hook up with someone else.

"I have a date tonight, y'know!" I said angrily, after a few minutes of silence.

"I'm sorry," Dad answered. "It might not take long."

"In Mineola!" I added, with disgust in my voice.

"Tony can do the work once I find out the problem," he answered.

I didn't speak the rest of the way to the plant, where we were greeted by a panicked Tony. Dad told Tony to calm down and tell him what was going on. Tony started telling him everything he had done. He had replaced the gaskets, the fuel pump, the fuses, the nozzles, the relay switches, the thermostats and just about everything that could be replaced.

"When you turn the boiler on, do you get ignition?" Dad asked Tony.

"Yeah," answered Tony, "and it runs for ten or fifteen minutes and then shuts down."

"Sounds like the safety shuts it down," Dad said. "Did you check the safety?"

"I changed the safety," answered Tony.

"Did you reset it?" Dad asked.

"Reset it?"

"Yeah, Tony. A safety has to be manually reset once it's thrown."

"But, Joe, I put a new one in," Tony exclaimed excitedly.

"Go start the boiler up," Dad said, reaching for his flashlight.

Tony went around to the other side of the huge boiler and threw the 'on' switch and returned to where we were talking.

"I've been here all day," Tony said to me.

"So I've heard," I answered.

"This is a real ball buster, this one is," Tony exclaimed, the frustration showing on his face.

Just then Dad emerged from the darkness behind the boiler and said that the safety switch was thrown and that he had reset it.

"Let's see what happens now," Dad said.

For the next few minutes as the boiler heated up, Tony told me the story of his day. The manager of the plant was apparently quite upset over the inability to get the boiler running and had expressed his frustration to Oscher and Reiss's office manager, Dave. Dave was who called us on the radio on the way home. Tony was worried. Both Dave and the plant manager suspected Tony didn't know what he was doing.

As the minutes went by, my anger and frustration grew. Finally the boiler was running smoothly and seemed to be functioning normally. Tony was bewildered and asked Dad to explain.

The explanation was that a short in a relay kept throwing the safety. Tony replaced the safety and started the boiler before he replaced the faulty relay and never reset the safety. Subsequently, each time Tony would start the boiler after changing something, it would shut off when it reached a certain point because the safety was thrown and hadn't been reset. Even I understood it!

After Dad told Tony what to tell the plant manager, we got in the car and resumed our trip home. The delay was well over an hour and I was fuming. When Dad covered for Tony by telling Dave that it was a tricky electrical problem that Tony had fixed before we arrived, I boiled over.

"How can you cover up for that asshole?" I said, shaking my head in exasperation. "He screwed up my whole night."

"I'll tell you how," Dad yelled back. Tony tries hard and he has a wife and three kids and needs this job. That's more important than you meeting some chippie in a bar and if you don't think so, you can go to hell!"

We didn't talk the rest of the way home. I cleaned up, skipped dinner, picked up Maureen's piece of shit car, and headed for Mineola. The date went well, but I felt badly about my attitude.

On Monday I told Dad I was sorry for my attitude.

"I don't know this girl very well and I didn't want to screw it up," I said.

"Yeah, well, if you want to be a man, act like a man," he said. "You were acting like a boy."

That really stung and I felt bad about it for a long time.

In the last week of Oscher and Riess, I screwed up and gave everybody (well, almost everybody) a good laugh. One of the top bosses was a guy named Ralph. Ralph drove a big white Cadillac and wasn't particularly well-liked by the servicemen. He drove his car in one day early that week and asked Vinnie to gas it up and check all the belts and fluids. Vinnie had me do it and I accidentally left a rag on the radiator after twisting the cap closed with it. Ralph left work soon after but didn't get far. The rag got caught in the fan and threw the fan belt off and the car overheated on the Parkway in Brooklyn. Ralph was pissed off, but everybody else loved it.

On my last day, everybody said good-bye and chipped in some words of wisdom.

"Stay in school as long as you can," "Keep it in your pants," "Listen to your father." "Study hard."

Vinnie hugged me and said, "Listen to me, Giuseppe . . . don't-a fuck up. You gotta good future if-a you don't-a fuck it up. You a good-a boy."

On the drive home, I asked Dad if he had any advice other than what I had just heard.

"Not really," he responded. "Just keep your head in the books. Education is the ticket to a good life."

"That's all?" I asked. "Don't you have a philosophy of life or a code you live by?" I asked, half sarcastically.

"Well," started Dad, "I believe in three words . . . 'please,' 'sorry,' and 'thanks.' Use them often and avoid people who don't. That's my advice. Don't work with or for them, don't befriend them, don't get involved with anyone who doesn't use those words."

There was a moment of silence as I thought about what Dad had said, but couldn't really connect with it.

"So you're saying only associate with polite people?"

"Polite hell! It goes much deeper than polite! Think about what it means to say 'please.' It means it's a request, not a command. It shows respect for that person and recognizes that they have a choice in the matter and are not under your control. Believe me, that can mean a lot."

Dad took his eyes off the road to see if I was really listening. Apparently satisfied that I was, he continued.

"Who wants to be around someone who can't say they are sorry when they have caused harm to someone or inconvenienced someone. It's either a person who cannot admit a mistake or someone who doesn't give a damn about anyone else. Either way, not a good person to be involved with."

We were nearing home now and I was amazed that Dad had given so much thought to this.

"How about 'thank you'?" I asked.

"A person who doesn't feel or express appreciation is a very self-centered person," he said, "again, not someone you want to be around very often or be involved with very deeply."

As we pulled into the driveway of our house, Dad saw an amused smile on my face.

"You can laugh if you want," he said. "It may sound stupid but it will make sense to you as you get older or you'll become like that and no one will want to be around you."

"I'm not laughing," I said quickly as we were getting out of the car, "I'm just amazed that I never heard this before."

"Do you know what arrogance means?" he asked.

"Yeah," I answered, although I wasn't totally sure.

"It doesn't cost anything to say, 'Please,' 'Sorry' and 'Thanks,' but an arrogant person doesn't see the need so doesn't bother."

"Thanks for getting me this job, by the way," I said smiling and showing that I understood.

"You're welcome," he said as he pushed open the door to the house.

In a few days I was back in Latrobe where I would soon start my first philosophy course. My amazement at my father's attempt at formulating a code or philosophy of life that could be expressed in three words would grow and my appreciation of the wisdom of his words would continue to grow and amaze me throughout my life.

There were one hundred and twenty-five thousand American soldiers in Vietnam . . .

CHAPTER TWENTY-TWO

♦ ♦ ♦ ♦ ♦

"GERRY III"

Now young faces grow sad and old
and hearts of fire grow cold,
We swore blood brothers against the wind
I'm ready to grow young again.
                    Bruce Springsteen—"No Surrender"

I returned to school a few days ahead of most of the other students because I was a member of the Orientation Committee and we needed the time to get organized. I had requested to live with Lou Posa and that request was granted. We were to share a room on the third floor of Gerard Hall. Most freshmen were housed in the freshman dorm, Aurelius Hall, but a few lucky freshmen got assigned to one of the two new better modern dormitories Gerard or Bonaventure Halls. The third floor of Gerard (which we nicknamed 'Gerry III') was where some freshman were housed in 1964-1965 and they had, for the most part stayed together which made me and Lou Posa and a few others the new guys on the floor.

Lou Posa was a big, strong, athletic accounting major from the Monongahela Valley near Pittsburgh. He acted tough, but was in reality a sensitive and great guy. When room assignments were announced, I was a little anxious about Gerry III because Billy and Glenn had both been assigned to Bonaventure Hall and I couldn't find anyone I knew well who was on Gerry III. My fears were completely allayed, however, once I met the guys. They immediately extended themselves and made us feel part of their craziness.

When I met Frank Bonati, he helped break the ice with others on the floor.

"You still a psych. major?" he asked.

"Yeah," I answered.

"How about your roommate?" he continued.

"Lou Posa," I answered.

"I don't care about his name, is he a science major?" Frank asked.

"No, accounting major," I answered, amused by Frank's attitude. "Why?"

"Because I hate science majors! They eat shit," Frank yelled loudly, just as Ed Heinrichs and Steve Bellich, two science majors, walked past.

"You're living between two sets of shit-eating science majors, you know," he went on, gesturing toward the rooms on each side of our room. "Over here, you have May and Pagano," he pointed, " . . . they are robots! You can set your watch by them. They live on a schedule. They go to breakfast at seven. They eat dinner at five. They shower at ten and lights out at eleven. They are fuckin' scary! On the other side of you there is Steve I-am-a-Robot Bellich and Ed Heinrichs who we call 'H'. H sometimes appears human but he'll cut your throat just like the rest of these science majors. Cut-throats, all of them. Cut-throat robots! Cut-throat shit-eating robots!!"

H and Bellich had entered their room, but heard the whole thing since they left their door open.

"Does that include your roommate?" a voice yelled from around the corner.

The voice belonged to Bill Lloyd who thrust out his hand and quickly introduced himself.

"I see you've met Frank," Lloyd said with a laugh.

"Yeah," I answered. "Are you a science major?"

"No, I . . . . ."

"He's not smart enough to be a science major," interrupted Bonati. He's a history major. He waits until long after something has happened and then forms an opinion. He's disorganized, lazy and a moocher. Don't even think about bringing any food up here. Lloyd will smell it and beg you for some. That's why I keep a large knife handy in my room. If he tries to take anything from me, I'll cut off his hand."

"He's not kidding," said Lloyd, looking at me and then looking at Bonati, added, "You're gonna hurt somebody with thing someday."

"Yeah, I know and I hope it's you," Bonati replied.

"Bonati calls other people crazy," piped up H, "but sleeps with an eighteen-inch bayonet. Now you tell me, who's crazy?"

"I'm not the crazy one," said Bonati. "I use it to protect me from the crazy ones."

"Like who?" asked Lloyd.

"Yeah," added H, "who's crazy?"

"How about Greenwood?" offered Bonati.

"Well, Greenwood's crazy, but he's harmless," replied H.

"Okay, then, how about Duffer or Muir?" said Bonati.

"Holy shit," said H, looking at Lloyd, "he's right. We better get guns or something!"

"That might be good thinking," Lloyd replied, "'cause I hear some crazies are moving in here from third floor Aurelius."

"Hey, hey, that's where I came from!" I said.

"I know," answered Lloyd, laughing.

"Well, I happen to be the picture a mental health," I said. "Who else is on this floor from Aurelius?"

"I have a master list right here," Lloyd said, unfolding a piece of paper, "Let's see, there's a Tim Zadai."

"He's not crazy," I said quickly. "He's a lot of fun, but perfectly sane."

"How about your roommate?" asked Bonati.

"Lou Posa? He's completely normal. You don't want to get him mad, but he's not crazy or anything. Who else?" I asked, looking at Lloyd who was consulting his list.

"How about Stock, Rakoczy, Dice, Gerlach, and Rose?" Lloyd asked.

"Okay, they *are* crazy," I laughed. "I guess you heard correctly.

Over the next two years, many of the guys living on Gerry III would forge friendships with each other that would last a lifetime. My six weeks being on the Orientation Committee went well. It felt a little like being a patrol boy again. I wanted to do well at helping freshmen get off on the right foot. We were introduced to them by the administration as the "leaders of the St. Vincent community, a community of scholars."

It was the first time anyone had ever referred to me as a scholar, even as indirect as it had been. When advising freshmen about studying strategies and techniques I would often think, 'If only they knew how mightily I struggled. If only they knew I had to be locked in my room and guarded by George Dixon. If only they knew I already had two Ds on my permanent record!'

I expressed these thoughts to George Dixon and John Degnan who were seniors and also Orientation Committee members and they both agreed I was a tremendous asset to the program.

"Whenever we come upon some poor freshmen who aren't cutting it, who made a mistake by coming here or who are just completely fucking things up, we'll just point to you," offered Degnan, laughing.

"You can be a beacon to those who are lost, those who are math-impaired," added George, "those with no discipline, those . . ."

"Okay, I get it," I said, cutting him off. "You guys are brutal! Great models of sensitivity for the freshmen."

"You're a sophomore now," said George, continuing to laugh heartily. "any weakness will be exploited—any vulnerability revealed."

Although I didn't feel like a scholar, I did take Father Ronald's words seriously. In the Spring semester, I signed up for twenty credits, the maximum allowed for the flat $950 tuition fee and took the work seriously. I chose many difficult electives and within limits, tried to learn as much as I could. Although mostly pleased with the results, I did have some difficulties.

The Psych. Department required twelve credits in either French, German or Russian. I had had Spanish in high school and I knew that if I took French, I'd be in a course where most of the students either had it in high school or loved languages. I went to Father Cuk, the head of the Psych. Department and asked him if I could take Spanish and satisfy the requirement.

Father Cuk was an odd man who had a reputation of being a prick. He had a nervous condition of some kind which caused him to noisily clear his throat every few seconds. I had avoided any significant contact with him in my freshman year, but now was going to have him for his specialties: Statistics and Experimental Psychology.

On the first day of our Statistics class I waited around after class to ask him about taking Spanish.

"Father," I started, "can I speak to you a minute?"

"What (*ahem*) about?" he answered.

"About the language requirement of the Psych. Department," I said.

"(*Ahem*) See me in my office," he said as he started toward the door.

I slowly followed him down the hall and watched him go into his office. I waited a few moments and knocked on the open door.

"(*Ahem*) Come in."

"Father, I was wondering if I could satisfy the language requirement by taking Spanish since I had it in high school and most of the guys in French had French in high school. I'm not very good at foreign languages and am starting at a disadvantage. Actually, I'll be at a disadvantage in Spanish too, but at least I'll have a chance," I said, as nicely and respectfully as I could.

"(*Ahem*) What's your name again?" Father Cuk asked.

"Farrell," I answered. "Joe Farrell."

"(*Ahem*) No," said Father Cuk.

Father Cuk was looking down on his desk reading what was apparently a message. I stood there for a moment, not sure if I had heard correctly or if he had more to say but was distracted by what was on his desk.

"Excuse me, Father?" I said.

"(*Ahem*) (*ahem*), No," he said, louder than before, never looking up from his desk.

I stood there for a minute and thought about asking him for an explanation, but given his reputation and the fact that I had him for Statistics, I left.

French class was hell. I was behind from the first day. Madame Carrass was the instructor. She was an adjunct faculty member who lived in Pittsburgh and drove to SVC to teach her two French classes on Monday, Wednesday and Friday. To make matters worse, my French class was at 8:00 a.m. I was not by any means a 'morning person,' but it soon became apparent to me that Madame Carrass was a vindictive, man-hating ex-nun who was determined to make me pay for everything I had even done wrong. After flunking a quiz and an exam, I asked to speak with her after class.

"Oui, M'sieur?" she said as I approached her desk.

"I guess you can tell that I'm not doing very well in this class," I began.

"Oui," she replied.

"I have to take either French, German or Russian to fulfill my foreign language requirement for my major and I had Spanish in high school," I began.

"You are always late for class, non?"

"Yeah, oui," I answered, looking contrite.

"How comes I am here on time for everee class and I come all zee way from Peetsburgh, yet you leev here and always you are late?"

I had no real answer for this question and after groping around for one, I said, "Perhaps I stay up later than you?"

"Apparently not studying Francais," she replied.

"Well, anyway," I continued, "I started behind the others and I'm not doing well catching up."

"Oui, m'sieur, dees ees not my probelem."

"Do you have any advice as to how I can get out of this mess?" I asked somberly.

"Oui, I vill geef you a 'D' if you do not come back," she answered.

"Hmmm," I thought for a moment. "Do you mean if I drop the course?"

"Oui, and nevaire return."

I stood there surprised and mulling over my options.

"Take zee D," Mme. Carrass said as she started walking toward the door.

"I'll check with Father Cuk," I said to her back as she was walking out the door. I was reluctant to take the deal and get another D.

"Do you know Father Cuk?" I yelled to her back.

I saw her shake her head 'no' without even looking back.

"I'm sure you'd like him," I said softly to myself. "He reminds me a lot of you!"

Later that day, I had Father Cuk for Statistics and waited after class to talk with him.

"Father, can I speak with you for a minute?" I asked, approaching his desk.

"(*Ahem*) Is it about Statistics?"

"No, it's about French."

"(*Ahem*) Well then, see me in my office," he replied. Once again, I slowly followed him down the hall and watched him go into his office. I waited a few moments and knocked on the open door.

"(*Ahem*) Come in."

"Father, as I predicted I am in trouble in French class," I began. "I flunked the first test and a quiz. Everybody in the class had French in high school (as far as I knew), and I don't think it's fair. Madame Carrass offered to give me a D if I drop it, but then I don't know what to do if you won't allow me to take Spanish."

"(*Ahem*) Take Russian," he said.

"Excuse me, Father?"

"(*Ahem*) (*Ahem*) Take Russian. (*Ahem*) Surely no one had Russian in high school."

I didn't know how to respond to this since it was true, but the thought of learning a language that used a whole new alphabet was *very* unappealing. Actually, foreign language in general was unappealing, no matter what alphabet. I hated Latin, I hated Spanish and now I hated French.

I couldn't tell if Father Cuk was smiling in amusement at my dilemma or was in pain (this was frequently the case with Fr. Cuk), but not seeing any logical argument I could make, I shifted gears and tried to avoid another D.

"Do you know Madame Carrass?" I asked.

"(*Ahem*) No."

"That's too bad, I continued. "She's very nice. I was wondering if you could talk to her about giving me a 'C' instead of a 'D' so it won't hurt my GPA so much and look bad on my transcript."

"(*Ahem*) No."

I stood there for an awkward moment after which I said, "Well, okay then, Father. I guess I'll see you Monday in class," and I left.

Back in the dorm that night, I told the gang about my bad day, much to their delight.

"Why does Cuk hate you?" asked. H.

"I don't know, I swear I have no idea. I haven't missed a class. I respond in class to questions and I aced the only exam we've had." I answered.

"Well, you know Farrell, you just rub some people the wrong way," offered Lloyd.

"Oh yeah, like who?" I asked.

"Well, me and H for starters," Lloyd laughed. "And Posa. Right, Lou?"

Posa had been staring at his 'Money and Banking' text and only half listening.

"What?" Posa said.

"Doesn't Farrell rub you the wrong way?"

"No," answered Lou, deadpan. "And if he tries to rub me, I'll break his head."

"Look on the bright side," said H. "When the Russians take over, you'll know what they're saying."

◆ ◆ ◆

Russian was taught by Father Ludwig Cepon. Father Cepon was a kind and merciful man. Over the fours semesters of Russian, I got a B and a C and two Ds. I loved listening to Fr. Cepon's stories of the Soviet Union and learning of their culture and history, but the time involved in memorizing was just too much for me. After my first two semesters of Russian, I asked Fr. Cuk if there was some way I could have the D in French expunged from my record. Take away the credits and the D as if it never happened.

"(Ahem) No," he answered.

Fr. Cepon also taught a course named *World Religions*, a survey of all the major religions in the world. I took it as an elective trying to learn about the world. It was an eye-opening course. Catholics and Christians in general imagine that no faith imparts the virtues of love and forgiveness more effectively than their own. Funny thing is that Jews, Muslims, Buddhists, Hindus and Taoists all believe that of their own religion. Billions of them had the same reasons for being a believer that Christians do. It occurred to me that most of them came to believe whatever was popular in their culture perhaps to meet a common human need. Fr. Cepon had started me thinking in new ways about my religious beliefs.

I carried this thought into a course called *Theology and Psychology* taught by the Dean of the Pittsburgh Theological Seminary. This was a Presbyterian institution of graduate theological education. The readings for this course included Freud's "Future of an Illusion" where Freud examines man's need to create an afterlife. He describes religion as an illusion in that it is a fulfillment of man's oldest, strongest and most urgent wish. These two courses fed my own doubt about my faith that went back to Catechism class and St. Margaret Mary Alacoque.

Other courses that had a lasting impact on me were a terrific *Logic* course and *Introduction to Philosophy* taught by Dennis Quinn. His classes inspired me subsequently to take a course in Epistemology and one in Metaphysics.

A two-semester *Major American Writers* course led me to take a poetry course and a drama course, both of which changed me and have had lasting effects on my life.

I also took a course in Political Science that had a big impact on me. The course was *American Government* and it was taught by a local lawyer named Gold. Mr. Gold was an excellent professor and I found myself looking forward to his class. I was surprised to be looking forward to any class and also surprised at how little I knew about our Constitution after all those years of Social Studies. I remember saying that this course should be mandatory. Mr. Gold's exams were difficult and yet interesting. They were open-book tests that required thought and an understanding of the material.

Since the course was an elective for me and had mostly Political Science majors in it, I elected to take it on a Pass / Fail basis. I got a P (which of course doesn't count toward a student's GPA.) Had I had more confidence in myself and taken it without the P/F option, I would have gotten an A.

The learning experiences were not, however, confined to the classroom. There were many speakers who came to campus and many seminars open to the whole student body. We had a whole week devoted to the study of Communism which brought picketing and protests from many in nearby communities. They must have felt that just listening to a Communist would damage us and put us under a spell that would either convert us or make us dupes for the international 'Communist Conspiracy.'

When Pete Seeger came to campus to speak and sing, someone called in a bomb threat. The President of St. Vincent, Father Maynard Brennan, took all the heat and criticism, believing that a good education included being exposed to unpopular, controversial or even radical points of view. He was quoted as saying he would invite Satan himself to campus in the quest for truth.

I personally met Saul Alinsky (the famous community organizer), James Farmer (CORE) and Stokely Carmichael (SNCC) and Milton Shapp. Shapp was running for governor of Pennsylvania at the time and being a New Yorker, I couldn't have cared less. I came out of Gerard Hall and walked right into him. He shook my hand and asked for my support. I told him I wasn't from Pennsylvania. "Well, maybe you should be," he said, smiling. (Four years later Shapp would run again and win the governorship and hire me to work on his staff!)

Many of us marched in demonstrations for civil rights and against the war and yes, we sang "We Shall Overcome" and "Kumbaya," often with a lump in our throats.

We marched in a lot of different demonstrations and were often jeered and once were threatened. A civil rights march in Jeanette, PA, brought a death threat phone call to the college. The caller said that if any of the college students marched in the planned demonstration, some of them wouldn't return. The administration did its job and let the students know of the threat. The result was even more marchers showing up than had planned to before the threat. In fact, many faculty members marched with us.

When hundreds of thousands were starving in Nigeria as a result of a civil war, we got the administration to agree to donate the cost of our dinners to the relief effort. Hundreds of students agreed and signed up to skip dinner.

We raised money for and bought and delivered toys for underprivileged kids in a Pittsburgh orphanage that Christmas. Jim Fink dressed up as Santa

Claus and passed out the toys. It touched us all to see such joy and gratitude in those little faces.

Life on Gerry III was also a huge learning experience of a different type from anything I had ever experienced before or have experienced since. I have often described it as intensive group therapy. We ate together, learned together, studied together, partied together and competed together. We shared bathrooms and showers and TVs and telephones as well as hopes, dreams, fears and worries.

You couldn't have a date or an exam or a visitor or a pimple on the end of your nose without everyone knowing about it and demanding details. If you were expecting a phone call and didn't want anyone to know who from, you'd better stand by the phone booth or sit in it, so you'd be sure to be the one to answer it. Otherwise, it was everybody's business.

"Hey, Shlopak," I heard someone yell in the hallway one night as I sat at my desk. "There's a girl named Penny on the phone for you. I told her your dick is only one inch long, but she wants to talk to you anyway!" If you refused to supply sufficient credible detail, the details were made up for you and circulated.

John Muir and I were walking toward Gerard Hall one night after dinner when we ran into Mike Polechko coming the other way.

"Hey, Polechko," John yelled as soon as he saw him. "Did you take a call for me last night?"

"Yeah," answered Polechko, "you got a call from Latrobe Hospital."

"Thanks for telling me, asswipe! What was the message?" Muir asked.

"Hey, I looked for you, but I couldn't find you," Polechko answered.

"Ever think of *leaving* . . . a . . . *note*!?" John screamed, his hands outstretched in frustration.

"I knew I'd see you eventually," answered Polechko with a laugh.

"Eventually?" John screamed, looking at me, his eyes bulging out, his hands palms up near his chest. "Eventually?" "What was the message?" he asked again shaking his head in disgust.

"Your blood test is done and you have the clap," Polechko answered, smiling broadly.

"I wish!" said Muir.

"You *wish*?" said Polechko. "You *wish* you had the clap?"

"Yeah," answered Muir. "You can treat the clap with shots. I'm so horny, I can't see straight. What do I do for that?"

"Do what I do," offered Polechko, "get drunk and slam it in a door. You won't think about sex for a while, I guarantee it!"

"Ugh, you're sick," responded Muir with a look of horror on his face at the thought of slamming his dingus in a door.

"I'm sick? *You're* the one who has VD."

"Again, I wish."

"Hey, you can always go to Brick Alley (a local whore house)," suggested Polechko, walking away. "You better get used to that 'cause it's the only way you'll ever get laid."

John Muir was one of the many colorful and unforgettable characters on Gerry III. Muir had a habit of drinking too much beer and when he did, he had trouble laying down. It seems that the room would start spinning and John would proceed to throw up. He tried putting one foot on the floor to stop or slow the spinning, but to no avail.

Dan Lovett was Muir's roommate and although a patient, caring, sensitive, intelligent guy, he got a little annoyed when he found vomit in his shoes. Muir responded to Dan's threats in the same thoughtful, rational way he approached any problem. Thereafter, when Muir came home drunk, he would remove all his clothes, grab his mattress by the convenient handles on the side, and drag it a few feet into the washroom. There he would turn out all the lights and sleep on the floor. This was so that when he threw up, the toilet or sink was just inches away and if he missed or didn't make it, the floor was tile and much more easily cleaned up than the carpet in his room. This solution worked quite well for a while. His mattress took a beating and one of the handles broke on each side and some say it had an unpleasant odor, but overall Muir was pretty proud of his problem-solving ability and ability to adapt to change.

Most of us were used to Muir being asleep on the washroom floor and if by chance, we opened the door and the lights were off, we'd quickly realize why and make a decision to just back out and leave him alone *or* that it was late enough in the day and time for him to get up.

Most of us were, that is. The student prefect Franny DeBennedetto, however, was not. Franny needed money and got paid, not only for being a prefect, but also for giving tours to prospective students on weekends for the admissions office.

One Saturday around noon, Franny was giving a tour to a high school senior and his parents. He brought them up to Gerry III to see what the dorms were like in general, but specifically he knew that Joe May and Charlie Pagano were gone for the weekend (as usual) and that their room would be neat and clean. He opened their door and sure enough, the beds were made, clothes were all hung up and everything was in its place. Not a typical situation, but Franny knew who he could count on to give a good impression to parents.

After locking up the May/Pagano room the foursome walked down the hall a bit while Franny answered questions. Then pausing by the shower room, Franny knocked on the door and hearing nothing, he slowly opened it until he could see that no one was in there.

"This is a typical shower room," he told the boy and his parents, "and this," Franny continued as he knocked on the washroom door next to the shower room, "is your basic wash room." His knock going unanswered, Franny opened the door slowly. When he saw it was dark inside he relaxed and holding the door open with his body so all could see, he reached across for the light switch and turned on the lights, and there for all to behold was John Muir in all his glory.

"Aagh! Turn the fucking lights out!" he screamed, hands over his eyes.

Franny, the boy and his parents were stunned. Franny backed out of the washroom, letting the door close and mumbling something to his guests about that being very unusual and maybe the student was ill.

A group of us who realized what had happened ducked into a room and were in convulsions of laughter. Franny walked by a few minutes later with the family and quickly stuck his head in the room and said, gritting his teeth "Tell Muir he's *dead!*" We gleefully went to tell Muir what had happened and to deliver Franny's message. Typical of Muir, he was the one who was pissed off. "Jesus Christ, can't a guy sleep in on a Saturday!" he yelled. "Turn those fuckin' lights out."

We coaxed Muir to at least move to his room so as not to make the situation worse if Franny returned. "Fuck Franny," said Muir, picking up his mattress and heading for his room. "Have him show me the rule that says you can't sleep in the washroom."

Strangely enough, the washroom was the setting for another classic Gerry III story. Paul Duffer, like a lot of college students, didn't really care for doing laundry. He did, however, like the comfort of socks. Many of us didn't wear socks to avoid doing laundry, but Duffer liked socks and frequently left them soaking in the sink in the washroom, sometimes for days. This really annoyed some guys. Duffer would come in to the washroom after days of his socks soaking, pull the plug to let the water out and then wring the rest of the water out of them with his hands. He would take the wet socks to his room to dry and often put more dirty socks in the sink. This ritual went on for some time until one day, someone put a turd in one of his socks soaking in the sink. Apparently using lab tongs, somebody took a turd (presumably their own) out of the toilet and put it in one of Duffer's socks. True to form, some time later, Duffer came in, pulled the plug and began wringing out his socks.

No one ever saw socks in the sink again.

Not all the craziness was on Gerry III, however.

One night I entered the building around 10:00 p.m. and saw a number of my classmates in the stairwell with handfuls of wire coat hangers.

"What's going on?" I asked, quizzically.

"Oh, nothing much," answered Larry Wagaman, "just getting Snappo Racko to snap. Wanna help?"

We reached the second floor and I followed to see what was going on. A group of guys was throwing hangers under Bob Racko's door as fast as they could. There was just enough of a gap between the floor and the door for a hanger to be easily slung under. They had already thrown hundreds under and were planning to continue as long as the supply lasted. They were getting them from a storeroom in the basement.

It seems Racko was trying to study and was known for having a short fuse, thus becoming known as Snappo. When they discovered that Snappo was studying, they naturally went to bother him. He told them he needed to study for an exam and asked to be left alone. When they wouldn't, he threw them out of his room and locked the door. The normal taunting and verbal abuse was ignored by Snappo, determined to study and firmly believing that if he just ignored them, they would eventually grow tired of this game and move on.

It might have worked too, but Snappo underestimated the creativity, energy and the enormous capacity for mayhem of his friends. Up and down the stairs they ran with more and more hangers, zipping them under the door as fast as they could.

After a while I left, believing Snappo wasn't going to break. I was wrong, I heard later that night. After thousands of hangers had been zipped under his door, he erupted. As soon as the guys heard his door unlocking, they ran. They ran and knew not to bother him again that night, but hearing the tirade of cursing and death threats, also knew that they could rely on the snap in Snappo.

Another part of the bonding process was sports. In a small male school, intramural sports can take on great significance and excitement. St. Vincent was one of those and intramurals were organized by floor. In my two years on Gerry III, we won two school championships: one in softball and one in football. Although it was exciting and rewarding to win the softball championship, the football championship was the stuff legends are made of.

The game was flag football and it was rough and played for keeps. There was no equipment (helmets, pads), but a mouthpiece was required. There was no tackling, but everything else was like real football. The hitting was intense and, without pads, bone-jarring. I did end my intramural football career in my Junior year with a dislocated shoulder.

No sophomore team had ever won the school championship, that is, until the fall of 1965. It would have been, I'm sure, an interesting sociological study as to how a group of about twenty guys could come together and without any preconceived roles, form a harmonious, smooth running, efficient, and hard-working team. We had no coaches, no sponsor, no one in charge. We made up our own plays, our own lineup, ran our own practices and meetings. We won our first few games and then really started to get good.

Our quarterback, Bob Davie, had played quarterback on his high school team in upstate New York and was a talented passer. Our running back, Jack Mihok, was a star running back in high school and only because of a serious knee injury wasn't playing college ball on a scholarship somewhere.

What made this championship so special was who we beat and how. St. Vincent had abolished varsity football abruptly after the 1962 season. Players who had come for football and given financial aid were allowed to keep their deal if they chose to stay. The last of those guys were in the Class of '66, were seniors now, and were dominating intramural football. They called their floor "The Jungle" and their team "The Jungle Bunnies." They were arrogant and expected to win and did in fact win every game until that fateful day.

Intimidation was their strong suit and what they relied on. We would have died before we showed any fear or gave an inch. We went into this game like we were going to war. It also helped that we scouted them by watching their last two playoff games, but in their arrogance, they saw no need to scout us.

It was about as intensely played a game as could be. Lou Posa, Rich Ruffalo, Greg Shlopak, and Jim Fink were terrific up front and their confidence grew as the game went on.

The hitting was fierce and every play intense as the half ended scoreless. During the half, the crowd had grown and almost everyone was rooting for us. Tom Castle and Tom Griffin both played for another sophomore class team, "The Radistats" (I have no idea what that means) from Gerry II, and they came right into our halftime meeting to urge us on.

"You can beat these fuckers!" said Griffin, shaking his fist.

"They are worried," added Castle, excitedly. "We just walked by them and they are arguing and finger pointing."

Word spread throughout the campus that the Jungle Bunnies were in trouble and the crowd grew bigger and louder. Tom Mateja, one of our linebackers, started taunting Frank Vukmanic, one of the Bunnies' wide receivers. Vukmanic was extremely cocky and after catching one pass early, Mateja and our defensive backs had shut him out. Now Mateja was yelling, "Voookie, Voookie," in an extremely high-pitched voice before and after every play. No matter which side Vukmanic would line up on, Mateja would go to that side and hit him at the line of scrimmage.

Soon some of the fans picked up on it and were screaming, "Voookie, Voookie." Vookie did seem rattled and the Bunnies could not score. Our defense was dominating, but we couldn't seem to score either.

Near the end, Bob Davie called a time out and said, "I think it's time for the sleeper play."

"You're right," answered Zadai. "Now would be a good time."

The sleeper play was a trick play where a few guys ran in as substitutions and a few guys ran out. The trick was that Tim Zadai, one of our receivers, would seem to leave as Joe Rose substituted for him, but in the shuffle that purposely looked confusing, Zadai did not leave the field, but stood near the sideline, looking in as if he was out of the game.

When the huddle broke, the Bunnies didn't notice it was one guy short. As we had discussed, Bob Davie went on a quick count to avoid detection. At the snap, Zadai turned and headed downfield. The deception worked and no one was near him. Davie threw a nice easy pass that seemed to take forever to reach Zadai. We all held our breath as Zadai caught it and ran for the end zone.

After that play, our defense was so pumped the Bunnies couldn't gain a yard.

"Voookie, Voookie, Voookie" was echoing all over the field.

We *won!* We had stood up to them physically as well as outsmarted them. The Sophomores from Gerry III had beaten the arrogant Seniors. How sweet it was! Guys from every class applauded as we walked off the field and back to Gerry III where we partied long into the night.

The Champs pose for a picture in Gerry III shortly after the game.

"... and we partied long into the night!"

Someone had a camera and snapped some pictures of us celebrating. After hours of drinking, someone suggested we take a picture of us mooning the Jungle Bunnies and we post it on the bulletin board on their floor. Ten guys who shall remain anonymous formed a pyramid of moons for a picture and a week later, after it was developed and copied, it was posted in the Jungle.

Events like these led to a huge banner being painted and hung from Gerry III across the width of Gerard Hall for Spring Weekend. It read: "Gerry III—The Greatest Show on Earth."

Although we bonded first as a floor, various events brought us together as a class as well. Our class 'keggers' were masterpieces. We collaborated on renting places, having beer and food delivered, getting dates, transportation, music and cleanup. We were underage in Pennsylvania at the time and yet nothing ever went wrong (unless you count stealing a school bus and knocking up our girlfriends). The details of our keg parties were communicated on signs posted openly in the dorms as a meeting of the Aviators Club. A typical sign would read: "Aviators Fly This Weekend" and below would be the details. Everyone understood.

One night I was studying in my room when I heard some commotion in the hall and then a knock on my door. As I opened the door, I heard yelling.

"We got guys in trouble at the Highway Diner. Head for the Highway Diner now. If you have a car, get it and take as many guys as you can."

I quickly grabbed a jacket and headed for the stairway. When I got there, it looked like a fire drill. The stairwell was full of guys running down. Once outside, there were guys piling into cars and speeding off toward the Highway Diner.

"I need a ride," I started yelling to no one in particular.

"Who's got a car?" someone yelled.

The student parking lot was about a quarter of a mile from Gerard Hall. A car pulled up driven by Bob Gondolf and about eight guys jumped in and we took off for the diner. There was one traffic light on the way, and when we stopped, we saw about eight cars full of Bearcats, and one pickup truck. The truck had about a dozen guys in it, and most of them had baseball bats in their hands. One of the guys was the equipment manager of the baseball team and he threw the bat bag in the truck.

"Oh my God," I said gleefully as I took in this sight. "Where'd they get a truck?"

Someone in the front seat with a better view of inside the cab of the truck answered, "It's Father Melvin driving!" Father Melvin was a prefect and did a great deal of gardening and landscape work on campus and had a truck to use for such work. When he heard of the trouble, he got his truck, and took whoever wanted to go.

Meanwhile, at the Highway Diner was a small group of our guys. Bill McGee was wearing a raincoat that was styled like a Paris policeman's. It had slits for your arms to come through and hung like a cape. A larger group of mean-looking locals were drunk and seemed to be offended by McGee's coat.

They called him a variety of non-flattering names and accused him openly of being a non-heterosexual. The entire time our guys were trying to eat, the taunting escalated. The locals were now on their feet and threatening our guys. The manager of the diner knew that trouble was about to happen and was only concerned that it not happen inside the diner. The manager pleaded with the locals to "take it outside."

The locals agreed.

"Finish up, boys, 'cause there's an ass-woopin' comin,'" one of them taunted. "I got you, college boy," one of them said, glaring at Greg Stock. "I'm gettin' me that fancy raincoat and giving it to my girlfriend," promised another.

What almost no one noticed was that Pete Hutchinson had pretended to go to the men's room and quietly ducked into a phone booth and called the second floor of Gerard Hall, where he lived. It only took a few seconds to say 'send help' and where the trouble was and he returned to the table. Hutch knew help was on the way although he had no idea how much help was on the way.

The rest of our guys were getting very nervous now as the waitresses, at the manager's urging, hurriedly collected what was owed them and the locals gathered around and started to get in our guys' faces, taunting them and urging them to get up.

Frank Bonati, unaware that Hutch had called the dorm for help, suddenly bolted for the phone booth. One of the locals chased after him, but Frank managed to close the door and held it closed while he made a call to Gerry III.

"Go ahead, call you mother, tell her you're a dead man," yelled the one of them.

Frank was frantic as the phone rang and rang and rang.

"Why doesn't someone answer the fucking phone?" he muttered to himself, leaning against the door with all his weight.

H and Pat Greco had just returned to Gerry III from the library where they were studying and H heard the phone ringing as he entered from the stairwell. He heard it ringing as he went into his room and put his books down on his desk. It was still ringing as he started down the hall toward the phone booth.

"Why doesn't someone answer the fucking phone?" he said loudly.

When H answered the phone, Bonati quickly told him that a group of them was in big trouble.

"Get as many guys as you can and get here fast or we are gonna get hurt."

He hung up and started yelling and going door to door, but found no one. Greco quickly ran down to Gerry II and also found no one. Stoically, the two of them headed down to the parking lot for H's car. They were confused and worried, but they were going.

Meanwhile back on the highway, by the time the light turned green, a few more cars full of Bearcats had arrived and the entire convoy of cars and the truck sped about a half mile further to the diner.

"Looks like we made it in time," someone said, as about fifty guys, some with bats, entered the Highway Diner.

The locals were stunned and suddenly acted like it was just a little joking around. There was some jostling and a few punches and one of the locals was bleeding badly. *Now* the manager called the police. Greg Stock was screaming for someone to smash the jukebox with a bat. Father Melvin, concerned that the police were on the way and feeling that the rescue had been accomplished, strongly urged everyone to leave immediately. Carloads of guys were still arriving as we quickly got back in vehicles and left.

As the caravan arrived back at school, we ran into a greatly relieved H and Greco. They had resigned themselves to taking a beating.

"Why didn't you call the cops?" asked Lloyd.

"Why didn't Bonati call the cops?" answered H, showing that he had given some thought to that course of action.

Although we avoided the police that time, we weren't so lucky a few months later in Greensburg. A bunch of us were in a bar called "Leonard's" partaking of their special on pitchers of Rolling Rock, when a group of locals, for some unknown reason, hit Mike Heaney in the head with an empty pitcher, and then tried to run out the door.

A brawl ensued. The pitcher shattered on Heaney's head, and glass flew everywhere, then tables, chairs, glasses, and bottles. I swung and hit one guy hard, but was a little off target and hit him in the forehead. I thought I broke a bone—my fist hurt so bad. One of the locals hit me from behind in the ear and I thought I had gone deaf. *It* hurt like hell and sounded like the ocean was in my head.

The police came quickly and arrested me, Greg Shlopak, and Kevin Coakley. No locals were arrested. All three of us had been sitting at the bar, away from where Heaney had been sitting and only were involved in defense of Mike Heaney. Of course, it didn't help that none of us were of legal drinking age. The police took us to the city jail, took our personal belongings, our belts, and locked us in cells.

Coakley, who was a pre-law student, informed the police that we had a right to a phone call and demanded to exercise this right.

The cop said, "No."

Coakley started telling the cop about Miranda and how no one has informed us of our rights and demanding to make a phone call.

The cop said, "No."

Greg and I were outraged and started screaming at the cops about the Constitution of the United States and our guys fighting and dying in Vietnam.

The cop calmly said that we weren't calling anyone. Shlopak said, "My father's a lawyer and he's going to be very upset when he hears about this."

"I hope so," replied the cop as he left and locked a big steel door behind him.

"Boy, what a crock of shit," said Coakley as he lay down on the bed in his cell.

"Is your dad really a lawyer?" asked Coakley, hoping it was true.

"Yeah," he answered without much enthusiasm.

"Well, that's cool," I said. "What's his name?"

"Igor," answered Shlopak.

"Igor?" I said, surprised.

"Yeah, Igor," said Shlopak, smiling.

"Will Igor help us?" I asked laughing.

"Igor? Help us," yelled Coakley and he broke up laughing.

Suddenly, Igor seemed very funny. We were all laughing and yelling for Igor to help us.

After a while, we settled down, and were all lying on our cell beds, getting sleepy.

Just before I dozed off, I asked Shlopak, "Seriously, Greg, will Igor help us?"

"Well," Shlopak answered, "there are two problems with that. One is that Igor is a patent attorney . . ." he said, his voice trailing off.

"What's the second problem?" I asked with hope dimming.

"The second is that I'm hoping Igor doesn't hear about this."

In the morning I awoke to the voice of Father Earl, the Dean of Men at SVC.

"Okay, guys, listen up and listen carefully," he began. "This is not the first time I've been here and, I suspect, it won't be the last. If you want to leave with me now, you walk out with me now, pick up your personal belongings on the table in the office, and proceed out the door without saying a word."

"But, Father . . ." we started, intending to tell him of the grave injustices we had endured.

"No buts!" he yelled. "I know the whole story. Either do what I ask or you're on you own."

Each of us in turn agreed and Father Earl went to tell the cops. One officer returned with Father Earl and unlocked our cells and led us to a table upon which were our wallets and belts. It was hard not to say something, but true to form, Greg Shlopak, without saying a word, picked up his wallet and very conspicuously, counted the money in it, as if checking to see that it was all there. We started to laugh, but a stern, "Let's go, guys" from Father Earl wiped the smiles off our faces, and we walked out into the late morning sun, with the charges against us dropped.

Police Arrest
Three Students

Three St. Vincent College students, all 20 years of age, were arrested by Greensburg police at 3 a.m. yesterday and charged with disorderly conduct.

They were Kevin Coakley, Gregory P. Sholpak and Joseph W. Farrell.

Greensburg police took the trio into custody at the corner of W. Otterman and Jefferson Sts. They were released to college officials.

The stories about those years living on Gerry III could go on and on. On any given night, just a walk through Gerry III was fun and uplifting. Just the music was worth the walk. The Mamas and the Papas, the Beatles, the Byrds, Bob Dylan, Simon and Garfunkel, The Righteous Brothers, The Association, the Beach Boys, Donovan and the Young Rascals all were likely to be heard as you passed by the rooms.

Often you would encounter Ed Kulnis or Don Morris or Ray Brannon playing guitar and leading a sing-along or Shlopak, Zadai, Bob McCarthy, and Kulnis working on their Four Tops imitation. Steve Dice would most likely be taking orders for a late night food run to Eat 'n' Park and Greg Stock would be writing a paper for someone else for his standard fee (he guaranteed an A for $10 or a B for $5. If you tried to get one cheaper for a C, he would say he just wasn't capable of C work and would refer you to Steve Dice.)

Kulnis, McCarthy, Zadai, and Shlopak working on their Four Tops' imitation.

If Muir wasn't asleep on the washroom floor, he would be studying Economics with Joe Campus and discussing whether or not to cut the upcoming exam. They once cut an exam just before Spring Break and sent the professor, Father Calistus, a postcard from Florida. "The weather is here, wish you were great," it read.

Once, while I was walking down the hall, Zadai suddenly came tear-assing around a corner, and darted into the shower room. Bonati came around the corner a few seconds later with his bayonet in his hands in hot pursuit, breathing heavily as if the chase had been going on for some time. He saw a door to a room open a crack and assumed that Zadai had gone in there and was in the process of closing the door.

He threw his body at the door to prevent it from closing. Bonati was wrong and the door flew open with loud crash against the wall. Inside, an unsuspecting Jim McCarthy was quietly studying at his desk and was startled by Bonati bursting into his room. He became more than startled, when he saw a wild-eyed Bonati brandishing a bayonet!

Each room in Gerard Hall had two tall recessed windows with drapes that could be drawn or opened for each window. It was possible to stand on the window sill—and with the drapes drawn, not be seen from inside the room. This is what Bonati thought Zadai had done. Since he didn't see him anywhere in the room, he thought Zadai was on McCarthy's window sill behind the drawn drapes.

"Come out!" he yelled, challenging the drapes.

"Come out, you fuck! I got you now!"

I stood in the hallway, watching with amusement. McCarthy remained seated at his desk as if frozen in terror.

"Come out now or I'll cut your balls off! I'll cut them off and feed them to wild dogs, you fuck!" screamed Bonati.

He got no response. Suddenly, Bonati saw a shoe on the floor that had a wooden shoe tree in it. (McCarthy was a science major and thus everything in his room was meticulously organized and he used shoe trees to keep his shoes nice.) The shoe tree made his shoe heavy and solid. Bonati grabbed it by the toe end and threw it hard at the window. I watched in amazement as the shoe hit the window with a loud crack.

"Whoa!" said Bonati, as he realized he had cracked the window. He pulled the drapes open, and saw that Zadai wasn't there.

"Sorry," said Frank, meekly, as he walked out of the room, and ran down the hall yelling that Zadai was a dead man. McCarthy's door slammed closed and I heard it lock. McCarthy never said anything to Bonati about it.

Bob Rakoczy was an unusual guy who lived on Gerry III. He loved going to flea markets and owned a lot of unusual stuff. Old clothes, old maps, old books, and a lot what most of us would call junk. One night, a bunch of us were in the hallway discussing world events and watching H and Greco play some handball game they had invented using a tennis ball and the wall at the end of the hall. Rakoczy suddenly appeared in a vest with a sheriff's badge on and announced that he was going to arrest Joe Rose on charges of being a "useless piece of shit" and wanted to know if anyone had any objection.

A short while later, Rakoczy shows up again in coat and tie, carrying a Bible and asks if there is anyone who would like to testify on Rose's behalf. No one did. A few of us offered to testify against him, but Rakoczy said he had plenty of evidence against him, but couldn't find anyone to testify on his behalf.

A short while later Rakoczy appeared again, this time wearing a judge's robe and holding a gavel. He says Rose has been found guilty of being a useless piece of shit and is about to sentence him to be hanged and does anyone have anything to say on his behalf. No one did again, so he polled each one of us, individually, "just to make it all official-like." Everyone voted thumbs down.

As the handball game ended and we started breaking up at the end of the hall, Rakoczy was seen heading toward Rose's room with a rope. Some of the guys followed to see what was going on. Later they reported that Rakoczy was going to carry out the sentence. He kept insisting that Justice be served when various guys tried to dissuade him. Only when someone pointed out that a hanging in the dorm could cause the scheduled kegger to be cancelled, did Rakoczy decide on a stay of execution. Joe Rose was greatly relieved.

When I left Gerry III in June of 1967, there were four hundred and sixty thousand soldiers in Vietnam.

CHAPTER TWENTY-THREE

♦ ♦ ♦ ♦ ♦

"THE PROMISE IS BROKEN"

When the promise is broken, you go on living
But it steals something from down in your soul
Like when the truth is spoken and it don't make no difference
Something in your heart goes cold . . .
                            Bruce Springsteen—"The Promise"

There were also some unsettling moments during these years at St. Vincent and we did feel anxiety and grief, dread and despair. These were unusual and tumultuous times and gave rise to unusual and new feelings.

The anxiety was more than the usual college student anxiety about exams, paying tuition, sex, love, and grade point averages. It was a more pervasive, sinister, divisive anxiety. The Civil Rights movement was one source of this anxiety. There was something deeply wrong in America and most of us agreed and did what we could about it. It was deeply disturbing to see black Americans beaten and lynched for trying to register to vote or for peacefully marching against discrimination. It was also disturbing to encounter someone amongst us *not* upset about it.

It was disturbing to see cities erupt in violence all across America and to have Stokely Carmichael come to our campus and blame us. As the violence spread and the rhetoric became more heated, lines became drawn that divided us, our families, the movement itself, and the nation. It was a very new type of anxiety and a new intellectual and emotional challenge.

Were you racist? Were you prejudiced? Were you upset by the institutionalized prejudice and racism that existed? Did you support Martin Luther King? Malcolm X? Eldridge Cleaver? How did you feel about the Black Muslims? The Black Panthers? "Black Power"? "Freedom Riders"? J. Edgar Hoover? George Wallace?

The answers to these questions divided us. No one felt the same way about all these things and with emotions running high all across America, a lot of assumptions were made and a lot of arguments ensued.

If you marched in a demonstration against discrimination, were you okay with the violence and rioting in the cities? If you spoke out against the violence, were you a bigot? If you read "Soul on Ice" and thought it was the rationalizations and sick rants of a psychopath, were you a narrow-minded prejudiced white man who didn't understand being black in America? If you said you liked it, was it because you felt too guilty to be critical of anything a black man did?

All through my college years, these issues raged and intensified and united us and divided us.

Another strange new feeling occurred when the District Attorney of New Orleans, Jim Garrison, claimed to have solved the JFK assassination. At the time, a documentary film based on Mark Lane's book, "Rush to Judgment," was making the rounds and due to the publicity, many of us read the book. When Jim Garrison claimed to have solved the murder of our president and made arrests for the murder of JFK, many of us were flabbergasted.

A group of us stayed up all night discussing the Warren Commission's findings and the criticisms offered in "Rush to Judgment." Not one of us believed that Lee Harvey Oswald acted alone or was the single shooter. Bill Lloyd led the discussion and having a copy of the book, read passages from it. As the hours passed, a spooky feeling started to infiltrate the room. Could it be that our national government purposely covered up the truth of what happened?

If so, why?

The first answer proposed was that the truth would lead to nuclear war and mutual annihilation. Oswald had a Russian wife and visited the Soviet Union. Surely this must be the reason! The Soviets were behind it. Oswald was a Soviet agent and if the public found out, they would demand retribution and our government didn't want a nuclear war. We were happy with that answer for a few minutes. Then some of us started poking holes in the theory.

Jack Ruby was no Soviet agent, so our government must have gotten him to kill Oswald. What threat could make Ruby kill Oswald in a police station on national television?

It didn't make sense.

"I can think of another reason the government would cover up the truth," said Lloyd.

"You're a history major," I replied. "You're supposed to wait until all the data is in before you draw any conclusions. You're supposed to wait until it's too late!" I chided.

"It *is* too late!" Lloyd replied.

"Come on, tell us," said Jim Fink. "Tell us the other reason the government would lie."

"Well," answered Lloyd, obviously enjoying being the center of attention, "maybe part of the government was involved . . ."

"Oh, man, don't tell me that," cried Fink.

"Hey, I'm just saying it makes sense."

"It can't be true. It can't be true," proclaimed Fink, shaking his head in disbelief.

"You just don't wanna believe it, but it's the only explanation that makes sense," responded Lloyd.

"But it doesn't make sense," insisted Fink. "The whole Warren Commission is in on a plot to kill the president?"

"No, that's not what I'm saying."

"Then what are you saying?"

"I'm saying that parts of our intelligence agencies were in on a plot to kill Kennedy and have tampered with evidence and testimony to mislead the Warren Commission."

"Oh, Jesus, that's scary," said Fink. "I'm going to bed. It's not safe to talk about it if what you say is true." Fink rose to leave the room and offered one last thought.

"How come it looks that way to us, but the Warren Commission didn't see it?"

"That's the beauty of being an historian," replied Lloyd. "They didn't have time to collect all the data and see the big picture. The book is called "*Rush* to Judgment" after all."

It did indeed bring on a strange feeling to think such a thing might have happened. To think that maybe a few rogue members of our government's intelligence community could and would have our president murdered and successfully keep the truth from being discovered was a disturbing thought to most of us, especially given the other tumultuous events of the 1960s.

And then there was Vietnam; always, there was Vietnam. It lurked in the background, hauntingly, slowly, relentlessly growing week by week, month by month, slowly eroding everything we believed about America. Vietnam was stalking us.

When we left high school, I doubt any of us could quickly find Vietnam on a map of the world. The only mention of Vietnam was an occasional reference on a news show. As we went through freshman year, there were articles in the news magazines about President Johnson authorizing bombing raids (Operation Rolling Thunder) in North Vietnam and then a few troops were sent to guard the air base from which we launched the bombs.

In our sophomore year, the war escalated greatly as did the anti-war protests. B-52s were used to carpet bomb the north, over one hundred thousand troops were sent and almost all of us knew of young Americans were being killed and wounded in the jungles of Vietnam. The footage on television showed the fighting in the rice paddies and hamlets with thatched huts, and in the thick jungle. Friends were signing up or getting drafted and some signing up to avoid getting drafted. There were protests in Congress, in our cities and on our campuses and around the world.

When we started our junior year, it was a pervasive issue that was tearing our campuses, our families, our communities, and our nation apart and directly threatening our lives. The draft was running full bore and although being a student exempted most of us from the draft, there was no guarantee.

Bob Flynn got drafted even though he was attending SVC. As Draft Boards exhausted the existing pools of 1A's, they started challenging student deferments. If a student flunked out or needed a semester off to work and earn money for tuition, they were sure to be drafted. Saying good-bye to Bob Flynn really got to me and others on Gerry III.

Then word came from home that Dennis Geoghan had been drafted into the Marines. I had never heard of anyone being drafted into the Marines and at first didn't believe it but Bill Landers talked to friends in New York and confirmed that indeed Dennis was in Boot Camp on Parris Island.

Almost all of us thought of Marine Basic Training on Parris Island as a nightmare. Being drafted into the Marines during a war? Well, forget it.

Dennis was smart and a terrific athlete so we shouldn't have been surprised when a letter arrived from him saying he had no problem at all with basic training and that he had excelled at everything. "It's all hype," Dennis wrote. "Nothing to it." The thing that scares me, Dennis wrote, is the guys I'm with. They like it! They think it's fun and exciting!

Shortly after Dennis was drafted, I heard that Eddie Haggerty had joined the Army and was in Basic Training. Eddie was tired of the threat of being drafted and was recruited by the Army to be in intelligence. Intelligence work sounded better than being in the infantry and so Eddie quit St. Francis College in Brooklyn and went in the service.

Both Dennis and Eddie were promptly sent to Vietnam.

Dennis wrote from California, then the Philippines, and finally from Pleiku, right smack in the middle of South Vietnam. Pleiku was the site of a Viet Cong attack on a special force base the year before, which led to further escalation by the U.S. It sounded horrible and whenever I watched the news on television, I would watch and listen for Pleiku to get a glimpse of what it was like.

Then word came that Dennis had been wounded in a mortar attack and was headed home. Fortunately, Dennis's wounds were not serious and we visited him in St. Albans' Naval Hospital where he was recovering.

I was a little nervous about what we were walking into as we were led in to see him, but Dennis quickly showed he was his old self by telling us all about meeting actress Jill St. John, who was visiting troops in military hospitals. "She was fucking gorgeous," Dennis kept repeating. "I'm telling ya. She is fucking gorgeous. Ya think those movie stars look good in movies with makeup and camera angles and lighting and all that shit, but she looks fantastic—better than in the movies."

Eddie ironically also wound up in Pleiku. He was there during the famous Tet Offensive, which was generally regarded as the turning point of the war. I had a hard time picturing Eddie in the Army but when I did, I felt pretty sure that he would be killed in Vietnam. The guy who wouldn't rat me out to Sister Charles Marie in seventh grade, despite being hit in the face repeatedly—the guy who thrust his hands in his pockets in determination to take whatever punishment was coming—was, it seemed to me, the type of guy who would get killed in combat. I figured either the Viet Cong would piss him off and he'd go after them or he'd piss off some officer who would put him in harm's way. Eddie didn't write to any of the guys very much, so I rarely heard anything about him except that he was in some radio Intelligence outfit in the jungle.

The war dragged on month after month, year after year with no end in sight. The flag draped caskets arriving home on the TV news and in the news magazines brought the reality of the suffering and sadness and the tragedy of it all to our minds regularly.

War is awful but this felt different than we imagined the wars our fathers and uncles had fought. "Why are we doing this?" we wondered. Why is the greatest and the most powerful country on earth waging war in a jungle, halfway around the world, against a peasant nation? Why were we dropping more bombs on a poor third world country the size of New Jersey than all parties dropped during World War II?

We were raised to believe that we were the most powerful and technically advanced country in the world but that we would only use our might in defense of our freedom. So how, we asked, do the peasants of Vietnam threaten our security and freedom? We wanted to believe in our government and that we were doing the right thing and our young men—our friends, our brothers—were dying out of necessity.

It was like we were promised that America could be trusted never to wage an unnecessary or immoral war and now that promise was being broken.

On Gerry III, one night, I walked into a discussion of the morality of war in Bonati's room. Guys were coming in and out of the room, and in and out of the discussion that covered the use of napalm, cluster bombs, and chemical agents as well as the morality of the war in general. When Jerry Greenwood raised the morality of killing, Bonati erupted. "That's a stupid argument," said Bonati to Greenwood when he mentioned that killing for any reason might be wrong.

"Why is it stupid?" asked Greenwood, his tone suggesting he had just hit on the crux of the argument.

"Because it is," shrugged Bonati, who was laying on his bed with his bayonet.

"Oh, that's very intelligent," challenged Greenwood. "Is that your imitation of Descartes? 'It's stupid because it is'?"

"I'm not familiar with Descartes but if he won't kill people that are trying to kill him, then he's nuts, and I don't care what he thinks."

"Descartes said 'I think, therefore I am,'" chipped in Bill Lloyd.

"Yeah, well, if he's dead, he won't be thinking, therefore he's not," countered Bonati.

We all laughed at Frank's witty response and then Greenwood asked, "Who do you think is trying to kill you, Frank?" with a tone that implied Bonati just might be paranoid.

"The Viet Cong, you moron," responded Bonati.

"The Viet Cong are trying to kill you?" said Greenwood with skepticism in his voice.

"Yeah, I believe so," answered Bonati.

"Oh, really? Why?" asked Greenwood.

"Well, I'm not sure why, really, since I've never talked to one of them, but I think it's because we invaded their country," responded Bonati.

"Oh, you mean they'd *be* trying to kill you if you were there?" asked Greenwood as if he had just made an important point.

"Of course that's what I mean, you fucking asshole. What did you think I meant? What are we talking about?" Bonati yelled, waving his bayonet.

"Well, I wasn't sure what you meant since you are brandishing a bayonet."

"This is for the assholes like you, Jerry, not the Viet Cong," said Bonati, to everyone's delight.

"So you'd kill Viet Cong or who you think are Viet Cong because they're trying to kill you?" Greenwood summarized.

"Fuckin' A."

"Suppose you're not sure if they are VC?" posed Greenwood.

"Dead," answered Bonati.

"You have *no* problem with that?" asked Greenwood.

"*I'll kill them all,*" screams Bonati swinging his bayonet wildly.

"Because you think they are trying to kill you?"

"That's right!"

"But they are only trying to kill you because you are in their country," chimed in Bill Lloyd.

"So?" answered Bonati.

"So doesn't that change the morality of it?" Lloyd asked.

"No," said Bonati.

"Why not?" asked Lloyd. "I'm not arguing with you. I'm just curious as to your view."

"Because," answered Bonati loudly as if he was frustrated with repeating himself, "they are trying to kill ME!"

"And the reason doesn't matter?" Greenwood asked.

"Not to me!" Bonati screamed. "Should I LET them kill me if they have a good reason?"

"You could leave their country," offered Greenwood.

"*You* are a fuckin' idiot. You know that?" erupted Bonati. "I wouldn't be in their fuckin' country if I had a choice, asshole."

"Well, you do have a free will," pointed out Greenwood. "Nobody can make you go."

"You just like pissin' people off, Greenwood?" answered Bonati. "I hope you go, get captured, they cut your nuts off, and feed them to wild pigs."

"I'd rather go to Canada," stated Greenwood.

"Or even back to Ohio," I interjected.

"You've been awful quiet, Farrell," said Greenwood. "I'd prefer Vietnam to Flushing for sure."

"It'd be just as dangerous for you," I responded.

"Ooooh, Mr. Macho," said Greenwood. "Where do you stand in this discussion?"

"You mean about killing?" I asked.

"Yeah."

"To be honest, I haven't thought about it," I answered. "All I've thought about is being killed or maybe worse, horribly injured for no good reason."

"That's big of you," laughed Lloyd.

"Well, I'm being honest," I answered. "I don't want to die. I don't want to kill. I don't want to go."

"Very patriotic," laughed Fink.

"Sounds like a protest song title," chipped in Conroy, who had just stepped in.

"I don't know what this fight is about, so I can't feel that I want to be in it much less die for it," I explained.

"It's about oil," said Lloyd.

"Oil?" a bunch of us said.

"Yeah, oil. I'll bet you there is oil in Vietnam and that's what this is about," said Lloyd.

"I never heard that before," I said.

"Oh, yeah," said Lloyd. "It makes sense, doesn't it?"

"More sense than LBJ or McNamara," I answered.

"I'm not dying for oil," shouted Bonati.

"But you'd kill for it," shouted Greenwood.

"Fucking Jerry Greenwood," said Bonati as he waved his bayonet and started to get up off his bed.

Greenwood ran out of the room and Bonati got to his feet and went to his door but instead of chasing after Greenwood, he slammed the door to his room.

"He's a screwy little fucker," said Frank shaking his head back and forth. "Did you know his parents moved and didn't tell him?"

"No, really?" asked Fink.

"Yeah," answered Bonati. "When Greenwood went home for Christmas, he went to his house and there were strangers living there. He asked the strangers what they were doing in his house and found that his family moved and forgot to tell him."

"Or at least that's what they told him," laughed Fink.

In a minute or so, the joviality of the moment wore off and talk turned to the reality that was facing all of us. In general, our choices were: to sign up for the branch of service we preferred and maybe even the type of assignment we'd prefer; wait to be drafted and hope somehow to get a deferment; flee to Canada; or go to jail.

Jail, of course, was not appealing to anyone. The prospect of fleeing to Canada was also very disturbing. Leaving behind friends and family and never being allowed back in the U.S. without being arrested was a sad alternative to jail. Enlisting meant we could pick our branch of service and if we made it to graduation, be an officer. Sometimes enlisting gave us choices of flight school, Intelligence work, or some sort of specialty. Waiting to be drafted meant we would lose complete control and most likely be sent to Vietnam as a grunt.

This was the situation that haunted us all through college as the war—a war we didn't understand—grew bigger and bigger.

CHAPTER TWENTY-FOUR

♦ ♦ ♦ ♦ ♦

"MY LUCKY DAY"

In a room where future falls
On a day when choice is all
In the dark of this exile
I felt the grace of your smile
       Bruce Springsteen—"My Lucky Day"

I have always been amazed and fascinated at the small, unexpected twists of fate that can turn out to be so important in a person's life and how most days that are supposed to be important aren't.

November 4, 1966, started like a normal Friday. I went to classes, worked in the cafeteria, ate dinner, put a six pack of Rolling Rock on the windowsill to chill and studied until 10:00 p.m.

There was a "mixer" on campus that night and buses filled with Seton Hill students—our all women sister school—had come over for the mixer.

By ten o'clock, I had finished about three beers and decided to head over to the mixer. I left the other three on the windowsill for the usual mixer post-mortem that took place when the buses returned to Seton Hill and we returned to Gerry III.

I had just broken up with a Seton Hill girl, who was rich, beautiful, and in love with me one week ago at an off campus party at the Cole Athletic Club in Greensburg. I had told her I didn't feel the same way about her. She asked me why and I told her the absolute truth, "I don't know why."

So as I walked into the mixer in Alcuin Hall, I had very low expectations. I felt bad about ending a relationship but also a sense of freedom that I hadn't felt in months. I knew Seton Hill was a small school and the girl was very popular and that some of her friends would probably think poorly of me. I didn't have another girlfriend. I just didn't feel the same way about her and honestly told her so. I didn't know why. There was nothing wrong with her. She was nice. She was smart. She was beautiful. She did nothing wrong. I felt boxed in and didn't really know how that had happened.

As I stood in Alcuin Hall taking in the scene, I noticed a beautiful girl with dark hair and blue eyes who was dancing with another girl. I watched her for a while and didn't see her with a guy, to my surprise. It took me about a half hour to work up the courage to ask her to dance. She danced with me and when I introduced myself, she told me that she knew who I was and all about the breakup with her friend.

"Sounds to me like you're a real prick," she said.

We left Alcuin Hall so we could more easily continue the conversation. We walked around aimlessly and wound up sitting on a bench on the soccer field. I told her why I had broken up with her friend and she seemed very skeptical of my story.

"I am supposed to keep an eye on you tonight and report back to her," she said.

"What do you mean?" I asked.

"I'm supposed to tell her if you were at the mixer and if you were with anyone. She thinks there's someone else."

Soon it was time for the buses to leave. We walked together to the bus and said goodnight.

"It was nice talking to you," I said. "Maybe I'll see you again sometime."

It was midnight and as I headed back to Gerry III, I still had no idea that it had been the most important day of my life, nor would I for quite some time.

On Gerry III, a bunch of guys were in H's room doing a post-mortem on the night. Things hadn't gone H's way with a girl he was interested in and he was crying the blues.

H was a lot of fun to pick on and so I went to my room, got a beer off the windowsill and hurried back to H's room.

"Who was that girl you were with?" asked Lloyd as I sat down on H's bed.

"Gracie Dirienzo," I answered.

"A new conquest?" he asked.

"What the hell does that mean?"

"Well, you two looked pretty intense when I saw you headed into the darkness." He continued.

"Calm down, Lloyd," I responded. "All we did was talk. Let's get back to H."

"You're a psych major," started H, "maybe you can figure out this girl. I'm sure having trouble."

"I don't think it's her," I answered. "I think it's you."

"Me?"

"Yep. You."

"Why do you say that?"

"Because you're too uptight. You need to relax," I started.

"Oh, good," said Lloyd. "He's going to psychoanalyze H. This ought to be good."

"Why do you say that?" asked H in earnestness failing to realize that I was just playing around.

"Well," I answered, "I'm sitting here on your perfectly made bed and as I look around, I see on your closet shelf sets of colored towels with matching washcloths all folded and piled neatly."

"Yeah. So . . . ?"

"So that's fucked up," I concluded. "Nobody does that."

"What's wrong with that?" H yelled.

"That's obsessive compulsive behavior," I answered, "or what we in the field of psychology call crazy."

"Bullshit." Yelled H. "Don't you have towels and washcloths?"

"I do, but they don't match," I replied. "And I don't use a washcloth. Who uses a washcloth anyway? Is there some part of your body you don't like to touch with your hand?"

Lloyd and Tim Zadai were loving this and acting like they were in complete agreement.

"This," I concluded, "is why girls don't like you."

"Who said girls don't' like me?" yelled H. "I didn't say that!"

"Well, they don't." I answered.

"Let me get this straight," said H in disbelief. "You're saying that girls don't like me because my towels match?"

"And you have matching washcloths," added Lloyd.

"And they're neatly folded," added Zadai.

"And your bed is neatly made," added Lloyd again.

"And that part about touching yourself," I added laughing.

"So that's why you think girls don't like me?" summed up H.

"No, no, no." I answered. "You are missing the whole point."

"Well, then what is the point?" yelled H, his hands held high, palms open.

"Those are just symptoms," I yelled, sipping on my beer.

"Symptoms of what?" H asked.

"Of rigidity, of obsessive compulsive behavior, of being over-controlling or to use a technical term, of being fucked up." I answered in a sorrowful voice.

There was a knock at the door and Bonati and Shlopak came in.

"Who's going for food?" asked Bonati brandishing his bayonet.

"Hey, Frank. You're a psych major, aren't you?" asked H.

"Yeah! What of it?" answered Bonati through clenched teeth, crouching, and holding the bayonet in a threatening way.

"Calm down," said H. "I have a question for you."

"Yeah, well, whatever it is, I didn't do it and I'm sick of being asked about it," Bonati said loudly now breathing heavily and glaring menacingly at all of us.

"It's not about you. It's about me," H said.

"Oh, okay." Bonati said softly as he abruptly sat down and crossed his legs as if he was anxious to help and relieved that it wasn't about him.

"Do you think I'm . . . what was the term you used?" asked H looking at me.

"Fucked up," I answered.

"Yes!" said Bonati quickly. "Who's going for food? I'm hungry."

We were all laughing at how Bonati answered without hesitation when Shlopak interrupted, "Hey, Farrell. Who was that girl you were with down on the soccer field?"

"Grace Dirienzo." I answered.

"Grace. Huh, how ironic." Shlopak said. "I bet neither of you is in a state of grace now!"

"We just talked," I responded.

"Just talked? I bet! You needed to go down to the soccer field to talk?" Shlopak said in mocking disbelief.

"I'm serious," I insisted.

"I'm sure you *were* serious," laughed Shlopak.

"I know your game. You don't talk much but you always have something going."

"Why would I lie?" I asked. "Do you think I was porking her down on the soccer field?"

"Speaking of pork," interjected Bonati, "let's get some food. I'm hungry."

"Why don't you believe him? H asked of Shlopak. "I'm curious."

"Because I know how he operates," answered Shlopak. "let us smell your hand."

"What?" I answered.

"Let us smell your hand," Shlopak repeated.

"*Smell my hand?*" I asked disbelievingly.

"Okay. Just your index finger," said Shlopak laughing.

"Get out of here, "I said shaking my head and rolling my eyes at Shlopak's request.

"And you think *I'm* fucked up?" yelled H.

"Why do you think H is fucked up?" asked Shlopak.

"Well, that's what we were talking about before you so rudely interrupted." I answered.

"Oh well, go on," said Shlopak. "I can get into this."

Just then, Greg Stock came in the room asking if anyone wanted food from the local Eat 'n Park.

"Get your order and money together and I will be leaving in a few minutes," Stock said.

We began getting our order together as Lloyd wrote it down on a piece of paper from H's desk.

"Put Farrell down for a pork platter," teased Shlopak.

Everyone thought that was hysterical and Stock came back for the order and the money.

"How are you going to carry all this?" asked Zadai.

"Don't worry. Steve Dice is going with me," Stock answered.

"No kidding?" How'd you manage to get Dice out of bed?" asked Lloyd.

"Every time I'd go for food, I'd fuck up Dice's order on purpose. Now he goes along to get it right," laughed Stock.

"He knows if I have to go alone, his order will be wrong."

We thanked Stock profusely and threw in a little extra money for gas, although he didn't do it for that reason

"Okay. Let's get back to H," prodded Lloyd.

"Yeah, so let's hear how H is fucked up," said Bonati.

"Hey, I don't have all night for this," laughed Shlopak. "Is there some specific aspect we can focus on?"

"Well," I began, "it started with H complaining that girls don't like him."

"I never said that," yelled H.

"So, I started telling him that it wasn't just girls. That we are the only ones that like him and we don't really like him that much."

"That's true!" said Bonati trying to be dead serious.

"Farrell says I'm fucked up 'cause my towels match my washcloths, and I'm neat," yelled H in disbelief.

"That is kinda strange," said Bonati

"And his bed is neatly made," added Lloyd.

"And don't forget his closet being all organized," added Zadai.

"Oh, and he doesn't like touching himself in the shower," I added.

"I never said that!!" H screamed.

"Okay." I amended my statement. "It makes him uncomfortable to touch certain parts of his body with his naked hand."

"I never said that either!!" H screamed.

"See how defensive he gets," I said softly to the group.

"It's okay, H," said Shlopak. "It's a normal part of growing up."

"What is?" responded H.

"Having those warm feelings in your loins," answered Shlopak trying to not crack up.

"Do you ever have a wonderful dream and you wake up with hot sticky stuff in your underpants?" asked Bonati.

"No," said H.

"Okay. Well, maybe that's just me then," laughed Bonati, "I hear it's normal."

"What would *you* know about normal?" asked Lloyd.

"I said I *heard* it was normal," yelled Bonati wide eyed and brandishing the bayonet. "I didn't say *I* was normal."

"Now see what you've done?" asked H looking at me. "you have gone and gotten Bonati all upset." "It scares me to think that you could be a psychologist some day."

"What else scares you?" I answered.

"Does it scare you that I could come in here while you're sleeping and cut your throat?" asked Bonati.

"Yes, it does," answered H. "That's why the door is always locked when I'm sleeping."

"What about you, Lloyd?" Bonati asked menacingly. "Is your door always locked?"

"It will be now," answered Lloyd.

Soon Stock came back with our food and we ate and drank beer in H's room.

"By the way," started up Zadai, "did I hear that you got a job at the Rolling Rock Brewery?"

"Yeah, maybe, I answered. "Thank God."

"What do you mean maybe?" asked Bonati

"Manoli gave the brewery my name and Lander's name to work part time but they haven't called us yet."

"Manoli as in Mr. Manoli, the history professor?" asked Lloyd.

"Yeah, he works there, too," I answered.

"I know," said Lloyd. "I wonder why he didn't ask me."

"Because he knows you are a loser," answered Bonati and then turning toward me added, "why do you say Thank God?"

"Because I need money and I think Father Earl hates me."

"What's up with you and Father Earl?" asked Zadai. "I heard something happened but I don't understand it."

"Wait a minute," interrupted Bonati. "What's Father Earl got to do with it?"

"He runs food services," I explained.

"So, he's your boss?" Bonati continued.

"Well, I've been working the cafeteria since first semester last year and he only took over this year and I hardly ever see him or speak to him, yeah, I guess he's my boss," I said.

"So, tell these guys what you did, Joe." Said Shlopak. "I heard all about it."

"Well," I began rolling my eyes and shaking my head in frustration, "guys keep giving Sister Monica a hard time about the food. It's just ridiculous. She just serves the food. She doesn't cook it and she doesn't have anything to do with the menu, yet, guys come in, see what she is dishing out, and give her a hard time. Especially some of the seniors."

"Which one is Sister Monica?" asked Lloyd.

"She's the younger one with the round face," I answered. "She speaks German and doesn't understand most of what the guys are saying but she knows by the tone that they are angry. She asked me last week why the boys are so angry."

"What'd you tell her?" asked H smiling and sensing he would like my answer.

"I told her they didn't like the food and that it wasn't her they were cursing about."

"Did she understand you?" asked H.

"It's hard to tell for sure but I gave her some advice . . ."

"Wait till you hear this," laughed Shlopak. "This is great."

"What'd you tell her?" asked Bonati anxiously.

"I told her that whenever someone was unhappy with the food, tell them 'Das is good shit.'"

The room burst into laughter.

"Ooh you didn't," moaned H gasping for air between laughs. "You didn't!"

"I did, and it was working!" I yelled over the laughing.

Lloyd was wiping tears from his eyes when he asked, "What do you mean it was working?"

"It was working. Guys were laughing when she said it. I swear! Guys were giving Sister Monica a hard time and she would say 'Das is good shit' and they would laugh. She was loving it."

"Well, then, what's the problem?" asked Lloyd.

"Well, last week Father Earl came into the cafeteria for some odd reason, I think he was checking to see how the new juice machine was working out and he heard Sister Monica saying it."

"Here," said Bonati holding out his bayonet.

"Do the honorable thing."

"Oh, God. This is great," said H holding his palm to his chest. "I almost choked on my Big Boy Burger."

"You guys can laugh but I feel sick about it," I said.

"Go on," said H putting some french fries in his mouth. "I'm almost done eating."

"So Father Earl hears her and asks her who told her to say that," I went on "and she, of course, says, 'Joe told me dat.' Father Earl then tells her its bad and not to do it anymore. She was very embarrassed."

"Kill yourself" said Bonati, again offering his bayonet.

"I'm serious. Kill yourself."

"I should have" I muttered "I might yet."

"And so did Father Earl say anything to you?" asked Zadai.

"Yeah, he came over to me and glared at me for a few seconds. I thought he was gonna punch me for a minute. Then he says 'That was pretty low,

Farrell." I told him I was just trying to help her. He said if you want to help her, why don't you speak up and tell these guys they are out of line?"

"That's a great idea" said Shlopak "then everyone will be pissed at *you* instead of food services."

"What'd you say," ask Lloyd.

"I told him I was trying to de-fuse the tenseness with a little bit of humor."

"That's a pretty good answer" observed H. "What'd he say to that."

"He said knocking them on their ass would de-fuse the tenseness."

"That's typical Father Earl" said Lloyd. "Did you say anything to that?"

I said, "I wouldn't think you'd want meals turning into a brawl."

"I would've said, not for a dollar and a quarter an hour" laughed Shlopak.

"What'd he say to that" asked H.

"He said, 'If you don't have the guts, Farrell, then send them to see me.'"

Everybody oooed and ahhhed and I finished the last can of Rolling Rock and smashed it on my forehead to show my frustration. "So that's why I need this Brewery job. That and the fact that it pays nearly three times what I make in the cafeteria."

Soon we were finished eating and drinking and Shlopak and Bonati left. H Started cleaning up the room and bitching about Shlopak and Bonati leaving their garbage behind on Fink's bed. Fink was H's roommate and home for the weekend. Then he announced it was time for the rest of us to leave. We teased him about being a prick ("another reason girls don't' like him" I jabbed') and I headed for my room. On the way to the room, I saw a naked John Muir dragging his mattress into the washroom. It was the end of another night on Gerry III. As I laid in bed, I thought about how much I loved my life at St. Vincent. I loved the guys, the social life and the learning and now without knowing it, I had just finished the luckiest day of my life.

CHAPTER TWENTY-FIVE

♦ ♦ ♦ ♦ ♦

"COMMUNION"

For the one who had a notion
a notion deep inside,
That it ain't no sin
to be glad you're alive.
Bruce Springsteen—"Badlands"

The Met Club had arranged for a group rate on the train from SVC to New York and back for the Christmas break of 1966.

As I settled into my seat at Grand Central Station preparing for the long ride to Latrobe, I had a lot of things on my mind. I was looking forward to the long ride through the night to think about all that happened in the last few weeks. To get the cheapest rate, the train we were on left New York at around 10:00 p.m. and would arrive in Latrobe at around 6:00 a.m. The clickity-clack of the tracks were hypnotic and soothing as the train moved through the night.

I felt I needed this downtime to think. I sat comfortably sprawled in my large train seat with my coat lying over my chest and tried to think about all that happened in some logical order. I knew I was exhausted from all the partying during the break and that I surely would sleep for a lot of the trip but I had a lot of thinking to do and organized them in my mind in the first hour.

I spent the time from New York to Trenton reviewing the horrible accident that had occurred at the SVC Med Club Dance. Billy Landers and Eileen Quinn were in the car ahead of the car I was in on the way home from the Met Club Christmas Party.

Billy was driving and it was raining hard as we left the venue for the party. Billy tried to make a left-hand turn, there was a head-on collision. I ran to their car and had an awful feeling. Eileen's side of the windshield was shattered and she was unresponsive and covered in blood. I thought for sure she was dead. Billy was conscious and dazed and had his hand in his mouth which was gushing blood. Then I noticed his jagged jaw bone was sticking through his cheek and blood was pulsing out.

"Billy, your jaw is broken. Is anything else hurt?" I yelled looking for the nearest phone.

Billy took his hand out of his mouth and said, "Look." I could see several bloody teeth in his hand

"Don't move," I yelled as I saw a phone booth on the corner and "I'll be right back," as I started to run toward it in the rain. I called 911, told them the details, and ran back to the wreck

To my amazement, Eileen was not dead and regaining consciousness. Some of our group were talking to her and trying to help. Billy was still dazed and now was touching his jagged jaw bone with his hand while he held his teeth in his other hand.

Only as I thought about it on the train did I remember the first emergency vehicle to arrive was a tow truck. The driver walked right up to us and asked where we wanted it towed and could he have a name and number. I yelled obscenities at him and was relieved to see police cars arriving followed shortly by an ambulance.

I rode in the ambulance with both of them. Billy kept asking if Eileen was okay and touching his jaw bone as if trying to figure out what was wrong. I assured him Eileen was okay (although I had my doubts) and that no one else had been hurt (miraculously) and that he had a broken jaw and a few missing teeth and would be fine. I didn't mention that those teeth had been driven out of his mouth as his jagged broken jaw bone was driven through his cheek and that I could hardly look at him without passing out

Once at the hospital, I took charge. I gave all their information to the intake staff, kept all their personal belongings and called both sets of parents. The staff in the Emergency Room at Queens General Hospital were very nice to me and appreciated my help. As each set of parents arrived, I greeted them, calmed them down, told them what had happened and took them into the room where Billy and Eileen lay awaiting treatment. Then I called my friends to get a ride home.

While sitting in the waiting room, I started to feel sick. I kept seeing Billy's bone and blood pulsing out where it had come through his cheek. I took some deep breaths and tried to calm down but I felt like I might throw up.

This mixture of wooziness and nausea persisted for a few minutes and then I could fight the urge to vomit no more and got up and raced for the restroom. I had, however, fought the urge for too long and didn't make it. All of the beer and food I had consumed for the past five or six hours was coming up on the floor of the Emergency Room of Queens General Hospital. After a couple of violent spewings on the floor, I was almost to the restroom when I slipped on the vomit and hit my head on the floor hard and lost consciousness.

I woke up laying in vomit with the smell of ammonia from the capsules the nurse held at my nose. Three nurses got me up and sat me on a bench. They took my vital signs, got me water, gave me a wet cloth to clean off the vomit and kept making me sniff smelling salts

Soon a doctor came out and shined a light in my eyes and asked me some questions to see if I had a concussion. I was completely embarrassed and tried to make light of what happened by making some comment about the vomit providing a cushion for the fall.

When my friends came for me, one of the nurses said, "Get him out of here! He was more trouble than both accident victims."

Billy and Eileen were okay now. Billy had his jaw wired shut and ate his meals through a straw. He was going to require extensive dental work when the wires were removed

As we pulled into Trenton, I was debating with myself. I was often amused by the notion of luck. "You were lucky no one was killed or seriously hurt" a number of people said. I agreed with that sentiment but also wondered if it was unlucky to be in that particular spot at that particular time in the rain. Was the other driver lucky or unlucky?

As we pulled out of Trenton, I thought about the physiological psychology course I dropped just before Thanksgiving. When my grades arrived during the Christmas break, I had received a WF (Withdrew Failing) as Father Cuk said I would. I wasn't surprised just a little disappointed. I couldn't understand Father Cuk. After three exams and only the final remaining, I had a solid C in the difficult course. Although I had plenty of Cs on my record already, I didn't have any in a psychology course and knowing I would be applying to graduate school, I didn't want a C in Psych.

I made an appointment with Father Cuk to discuss my dilemma. I thought my reluctance to take a C was a good thing. I was willing to take the whole course again, determined to do better. I really didn't see any other way to look at it.

Once again, Father Cuk and I would clash. He told me that if I dropped the course I would get a WF (Withdrew Failing.) I argued it should be a WP (Withdrew Passing). He said he doesn't give WPs only WFs and added that if I take it again and complete it, the WF would drop off my transcript. (It didn't. It doesn't count but it still shows.)

No matter how hard I argued, he refused to change his decision or explain it. He acted as though I had some kind of trick up my sleeve and he was too smart to be suckered in. I wondered why he seemed to hate me and how it would affect me in his next class, which was his precious legendary Experimental Psychology course. This was Father Cuk's litmus test. This is where he washed out many psych majors. "I better be ready from Day One," I thought to myself as we pulled out of Philadelphia.

"I can't give him any opportunity to screw me."

Realizing that, my thoughts went to the Latrobe Brewery; I did get the job there and was working about two nights a week from four until midnight. The Brewery pad $3.65 per hour and I loved having the money.

The Experimental Psych course was a demanding four credit course and Russian was getting harder and harder demanding more and more memorization which I hated. I was determined to manage my time well and as we pulled into Paoli, I decided that I would study in the library away from the distractions on Gerry III

As we pulled out of Paoli, I sat back and put my coat over me like a blanket. I was hoping to fall asleep thinking about the last item on my list, Gracie DiRienzo.

Since that night we met, I had had a few dates with Gracie. It all started when Ray Brannon, a wrestler, got free tickets to the Varsity Ball and wanted me to double date with him. He promised he would be able to get his father's car and provide the transportation.

His girlfriend Margie went to Seton Hill and, unbeknownst to me, was good friends with Gracie.

"I don't have anyone to take to the Varsity Ball" I told him

"You should ask Gracie" responded Ray. "She likes you."

"What the hell are you talking about?" I asked.

"She accused me of being a prick for breaking up with her friend, Cathy."

"Yeah. Well, she told Margie 'now I see why Cathy was so upset!' How about that!"

"Why am I first hearing about this now you bastard?" How long did you know this?" I screamed.

"Margie just told me today when we talked about going to the Varsity Ball," said Ray holding up his hands defensively although being a wrestler, he could probably have twisted me into a pretzel.

I paced around Ray's room trying to decide what to do while Ray played the guitar and said "Call her" every minute or two.

Finally, I did call her but instead of asking on the phone, I said, "Gracie, this is Joe. I'd like to come over and talk to you, if I could?"

"Sure," she said. "How about seven o'clock in the Tea Room?"

"Okay. I'll see you then," I answered.

I was elated and so was Ray. "I told you she liked you" he started singing while strumming the guitar.

I borrowed Bob Rakoczy's car and drove over to Seton Hill. When I arrived at the Tea Room, Gracie was sitting with a bunch of friends and as I approached made no move to get up or acknowledge me in any way.

I said "Hi" and stood there awkwardly for what seemed like a long time but was probably ten seconds when suddenly it hit her.

"Oh, it was you that called! I thought it was Joe Dunn," she exclaimed. All the girls laughed and I felt very embarrassed. Joe Dunn was a sophomore at SVC. I muttered something about being sorry to disappoint her and felt my face getting hot.

She got up and apologized and we went for a walk. During the walk, I kept apologizing for not being Joe Dunn and finally asked her to the Ball. She accepted and we had a good time. I kept her on the defensive by introducing myself a Joe Dunn whenever we'd encounter a friend of hers.

We had a few more dates and I really liked her. I couldn't figure out why I had just broken up with a girl and now was going was another girl and felt completely different about it. I had actually done something at the train station that I hid from Billy and the rest of the guys. I bought a little stuffed tiger in a gift store and stuffed it quickly in my bag so no one would see it. It said, "you bring out the tiger in me. All of the rest of the trip I slept and thought about Gracie and showing up with the stuffed tiger.

A few days later, I went to Seton Hill and gave her the tiger. She said it was sweet and kissed me. I was real pleased with myself. I wondered in the following days if she slept with it. I pictured it on her bed or on her desk where she would look at it and think of me and sigh.

Then Ray Brannon came bursting in my room one night and said, "Hey. I was just talking to Margie on the phone and she told me a funny story."

"Tell me," I said.

"Did you give Gracie a stuffed animal recently?" he asked.

"Yeah," I said sheepishly, "Why?"

"What kind of animal?"

"A tiger. Why?"

"Well, Gracie and her friend Betty named it Jack-off and last night they tied a rope around Jack-offs neck and hung him out the sixth floor window and terrified the girls on the floor below by banging Jack off on their windows."

Despite this horrible abuse of a token of my affection, I continued to date Gracie throughout that hectic semester. The brewery job averaged two or three nights a week. The time pressure made me more efficient and I was handling most of my classes well except for Russian. The time needed for memorization was enormous and I was falling further and further behind. The actual work at the brewery was easy and the $3.65 an hour was fantastic. Billy and I were known as relief workers and were given a rotation of posts in the bottling plant to relieve for twenty minutes each. On the four to midnight shift each worker got three twenty minute breaks instead of an hour lunch break. We were supposed to take our break after each rotation. The regular brewery workers loved us. They teased us a lot but seemed to respect us. They asked us a lot about the war and the Civil Rights events. We knew not to come on strong and alienate them so we always came across as skeptical of the war and supportive of Civil Rights but not of violence. Often, you could tell that Chuck Manoli had been talking to them as they would ask us if he was telling us the same things he was telling them. We were allowed a case of beer at a discount and we got one every time. No one ever asked if we were twenty-one and we weren't that whole semester. On Fridays, if we worked, we would save our breaks until the end and have the last hour to guzzle ice cold beer.

At Easter break at long last, I got a car. My grandfather was dying of throat cancer and was no longer able to drive and so I paid $500 for his

1963 Chevrolet Bel Air. According to my mother, my grandfather had done nothing but sit and stare out his kitchen window in Rockaway drinking beer and smoking Luckies since 1931, so throat cancer was no big surprise. The car was four years old but hadn't been driven much. Although this sounds good if you know about cars, not being driven much has its own problems and the car broke down on the Turnpike on the way back to school. The car had a lot of problems but it was *my* car, my independence, my freedom.

Also, during Easter break, I had nailed down a job for the summer at Cross Armored Carrier. It seemed business had picked up and they expected a huge summer for coin rolling. They had gotten some amusement park business and would allow me all the hours I wanted at $1.90 an hour.

This was very important to me since not only did I have the expense of a car but John Muir, Pal Gierlach, and I had agreed to live off campus for our senior year and had rented an apartment in Latrobe. I wanted to stockpile money so I could have a senior year to remember.

After finals, I drove home for the first time in *my* car. When my grades came, I was disappointed even though I had done well. I was hoping for a C in Russian thinking that Father Cepon was such a nice guy and Russian so difficult that he wouldn't give a D. I never missed class and participated in discussions about Russian culture and history. I was wrong however and I did indeed get a D. I had busted my ass in Father Cuk's notorious Experimental Psychology course and expected an A but I got a B. Cuk did not like me and I could not seem to win him over no matter what I did.

I worked about sixty hours a week that summer and never missed a day. The thoughts of having my own apartment and having girls over were an enormous motivator. Most of the hours I worked, I was working alone. Just me, my transistor radio, and my coin-rolling machine—I listened and sang the hours away. It was a great summer for music on the radio. The Beatles, Sonny and Cher, The MaMas and The PaPas, Fifth Dimension, Paul Revere and the Raiders, The Temptations, and the Four Tops were all on the charts. I could get so lost in the music that the hours just melted away.

Early that summer of 1967, Muhammad Ali was convicted of draft evasion, stripped of his crown and sentenced to five years in prison. It was quite a turn of events and magnified the growing opposition to the war. Also, that summer there were race riots in Memphis, Detroit (forty-three killed), Milwaukee, Durham, and Cambridge, Md.

Later that summer, I got a horrible call from Paul Gerlach saying that Ed Ryan had been killed in an auto accident. He told me of the details of the funeral and offered his house in York, PA, for anybody that needed a place to sleep. Ed Ryan was from Harrisburg, PA, and was a wonderful, happy, smart, good-looking guy. Everybody loved him. He had a baby face and was, in fact, a year younger than most of us as a result of skipping a grade in elementary school. We teased him about being a kid and if we talking about girls or sex when he walked in the room, we would stop and claim he was too young for such talk. Bill Landers and I made the trip to Harrisburg and when we arrived, found a large group of guys from our class had arrived. Ed had been in Washington, DC, visiting his girlfriend Dee Dee Williams. On his way home, he apparently fell asleep while driving on Interstate 83 and hit a bridge abutment. His mother was heavily sedated and in shock. Her eldest child of whom she was so proud was dead. Despite the grief and sadness, Mrs. Ryan was impressed and pleased to see the St. Vincent delegation arrive. She fussed over every one of us. She told us how much we meant to Ed, how many names she recognized and briefly told a few stories that proved she was telling the truth. It brought me and many of us to tears. She talked about how Ed loved the guys on Gerry III and how he wore his Gerry III shirt all the time when he was home. We had gotten red and white "Gerry III" T-shirts after our football championship. We also used them for intramural softball and won that school championship as well. The shirt, which we all wore so proudly meant, a lot more than athletic prowess; it stood for the solidarity and camaraderie and spirit of the guys on Gerry III. If you lived on Gerry III, you were not alone in the world.

Mrs. Ryan suddenly got the idea that Ed should be buried with his Gerry III shirt, went to Ed's room, and returned with it. One of us, I think Paul Gierlach, put the shirt in the casket. Mrs. Ryan claimed she couldn't bear to do it.

The next day after the mass and graveside service, we all were invited to a reception in a little facility on the cemetery grounds. We ate sandwiches, drank beer, and talked very quietly. Paul suggested we all meet at the grave in a few minutes for our own private tribute. We did, and the casket had already been lowered in the hole but was uncovered. Paul muttered something about life being absurd and this being proof but that we should use Ed's memory as inspiration to try to put some meaning in our sorry lives. We passed around a bottle of beer each of us taking a sip and then poured the remainder in the grave and walked away silently. It was our form of communion.

I spent a lot of time that summer drinking beer with Pat Kelly. He was going to marry Eileen Fenchak and that made us both happy. They seemed perfect for each other and had met through me. Pat asked me to be in the wedding and I, of course, agreed. I remember talking one night about us being Irish and how we fit the Irish stereotype of loving to drink. As we talked about all the Irish we knew, and how it seemed like they all drank heavily except for my dad, who was the son of an alcoholic and whose uncles were all alcoholics. Gradually, the discussion turned to how some of these Irish were happy drinkers and some not so much. Pat's dad was apparently an unhappy guy when he drank. My Uncle Pat Nash was the opposite. Give him a few beers and prepare to laugh. We knew other young guys who got in lots of fights in bars and at parties when drinking. That's when I told Pat my theory about the Irish and drinking. I theorized that the Irish people have a deep sadness within them from eight hundred years of exploitation, starvation, premature death, poverty, and betrayal. It's like Jung's collected unconscious or original sin I speculated. Irish behavior can be running from the sadness when it becomes intense or running toward the sadness if it begins to fade. If you can't feel the sadness, it scares you as if you might not be able to feel anything. When drinking, I theorized, happy, funny, loud behavior is running from the sadness; sad belligerent, cynical behavior is running toward it.

"Wow!" said Pat. "That is fucking heavy. Wow! That *is* heavy." He took a big swallow from his glass of Schaeffer beer. "I need to think on that some but that is an amazing theory."

In late August 1967, I finished up at Cross Armored and anxiously headed back to SVC for my senior year. I was never so anxious for a summer to be over. I went back a few days early so that I could watch the Steelers practice on our campus and set up things at our apartment. It was supposed to be three of us sharing a small house attached to our landlord's house. Mrs. Matusek was the landlord. She had a grown son and a daughter in college and was very motherly to us. We liked her even more when we found out she did our laundry. It was never discussed as part of the deal but one day in early September, we came home and found each of our beds had clean, folded clothes on it. We figured she took pity on us and decided to help us out. We were grateful, thanked her, and fussed over her profusely.

"Once I get started on laundry," she said, "I might as well do everybody's."

The three of us were supposed to be me, John Muir and Paul Gierlach. I worked at the Rolling Rock Brewery, which struck everybody as appropriate. John worked at Latrobe Hospital, which struck everybody as absurd and frightening. We and three other model citizens who also were in the Class of '68 also worked in the Inhalation Therapy Department of Latrobe Hospital. All well-known drunks and party animals, it would have been disconcerting if they had worked in food services but inhalation therapy. We were horrified at the thought of ever being a patient in that hospital. Sometimes John would come home in his hospital clothes with a lot of tubes and breathing apparatus in his pockets. Paul and I would look at each other in horror and disbelief. Paul didn't have a job that I can remember but he worked hard at fighting depression and sinking into an existential abyss. Paul was an English major

411

and almost always had his nose in a book. He favored Existentialism and theater of the absurd. Sartre, Camus, Nietzsche, Kierkegaard, and Hegal were his friends. I called him the Black Knight and had considerable success in lightening his moods

I said it was supposed to be the three of us because a few days later Bob Rakoczy came to our door and asked if he could live with us. He said his mother screwed up his room deposit and SVC never received it and thus he had no room in the dorm. At first, we said no because there were only three beds in this small two-bedroom house. Rakoczy said he would sleep on the living room couch but we told him we expected to have a lot of visitors of female variety and would be needing the living room. Finally, Rakoczy said he would live in the basement, sleep on the floor, and pay one fourth of the rent. We agreed. The basement had its own entrance from outside and we hardly ever saw Rakoczy except for our marathon games of Risk.

A few weeks into the semester, John showed up with a puppy named Judd. Paul and I argued with John that we didn't want a puppy and our lifestyle didn't fit with a puppy and we didn't want to train a puppy, and feed a puppy and walk a puppy and listen to a puppy bark. John said a puppy would help us score with girls. We kept the puppy.

One Sunday night, we were drinking beer and playing Risk and John poured some beer into Judd's water dish. Judd lapped it up. John gave him more and Judd lapped it up. Soon Judd was drunk and stumbling around the house. It was funny to see a drunk dog slipping and trying to keep its balance. We all laughed but also felt sorry for the dog. John picked him up, held him on his lap, and comforted him. Judd fell into a deep sleep and was snoring. When John finally had to get up to pee, he put Judd on the couch. Judd slept on the couch snoring and limp until we woke up the next day. All the next day Judd was sluggish and sad. A few nights later, Judd had returned to normal and we resumed our game of Risk. John once again poured some beer into Judd's bowl but this time Judd would not drink it!

Life was good at 1201 Grant Avenue in Latrobe in the fall of 1967. We drank a lot of Rolling Rock, watched a lot of football, played a lot of Risk and APBA Football, played a lot of music on the stereo, and had a lot of young women to our humble home under various pretenses, but mostly, we laughed. We missed Ed Ryan and thought about him a lot. We worried about the country and we fretted about the war and we talked anxiously about our immediate future but mostly we laughed.

There were yet some hurdles to clear if I was to become the first Farrell to graduate from college. One was Russian, which was a constant drain on my morale. I was struggling just to pass and if I failed either semester, I could not graduate. On Christmas break when the grades came, I had gotten another

D. I was relieved to know I hadn't failed but worried about another semester of relying on Father Cepon's mercy and kindness.

Father Cuk on the other hand showed no mercy or kindness. I was retaking his difficult Physiological Psych course because I didn't want a C in Psych. I had decided to apply to graduate schools and didn't want a C in Psych on my transcript. I had worked hard in this course and had a B going into the final. On one of my exams, he had written a note that I should have done better since this was my second time with this material. I had gotten a B on the exam and so I didn't think much about it. Just as finals were scheduled, Father Cuk announces that the final would be an oral exam and gives each of us a time to come to his office to take the exam. I asked why he was doing this and he said because it was such a small class (of eight) he thought it more convenient. The exam would be comprehensive, he added, covering the entire semester. This development pissed me off to no end. Now, I had to study the whole book for an oral exam where he would control the questions and subjectively score the answers. I studied very hard for the final. I even studied at the Brewery. I had what I thought was a great idea and studied from the exams we had already taken figuring that he considered those areas to be the most important. I arrived at Cuk's office early hoping to get some clue from the guys going before me as to what he asked but got no real help.

During the exam, Father Cuk was very cordial. He asked me very vague questions like "explain the Limbic System" or "What role does the Hypothalamus play?" I felt torn by the idea that if I give too much info, I might get something wrong and too little info, and he may think I don't know the answer. At the end of the exam, Father Cuk decided on a C for my grade. I asked why and he explained that I was too vague, considering that this was my second time in the course.

"Father," I said feeling the rage rising in my body, "I don't want a C in a Psych course. That's the reason I took it over."

"Cough, Cough, I understand but you see you have to earn it. You don't get a B just because it's your second time"

"But Father," I pleaded, "it's not fair to hold me to a higher standard because I'm repeating the course." "Cough, Cough, I'm not," he answered.

"Father, you just indicated that you are," I said my voice rising.

"Cough, Cough, no, I'm not," Father Cuk said. "I just feel that a C is the proper grade for the exam."

I realized that he could still give me a B for the course even with a C on the final and that I still had to get a thesis approved by him in order to graduate. I therefore lowered my voice and respectfully reiterated that I repeated the course because I didn't want a C in Psych since I intended to apply to Graduate School.

"Cough, Cough, well, I don't know yet what your grade will be. I have to look at your other grades and those of the other students and decide on the final grades."

"Well, okay, Father," I said softly, "just so you understand why I took this course a second time."

"Cough, Cough, we'll see how it works out, Cough," Father Cuk said as if to end the discussion.

I left feeling like I would get a B. I felt like I had made my arguments clear. I should not be penalized because I was repeating the course and I was only repeating to avoid a C.

If I had been paranoid, I would have thought Father Cuk had decided on an oral final just so he could screw me but I was a psychology major and I could find no motive for him to want to screw me and didn't think I was important enough for him to *plan* to screw me. When the grades came, I got a C in the course.

CHAPTER TWENTY-SIX

◆ ◆ ◆ ◆ ◆

"AMEN"

Time it was and what a time it was
a time of innocence
a time of confidences.
Long ago it must be,
I have a photograph
Preserve your memories,
they're all that's left you.
                    Simon and Garfunkel ~ "Bookends"

As 1968 arrived, it looked to the casual eye as though I might actually graduate from college. There were however two major hurdles to clear in order for me to achieve this life-altering climax. One was that I needed to pass Russian, which wasn't going to be easy given I had gotten D's the last two semesters and was sinking further and further into an abyss. The second hurdle was an unusual little gem dreamt up by Father Cuk. I needed to do a thesis and get it approved by him. An undergraduate thesis was a requirement of the Psych Department and given my history with Father Cuk, this could be a major problem.

1968 was to be a year of great tumult and change on this planet, in this country and in my life. Almost immediately upon returning to St. Vincent for my last semester, the Siege of Khe Sanh began. A marine base with 6,000 troops was isolate and surrounded by 20,000-30,000 North Vietnamese troops and under constant ground, artillery, mortar, and rocket attacks. The battle lasted for seventy-seven days with heavy U.S. casualties.

Days after the siege began, the North Vietnamese launched the Tet Offensive. Nearly 70,000 North Vietnamese Troops took the battle from the jungle to the cities. Almost every major city and province was attacked by Communist forces. The fact that North Vietnam could launch such an attack at this point in the war was a shock and caused many to question anew what was being accomplished. In February, Walter Cronkite questioned our leaders and advised negotiation to end the war.

I had applied to a number of graduate schools in Psychology and Alfred University invited me to interview for a possible assistantship, which would pay room and tuition. I was on my way to Alfred, NY, for the interview when I heard that U.S. casualties had been the highest the week before than at any time since the war began. It was a sunny, but cold, day and there was snow covering the ground from recent snowfalls. I thought how strange it was that mere months from now, I could be in a jungle fighting in a war that seemed to make no sense. We all were haunted by the war and found it difficult to think about or plan for the future knowing we were likely to be drafted when we lost our student deferments.

It was a long drive through many small towns to Alfred, NY, from Latrobe and I winced at how I might be doing this a lot if I went to Alfred and wanted to see Gracie Dirienzo who would be a senior next year at Seton Hill.

The interview at Alfred went well I thought except maybe for one question. I was interviewed by a committee of faculty and it was the head of the Department who asked me why I had so many D's on my transcript. She said for someone with my GPA, she found my transcript to be a bit "bizarre." Her use of the term "bizarre" kind of bothered me. She said there were an unusual number of D's (six) and also a lot of A's (nine) and how did

I account for that. I answered that I had difficulty working hard when I don't see the point. I explained as best I could my foreign language situation and mumbled something about poor math teachers in high school. I mentioned that every D on my transcript was in a course that I had to take to meet some requirement that I didn't see the need for. I thought I had wrapped up the answer extremely well, considering I was talking to psychologists by saying it was basically a "motivation problem."

I was excited to learn that the assistantship I was being considered for was to be a prefect or an RA as they called it, in an undergraduate dorm. I had visions of having special access to numerous undergraduate women. I thought about this all the way back to Latrobe.

When I arrived back at our apartment, both John Muir and Paul Gerlach were there. John had just arrived home from work and was dressed in his hospital smock and drinking a Rolling Rock pony bottle. Paul was drinking black coffee and reading Camus. I told them what the assistantship would be and they both reacted sharply. Paul said "Remember, Farrell, you have existence but your essence is determined by your decisions and actions."

"I'll keep that in mind," I answered smiling with delight.

"And you have had the audacity to mock and criticize Latrobe Hospital for employing *me*," John yelled his eyes wide in mock outrage. "How could any sane organization put you in charge of young women. It figures that any university that would accept you, would be that fucked up!" He chugged the rest of his beer and got up to get another. "Jesus Christ. I don't know what's happening to our society. I swear nothing seems to make sense anymore."

"It's all part of the absurdity of the human existence," said Paul "don't try to make sense out of it."

"I quite trying to make sense out of you," answered John. "I should get some credit for that."

"Hey! Hey!" I yelled. "You are insulting me."

"We're certainly trying to," responded John.

"Don't you guys think I'm mature enough to use proper judgment even if there are young women involved?"

"Noooooo!" they both yelled simultaneously.

"Really?" I said with utter disbelief on my face. There were a series of insults hurled at me. "Really."

"What a joke!" "Are you kidding me?" "You've got to be shitting me?" John asked how he could apply to Graduate School at Alfred U.

"You guys can take solace in the fact that I didn't get the job yet, and maybe won't get it," I responded.

"Here's to hope," yelled John holding his beer high in a toast and them finishing it. He got up and went to the fridge for another.

"I suppose you're on call tonight," I said as he walked back into the room with a fresh beer.

"Fucking A," he answered. "If anyone has breathing problems tonight, I'm the guy to call. I'll jam one of these suckers down their throat," he said holding up an S tube.

"This is like one of Sartre's plays," said Paul. "I'm living in the Theater of the Absurd."

"Oh, yeah, what particular play?" asked John acting like he would know what Paul was talking about.

"Nausea" shot back Paul as we all laughed.

"What's so fuckin' funny?" said Bob Rakoczy who suddenly appeared in the doorway dressed in a coat and hat that made him look like a Russian Cossack.

"See what I mean?" exclaimed Paul. "This is like a Fellini movie now! Why do drugs when you can live here?"

Rakoczy loved to go to flea markets and had lots of costumes and weird things, so it wasn't unusual for him to dress or act strangely.

"Wait till you hear this!" yelled John as he proceeded to tell Rakoczy about my interview.

"Well, don't worry boys," Rakoczy counseled. "they'll never give him the position, In fact, now that they've met him, they'll probably revoke his admission. Besides, the war is waiting for all three of you."

Rakoczy was wrong. About three weeks later, I was offered the assistantship and I accepted it, hoping I could avoid the draft.

On Saturday, March 16, John, Paul, and I and Gracie and two of her friends all huddled around a radio and listened to Robert Kennedy declare his candidacy for President. President Johnson had shown his vulnerability in the New Hampshire Primary that Tuesday and we were sure Kennedy would win the nomination and end the war.

Father Cuk and I were having our own war over my thesis. As incoming freshman, we had all taken a basic psychological test called the California Psychological Inventory (CPI). I had retested a random sample of seniors to examine for any significant changes on any of the eighteen scales the test measures. I researched all the literature, did all the math, and rechecked everything. It was all good. I was feeling confident that I could get this done and then focus on learning enough Russian to get a D. I typed it all myself which was annoying because of all the charts and statistics involved and handled it in on the last week of March.

On Sunday night, I was in the Library when I went to isolate myself from all distractions in an effort to pound some Russian words or tenses into my head. It seemed futile at times but Father Cepon was a good man and if he saw effort and progress I believed he wouldn't flunk me and deny me graduation. As I was studying, I thought I heard yelling and then murmuring out in the lobby area of the library. I got up and asked another student what was going on. Some student, I was told burst into the library and yelled the LBJ had quit the race.

"Is it true?" I asked.

"I don't know," answered the student as he gathered up his books, "but I'm going to go and find out."

I too gathered up my books and headed to see what was going on. I went to Gerry III, which I often did when I was on campus. There were various discussions going on about the announcement, that indeed, LBJ was not running. I listened to the discussion and the bantering back and forth and remember hearing Bill Isler, our Class President, say that 1968 is turning into a historical year. "This makes you wonder what will happen next." He said.

We found out four days later when Martin Luther King was murdered in Memphis and rioting broke out all across America.

Indeed it seemed as if the world had gone mad. A war was raging that seemed to make no sense and political turmoil and racial violence and rioting all across America.

Father Cuk returned my thesis about a week later and he had made a whole bunch of red marks where he said things needed corrections. He had no substantive corrections but wanted the data displayed differently. He wanted some double lines where I had single lines between rows or columns of data. He wanted some labels changed from "Figure" to "Table" and vice versa. It seemed like chicken shit to me but with a month to go until graduation, I went back to work on making the changes he wanted. It meant retyping most of the thesis being very careful not to make any mistakes. It took hours and hours. When I was finally finished, I took it over to Father Cuk's office and handed it in. I was hoping that he would look at it on the spot and sign off on it so I could feel relief and celebrate but he said to check back with him on Monday.

I wasn't working that night and John Muir and I were in a Shuffle Bowling tournament at a bar called The Cove. We loved this bowling game where you slide a puck-type disk at the pins and score it like real bowling. We were good at it and I thought we had a good chance to win. John never showed up, however, and I had to forfeit in the opening round. When I got back to the apartment, John was sitting quietly in the living room alone drinking a beer.

"Where the fuck were you?" I asked with disgust.

John just looked at me expressionless."

"We forfeited the tournament!" I added.

"Sorry" responded John softly. "I had other things on my mind."

"You mean on your *alleged* mind," I added smartly. "What could possibly have distracted you from the Shuffle Bowl tournament?"

"I joined the Marines," John answered quietly.

"Very funny" I said as I went to the kitchen for a beer.

When I came back and sat down, I noticed John wasn't showing any signs of clowning around.

"So tell me . . . what really happened?"

John went on to tell me that he had, in fact, joined the Marines. He said he couldn't take the anxiety of wondering what was going to happen after graduation. Faced with being drafted into the Army and being sent to Vietnam as an enlisted man he chose to go to the Marines as an officer and a promise of flight school.

As we proceeded to get very drunk, John explained his thinking. If he did nothing, he would lose control of his fate and most likely get drafted within months. He would be sent to Vietnam as an infantry soldier and if he survived, he would come home with nothing but a bad experience. By joining the Marines, he would be an officer and a pilot. There was a chance that by the time he was trained and combat ready, the war would be over and if not and he survived, he would probably be a Captain and a trained pilot which should be useful in the rest of his life.

I countered by speculating that there were probably thousands of Marines in the Vietnamese jungle right then laying in the wet rice paddies with rifles in their hands that were promised flight school and officer training or at least flight school.

Later that night, Paul came home and we were pretty drunk. I told Paul what John had done as John was having difficulty speaking.

"That's pretty ironic," said Paul. "I decided to go to Canada and made my plans today!"

Paul had discussed the Canada option with us a few times before so I knew he was serious.

"I just heard the new troop level in Vietnam was raised to 550,000. Well, I won't be one of them. The war is absurd and I won't play a part in it," he said.

John and I slept past noon the next day and when John woke up, he said that he was really hammered last night.

"I know you were," I said. "I was, too." "I had a dream that Paul came home and said he was going to Canada," said John laughing.

"That wasn't a dream," I answered. "he did and he is."

"Jesus," sighed John. "What will become of us? This sucks! This *really* sucks."

On Monday, I went to see Father Cuk believing and hoping that he signed my thesis and I could then concentrate on Russian. My other courses were wrapped up. I had a solid C in Epistemology, which given who was in that class (mostly Philosophy majors and seminarians) I was quite pleased with. I had a Social Psych class that I could cut the final and still pass. I had a Drama class for which there was no final and I would most likely get a C and another Psych course offered at Seton Hill College that our department accepted the credits for. It was the Psychology of Exceptional Children and there were women in this class since it was at Seton Hill. I, of course, had a solid A. It made me wonder what effect having girls in my classes in high school or at St. Vincent would have had on me. I always came to this class prepared and hoping that the girls would notice my brilliance. Especially one named C. J. Riker. If she ever noticed she was quiet about it.

Father Cuk had not signed off on my thesis. Instead, he had more changes he wanted me to make. Some of the changes were new, meaning he hadn't pointed them out before, and a few were back to the way it was originally. This sent me into orbit.

"Father, I don't have time for this," I said loudly. "You didn't ask for these changes last time. I have a Russian final I have to pass because you couldn't let me take Spanish! Some of these changes are the way I had it originally!" I was close to losing control. I felt like I was having an out of body experience—like I was watching this happen as an observer.

Then I noticed that Father Cuk looked shaken, like he was frightened. He coughed nervously like always and asked me for the thesis back. He looked it over and said that with a few minor changes, he would sign it.

"But Father, you *marked* it up in *red*! I'll have to type it all over again." I said plaintively.

To my amazement, Father Cuk said the marks were in red pencil and could be erased and some changes made on the existing page.

"If you just make these change . . . cough, cough . . . I will sign it," Cuk said.

I went back to my apartment, made the changes that were easy to make, and ignored any that weren't. I retyped a few pages and raced back to Cuk's office. I wanted to end this now.

Cuk saw me and summoned me in to his office.

"Cough, cough. Did you make the changes we talked about?" he asked in a friendly upbeat manner.

"Yes, Father," I answered handing him the document. Without even checking to see the changes, he signed the thesis as approved.

I bounded out of the building and wanted to get drunk right away but decided instead to study Russian. Father Cepon was the only thing that stood between me and a Bachelors degree.

My determination to study Russian, however, quickly turned to feelings of futility and after a couple of hours isolated in the library, I went out and got drunk.

Father Cepon was a wonderful man. He spoke with a very deep voice in what seemed like a Russian accent and always was a gentleman. I had taken his World Religion class, which was truly a course that contributed to the formation of my values and my view of the world. He had given me a B in the first semester of Russian and then D's in the next two semesters. Both deserved. Now, I had very low scores in the two previous exams and could easily flunk. I took the final and knew very little for sure. I guessed and fumbled my way through it. When I handed in my exam, I asked Father Cepon when he would have the grades prepared. I told him my graduation depended on my passing this course and I'd like to know if need to call my parents and tell them not to come. He laughed, which I took to be a good sign, and told me to come around in about an hour, as he would do the seniors' grades first.

I went to Gerry III to wait and shoot the breeze with the guys. Most of them felt that Cepon wouldn't flunk a senior. After an hour, I headed for Cepon's office. My anxiety was extremely high as I knocked on his door.

"Ah, Mr. Faddle," he said with his deep voice and accent. "I'm afraid you will have to call your parents," he continued with a serious tone and then he paused "and tell them they should come to graduation." He broke into a big smile and said, "I have given you a C for the semester."

"A 'C'?" I stupidly asked as if there was some mistake.

"I appreciate your humor in class and your interest in the Russian culture and politics, so I gave you extra credit for class participation."

"Thank you, Father" I said my voice cracking with emotion. "Thank you very much."

Father Cepon stood up and extended his hand for a handshake. "Congratulations," he said.

I fought the urge to hug him and shook his hand. "Thank you, Father" was all I could manage to say.

A few days later, I graduated from St. Vincent College. I don't remember who the speaker was or who handed me my diploma. After the official ceremony in the Gymnasium, the class members all assembled outside Kennedy Hall for the traditional ringing of the Ave Maria bell by the Class President, which in our case was Bill Isler.

As I stood there surrounded by friends I loved and had shared such important times with, I found it difficult to breathe. I thought about our yearbook cover, which I was so proud of. It was a black cover with green script that simply said: St. Vincent. Where one gets involved in the situation and asks why. Looks for truth in classes, books, discussions at bars and dances and then must choose a direction.

It seemed to capture what my experience had been and now sadly, it was over. I thought about Muir asking, "What will become of us?"

I tried not to make eye contact with anyone for fear they would see me crying. I felt better when I saw Bill Isler fail to ring the bell on his first try. He was so choked up with emotion that when he pulled on the heavy rope to ring the bell, it slipped out of his hand. He succeeded on his second try and it was over.

I turned away from the crowd and tried to gain control of my emotions. I couldn't bear to say good-bye to anyone. I had learned a lot at St. Vincent and grown a lot as a person. "It was like four years of group therapy," I always liked to say. I had learned about the forces that Father Ronald had told us about and I had learned how to learn.

I had learned and believed that success is a journey and not a destination. I had been exposed to the sciences and the arts and to the great writers and thinkers on our planet. We had discussed and debated the great issues of our time. I had loved it. I was the first of our Farrell clan to graduate from college and now it was time to choose a direction.

Indeed, what would become of us?

Amen.

Breinigsville, PA USA
12 January 2011
253208BV00002B/13/P